La Florida

UNIVERSITY PRESS OF FLORIDA

Florida A&M University, Tallahassee
Florida Atlantic University, Boca Raton
Florida Gulf Coast University, Ft. Myers
Florida International University, Miami
Florida State University, Tallahassee
New College of Florida, Sarasota
University of Central Florida, Orlando
University of Florida, Gainesville
University of North Florida, Jacksonville
University of South Florida, Tampa
University of West Florida, Pensacola

La Florida

Five Hundred Years of Hispanic Presence

Edited by Viviana Díaz Balsera and Rachel A. May

University Press of Florida
Gainesville · Tallahassee · Tampa · Boca Raton
Pensacola · Orlando · Miami · Jacksonville · Ft. Myers · Sarasota

Copyright 2014 by Viviana Díaz Balsera and Rachel A. May
All rights reserved
Printed in the United States of America on acid-free paper

The publication of this book is made possible by direct support of the University of Miami as well as by related programming support of the Florida Humanities Council and the National Endowment for the Humanities.
This book may be available in an electronic edition.

21 20 19 18 17 16   6 5 4 3 2 1

First cloth printing, 2014
First paperback printing, 2016

Library of Congress Control Number: 2014939126
ISBN 978-0-8130-6011-8 (cloth)
ISBN 978-0-8130-6203-7 (pbk.)

The University Press of Florida is the scholarly publishing agency for the State University System of Florida, comprising Florida A&M University, Florida Atlantic University, Florida Gulf Coast University, Florida International University, Florida State University, New College of Florida, University of Central Florida, University of Florida, University of North Florida, University of South Florida, and University of West Florida.

University Press of Florida
15 Northwest 15th Street
Gainesville, FL 32611-2079
http://www.upf.com

Contents

List of Figures   vii
List of Tables   ix
Preface   xi
Acknowledgments   xv

Introduction. Ponce's Ghosts: Spain and Florida, 1513–2013   1
　Gary R. Mormino

Part I. La Florida: First and Second Spanish Periods

　Introduction: Three Hundred Years of La Florida   43
　Viviana Díaz Balsera

1. Charting Juan Ponce de León's 1513 Voyage to Florida: The Calusa Indians amid Latitudes of Controversy   49
　Jerald T. Milanich

2. "Until the Land Was Understood": Spaniards Confront La Florida, 1500–1600   69
　Paul E. Hoffman

3. On the Trail of Texts from Early Spanish Florida: Garcilaso's *La Florida del Inca* and Oré's *Relación de los mártires*   83
　Raquel Chang-Rodríguez

4. A Land Renowned for War: Florida as a Maritime Marchland   103
　Amy Turner Bushnell

5. "Giving Liberty to All": Spanish Florida as a Black Sanctuary, 1673–1790   117
　Jane Landers

6. The Experience of a Loss: Spain, Florida, and the United States (1783–1833)   141
　Carmen de la Guardia Herrero

PART II. POSTCOLONIAL AND CONTEMPORARY FLORIDA

Introduction: Florida in the Modern World 167
Rachel A. May

7. Fireworks over Fernandina: The Atlantic Dimension of the Amelia Island Episode, 1817 171
Karen Racine

8. The Old World in the New: Florida Discovers the Arts of Spain, 1885–1930 192
Richard L. Kagan

9. Performing Diasporas, or *Cubanidad* Meets Jim Crow: Miami in a Period of Demographic Transition before the Cuban Revolution 209
Darién J. Davis

10. Mickey Ricans? The Recent Puerto Rican Diaspora to Florida 224
Jorge Duany

11. Miami in the Twenty-First Century: Still on the Edge? 242
Alex Stepick and Marcos Feldman

12. How Cubans Transformed Florida Politics and Gained National Influence 263
Susan Eckstein

List of Contributors 285
Index 287

Figures

1.1. Florida depicted on the Freducci map 51
1.2. Modern locations mentioned in the text 55
3.1. Title page of *La Florida del Inca* 85
3.2. First folio of Oré's *Relación* 86
3.3. Hernando de Soto, engraving from *Retratos de los españoles ilustres* 87
8.1. George R. Fairbanks 196
8.2. Program from the Ponce de Leon Celebration 197
8.3. Flagler hotels in St. Augustine 200
8.4. Addison Mizner, 1920 202
8.5. Mirasol postcard, 1923 203
10.1. Main destinations of migrants from Puerto Rico to the United States, 2000–2009 228
10.2. Racial self-classification of Puerto Ricans in Florida and the United States, 2006–2010 233
11.1. Race and ethnicity of Miami-Dade County population, 1990 and 2010 244
11.2. Share of racial/ethnic group by personal income bracket, 1990 and 2010 245
11.3. Share of personal income bracket by race/ethnicity, 1990 and 2010 246
11.4. Map of gentrifying central city neighborhoods 250

Tables

10.1. Geographic Distribution of the Puerto Rican Population in the United States, by State, 1960–2010   226

10.2. Puerto Rican–Origin Population in Florida, by County, 2010   227

10.3. Top Ten U.S. Metropolitan Areas for Number of Puerto Rican Residents, 2010   229

10.4. Occupational Distribution of Latinos in the Orlando-Kissimmee Metropolitan Area, by National Origin, 2007–2009   230

12.1. Summary of U.S. Embargo Tightening and Loosening Measures and Whether Incumbent President Won Florida   271

Preface

La Florida was the first region in the present-day United States to be globalized by European contact. Spurred by the 2013 quincentenary of Juan Ponce de León's landfall on the Atlantic coast of Florida, *La Florida: Five Hundred Years of Hispanic Presence* provides a richly textured analysis of five centuries of transatlantic exchange. The volume brings together contributions by prominent scholars from several academic disciplines who participated in at least one of the three conferences sponsored by the Florida Humanities Council in 2012 to commemorate this momentous occasion for the state of Florida.

La Florida: Five Hundred Years of Hispanic Presence is structured in two parts containing six essays each. Florida historian Gary R. Mormino's essay "Ponce's Ghosts" introduces the volume. Ranging from the wild dreams of a fountain of youth to the demanding paradise of the Sunshine State, "Ponce's Ghosts" is an authoritative synthesis of Florida's relationship with its Spanish past since its christening by Ponce de León. Masterfully written and full of wit, the essay fearlessly weaves past and present, myth and history, gains and awful losses, into a tightly braided tapestry of Florida's unique identity and character.

Subsequently, part 1 is framed by Florida as a Spanish territory and part 2 by Florida as a U.S. state with an indelible Hispanic presence. From different academic perspectives, the twelve essays engage with significant—and at times lesser known—episodes that evince Florida's Spanish imprint from Ponce de León's landfall to the current influence of Hispanic politics in the peninsula and on the national scene. This format offers the reader both a panoramic view and focal interdisciplinary reflections on the Spanish legacy. It shows that far from being "a subterranean river, dipping invisibly" in the words of Walt Whitman regarding the Spanish heritage in the Southwest,[1] in Florida this heritage has always streamed in open daylight.

Although the volume does not pretend to offer a neat chronological narrative, the collection as a whole does tap the breadth of five centuries of Florida's history and culture. Each chapter in the book is fully independent from the others. But by virtue of the chronological order of their presentation, their interdisciplinary topics, perspectives, and contexts produce a web of connections that give the volume temporal consistency, balance, and continuity. Thus part 1, on Florida's Spanish period, opens with an essay on controversies over the specific landing site of Ponce de León in 1513, and his first contacts with the Calusa Indians. Subsequent chapters address daring and fruitless attempts by the Spaniards to reconnoiter the riches of the land; major chronicles on the perils of globalizing Florida written by Spanish subjects from faraway Peru; the hardships of St. Augustine as a loyal war post resisting Spain's foes from land and sea; Fort Mose as the first free African American community, which paid for its liberty by resisting deadly British assaults. The first part of the volume fittingly comes to a close with a chapter on the intricate chain of events leading to the end of the Spanish period, when Florida was ceded to the young U.S. republic.

Moving from the story of the anointment of a paradise that quickly turned hostile to the tale of its ultimate loss, the reader then enters the second, more contemporary part of the book, which considers how Spain's presence is felt into the modern, or "American," period.

Like Florida's colonial history, its modern history is complex and marked by conflict and the influence of global forces that place Florida firmly in the circuit of the Caribbean Basin and the Atlantic World. The six chapters in part 2 take the reader from complicated international dynamics that accompanied the collapse of the Spanish Empire through the "Spanish craze" at the turn of the twentieth century. The book then moves on to have the reader consider the racial dynamics of the migration patterns between the Afro-Hispanic Caribbean and Florida in the Jim Crow era preceding the Cuban Revolution, as well as the changing patterns and influence of Hispanic-Caribbean migration into Florida in the last decades of the twentieth century and into the twenty-first.

All of the chapters in this book work together to facilitate an understanding of the deep and complex transatlantic connections between Spain, Africa, and the Americas that influenced Florida's past; the demands that Florida faces in its present as a crossroad of cultures, peoples, and legacies; and the ensuing challenges that will continue to shape its future as one of the most diverse states in the nation.

Note

1. The phrase comes from Walt Whitman's letter to government officials from Santa Fe, New Mexico, on the 333rd anniversary of the founding of the city by the Spaniards, entitled "The Spanish Element in Our Nationality." The letter was published in the *Philadelphia Press* on August 5, 1883. Some passages from the letter are also quoted in Richard Kagan's essay (chapter 8).

Acknowledgments

We acknowledge the support of the Florida Humanities Council, the University of Miami Center for the Humanities, and the Institute for the Study of Latin America and the Caribbean (ISLAC) at the University of South Florida. In addition to contributing the introduction, Gary R. Mormino was the original editor of this book. Without his generosity and advice, we never would have been able to see it through. And lastly, we owe a special debt of gratitude to Sian Hunter from University Press of Florida, who has been most patient and kind with us and has made bringing forth this book a pleasure.

Introduction

Ponce's Ghosts

Spain and Florida, 1513–2013

GARY R. MORMINO

Founded in legend by Hercules, settled by the Romans in 206 BC, occupied by the Visigoths in the sixth century, and wrested from the Moors in 1248, Seville had become the wealthiest city in the world by the mid-sixteenth century as a result of Spanish conquest and empire. The seemingly inexhaustible silver mines of Potosí in Bolivia and gold mines of Mexico were the sources of new wealth. Annually, the silver plate fleets sailed from Lima and Veracruz, bound for Spain.

When sixteenth-century Spanish seafarers returned from their global voyages, they sought the mouth of the Guadalquivir River then sailed sixty miles upstream to Seville. There, they reported to the most secret room in Spain. In La Casa de Contratación (the House of Trade), cartographers and cosmographers scrutinized logs and navigational charts. Amerigo Vespucci—he of the eponymous name—proposed in 1508 that Spain create an official set of maps, *el padrón real* (the royal register), a master chart of the known world, an official record of discoveries. Contours of a New World appeared on vellum and linen, adorned with ornate cartouches displaying terrifying and fascinating images: human-eating cannibals, fierce tribes of female warriors, and emerald cities. The contours of a New World unfolded.[1]

In the chapel of the House of Trade, explorers prayed in front of a remarkable painting. Alejo Fernández's *La Virgen de los Navegantes* (The Virgin of the Navigators) straddles the oceans and offers sailors a safe harbor and calm waters. Painted in the early 1530s, the altarpiece depicts the Virgin flanked by Holy Roman Emperor Charles V, King Ferdinand of Aragon, a kneeling Christopher Columbus, and Amerigo Vespucci. In the background, natives of the New World cower.

At some point in the early sixteenth century, a royal cosmographer identified a spit of land north of Cuba. Carib Indians spoke of an island called Bimini north of Cuba. As Lucas Vázquez de Ayllón, Alonso Álvarez de Piñeda, Juan Ponce de León, Francisco Hernández de Córdoba, and Sebastian Cabot explored the Gulf coast, the body of land became a peninsula; in time it was revealed that La Florida was no mere island but an appendage of a great continent. Janus-faced, with one side facing North America and the other looking toward the Bahamas and Cuba, Florida became the pathway between the Americas. Five hundred years later, Florida occupies the distinctive position of being the southernmost state of the United States *and* the northernmost province of the Caribbean.[2]

Ponce de León

Ponce accompanied Columbus on his second voyage to the New World in 1493. Burnishing his reputation as a fierce fighter on the island of Hispaniola, he helped conquer and later govern the province of Higüey (northeastern Haiti). In 1506, leading an expedition to the island of Borinquen (Puerto Rico), he ruthlessly put down Taino uprisings, earning the governorship for his deeds. He later plundered the Lucayas (Bahamas).

During the quarter century after 1492, the Caribbean had become a proverbial Spanish lake. But feats of navigation and military triumph had yielded precious little treasure. Ominously, the Tainos, Arawaks, and Caribs perished at alarming rates, victims of what conquest wrought: disease, warfare, and labor tribute. In 1512, King Ferdinand rewarded Ponce with an *asiento* (charter) to discover and conquer the island of Bimini. The contract stipulated

> Firstly, that with the ships you wish to take at your own cost and expense,
> You may go to discover, and you shall discover, the island aforesaid . . .
> That when you find the island you shall be obliged to settle at your cost in the sites and places you can best do it.

The expedition sailed from San Germán, Puerto Rico, on March 3, 1513, in three ships "well provided with food, men, and mariners." The manifest of the *Santa María de Consolación, Santiago,* and *San Cristóbal* included one woman, Juana Ruiz; an Italian named Juan or Giovanni Bono; a cabin boy identified as Jorge Negro; a free West African black identified as Juan Garrido; a black man listed as "Fernandico, Indian, slave"; and two Taino seafarers.[3]

Guided by a brilliant pilot, Antón de Alaminos, the voyagers sighted land after a month at sea. According to Antonio Herrera, the court historian who had access to the now lost journal of the voyage, "They ran along the coast seeking harbor. . . . Believing that land to be an island, they named it La Florida, because it appeared very delightful, having many fresh groves, and it was all level, and also because they discovered it at the season which the Spaniards call Flowery Easter [Pascua Florida] . . . they went ashore to discover and take possession."[4]

The ships turned and sailed southward, hugging the coastline. Sailors spotted a cape of land jutting into the ocean and named the site Cabo Cañaveral (Cape of Canes) because the reeds reminded them of sugarcane. It remains one of America's oldest place-names. They anchored near a river they christened Santa Cruz (Sacred Cross), believed to be present-day Jupiter Inlet, where sailors took on water and wood. They later noted the Indian village of Chequescha, probably the site of today's Key Biscayne, home of the Tequesta people.

On April 21, 1513, in the vicinity of today's Key Biscayne, Alaminos encountered "El Cabo de las Corrientes" (the Cape of Currents). Arguably, this was the greatest "discovery" of the expedition: the Gulf Stream. The thirty-eight-year-old Alaminos—a native of Palos, Spain, who had been a cabin boy on Columbus's fourth and final journey—was awestruck by the rush of water so powerful that it forced his ships backward: "So great was the current that it was more powerful than the wind . . . the current was so strong it made the cables tremble." Six years later, the mariner was sailing across the Straits of Florida on his return voyage to Spain when he again encountered the Gulf Stream. He became the first to chart and understand how the winds and currents could guide future voyagers to and from Spain and the West Indies.[5]

Turning northward, Ponce's ships anchored off one of the many barrier islands, exploring San Carlos Bay (Charlotte Harbor) and the mouth of the Caloosahatchee River. There they gathered freshwater and firewood. The visitors also encountered fierce resistance from Calusa Indians who attacked them in dugout canoes. Ponce commemorated the first Spaniards to die on La Florida's shores by naming the island Matanzas (massacre). (The island appears on historic maps as Puerto de S. Nivel, Santa Ybel, Santa Isabel, and finally Sanibel.) Returning to Puerto Rico, the expedition "sailed among islands . . . called Las Tortugas, or Tortoises, because they took 170 of them in a short time."[6]

The decade following the exploration of La Florida witnessed Hernán Cortés's conquest of Tenochtitlán and the fabulous treasures of the Aztec

Empire. The ambitious Ponce wrote Emperor Charles V in February 1521: "Among my services I discovered at my own cost and charge, the Island of Florida . . . and now I return to that Island, if it pleases God's will, to settle it." The emperor awarded Ponce the position of *adelantado* (governor) of this new land.[7]

The second voyage aimed to conquer and colonize La Florida. The journal of the expedition is lost, but a contemporary court historian, Gonzalo Fernández de Oviedo, left an extended account. "Not exhausted by his outlays and labors," Ponce de León sailed from the future city of San Juan with a formidable force, described by Oviedo as consisting of "200 men and fifty horses . . . and as a good colonist, he took mares and heifers and swine and sheep and goats." His caravan also included "seeds for planting" as well as missionaries and priests.[8]

In the spring of 1521, brigantines sailed up the southwest coast of the peninsula, anchoring off one of the islands in today's Charlotte Harbor (a name derived from the Spanish transcription of Calusa/Caloosa as "Bahia de Carlos"). "The natives," wrote Oviedo, "were rough and savage and untamed and not accustomed to peace." The belligerent Calusa assailed the invaders, killing several Spaniards. Ponce suffered a mortal leg wound. Thwarted, the would-be colonists sailed to Havana, Cuba, where the leader died in July 1521. His body was later shipped to Puerto Rico, where his remains rest in the Cathedral of San Juan. Ponce became the first of a series of conquistadores to fail in La Florida, the graveyard of dreams.[9]

Naming Rights and Rites

We know when Ponce first sighted land in 1513, but no one is certain as to the exact location. Most scholars believe the hallowed shoreline lay somewhere between Daytona Beach and Melbourne Beach. The city of St. Augustine, along with other places, claims the Ponce landing sweepstakes. In 1945, a state senator from St. Augustine took a Miami historian to court because the impertinent scholar doubted the Ancient City's claim.[10]

The lyrical name La Florida has endured. The origin of this name has been mythologized and popularized. In the nineteenth century, Washington Irving romantically believed that since "the trees were gay with blossoms and the fields covered with flowers," the exotic landscape must have seemed like sirens seducing the Spanish sailors. Of course, Ponce chose the name La Florida not solely because of the lush landscape, but also because of the time of year, La Pascua Florida (The Paschal Season of Flowers).

The historian Samuel Eliot Morison stubbornly backed Florida's secular allusions. "One tires of the repetitious Spanish names," he wrote, "so many Trinidads, Santa Marías, Espíritu Santos, Santa Fes, Concepciones and the like." The poet Elizabeth Bishop may have written the shortest and most beautiful sentence about the subject of state names: "Florida," she mused, "the state with the prettiest name."[11]

Scholar David Weber explained the portents of Spanish flags planted on a distant Florida beach. "Natives would surely reject such presumption," he writes, "but until the late eighteenth century, most European nations recognized the rituals of possession as establishing legal validity of claims to sovereignty over *terra nullius*—land previously unknown to Europeans. Native rulers, Europeans supposed, lacked legitimate dominion over their lands and subjects for they were neither Christians nor did they live according to what Christians understood as 'natural law.'"[12] By authority of the Treaty of Tordesillas (1494) and Spanish claims, La Florida ranged from the Florida Keys north to Newfoundland and lands to the west of the Georgia Sea Islands and beyond.

Fountains of Youth

Literary and folk allusions to the Fountain of Youth can be found in the ancient and early modern world. In the modern era, an account appears in the works of a remarkable Italian cleric, Pietro Martire d'Anghiera (Peter Martyr). A humanist attendant to the court of Ferdinand and Isabella, Martyr interviewed returning navigators between 1493 and 1526.

For centuries, the notion of a fountain of youth has tantalized businessmen and vexed historians. Oviedo, a contemporary who had access to Ponce's journal, supposedly scoffed at the idea of a spring turning old men into boys. Bernal Díaz del Castillo, a veteran of the Cortés siege of Tenochtitlán, was more honest in his memoir. "We came to serve God and his Majesty, and to give light to those in darkness," adding, without shame, that another reason was to "acquire the wealth that most men covet."[13]

If the Fountain of Youth was a thin veneer for greed and rapacity, it has endured as a popular myth and invented tradition. Addressing members of the Florida Advertising Association in 1950, an executive speculated, "Had one of our modern high-pressure publicity organizations been in existence at the time, we might have capitalized on the Fountain of Youth story more extensively." He need not have worried. Since the late nineteenth century, tourists have sipped the restorative elixir at St. Augustine's Fountain of Youth, at Warm Mineral Springs along U.S. 41, and at countless other sites. Curiously, perhaps even providentially, the St. Augustine Fountain of Youth and Warm Mineral Springs have both yielded fabulous archaeological secrets.[14]

Is there a legitimate place for the Fountain of Youth in the history or folklore of Florida? Consider the sixteenth-century European worldview. Legends of Amazonian women, cities of gold, and fountains of youth do not seem too phantasmagorical when contrasted to the real-world encounters with the Gulf Stream, the Alachua Savanna, flying squirrels, hummingbirds, long-beaked toucans, menacing anacondas, serpents posing as alligators and iguanas, and ferocious storms that natives called *huracanes*.

The American Dream, an elixir of inextinguishable optimism, begins with yearnings for new and better worlds. "Thank you, Ponce de Leon" writes the Florida poet Campbell McGrath, "because if local history teaches us anything it is the Fountain of Youth is no illusion—it is real and it flows around us, everywhere, always—and that the eternal font is youth itself, each generation encountering the old planet with fresh eyes and minds, remaking the world as it sees fit."[15] Literary scholars often point to F. Scott Fitzgerald as having penned the most optimistic sentences in American prose. "And as the moon rose higher," he wrote in *The Great Gatsby*, "the inessential houses began to melt away until gradually I became aware of the old island here that flowered once for Dutch sailors' eyes—a fresh green breast of the new world. Its vanished trees, the trees that had made way for Gatsby's house, had once pandered in whispers to the last and greatest of all human desires; for a transitory enchanted moment, man must have held his breath in the presence of this continent, compelled into an aesthetic contemplation he neither understood nor desired, face to face with something commensurate to his capacity for wonder."[16] Spanish sailors, soldiers, and priests also expressed wonderment about the new continent and its possibilities. After all, the Spanish creed may well have been expressed in the words so oft linked with the quest for New World discovery: ¡Más allá! Farther on!

The Florida Dream incorporated the birth myth of the Fountain of Youth into a publicity campaign that lured millions of senior citizens to the Sunshine State. "Come to Florida," the dream promised, and gray-haired auto workers and accountants from Kokomo and Kankakee migrated in hopes of palm trees, balmy Februarys, and youthful vitality. A refuge and dream, a time warp and brave new world, Florida provided a new home to millions of Americans wishing to reinvent themselves.[17]

Columbian Exchange

The most momentous event in the history of Florida occurred sometime in the early sixteenth century. No chronicler recorded the exact time, place, and details, but it most likely involved a Spanish sailor or soldier wading ashore to encounter an Ays or Tequesta warrior or shaman. Perhaps the inhaling of strange body smells, the pain inflicted by Toledo steel- or stone-tipped spears, or the unintelligible words marked Florida's chapter of genesis.

The significance of 1513 lies not so much in what Ponce discovered but in the interaction that followed. The historian William H. McNeill's observation about Columbus aptly applies to his successors: "What Columbus did was to change the world in which he lived and the world in which the American Indians lived by connecting the two in a way that lasted half a millennium."[18] The environmental scholar Alfred Crosby provided an apt name for this seminal moment: the Columbian Exchange.

For centuries, textbooks hailed Columbus and Ponce for "discovering" America and Florida. The term carries uncomfortable implications. If there was any discovery made, it was mutual, between peoples and cultures alien to one another. Ponce, Narváez, and de Soto brought Spain to Florida, and the exchange of plants and animals, foods and microbes, was reciprocal. The encounters among Europeans, Africans, and natives wrought disastrous consequences for the inhabitants of Florida. The Mexican writer Carlos Fuentes suggests that we reconsider the conquest as a "shared defeat," leading to the possibility of a shared victory in the form of greater understanding.[19]

Upon first contact between Europeans and natives, the indigenous population of Florida may have numbered in the hundreds of thousands. Estimates of the pre-contact population have provoked fierce debates. The debates over the population and fate of Florida's tribes are complex, especially when one considers outward migration, slave-raiding, ethnogenesis, disease, and miscegenation. Regardless of their numbers, density, and protein-carrying capacity, Florida's Indians succumbed to Old World diseases. Natives might resist mounted knights and harquebuses, but they lacked defense against diseases that had ravaged Europe, Africa, and Asia for thousands of years. Smallpox, yellow fever, influenza, measles, and other "vectors of death" decimated every pre-contact tribe and confederation in La Florida, breaching ancient boundaries and borders, reaching villages deep within the American Southeast and beyond. Keep in mind that in spite of such chaos and destruction inflicted upon Florida's natives, Spanish Florida remained predominantly Indian Florida. And when the pre-contact tribes faded, new bands of Indians poured in from Georgia and Alabama.[20]

Between contact and extinction, between colonization and assimilation, new multi-tiered societies evolved that required a new racial lexicon: *mestizos* and *mestizaje* (offspring of Europeans and Indians and the process of this mixture); *criollos* (children of Spanish immigrants born in the New World); *cimarrones* (Maroons, or fugitive slaves); *lobos* (half-breeds); *chinos* (Chinese or mixed race); *bozales* (unacculturated African slaves); *ladinos* (Spanish-speaking Catholic slaves); *conversos* (converted Jews); *moriscos* (converted Moors); *forzados* (convicts); and mulattos, octoroons, and quadroons. *Floridanos* lived in cities (Pensacola and St. Augustine), on *ranchos* (fishing settlements located along the barrier islands) and *haciendas* (rural estates), and within the 140 missions established along the peninsula. Always, *peninsulares* (Spaniards born in Spain) were a distinct minority. New groups emerged in this "middle ground," challenging established notions of race, nationality, and ethnicity in a fluid, hybrid society.[21]

The historian Bernard Bailyn imagined the metaphor of a circling satellite to understand the profound demographic changes affecting the Americas between 1500 and 1800. The circling satellite recorded unfathomable population losses in the American Southeast, the Central Valley of Mexico, and the Andes, but also monumental population shifts from West Africa to the Caribbean and from Western Europe to the Americas. "Neo-Europes" composed of settlers and descendants of Scots, Welsh, Irish, Britons, Swedes, French, Dutch, Portuguese, and Spanish, spread out from the Old World and settled across the Americas. Consider that if pre-contact Florida's population was two hundred thousand, a conservative estimate, modern Florida did not reach that demographic plateau until the late 1870s.[22]

No single event obliterated Florida's occupants. Rather, a series of epidemics scoured La Florida: Francis Drake's scurvy crew brought a typhus outbreak in 1585; between 1613 and 1617, half of the region's Indians died because of "pests & contagions"; in 1649, yellow fever killed the governor, treasurer, and many friars, as well as large numbers of Indians; smallpox spread rapidly in 1653, followed by measles in 1659. Spanish soldiers who came in the late seventeenth century referred to Florida as the "uninhabited land." The population of Timucuans, estimated at ten thousand in 1600, had plummeted to fourteen by 1727. When Bishop Dionisio Resino arrived in 1709, he quickly realized La Florida was barren of Indians to convert. Crestfallen, Florida's first resident bishop returned to Cuba two weeks later.[23]

A Calusa warrior returning to his ancestral home on the Caloosahatchee River after fifty years of isolation would have been startled to witness the changes on the land. An amazing variety of new animals inhabited his world. Horses, cows, burros, pigs, sheep, goats, chickens, ducks, swans, geese, rats, and even earthworms that accompanied the Spaniards now called Charlotte Harbor home. In new environments, not all species survive what scientists call "ecological release." In a root hog or die setting, the omnivorous razorback hog devoured weeds, grasses, roots, nuts, birds, eggs, shellfish, and fruit, while providing settlers an almost limitless supply of fresh meat. Swineherds and pigs accompanied de Soto and his armed expedition, providing what Alfred Crosby called an "ambulatory meat locker." In the Spanish hinterlands, *la tierra de bravos toros,* Castilians bred an especially tough breed of cattle. Ponce brought the first cattle to Charlotte Harbor in 1521. By 1737, a Spanish engineer observed "the country seems to be well stocked with horned cattle and wild horses." Not all new animals thrived in their new setting, however. Sheep died by the flock, unaccustomed to the hot weather and hostile predators.[24]

Globalization

Floridanos became agents, willingly and unwillingly, of a powerful new force: globalization. Increasingly, events in Madrid, Paris, London, Rome, Havana, Mexico City, Cartagena, Pelosí, Charleston, and Mobile affected pious friars and flinty merchants, Apalachee *caciques* and African slaves. Failed wheat harvests in Castile, a devastating hurricane in Hispaniola, and the price of tanned leather in Córdoba affected the lives of distant colonists.

Between 1500 and 1700 two vast, seemingly contradictory forces unfolded: global integration and tribal disintegration. In 1513, the identities defining and separating Indian peoples by territory, clan, and language were bewildering. By 1800, the Apalachicola, Guale, and Tocobaga were extinct. Natives who had lived on the Florida peninsula for thousands of years, having survived alternating cycles of global heating and cooling and the loss of Ice Age mega-mammals, fell victim to global pathogens.

La Florida's worldwide connections are well documented. Archaeologist Judith Bense described the findings at the Presidio de Santa María: "We discovered that the first Hispanic Pensacolians smoked Dutch pipes and drank tea from Chinese porcelain cups. They had French and Italian rosaries, German stoneware mugs, Swedish cannons, and an abundance of Mexican pottery." Pensacola's first settlement included one hundred Aztec warriors. St. Augustine wills document velvet gowns and linen sheets woven in Flanders, books printed in Amsterdam, and majolica earthenware baked in Venetian kilns. The Catholic Church fused old and new images and worlds. A religious medallion survives that incorporates the Mexican Virgin of Guadalupe, the Aztec goddess Tonantzin, and the Catholic Virgin Mary.[25]

Florida's global connections transcended boundaries and nation-states. Russell D. James described Panton, Leslie & Co., headquartered in Pensacola, in the following way: "The firm was run by Scots, with British citizenship who spoke English, French, Spanish, and in some cases, Portuguese, not to mention Native languages. The firm's partners worked under Spanish, British, and American rule in Florida and were friendly with colonial governments of the Portuguese, Dutch, French, and Danish, as well as others."[26]

Consider the remarkable life of the Mandinga Francisco Menéndez. Born in Africa, he became a British slave who, with the timely assistance of Yamasee Indians, escaped to Spanish Florida, where he converted to Catholicism, married an African woman, and rose to the position of captain of the militia for the free black settlement of Fort Mose, just north of St. Augustine. During the 1740 siege of St. Augustine, General James Oglethorpe and his Georgia troops invaded Florida, overrunning Fort Mose. Under the command of Menéndez, black troops counterattacked, reclaiming the prized possession. While serving as a corsair on a Spanish pirate ship, he was captured and re-enslaved in the British Bahamas. He somehow managed to win his freedom, whether by escape, purchase, or perseverance in the British courts, and returned to St. Augustine where he resumed command of the Mose militia. In 1763, when Spain ceded La Florida to the British, Menéndez moved again, taking his Mandinga wife and four children to Cuba.[27]

Black Legends and Legacies

Victors write textbooks, establish moral codes, and enforce orthodoxy. To win holy wars, enemies must be demonized. In the sixteenth and seventeenth centuries, Imperial Spain waged war against Protestants in Europe and America, fought Ottoman armies and navies across the Mediterranean, and toppled empires and chiefdoms on four continents. Powerful forces of religious reform steeled the Protestant Reformation. The same passionate, creative energies that inspired and spread the artistry of Dürer, de Bry, and Brueghel also championed *la leyenda negra* (the black legend). Contemporary broadsides, essays, and engravings pilloried the Spanish as tyrannical, cruel, and fanatical, sinister tools of a papal conspiracy. From early wooden engravings to the nineteenth-century writings of the historian William Hickling Prescott to *Zoro*, high and low popular culture has reinforced the image of Spain in America. In his 1898 history, *The Jesuits in North America*, the acclaimed historian Francis Parkman neatly summarized the comparative histories of Canada and South America: "Spanish civilization crushed the Indian; British civilization scorned and neglected him; French civilization embraced and cherished him."[28]

Tales of Spanish cruelty must not be dismissed as merely the product of Protestant propagandists. Spaniards, indeed, slaughtered French Huguenots, enslaved Africans, tortured Catholics, impressed Native Americans, and expelled Jews and Muslims. But moral indictments imposed across centuries ignore changing sensibilities and the harsh realities of earlier ages. History records few examples of conquest without violence and cruelty. Commentator Charles Krauthammer observed sardonically that Columbus is "the deadest white male now offered for our detestation." He adds, "If any historical figure can appropriately be loaded with all of the heresies of our time—Eurocentrism, phallocentrism, imperialism, élitism, and all-bad-things-generally-ism—Columbus is the man."[29]

Britain and Spain both lost colonies in America. But as Otto von Bismarck observed famously, "The most important fact of the modern world is that Americans speak English, and not German." The Iron Chancellor might have added that Americans also largely embraced Protestantism until the mid-nineteenth century. From Lord North to Winston Churchill, from Thomas Paine to George W. Bush, British and American leaders have expressed visions of the Anglo-American world. Colonial governors, revolutionaries, and modern writers have also articulated the Hispano-American world, but such visions are blurred because of fate and fortune.

In 1988, *National Geographic* lamented that the sixteenth century had been labeled "The Forgotten Century." Stewart Udall asked, "How can a nation that celebrates John Smith and William Bradford slight founders who preceded them in other parts of the United States? And why have we been so grudging in acknowledging contributions made in the dawn years of our history by people with Spanish surnames?" Historians, archaeologists, anthropologists, and others have contributed mightily to our understanding of this era of quixotic adventures and shattered dreams, but also spectacular advances and creativity.[30]

Freedom and Slavery

Spanish slavery differed markedly from the chattel slavery found in the Carolinas and the British Caribbean. Spain fully expected to exploit native Floridians, but epidemics drastically reduced their numbers. To make Florida work, Spanish officials relied upon a feudal institution of labor tribute. Some have called this system "conquest by contract." Imposed by the Crown and not by private individuals, tribute consisted of obligations to provide food to the garrison or labor on public works. Spanish authority in Florida was at best tenuous, and governors never imposed a formal system of *encomienda*, as existed in most of the Americas.[31]

The history of African slavery in Spanish Florida was not a mirror of its counterpart in Jamestown or the Carolinas. The first African believed to have set foot on Florida soil was Esteban, or Esteve, the Moor, a slave and scout accompanying Pánfilo Narváez in 1528. Heroically, Esteve (along with the more celebrated Cabeza de Vaca) survived the harrowing expedition to Mexico, only to die a decade later as an interpreter for the Coronado expedition.[32]

Spanish law held that human slavery insulted the laws of nature. The Catholic Church served as a moral and legal buffer, pontificating that slaves held legal as well as natural rights. Slaves could sue their masters on the grounds of cruelty and purchase their freedom.

Lives lived, however, are always more complicated than law. The harsh reality remains that for most African slaves brought to the Spanish Caribbean or Americas, their lives were brutish and short. Overworked on sugar plantations and exposed to new diseases, slaves also confronted cruel demographics: a persistent shortage of women. Such was not the case on most North American plantations, where tobacco and later cotton, not sugar, was the cash crop. Moreover, the presence of women fueled a population boom among slave families, which provided a new cash crop: the trafficking of humans. American roulette meant that slaves in Spanish possessions were less likely to survive but those who did could expect their children to have lives of freedom and mobility, whereas slaves in British North America were likely to live and procreate children whose prospects of freedom were bleak.

A buffer between the Protestant North and the Catholic South, La Florida became a sanctuary for escaped slaves from the Carolinas. Spain offered runaway slaves freedom, provided that the newcomers accepted the "True Faith" and swore obedience to and bore arms for the crown. In 1738, Governor Manuel de Montiano approved a refugee community for British ex-slaves north of St. Augustine. Gracia Real de Santa Teresa de Mose became the first legally sanctioned free town in the present-day United States. Spanish motivations for granting freedom were partly religious and partly pragmatic. Precariously situated, La Florida was surrounded by enemies and constantly at war. Everyone was expected to bear arms.[33]

Cradle of Institutions

In Spanish history, the year 1492 is memorable because of four significant events: the voyage of Columbus, the completion of *la reconquista*, the expulsion of the Jews by edict of Queen Isabella and King Ferdinand II, and the publication of the first book of Spanish grammar. The last achievement may be the most significant. A nation that has codified rules of grammar has the capacity, in triplicate form, for administration, empire, and rule.

The Spanish legacy includes institution building in Florida. "Here were founded the first school and seminary," notes historian Michael Gannon, "the first hospital, first court of law, and first institutions of banking and commerce." The Catholic Church in Florida expressed a Spanish zeal for organization, discipline, and salvation. Over several centuries, Jesuits, Franciscans, and Dominicans established scores of missions. The products of superb training, missionaries studied the native languages, presided over mass while competing with suspicious shamans, and faced the threat of invasion and Indian revolts. Their accomplishments included Fray Francisco Pareja's compilation of a Timucuan dictionary and grammar book. By the mid-seventeenth century, more than twenty-six thousand Christian Indians were part of the Florida network connected by El Camino Real.[34]

By 1702, the mission system had collapsed, the result of devastating diseases, British marauders, and rebellious Indians. Because the mission buildings were constructed of pine, clay, and thatch, no architectural legacy equivalent to the California missions survived. There was never a Florida mission architectural style to become the rage in nineteenth-century Florida, nor did any fictional or real-life *floridanos* capture the public imagination the way El Zorro, "The Curse of Capistrano," did.[35]

The first planned, civic-centered cities on the American continent were built in Florida. Spanish St. Augustine was designed according to the town ordinances promulgated by Spain in 1563, an imperial custom harkening back to ancient Rome. "If the great symbol of the English colonist is the frontiersman clearing the wilderness," writes Donald Meinig, "the symbol of the Spanish colonist is the *adelantado*, pacing out the grids of a Spanish town." Despite all of the planning and hopes, St. Augustine remained a small outpost, never numbering more than a few thousand inhabitants until the late nineteenth century.[36]

In 1598, Governor Méndez de Canzo located St. Augustine's public market on the *plaza mayor*. Royal policies and law ensured proper weights and measures and set the price of bread. During religious fiestas and the festivities surrounding royal weddings and ascensions of monarchs, the central plaza provided public space for St. Augustinians to celebrate the generosity of the governor.[37]

Far away from the relative comforts of urban St. Augustine, new institutions emerged. In the seventeenth century, one of the largest cattle ranches in North America, La Chua Ranch, sprawled across north-central Florida. (*Chua* is a Timucuan name for the large sinkholes found along Paynes Prairie; today's Alachua County derives its name from the historic site.) This ranch ranged from the St. Johns River across the peninsula to the Gulf coast marshlands, from the Santa Fé River to Lake George. The patriarch of La Chua, Thomás Menéndez Márquez, established an empire, at its peak numbering seven thousand cattle, with trade routes running along the Suwannee and Ocklawaha Rivers, as well as trails connecting it to St. Augustine 120 miles away. Ranch hands included African slaves, Mexicans, and Indians. His *estancias* supplied St. Augustine and Havana with fresh beef and hides, but also Cuban rum, Apalachee corn, and Indian deerskins. Menéndez Márquez clashed with rebellious Indians and French buccaneers (a name derived from the spit, *boucan*, on which the pirates smoked and roasted their beef). La Chua Ranch could not, however, survive James Moore's raid in 1704.[38]

The New American Table

Spanish *ranchos* may have vanished, but the black, briary Andalusian horned cattle introduced into La Florida endure. The world of *los rancheros y vaqueros* has also endured. The lexicon of ranching still resonates with familiar Spanish words: *lariat, mustang, pinto, lasso, bronco, reata,* and *rodeo.* Even the all-American word *buckaroo* derived from the Spanish name for cowboy, *el vaquero.*

A charred porterhouse or T-bone accompanied by baked or fried potatoes, long a favorite meal, represents a perfect example of how Americans blended foods from the New and Old Worlds. The Columbian Exchange created a new American table.

Perhaps the first contact between Europeans and natives involved not a clash of civilizations or the clank of steel, but rather an offering of maize porridge, oysters, or a gourd containing *Ilex vomitoria*, the black drink, a powerful caffeinated drink. Food is power. To the Calusa and Apalachee, the Spanish fondness for salted pork, weevil-infested bread, and rotted anchovies was as revealing as it was revolting. To Spaniards who were in the process of creating the greatest empire since Ancient Rome, the food they carried heightened their sense of moral superiority. The facts that Indian women performed agricultural work, that heredity depended upon matriarchal order, and that natives did not plant crops in orderly European-style rows only reinforced their notions of superiority.

When Pedro Menéndez de Avilés asked the Lord for thanksgiving in 1565 St. Augustine—fifty-five years before pious Pilgrims of Plymouth Colony paused to ask such a blessing—the table was laden with salted pork preserved in lard, a *cocido* made from dried fava or garbanzo beans, and hardtack. Food defined and divided Europe and America, invaders and hosts.[39]

Food also identified Spaniards and their subjects. Rank, race, and fortune determined what and how one ate in La Florida. "An *hidalgo's* table was set with Mexican majolica rather than Guale pottery and sea shells," writes Amy Bushnell, adding, "Instead of a soldier's diet of salt meat, fish and gruel, the *hidalgo* [a gentleman and a warrior, one certified to be of noble birth] dined on wheaten bread, pork and chicken raised on shellfish." Rank-and-file soldiers dined on Indian food.[40]

Determined to impose a Nueva España upon a new land, Spain faced environmental, cultural, and political obstacles. The Andalusian plow replaced Indian tools, but maintaining and supplying a traditional Spanish diet of wheat, oil, lamb, and wine proved logistically and environmentally impossible. Florida's hot, humid climate doomed the cultivation of vineyards, wheat fields, and olive groves. Dreams of large herds of sheep grazing in Florida meadows were dashed as well, as the animals fell victim to climate and predators. The Spanish diet evolved in Florida, as did native tastes. Borrowing from 1,500 years of ranching tradition, *vaqueros* introduced hardy Castilian range cattle to the grassy interior. For a century and a half, the feral cattle feasted on spring grasses, resisted wolves and bears, and bore calves. By the early nineteenth century, tens of thousands of wild cattle, survivors of the open range, greeted Seminoles and Americans. By the late 1850s, Captain James McKay pioneered the cattle trade with Cuba, rounding up wild herds in the interior and driving them first to Tampa and later to Punta Rassa for shipping.[41]

If Spanish cattle expanded gradually along meadows and prairies, black Ibérico pigs multiplied prolifically in forests and wetlands. They were only the most dramatic symbols of the Columbian Exchange. Minorcan Reds and Andalusian Blues, along with white-faced black Spanish chickens dubbed "the fowls of Seville," became familiar sights in backyards. Spanish brush and scrub goats also survived the voyage and became a source of meat and milk.[42]

Spaniards, along with Africans, Italians, and Greeks, adapted to Indian corn, snap beans, squash, pumpkins, and sassafras. "Maize, not wheat," contends Amy Bushnell, "was the staff of life in Florida." Tomatoes and potatoes, New World crops, arrived relatively late in Florida. Old World crops—such as Minorcan datil peppers; Valencia oranges; Canary Island sugarcane; and African okra, bananas, and watermelons—thrived in the new setting. Archaeologists excavating Pensacola's earliest settlements have found evidence of persimmons and papayas that originated in Mexico, as well as of almonds, plums, and cherries that may have crossed the ocean from Spain to Veracruz, then been loaded aboard ships to Florida. Not everyone accepted the new dietary order. In 1573, a soldier stationed in St. Augustine complained of a diet of "herbs, fish and other scum and vermin."[43]

Failed harvests, too, frustrated residents and alarmed officials. The spring of 1662 witnessed "starving times," while the year 1712 was known as *el gran hambre* (the great hunger).

Strategies and Distances, Disasters and Dependencies

St. Augustine and Pensacola played myriad roles: buffers to the Protestant North and barriers to dreams of a French Gulf coast, a vast frontier for exploration and redemption, and a middle ground for exchanging trades and customs. The mere occupation of St. Augustine and Pensacola—poor but strategic outposts on the fringes of a far-flung empire—validated Spanish territorial claims of legitimacy. The riches of New Spain—silver bars mined at Potosí, gold melted from Aztec temples, sugar and coffee from Jamaica and Cuba—traveled the Spanish Main, skirting St. Augustine and riding the Gulf Stream. St. Augustine and Pensacola functioned as sentinels for Spanish ships fleeing Dutch and British pirates and as havens for the shipwrecked. Lacking precious metals and self-sufficiency, La Florida's towns, forts, and interior depended upon the imperial granaries and treasuries of Havana and Mexico City. The annual royal subsidy (*el situado*) mostly arrived regularly but occasionally not at all. Colonial officials understood that physical distances allowed for bureaucratic latitude. The expression *Obedezco pero no cumplo* (I obey but do not comply) eloquently and prosaically underscored one of the few advantages of isolation. A royal appointment to St. Augustine or Pensacola must have been a shattering disappointment, compared to assignments in Cartagena, Buenos Aires, or Veracruz. An eighteenth-century governor, complaining of a shortage of troops to defend St. Augustine, explained that Spaniards recoil with "horror . . . when they even hear the name Florida."[44]

St. Augustine's survival depended upon provisions and coin from Cuba, along with bushels of corn harvested from native fields and transported to workers at El Castillo de San Marcos and friars in the hinterlands. Pensacola's survival was even more precarious when one considers the hostile natives, frequent hurricanes, and impoverished soil. The besieged presidio survived because of provisions purchased from French traders in Mobile and royal officials in Mexico.

New Spain, when compared to imperial rivals New England, New Netherland, and New France, maintained centralized control of its American possessions. The Archives of the Indies stands as a monument to imperial efforts to duplicate Old Spain in New Spain. Geographer Donald Meinig contends "[Spain's] transatlantic connection was an exact opposite" of patterns found in northern America: "a singular route from a single port connecting to two portals on the American mainland, one the focus for the traffic of Mexico and the other for that of Peru; a rigidly controlled maritime axis of an enormous imperial system that asserted exclusive territorial rights to most of the American world." Yet for all of the bureaucratic commands and directives, New Spain's northern borders were notoriously porous and ungoverned.[45]

Life in La Florida, as governors and slaves came to understand, depended upon the shifting winds of fortune. Literally. The Tainos of the West Indies called the ferocious storms that brewed toward the end of summer *huracanes*. Combining unimaginable power and fury, *el huracán* was a natural wonder and a political nightmare. Hurricanes dashed the dreams of Spanish kings and Creole planters, altering the arc of Spanish Florida. The star-crossed French Huguenots encountered a hurricane that blew their vessels southward until they foundered at Florida's Matanzas Inlet. "During the night of the nineteenth of this month of September [1559]," wrote Tristán de Luna, governor of Florida, to Phillip II, king of Spain, "there came up from the north a fierce tempest, blowing for twenty-four hours from all directions . . . [which] without stopping but increasing continuously, did irreparable damage to the ships of the fleet." The Spanish fort on Pensacola Bay was destroyed. Four years later, a hurricane scattered Ribault's French fleet sailing to relieve Fort Caroline. Spanish forces destroyed the French settlement and put to the sword storm-tossed French Huguenots.[46]

Ultimately, the survival of the St. Augustine settlement depended upon an unlikely natural element: coquina. What St. Augustine lacked in its natural harbor and hot, humid environment was surpassed by abundant deposits of easily quarried soft shell stone. Coquina became St. Augustine's most enduring and embattled image, in the case of the Old City Gate(s) and El Castillo de San Marcos. Spanish engineers understood the special qualities of coquina. Following the construction and destruction of eight wooden forts, the Spanish Crown financed and, between 1672 and 1696, constructed a permanent stone fort. The construction cost a staggering 138,000 pesos and required great numbers of Indian laborers. To find a harbor with stone quarries equal to Anastasia Island, a barrier island off St. Augustine, one had to travel north to New York's Staten Island.[47]

Literature and Culture

The quixotic and mythical search for the Fountain of Youth set a tone for the literature that defined Florida. The doomed 1528 *entrada* led by Pánfilo Narváez begat Alvar Núñez Cabeza de Vaca's *Relación,* a work whose fantastic journey and half-believable resurrection blur the boundary between literal and fantastic. Published in 1542, this was the first book to describe the vast continent north of Mesoamerica. As a reward for Cabeza de Vaca's remarkable deeds, Emperor Charles V appointed him *adelantado* for the South American province of Río de la Plata.[48]

Meanwhile, Narváez's wife dispatched a small party to reconnoiter Tampa Bay in hopes of finding her beloved husband. The Tocobaga Indians slaughtered the hapless Spaniards, sparing only one young man, Juan Ortiz. After torturing Ortiz, the chief prepared to fling him upon the fire, but a young Indian woman pleaded for his life. Thus began the first great captivity narrative in American history. Eight decades later, the Englishman John Smith may well have pirated the Florida tale and transplanted the story line to Pocahontas's Virginia.[49]

Hernando d'Escalante Fontaneda offers another of the early great captivity narratives. Born in Cartagena in 1538 of Spanish parents, he was en route to Spain when his boat was shipwrecked off Florida's Ten Thousand Islands. Rescued, the young boy lived among the Calusa, whom he described as "a fierce people," for four decades until discovered by an exploring party led by Menéndez de Avilés. Upon returning to Spain, Fontaneda wrote *Memoria de las cosas y yndios de la Florida.* "These Indians have no gold, less silver, and less clothing," he recounted to a captivated public. He also—rather ungratefully—recommended Florida's Indians be sold into slavery, so that "their number become thinned." Fontaneda's *Memoria* also introduced a number of place-names that would be familiar to later generations: Mayaimi, Tequesta, and Tampa. Buckingham Smith, a resident of St. Augustine and a remarkable scholar, first translated Fontaneda's volume into English in 1861.[50]

In 1539, the intrepid Hernando de Soto set out from Cuba with 600 men, 237 horses, 200 pigs, a dozen Catholic priests, and two women to conquer

La Florida. His audacious adventure across the continent yielded four precious accounts, including a work that many claim to be the first book set in the present-day United States by a native "American" author, *La Florida del Inca*, by Garcilaso de la Vega. In addition, de Soto's audacious endeavor rescued the seemingly doomed Juan Ortiz, whose skills at speaking and translating native dialects proved useful.[51]

In 1587, the first Franciscans arrived in St. Augustine. One of the friars, Father Alonso Escobedo, left behind a rhyming narrative, *La Florida*, considered to be the first work of literature written in Florida, and an invaluable source on Native American life.[52]

Florida continues to enchant writers. The state has a peculiar way of inspiring and bewitching authors who, in the spirit of Ponce's journey, find themselves shuttled between a place both real and imagined. "The Spaniards," wrote Henry Wiencek, "were the first to learn about the transforming power of the New World that this is a place of mirage and miracle that the two are forever getting mixed up."[53]

From Ball to Bolita

In 1676, Father Juan de Paiva served as a pastor at San Luis de Talimali, an important mission near present-day Tallahassee. He confronted grave challenges—a persistent shortage of dedicated friars, native revolts, and conflicts with secular officials—but he also grappled with an issue challenging men of the cloth today: Is the love of sport compatible with Christian virtues? The Indians' fondness for ball games (*el juego de la pelota*) perplexed missionaries. Their writings include a drawing of a goalpost (a pole topped by a nest cradled by a stuffed eagle). If an Apalachee player kicked the ball into the nest, his team was awarded two points. The players, dressed only in deerskin loincloths, painted their bodies with fetid bear grease. A bishop criticized the game as "barbaric and bestial," and called for its abolition. "And they fall upon one another at full tilt," he wrote, adding that "when the pile is broken up, four or five are lifeless, others have their eyes gouged out, and many arms and legs are broken." Three and a half centuries later, Tallahassee remains the site of ball games played with religious passion.[54] Proving that there is nothing new under the sun, a professor of religion describes our modern obsession with ball games: "Thousands of faithful followers, dressed in ritual clothing, go on long pilgrimages to sacred shrines where they writhe in emotional fervor, enacting bizarre rituals of worship of their god-like leaders." He was, of course, describing the annual Florida–Florida State football match.[55]

Perhaps no ball game enjoyed more fervent support and brought more pleasure than the Cuban game of *bolita*. The Cuban game derived from the Spanish Royal Lottery, which had its beginnings in the eighteenth century, although some have argued that the game of *bolita* may have preceded the introduction of the Spanish lottery in Cuba. Variations have occurred over time. The importation of Chinese immigrants popularized *La china charada* (the Chinese dream book), a pamphlet associating numbers with figures (1 = horse; 14 = frying pan, etc.). Whereas in Cuba the Lotería Nacional Cubana functioned under the aegis of the national government, *bolita* flourished in Florida's free-enterprise economy at the hands of ingenious businessmen and with the unofficial blessing of politicians and law enforcement. *Bolita* can be described as a Latin variation of the numbers game as was played in New York City. *El bolitero* (the numbers man) sold tickets indicating the number patrons guessed would turn up Saturday evening at various gambling emporiums, such as El Dorado in Ybor City. If their number was drawn from a bag of one hundred bolita balls, winning patrons received a payout ranging from 80-1 to 60-1.[56]

The Fourteenth Colony and the American Revolution

Schoolbooks typically ignore the American Revolution's Florida theater. A pawn on the great diplomatic chessboard, Florida became a British possession in 1763, as a result of Spanish missteps in the Seven Years' War/French and Indian War. Britain had taken possession of Havana, and Spain offered Florida in return for the valuable Cuban port city. King George III wrote Lord Butte in November 1762, "Mr. Townshend [colonial secretary of state] was here today . . . said he heard Florida was given us instead of Puerto Rico, that it was an uninhabited country." Britain's fourteenth colony, Florida remained loyal to the British Crown during the American Revolution, while Spain aided the American cause. To this day, Spaniards affectionately call the Málaga Cathedral by the nickname "La Manca" because funds that would have financed the "missing tower" instead supported the revolution across the ocean.[57]

Spain supported the Revolution militarily as well as financially. Spanish general and governor of Louisiana Bernardo de Gálvez expelled British merchants from New Orleans, financed American privateers, assaulted Fort Baton Rouge, bedeviled the British fleet in the Gulf of Mexico, and captured Mobile. He laid siege to Pensacola, capturing the strategic port town on May 8, 1781. When some of the Spanish warships tarried in Pensacola Harbor, Gálvez sent one retiring admiral a message: "Whoever has valor and honor will follow me." King Carlos III of Spain conferred the title of *conde* (count) upon the dashing and decorated hero, who emblazoned upon his coat of arms the inscription "Yo Solo" (I Alone). Galveston, Texas, honors his memory, as does an equestrian statue at the entrance to the U.S. State Department.[58]

Imperial Misfortune

Emblazoned on Spain's royal coat of arms, the words "Plus Ultra" (Farther Beyond) reminded the world of Emperor Charles V's favorite motto. Between the Columbian voyages and 1790, the year the last treasure fleet sailed the Spanish Main, Spain forged an empire ranging from Central and Western Europe to North Africa, from Florida to Texas to Patagonia, from California to the Philippines. Alas, Spain overreached and underachieved. In his influential book *The Rise and Fall of Great Empires,* Paul Kennedy contended that Spain frittered away its tons of bullion and silver: like "water on a roof—it poured on and then was drained away." In slow motion, the Netherlands, and then one by one Spanish colonies in the New World, gained their independence.[59]

Spain surrendered Florida twice, a result of geopolitical misfortune, internal decay, and restless neighbors. A backwater during the epic Seven Years' War, Florida became a diplomatic prize, ceded to Great Britain, which ruled it between 1763 and 1783. When Britain lost the American Revolution, Florida was returned to Spain. The second Spanish period Florida Governor Manuel de Zéspedes (1783–90) famously predicted, "The best fortification would be a living wall of industrious citizens." Land-hungry Americans poured across the porous borders along with Miccosukee-speaking Indians, Swiss planters, African slaves, and Italian and Minorcan escapees. Spain's imperial grasp may have displayed signs of overreaching, but the royal flag still flew across the peninsula as well as a critical but narrow panhandle from the St. Marys River to Mobile Bay across the Pearl River.[60]

The dawn of the nineteenth century ushered in a hurly-burly of Indian rebellions, patriot wars, slave revolts, and shadowy republics, a sideshow and panorama featuring towering and feckless leaders amidst the clashing of empires. Escaped slaves sought sanctuary in Seminole settlements while white Southerners mocked perfumed Spanish dons and Florida's porous, undefended borders. "Florida had always been a disturber of her [Georgia's] peace," wrote historian E. Merton Coulter, and when the opportunity arose to punish Great Britain and expel Spain, Georgians and other Southerners seized the moment to overrun the "corrupt and corrupting province."

Across the southern frontier, so-called American War Hawks cheered the onset of war with Great Britain in 1812. Some blamed the British for the Creek uprisings in the American Southeast; others urged America to seize the moment and oust Spain from the Gulf region. General Andrew Jackson, in a series of military expeditions, methodically crushed the Red Stick Creeks, tweaked the Spanish in Pensacola, and in January 1815 mauled the vaunted British forces at the Battle of New Orleans. What Jackson lacked in diplomacy and portfolio, he made up for in bravado and braggadocio. Accusing the Spanish governor of Pensacola of harboring "refugee banditti from the Creek Nation," he vowed to take "an eye for an eye." While critics in Washington gasped at Jackson's brazen conduct, supporters cheered the Tennessean, even if his conduct violated international niceties. "Old Hickory" marched again to Florida in 1818, ostensibly to demand the return of runaway slaves and to punish unrepentant Seminoles. In two months, the brazen general hanged two British citizens, destroyed a handful of Seminole towns, and captured Pensacola, all the while enraging imperial leaders and more than a few congressmen on two continents.[61]

Secretary of State John Quincy Adams, realizing Jackson's actions, delivered a message the equivalent of a diplomatic battering ram, defended the Hero of New Orleans. The New Englander bluntly told the Spanish minister that if Spain did not surrender Florida, "Spain would not have the possession of Florida to give us." In Madrid, King Ferdinand VII realized imperial troops could not possibly defend Florida. The Spanish Empire was crumbling, not only in Mexico and Florida but also in South America. The only remaining question was when, not if, the aggressive neighbor to the north would seize Florida. The Treaty of Amity, Settlement, and the Limits between the United States of America and His Catholic Majesty, better known as the Adams-Onís Treaty of 1819, was signed, and two years later ratified in Washington and Madrid. The treaty renounced any U.S. claim to Texas, fixed the western boundary of the Louisiana Purchase, and ceded Florida to the United States, providing a semblance of face-saving for humiliated Spain.

The Eagle Screams

The Jacksons left the Hermitage in Nashville for Florida in 1821. Jackson had been appointed Florida's first territorial governor. As the impetuous Tennessean learned of Governor José Callava's delaying tactics, his fiery temper erupted. When the new governor arrived in Pensacola on June 21—his third "visit" to the city—he was prepared to take military action, if necessary, to speed the transfer of power. On July 17, 1821, flag-raising ceremonies in St. Augustine and Pensacola signified a new chapter in Florida history. Once again, boats awaited Spaniards and *floridanos* bound for Cuba. In St. Augustine, Alcalde Juan Entralgo's delays so annoyed American authorities that they forcibly ousted him from his office.[62]

New accents could be heard in Pensacola and St. Augustine. As the Ancient City attracted increasing numbers of northern Protestants, the newcomers disapproved of old customs, labeling the celebration of Carnival and the trafficking of goods on Sunday as "vulgar and gross." Symbolic of the new order was the Americanization and de-Catholicization of El Castillo de San Marcos to Fort Marion, in honor of the Revolutionary War hero. Reinvented as a sanitarium, St. Augustine offered tubercular New Englanders a warm winter sanctuary. Ralph Waldo Emerson arrived in 1827, describing his winter home as "a queer place." The city captivated him. "The Americans live on their offices," he observed, "the Spaniards keep billiard tables, or if not, they send their Negroes to the mud bank to bring oysters . . . and the rest of the time fiddle, masque, and dance." When George R. Fairbanks first set eyes upon St. Augustine in 1842, he described it to his brother as "the oddest looking little old place you can imagine—there is not a thing in it scarcely that looks less than a hundred years old."[63]

As a child, Joseph Marion Hernández walked the hallowed grounds of El Castillo; as a young man he acquired fame as an Indian fighter and statesman. Born in St. Augustine in 1788, he pledged allegiance to the United States, becoming a territorial delegate to the U.S. House of Representatives in 1823 (the first Hispanic to serve in Congress). His reputation as a patriot was burnished by a series of actions in the Second Seminole War, 1835–42. Appointed brigadier general of the mounted volunteers in the U.S. Army, he patrolled the area east of the St. Johns River. In October 1837, General Hernández captured Osceola while the latter displayed a white flag of truce, an event historian John J. Mahon characterized as "the most notorious treachery" of the war. In retaliation the Seminoles burned Hernández's beloved plantation in 1836. Affectionately named Mala Compra (Bad Bargain!), the plantation stood in present-day Flagler County and was the largest such operation in northeast Florida. Later, in 1845, Hernández ran as an unsuccessful Whig candidate for the U.S. Senate before moving to Cuba.[64]

St. Augustine's influence, prestige, and population diminished. Meanwhile, following a devastating yellow fever outbreak in 1822, Pensacola's strategic importance as a naval base and its population grew, the latter reaching 2,300 in 1839. Rachel Jackson, the embattled wife of Florida's first territorial governor, arrived in Pensacola in the summer of 1821. "The inhabitants all speak Spanish and French," she exclaimed. "Some speak four languages. Such a mixed multitude! . . . Fewer white people by far than any other." Horrified at the lack of morality she found in Pensacola, Mrs. Jackson was especially alarmed at how the Spanish kept "the Sabbath profanely." Still, she was charmed by the physical setting. "The most beautiful water prospect I ever saw," Rachel wrote. "There is something in it so exhilarating, so pure, so wholesome, it enlivens the whole system." Claiming injuries to his pocketbook and his family's health, Governor Jackson resigned his appointment and left Florida in October 1821.[65]

For centuries, the presence of Creoles, the result of miscegenation, attracted little concern. As Florida and the Deep South became increasingly paranoid and obsessed over slavery and its future, however, race became a central concern. The "colored Creoles" of Pensacola had enjoyed freedoms not shared by other African Americans, such as the right to carry firearms and the occasional right to serve on juries. Nat Turner's Virginia rebellion in 1831 served as a "fire bell in the night" for white Southerners. State laws tightened control over urban blacks, free blacks, and slave education. A Pensacola editor wrote in 1848, "Some of the Negroes of the town are in the habit of assembling . . . on Sunday evenings to amuse themselves in the way of congo dancing." In 1848, the Florida legislature passed a law demanding that all free Negroes have guardians. When the law was tightened in 1856, almost half of Pensacola's 320 Creoles fled to Mexico.[66]

Spanish accents could still be heard in some of Florida's more remote outposts. In 1824, concerned that the Spanish or British might trade weapons to Florida's newest threat—the Seminole Indians—Colonel George Mercer Brooke supervised construction of a fort at the confluence of Hillsborough Bay and the Hillsborough River. Troops discovered an encampment of Spaniards, Cubans, and "Spanish Indians" on what became known as Spanishtown Creek. For centuries, such fishing *ranchos* had dotted the Gulf coast of Florida. The fishermen built shacks along Charlotte Harbor, Sarasota Bay, and the Ten Thousand Islands, where they salted, smoked, and dried vast catches of mullet, pompano, and red snapper to sell during Lenten season in Cuba. On the southern tip of the sparsely inhabited Pinellas Peninsula, Antonio Máximo Hernández supplied fresh turtle meat and fish from his kraal and *rancho* at Máximo Point. The Spaniards Joe Silva, Juan Levique, and William Papy settled along the peninsula. Impressed by the number and influence of mid-nineteenth-century Spanish settlers in Tampa, Tony Pizzo called Tampa "a cracker village with a Latin accent."[67]

New Spanish Accents in Key West and Tampa

The place-name Cayo Hueso (Bone Key) on ancient Spanish maps became Americanized as Key West. The archipelago of the Florida Keys had long provided a haven for pirates of the Caribbean. In 1823, Commodore David Porter, a hero of the Barbary campaign, arrived to command a new antipiracy naval force based in Key West.

In 1868, Americans were reminded—not for the first or last time—that Cuba lurked only ninety miles from Florida. Key West suddenly became an expatriate center as a violent rebellion enveloped the island. Cuban émigrés, including cigar manufacturers, made Key West an industrial power as well as the largest city in 1890s Florida. "To a person who has never visited this island," wrote Silvia Sunshine in 1879, "it is impossible to imagine that only miles from the mainland of Florida is a city so nearly in appearance to the Spanish dominions of the Old World where hardly a sentence in English is heard."[68]

In 1886 a new Cuban exile community rivaled Key West. Don Vicente Martínez Ybor, a Spanish patron who had fled Cuba for Key West, founded Ybor City, near Tampa. Thousands of Cubans (white and black), Spaniards, and later Italians created one of America's most extraordinary industrial towns. *Lectores* (readers) in Ybor City and Key West read novels of Cervantes, Pérez-Galdós, and Hugo to *tabaqueros* (cigar workers).[69]

Ybor City and Key West were cities of ideas and intellectuals. A vibrant and prolific Latin culture and Spanish-language press flourished. Scores of long-forgotten newspapers and magazines sprang to life between the 1870s and 1920s: *Eco de Florida, El Yara, Cuba, El Cubano, La Contienda, El Internacional, La Traducción, La Gaceta, El Porvenir, El Avisador Cubano,* and *Hispano-Americano*.[70]

In Tampa, Spaniards built enduring institutions. In 1891, they organized El Centro Español, a mutual-aid society. The club's bylaws stipulated that all members "be Spaniards by birth and by patriotic inclination *or* they be loyal to Spain and to its prestige in America." In 1892, members dedicated an ornate wooden structure, an event highlighted by fireworks and several lyric operas. In 1910, the Spanish community was so confident of its future that it dedicated two elaborate brick structures, one in Ybor City and another in West Tampa. Asturian immigrants eventually organized their own society. El Centro Asturiano became a North American auxiliary of Havana's renowned namesake building and club. Cuban leaders approved the new charter in 1902. A decade later, work began on a new clubhouse that the local paper described as "the most beautiful building in the South." The

$110,000 structure featured a 1,200-seat theater, a *cantina*, and a modern *biblioteca* (library). By 1919, El Centro Asturiano boasted 3,600 members. During the New Deal, the club housed America's only Spanish-language theater.[71]

The most far-reaching and progressive achievement by Tampa's Spanish mutual-aid societies occurred in the field of cooperative health care. Spaniards built two modern hospitals and several medical clinics that offered free care to members. The American Medical Association condemned "collectivized medicine" and blackballed physicians who worked for the Latin medical clinics.

Immigrants from the provinces of Galicia and Asturias recalled injustices inflicted upon their families by two despised institutions: the Spanish army and the Catholic Church. It was no coincidence that the doctrine of anarchism flourished in Galicia and Asturias. In 1913, Manuel Padrinas, a Spanish anarchist who had lived in Tampa, assassinated Spain's premier José Canalejas y Méndez.[72]

Cuban Wars of Independence

If the blood of the martyrs was the seed of the Church, Captain Joseph Fry appeared an unlikely candidate for martyrdom. Born in 1826 in Fort Brooke, the military cantonment that evolved into the city of Tampa, Fry graduated from the U.S. Naval Academy. Following the Civil War, Fry became captain of the *Virginius*, a side-wheel steamer. Its cargo, however, did not include tourists but rather guns targeted for Cuban rebels. In 1868, a rebellion erupted in Cuba known as the Ten Years' War. As Captain Fry sailed near Guantánamo, Cuba, a Spanish corvette commandeered the American vessel. In drumhead courts-martial, Captain Fry and his crew were convicted of piracy. The penalty was death. On November 7, 1873, Spanish firing squads shot Fry, fifty-seven other Cuban revolutionaries, and some Americans.[73] The incident became an international cause célèbre.

The Ten Years' War created a pantheon of heroes. The Cuban-born José Martí, son of Spanish immigrants, was exiled following his arrest for treason and sedition in the conflict. He became a fiery revolutionary following his visits to Ybor City and Key West in the early 1890s. "In Tampa, the eagle screamed," he wrote; "in Key West, the sun shone." In 1895, Martí and other expatriates launched a second uprising known as the Cuban War of Independence. Cubans in Tampa and Key West pledged "*un día para la patria*," one's day's wages for Mother Cuba. Motivated by prophets and profits, the cause brought together a strange coalition in Florida. Insurgents battling Spanish *voluntarios* needed arms and ammunition. In 1896 alone, thirty gunrunners managed to smuggle cargos along the Cuban coastline. The filibusters included a future Florida governor, Napoleon Bonaparte Broward.[74]

Martí admired American freedoms and values but feared American power. His fears became reality three years after he was killed on the battlefield in 1895, when the USS *Maine* exploded in Havana harbor. The Cuban War of Independence quickly morphed into the Spanish-American War, famously encapsulated in a contemporary slogan, "Remember the *Maine*; To Hell with Spain."

The young author Sherwood Anderson shared his countrymen's contempt of Spain, likening this war to "robbing an old Gypsy woman in a vacant lot after a fair." The war came to Florida fast and furiously. Secretary of War Russell Alger announced that Tampa would serve as the base of military operations for the invasion. American soldiers also gathered in Fernandina, Jacksonville, Lakeland, Miami, and Key West. War fever spiked a virulent hatred of all things Spanish. A *New York Times* reporter noted in Tampa, "Dark scowls lurk upon the faces of American men as Spanish is heard spoken. Whether by Cuban or Spanish refugee, the language is hated." Fearing a fifth column, the U.S. military took possession of El Centro Español.[75]

Neo-Spanish Revival: Gilded Age St. Augustine

In 1884 one of America's greatest robber barons, Henry Morrison Flagler, made a fateful trip to Florida. Newly wed, Flagler fell in love with the Ancient City. "We can make St. Augustine," he announced, "the Newport of the South." With an iron wheel and millions of dollars, Flagler did not so much create a southern Newport as reinvent St. Augustine.

In one astonishing decade, Flagler built three of the grandest hotels in Florida history, reshaping St. Augustine and recasting Florida tourism and transportation. The architectural team of John Merven Carrère and Thomas Hastings designed on a grand scale, and the Ponce de Leon was grand. Louis Tiffany stained glass decorated the interiors. Dedicated in 1888, the Spanish revival hotel ushered in Florida's Gilded Age. Flagler built two additional hotels, the Cordova and Alcazar, which also dazzled visitors with their Spanish Renaissance motifs.[76]

In Tampa, Flagler's fellow robber baron and talented rival, Henry Bradley Plant, built the grandiose Tampa Bay Hotel in 1891. The Tampa Bay Hotel's thirteen minarets atop curved onion domes dazzled critics who never quite agreed whether the architectural style was Spanish Moorish, Moorish revival, or Ottoman baroque.[77]

America in general and Florida in particular was in the midst of a powerful transition. Once a society committed to production and the Protestant work ethic, America was increasingly being reorganized around consumption and leisure. Recreation, once the antithesis of hard work, was now becoming its restorative tonic. The elites vacationing in Florida engaged in conspicuous consumption to confirm their social standing. A month of rest and recreation in a Florida hotel or palace that resembled Old Spain became the prescription for Americans whose nerves needed restoring.

Florida, along with America, had embraced a newly invented Spanish style of architecture. Robber barons needed a grandiose style and the rediscovery of Spanish Renaissance/Moorish castles, fountains, and courtyards worked its magic in Tampa and St. Augustine. The Ponce de Leon and Alcazar owed as much to the popularity of Washington Irving's *The Alhambra* (1832) as any authentic interest in or evidence of Spanish ruins in Florida. To the upper classes who flocked to Florida for the high winter season, the vision of romantic courtyards and lush Gardens of Earthly Delights evoked a welcome relief and escape from a world that was increasingly preoccupied with busy schedules and clockwork efficiency.[78]

Florida Discovers Spain: The 1920s

The decade of the 1920s introduced Florida to America through the newsreels of land booms, bathing-beauty pageants, and new architectural styles. Redefined and reimagined once again in the 1920s, Florida became a spot Americans wanted to visit, a fast-paced dreamy setting. Places not yet born or not yet part of Wall Street or Main Street conversation—Miami Beach and Coral Gables, Boca Raton, and Opa-locka—symbolized the new Florida.

A new or newly adapted architecture defined Florida and California, the two great American dream states. The mission and Mediterranean revival styles stamped a new identity upon the Sunshine State. Ironically, the California mission style caught on in a way that the Florida mission style never did. Florida's missions, built of palmetto thatch and wood, did not survive, whereas California's missions survived because of their stucco construction.

Florida became identified as the Mediterranean of America, a place of escape for businessmen who needed a Spanish vacation but did not like Spanish waiters or Spanish accents. Why travel to Córdoba or Barcelona when one could drive the Model T to Sarasota or Palm Beach and be surrounded by buildings that looked like they belonged in Andalusia? Architects, many of whom had traveled to Europe and Latin America, created an American style called Med rev, or Mediterranean revival. Alexander Moore, once ambassador to Spain, is said to have gasped upon first seeing Addison Mizner's Palm Beach: "It's more Spanish than anything I ever saw in Spain!" To romanticize and reinvent the newest forms, Americans incorporated the words *patio, plaza,* and *loggia* into the lexicon.[79]

The most dramatic Spain-in-America motif appeared along the shores of Key Biscayne in 1913–14. Charles Deering, the scion of an agricultural machinery fortune, wished to re-create palaces he had admired in Italy and Spain. He christened his forty-room, 180-acre fantasy Villa Vizcaya. Completed in 1916, Vizcaya—named after a province in the Basque region—borrowed architectural inspiration as well as purchases of tapestries, paintings, and pottery from Spain.[80]

While some critics lampooned Florida's Mediterranean revival style, historians and archivists cheered the efforts of John Stetson and Jeanette Thurber Connor to secure the oldest records of Florida's Spanish past. In 1913, the fabulously wealthy stockbroker Washington Connor married Jeanette Thurber. Having moved to and built a mansion in New Smyrna, Florida, Connor became fascinated with antiquities. Jeannette Thurber came from a cultured family and shared her new husband's fascination with the past. After scouring Spanish archives for precious Florida documents, she met John B. Stetson (1884–1952), the son of the famous hatmaker and college namesake in DeLand. "Together," writes Kevin McCarthy, "they founded the Florida State Historical Society (not to be confused with the Florida Historical Society) in 1921." Connor, Stetson, and the Florida State Historical Society began in earnest to microfilm and make copies of thousands of documents in Spain, most notably in the Archives of the Indies.[81]

What wealthy Americans could not duplicate, they literally excavated, boxed, and moved to the Sunshine State. In 1924, a delegation of Americans visited Asturias, Spain, to pay their respects to Pedro Menéndez de Avilés, the founder of St. Augustine. The occasion was the reinterment of Avilés's most famous son. One of the delegates was Angel L. Cuesta, an emigrant from Asturias who had become a wealthy cigar manufacturer in Tampa. Cuesta, with King Alfonso's help, left Spain with a valuable relic: the coffin of Menéndez. St. Augustine became the final resting place for the daring *adelantado*.[82]

Fears and Hopes: The 1930s

Between the Great Depression and Pearl Harbor, events in Europe and Asia alarmed Floridians, already reeling economically and desperate to avoid another military catastrophe. Floridians who once called Germany, Britain, and Czechoslovakia home watched in horror as their ancestral homelands were swept into the maelstrom of war. Nowhere was the "coming of war" felt more intensely than in Tampa and its Spanish communities.

In April 1931 Tampeños cheered the news that their beloved Spain had deposed the decaying Bourbon monarchy and embraced republicanism. In Tampa the moment was remembered for two searing events: the twilight of *la lectura* (*los lectores'* readings), a beloved custom that vanished forever because of labor disturbances, and the Great Depression that swept away the old order, and with it the popularity of premium Tampa-made cigars. While neither the cigar industry nor the custom of *la lectura* ever recovered, Tampa's five thousand Spaniards cheered Spain's democratic yearnings.[83]

But the Republican government splintered, leading to social, economic, and political tumult. In 1936, the Popular Front (a coalition of socialists and communists) took power back from the right. By July, Spain drifted into a hellish civil war, one that would result in hundreds of thousands of deaths. Tampa's Spaniards faithfully and vigorously supported the Popular Front, raising a staggering $200,000 for the Republic, and purchasing four ambulances for the Spanish Red Cross. Latin women collected clothing and milk for war-torn Spain; children organized paper drives and joined the Juventud Democrática Antifascista de West Tampa. "Everybody gave 10 percent of their pay to the Republic," remembered West Tampa native and writer Jose Yglesias. He later wrote about his father's native Galicia in the book *The Goodbye Land*. Almost daily, Florida newspapers reported the frightening struggle for Spain's future. One such article began, "Senorita Pilara La Fuente, 22-year-old girl anarchist of the Spanish loyalists, who boasts of having slit the throats of 1000 wounded rebels. . . ." Although not everyone understood the war's meaning, many feared it was a dress rehearsal for World War II, as Germany, Italy, and the Soviet Union sent troops and munitions to support their respective sides. When General Francisco Franco triumphed in 1938, Tampeños wept.[84]

The last glimpse of what had once been one of the most radical communities in the United States occurred in 1948, in an unlikely setting. The U.S. presidential race of 1948 featured four candidates: the incumbent Harry S. Truman, the GOP nominee Thomas Dewey, the Dixiecrat Strom Thurmond, and the Progressive Party's Henry Wallace. The Iowa-born Wallace had served as Franklin Roosevelt's vice president (1941–45), but the president unceremoniously dumped Wallace because of his strident liberalism and overtures to the Soviet Union. Wallace asked the great black tenor Paul Robeson to perform a benefit concert for the ill-funded Progressives in Tampa. Robeson agreed, but only if Tampa's Phillips Field permitted desegregated seating. Robeson began by expressing words that cheered the crowd: "¡Viva España! ¡Viva España!" Robeson understood the audience was composed largely of elderly Latins who had passionately supported the Republican cause in Spain. One Spanish family named their son Henry Wallace Lavandera. The other Henry Wallace won six precincts in Tampa, his only such victories in the Deep South that election.[85]

St. Augustine Reinvented, Again

American tourists motoring south along U.S. 1 or Highway A1A fell in love, once again, with St. Augustine. New technologies allowed more Americans than ever to walk the narrow streets and take etchings from the gravestones of Tolomato Cemetery. St. Augustine accommodated motorists so eagerly that for years cars drove through the Old City Gates. In 1937, the city's first radio station took the call letters WFOY, "Wonderful Fountain of Youth." In 1959 a massive restoration of the city began.[86]

Revolutions in Our Midst

In 1955, a new revolutionary visited Tampa. Like Martí, he was a Creole born in Cuba. Like his predecessor, he also had been jailed for revolutionary activities. But Fidel Castro was determined to finish Martí's dream of Cuba Libre. His first words to the 26th of July Club supporters in Tampa had been the first sentence Martí had uttered in 1891: "Para Cuba que sufre, la primera palabra" (For Cuba who suffers, the first word). Fidel understood the symbolic role of Tampa in Cuban history. "The Republic of Cuba," a beardless Fidel stated, "was the daughter of the cigarmakers of Tampa." On December 31, 1958, *los barbudos* (the bearded guerrillas) seized Havana when dictator Fulgencio Batista abdicated. Batista had already sent his extensive art collection to his Daytona Beach mansion. Few Floridians or *floridanos* understood the repercussions. Fifty years later a Castro still holds the reins of Cuba, but other revolutions, more cultural than political, more economic than ideological, have taken hold across the Straits of Florida.[87]

The first wave of Cubans arrived in 1959. Defiantly insisting that they were exiles, not emigrants, the largely middle- and upper-middle-class émigrés were welcomed by civic, humanitarian, and federal agencies. Day by day, throughout the 1950s, 1960s, and 1970s, small groups of Cubans landed in Miami, determined to achieve the American and Florida Dream. A million dreams later, sociologists argue that the Cuban experience in South Florida constitutes the greatest immigrant success story in American history. In the process, Cubans profoundly changed Florida as much as Florida changed them. Today, an astonishing 60 percent of Miami-Dade County residents were born abroad. More than half the population speaks a language other than English at home. Miami-Dade County boasts the highest proportion of foreign-born residents of any county in America. But perhaps most remarkably, the Spanish accents in Miami-Dade and Florida are no longer exclusively Cuban; indeed, among the burgeoning Hispanic population in the state, Cubans are a minority.[88]

In Central Florida, surging numbers of Puerto Ricans have altered the politics and the accents of the region. In other places, Mexicans represent the demographic future. Hispanics now outnumber African Americans in Florida, a development considered as unimaginable as it was improbable a half century earlier.

Since the 1980s, each new Hispanic accomplishment—the first election of a Cuban-born congresswoman, the success of Univisión, the election of the first U.S. senator who was a Pedro Pan refugee—has reverberated across the state and nation. But in a place with deep Spanish roots, what may appear to be a "first" can too often turn out not to be. When Tampa's Bob Martínez took his inaugural oath in January 1987, journalists noted the historic meaning of the day: Florida now had its first Hispanic governor. Historian Bill Coker reminded the Fourth Estate that Bob Martínez, the grandson of Spanish immigrants, was actually the fiftieth Hispanic governor of Florida![89]

The reverberations of the Columbian Exchange can be felt at the dawn of a new century and millennium. Supermarkets, *bodegas, taquerías, tapas* bars, *heladerías,* and cafes serving *café con leche*—Behold the Florida cornucopia! Floridians and *floridanos* can with ease indulge in the new Columbian Exchange: mamey *batidos,* guava *pasteles,* mango *helados,* fried Cuban-Chinese rice, African cassava, Jamaican jerk spices, Honduran tomatillos, African yams, delicatessens serving *jamón ibérico,* Polish pierogi, Korean kimchi, and fresh mozzarella made from water buffalo. The cooking pot may prove to be more powerful than the melting pot. A history of Florida foodways presents a parade of cultures both resistant to change and eager to adapt, a virulent fear of outsiders and an innate curiosity about the "other's" stockpot.

Fittingly, Florida's oldest eating establishment is the Columbia, "the Gem of Spanish Restaurants." In a state of bewildering mobility and change, the Columbia, founded in Tampa's Ybor City in 1905, symbolizes deep roots and cultural persistence. Several dishes especially emphasize the importance of tradition and memory, but also change and adaptability: *caldo gallego* (Galician soup) and Spanish bean soup. An iconic dish in northern Spain, *caldo gallego* contains white beans (typically fabe beans), greens, ham, broth, and potatoes (the last ingredient added after the sixteenth century). In Spain, *cocido madrileño* remains a classic dish. The soup or stew consists of chickpeas or garbanzo beans, flavored with pork, chorizo, beef shank, and chicken, along with vegetables. The time-consuming dish is then disassembled and served in courses: broth with noodles, followed by chickpeas and vegetables, then the meats. In Tampa, Spanish bean soup was stripped of its time-consuming elegance and became a working-class one-dish soup. Hearty soups fit for cold Galician and Asturian winters, they seem out of place in Florida's hot and humid climate. Gazpacho, a cold tomato soup popular in southern Spain, would seem better suited. But Galicians and Asturians, not Andalusians, immigrated to Tampa, and they brought with them the memories and recipes of their beloved *cocidos* and *caldo gallego*.[90]

La Florida in the New Millennium

Florida's historic trajectory is complete. How fitting and symmetrical that a place called La Florida in 1513—a colony, territory, and state shaped by Spanish-speaking *floridanos*—has become a lodestar for Hispanics at the dawn of a new millennium.

Notes

1. Carla Rahn Phillips, *Six Galleons for the King of Spain: Imperial Defense in the Early Seventeenth Century* (Baltimore: Johns Hopkins University Press, 1986), 9.

2. Gary R. Mormino, *Land of Sunshine, State of Dreams: A Social History of Modern Florida* (Gainesville: University Press of Florida, 2008), 7.

3. Samuel Eliot Morison, *The European Discovery of America: The Southern Voyages, a.d. 1492–1616* (New York: Oxford University Press, 1974), 506. See also "Ponce de León's Quest," 502–16; Robert H. Fuson, *Juan Ponce de León and the Spanish Discovery of Puerto Rico and Florida* (Blacksburg, VA: McDonald and Woodward, 2000).

4. Herrera quoted in Edward W. Lawson, *The Discovery of Florida and Its Discoverer Juan Ponce de León* (St. Augustine: n.p., 1946), 14–16.

5. Alfred W. Crosby, *Ecological Imperialism: The Biological Expansion of Europe, 900–1900*, 2nd ed. (Cambridge: Cambridge University Press, 2004), 127–28; Fuson, *Juan Ponce de León*, 106, 120–21.

6. L. D. Scisco, "The Track of Ponce de León in 1513," *Bulletin of the American Geographic Society* 45 (1913): 721.

7. Herbert Eugene Bolton, *The Spanish Borderlands: A Chronicle of Old Florida and the Southwest* (New Haven, CT: Yale University Press, 1921), 7.

8. T. Frederick Davis, "Ponce de León's Second Voyage and Attempt to Colonize Florida," *Florida Historical Quarterly* 14 (July 1935): 51, 59.

9. Ibid., 60–62.

10. "Ponce," *Miami Herald*, November 25, 1945.

11. Morison, *European Discovery of America*, 505; George Monteiro, ed., *Conversations with Elizabeth Bishop* (Oxford: University Press of Mississippi, 1996), 1.

12. David J. Weber, *The Spanish Frontier in North America* (New Haven, CT: Yale University Press, 2009), 29.

13. Bernal Díaz del Castillo, *The Conquest of New Spain*, trans. J. M. Cohen (New York: Penguin Books, 1963). For an excellent overview of the Fountain of Youth controversies, see Michael J. Francis, "Who Started the Myth about a Fountain of Youth?" (Florida Humanities Council) *Forum* 35 (Fall 2011): 6–9.

14. "Ponce de Leon Began State Publicity," *Florida Times-Union*, January 18, 1950.

15. "'Another Beautiful Day in Miami,' with poet Campbell McGrath." *FIU News*, August 31, 2009.

16. F. Scott Fitzgerald, *The Great Gatsby* (Peterborough, ON: Broadview Editions, 2007), 176.

17. Mormino, *Land of Sunshine*, 123–48.

18. William H. McNeill, "How Columbus Remade the World," *Humanities* 6 (December 1985): 3–7.

19. Carlos Fuentes, *A New Time for Mexico*, trans. Marina Gutman Castañeda and Carlos Fuentes (Berkeley: University of California Press, 1997), 192.

20. Alfred Crosby, *The Columbian Exchange: Biological and Cultural Consequences of 1492* (Westport, CT: Greenwood, 1972); Ann F. Ramenofsky, *Vectors of Death: The Archaeology of European Contact* (Albuquerque: University of New Mexico Press, 1987); Henry F. Dobyns, *Their Numbers Become Thinned: Native American Population Dynamics in Eastern North America* (Knoxville: University of Tennessee Press, 1983), 15–23. Dobyns's assertion that Florida's pre-Columbian Indian population may have numbered one to two million inhabitants set off contentious debate; see Amy Bushnell, *The King's Coffer: Proprietors of the Spanish Florida Treasury, 1565–1702* (Gainesville: University Presses of Florida, 1981), 13–14.

21. Richard A. White, *The Middle Ground: Indians, Empires, and Republics in the Great Lakes Region, 1650–1815* (Cambridge: Cambridge University Press, 1990); Jane G. Landers, *Atlantic Creoles in the Age of Revolutions* (Cambridge, MA: Harvard University Press, 2010); James H. Merrell, *The Indians' New World: Catawbas and Their Neighbors from European Contact through the Era of Removal* (New York: W. W. Norton, 1991), 543–45.

22. Bernard Bailyn, *The Peopling of British North America: An Introduction* (New York: Alfred A. Knopf, 1986), 3–6. The term *Neo-Europes* was coined by Alfred Crosby in *Ecological Imperialism*, 2–3.

23. Michael Gannon, *The Cross in the Sand: The Early Catholic Church in Florida, 1513–1870* (Gainesville: University of Florida Press, 1965), 78–79.

24. Engineer quoted in Woodbury Lowery, *The Lowery Collection: A Descriptive List of Maps of the Spanish Possessions within the Present Limits of the United States, 1502–1820* (Washington, DC: Government Printing Office, 1912), 270; Crosby, *Columbian Exchange*, 114; Deb Bennett and Robert S. Hoffman, "Ranching in the New World," in *Seeds of Change: A Quincentennial Commemoration*, ed. Herman J. Viola and Carolyn Margolis (Washington, DC: Smithsonian Institution Press, 1991), 90–111.

25. John J. Clune Jr. and Margo S. Stringfield, *Historic Pensacola* (Gainesville: University Press of Florida, 2009), 57; *Presidio Santa María de Galve: A Struggle for Survival in Colonial Spanish Pensacola*, ed. Judith A. Bense (Gainesville: University Press of Florida, 2003).

26. Quoted by permission of Russell D. James, e-mail to the author July 12, 2013.

27. Landers, *Atlantic Creoles*, 1–4, 6, 9, 11, 12, 36, 210, 238.

28. Francis Parkman, *The Jesuits in North America in the Seventeenth Century* (London: Macmillan, 1905), 131; Richard L. Kagan, "From Noah to Moses: The Genesis of Historical Scholarship on Spain in the United States," in *Spain in America: The Origins of Hispanicism in the United States*, ed. Richard L. Kagan (Urbana: University of Illinois Press, 2002) 21–48; Weber, *Spanish Frontier in North America*, 64–65: Charles Gibson, *The Black Legend: Anti-Spanish Attitudes in the Old World and New* (New York: Knopf, 1971).

29. Charles Krauthammer, "Hail Columbus, Dead White Male," *Time*, May 27, 1991, 74.

30. Udall quoted in Joseph Judge, "Exploring Our Forgotten Century," *National Geographic* (March 1988): 331–62.

31. John H. Hann, *Apalachee: The Land Between the Rivers* (Gainesville: University Presses of Florida, 1988), 143–44; Weber, *Spanish Frontier in North America*, 94–96.

32. Paul Schneider, *Brutal Journey: The Epic Story of the First Crossing of North America* (New York: Henry Holt, 2006), 5, 27–28, 261–62, 313–18; Weber, *Spanish Frontier in North America*, 16, 36–37.

33. Jane Landers, "Gracia Real de Santa Teresa de Mose: A Free Black Town in Spanish Colonial Florida," *American Historical Review* 95 (February 1990): 9–30.

34. Michael V. Gannon, "The Columbian Quincentenary: What Will We Celebrate?" in *Spanish Pathways in Florida, 1492–1992*, ed. Ann L. Henderson and Gary R. Mormino (Sarasota, FL: Pineapple Press, 1991), 332; John H. Hann, *A History of the Timucua Indians and Missions* (Gainesville: University Press of Florida, 1996), 6–8, 122–26, 130–31; Jerald T. Milanich, *Laboring in the Fields of the Lord: Spanish Missions and Southeastern Indians* (Gainesville: University Press of Florida, 1999); James Axtell, *The Invasion Within: The Control of Culture in North America* (New York: Oxford University Press, 1985), 54, 81.

35. Weber, *Spanish Frontier in North America*, 179–94, 243–58.

36. Donald W. Meinig, *The Shaping of America*, vol. 1, *Atlantic America, 1492–1800* (New Haven: Yale University Press, 1986), 14.

37. Amy Bushnell, "The Noble and Loyal City, 1565–1763," in *The Oldest City: St. Augustine, Saga of Survival*, ed. Jean Parker Waterbury (St. Augustine, FL: St. Augustine Historical Society, 1983), 38–39.

38. Amy Turner Bushnell, "Thomás Menéndez Márquez: *Criollo*, Cattleman and *Contador*," in *Spanish Pathways in Florida*, 118–39.

39. "First Thanksgiving Dinner in U.S." *Huffington Post*, July 11, 2013; "Historian: St. Augustine Had First Thanksgiving," *St. Augustine Record*, November 25, 2005; Robyn Gioia, *America's Real First Thanksgiving* (St. Petersburg, FL: Pineapple Press, 2007).

40. Bushnell, *King's Coffer*, 11, 25-26.

41. Crosby, *Columbian Exchange*, 76-77; Weber, *Spanish Frontier in North America*, 23-24, 232; Charles C. Mann, *1493: Uncovering the New World Columbus Created* (New York: Alfred A. Knopf, 2011), 9, 10, 43-45; Canter Brown Jr., *Florida's Peace River Frontier* (Gainesville: University Press of Florida, 1991), 198; Henry Hobhouse, *Seeds of Change: Six Plants That Transformed Mankind* (New York: Shoemaker and Hoard, 2005), 96; Kathleen A. Deagan and Edward Chaney, "St. Augustine and the La Florida Colony: New Life-Styles in a New Land," in *First Encounters: Spanish Explorations in the Caribbean and the United States, 1492-1570*, ed. Jerald T. Milanich and Susan Milbrath (Gainesville: University Presses of Florida, 1989), 179-80.

42. Charles Mann's book *1493* offers a fresh perspective on how globalization shaped a new diet in the centuries following Columbus and Ponce.

43. Soldier quoted in Weber, *Spanish Frontier in North America*, 232; Bushnell, *King's Coffer*, 11, 81; Sidney Mintz, *Sweetness and Power: The Place of Sugar in Modern History* (New York: Penguin, 1985); Jean Andrew, "A Botanical Mystery: The Elusive Trail of the Datil Pepper to St. Augustine," *Florida Historical Quarterly* 74 (1995): 132-47.

44. Bushnell, *King's Coffer*, 5-6; Dobyns, *Their Numbers Become Thinned*, 49; John Tepaske, *The Governorship of Spanish Florida* (Durham, NC: Duke University Press, 1964), 3, 6, 12.

45. Meinig, *Atlantic America*, 38.

46. Louis A. Pérez, *Winds of Change: Hurricanes and the Transformation of Nineteenth-Century Cuba* (Chapel Hill: University of North Carolina Press, 2001); Sherry Johnson, *Climate and Catastrophe in Cuba and the Atlantic World in the Age of Revolution* (Chapel Hill: University of North Carolina Press, 2011), 71-72, 76, 153-59.

47. Jean Parker Waterbury, "The Castillo Years, 1668-1763," in *Oldest City*, 57-90; Luis Rafael Arana and Albert Manucey, *The Building of Castillo de San Marcos* (n.p.: Eastern National Park and Monument Assoc., 1977).

48. *The Narrative of Cabeza de Vaca*, ed. and trans. with an introduction by Rolena Adorno and Patrick Charles Pautz (Lincoln: University of Nebraska Press, 2003). José Fernández, "Opposing Views of La Florida by Alvar Núñez Cabeza de Vaca and El Inca Garcilaso de la Vega," *Florida Historical Quarterly* 54 (1976): 170-80; John McGrath, "Sixteenth-Century Florida in the European Imagination," *Florida Historical Quarterly* 91 (Winter 2013): 401-18.

49. Schneider, *Brutal Journey*, 96-100; "Florida, 1528: A Tale with the Same Twist," *New York Times*, July 12, 1995; "'Pocahontas' Tale Likened to Earlier Rescue of Spaniard in Florida," *Los Angeles Times*, July 12, 1995.

50. *Memoir of Hernando d'Escalante Fontaneda on the Country and Ancient Indian Tribes of Florida*, trans. and ed. Buckingham Smith (St. Augustine: n.p., 1861).

51. Charles Hudson, "The Hernando de Soto Expedition, 1539-1543," in *The Forgotten Centuries: Indians and Europeans in the American South, 1521-1704*, ed. Charles Hudson and Carmen Chaves Tesser (Athens: University of Georgia Press, 1994), 74-103; Milanich, *Laboring in the Fields of the Lord*, 23-26, 68-76.

52. Gannon, *Cross in the Sand*, 38.

53. Henry Wiencek, "The Spain Among Us," *American Heritage* 44 (April 1993): 52-63.

54. John H. Hann, "Father Juan de Paiva: Spanish Friar of Colonial Florida," in *Spanish Pathways*, 140–67.

55. David G. Hackett, "Is Football a Religion?" (Florida Humanities Council) *Forum* 21 (Fall 1998): 50.

56. Gary R. Mormino and George E. Pozzetta, *The Immigrant World of City: Italians and Their Latin Neighbors in Tampa, 1885–1985* (Urbana: University of Illinois Press, 1987), 281–84, 301–2.

57. King George III's letter in Donna T. McCaffrey, "Charles Townshend and Plans for British East Florida," *Florida Historical Quarterly* 68 (January 1990): 325; Weber, *Spanish Frontier in North America*, 155.

58. Weber, *Spanish Frontier in North America*, 169, 195–97; John Francis Bannon, *The Spanish Borderlands Frontier, 1513–1821* (Albuquerque: University of New Mexico Press, 1970), 187, 201, 221.

59. Paul Kennedy, *The Rise and Fall of the Great Powers: Economic Change and Military Conflict from 1500 to 2000* (New York: Random House, 1987); Weber, *Spanish Frontier in North America*, 201–3.

60. Helen Hornbeck Tanner, *Zéspedes in East Florida, 1784–1790* (Miami, FL: University of Miami Press, 1963); Susan Parker, "Men Without God or King: Rural Settlers of East Florida, 1784–1790," *Florida Historical Quarterly* 69 (October 1990): 135–55; Weber, *Spanish Frontier in North America*, 199–220.

61. James G. Cusick, *The Other War of 1812: The Patriot War and the American Invasion of Spanish East Florida* (Gainesville: University Press of Florida, 2003); E. Merton Coulter, *Georgia: A Short History* (Chapel Hill: University of North Carolina Press, 1933), 210; Robert L. Gold, *Borderland Empires in Transition: The Triple-Nation Transfer of Florida* (Carbondale: Southern Illinois University Press, 1969).

62. William S. Coker and Susan R. Parker, "The Second Spanish Period in the Two Floridas," in *New History of Florida*, ed. Michael Gannon (Gainesville: University Press of Florida, 1996), 150–66.

63. Daniel L. Schaefer, "U.S. Territory and State," in *New History of Florida*, 207–30.

64. Ibid., 210–11; George E. Buker, "The Americanization of St. Augustine," in *Oldest City*, 165–68.

65. Clune and Stringfield, *Historic Pensacola*, 148–52.

66. Ira Berlin, *Slaves without Masters: The Free Negro in the Antebellum South* (New York: New Press, 1992), 131–32; Ruth B. Barr and Modest Hargis, "The Voluntary Exile of Free Negroes of Pensacola," *Florida Historical Quarterly* 17 (July 1938): 1–14.

67. Canter Brown Jr., *Tampa before the Civil War* (Tampa, FL: University of Tampa Press, 1999); James Covington, "Trade Relations between Southwestern Florida and Cuba, 1600–1840," *Florida Historical Quarterly* 38 (October 1959): 114–28; Covington, "The Cuban Fishing Rancho: A Spanish Enclave within British Florida," in *Anglo-Spanish Confrontation on the Gulf Coast during the American Revolution*, ed. William Coker and Robert Rea (Pensacola, FL: Pensacola Gulf Coast History and Humanities Conference, 1982), 17–24; Tony Pizzo, *Tampa Town, 1824–1886: The Cracker Village with a Latin Accent* (Miami, FL: Hurricane House, 1968).

68. Silvia Sunshine, *Petals Plucked from Sunny Climes* (Nashville, TN: Southern Methodist Publishing, 1880), 316.

69. Mormino and Pozzetta, *Immigrant World;* Susan D. Greenbaum, *More Than Black: Afro-Cubans in Tampa* (Gainesville: University Press of Florida, 2002); Nancy A. Hewitt, *Southern Discomfort: Women's Activism in Tampa, Florida, 1880s–1920s* (Urbana: University of Illinois Press, 2001).

70. Mormino and Pozzetta, *Immigrant World,* 102–3, 143–74; Louis A. Pérez, "Reminiscences of a *Lector*: Cuban Cigar Workers in Tampa," *Florida Historical Quarterly* 53 (April 1975): 443–49.

71. Mormino and Pozzetta, *Immigrant World,* 175–209; Miguel A. Bretos, *Cuba and Florida: Exploration of an Historic Connection, 1539–1991* (Miami: Historical Association of Southern Florida, 1991), 98–101, 106.

72. Gary R. Mormino and George E. Pozzetta, "Spanish Anarchism in Tampa, Florida, 1886–1931," in *Struggle a Hard Battle: Essays on Working-Class Immigrants,* ed. Dirk Hoerder (DeKalb: Northern Illinois University Press, 1985), 170–98.

73. Richard Bradford, *The Virginius Affair* (Boulder: Colorado University Press, 1980).

74. Bretos, *Cuba and Florida,* 79–90. Gerald Eugene Poyo, "*With All and for the Good of All*": *The Emergence of Popular Nationalism in the Cuban Communities in the United States, 1848–1898* (Durham, NC: Duke University Press, 1989).

75. Gary R. Mormino, "Tampa's Splendid Little War: Local History and the Cuban War of Independence," *OAH Magazine of History* 12 (Spring 1998): 37–42; Mormino, "Cuba Libre, Florida, and the Spanish-American War," *Theodore Roosevelt Association Journal* 31 (Winter–Spring 2010): 43–54; Louis A. Pérez, "Cubans in Tampa: From Exiles to Immigrants, 1892–1901," *Florida Historical Quarterly* 57 (October 1978): 129–40.

76. Thomas Graham, "The Flagler Era, 1865–1913," in *Oldest City,* 192–203; Susan R. Braden, *The Architecture of Leisure: The Florida Resort Hotels of Henry Flagler and Henry Plant* (Gainesville: University Press of Florida, 2002).

77. Braden, *Architecture of Leisure*; James Covington, *Henry B. Plant and the Tampa Bay Hotel* (Louisville, KY: Harmony House, 1991).

78. "Americans Visit Spain," *New York Times,* November 5, 1925; Rolena Adorno, "Washington Irving's Romantic Hispanism and Its Columbian Legacies," in *Spain in America,* 49–105.

79. Donald Curl, *Mizner's Florida: America's Resort Architecture* (Cambridge, MA: MIT Press, 1987); Beth Dunlop, "Inventing Antiquity: The Art and Craft of Mediterranean Revival Architecture," *Journal of Decorative and Propaganda Arts* 23 (1998): 191–206; Walter Rendell Story, "Old Spain Enters the American Home," *New York Times,* March 7, 1926; Aristides J. Millas, *Coral Gables, Miami Riviera: An Architectural Guide* (Miami, FL: Dade Heritage Trust, 2003).

80. Witold Rybczynski, *Vizcaya: An American Villa and Its Makers* (Philadelphia: University of Pennsylvania Press, 2007).

81. Kevin M. McCarthy, *The Book Lover's Guide to Florida* (Sarasota, FL: Pineapple Press, 1992), 101–2.

82. Ana María Varela-Lago, "Conquerors, Immigrants, Exiles: The Spanish Diaspora in the United States, 1848–1948," PhD diss., University of California, San Diego, 2008, 119–21.

83. Gary R. Mormino and George E. Pozzetta, "The Reader and the Worker: '*Los Lectores*" and the Culture of Cigarmaking in Cuba and Florida," *International Labor and Working-Class History* 54 (Fall 1998): 1–18.

84. Varela-Lago, "Conquerors, Immigrants, Exiles," 225–55; Varela-Lago, "'¡No Pasarán!' The Spanish Civil War's Impact on Tampa's Latin Community," *Tampa Bay History* 19 (1997): 5–35; Jose Yglesias, quoted in Studs Terkel, *Hard Times: An Oral History of the Great Depression* (New York: Pantheon Books, 1970), 109.

85. "Robeson Sings and Talks Here," *Tampa Daily Times,* October 5, 1948; "2,500 Hear Wallace Rap Both Parties," and "Crowd Shouts Viva Wallace," *Tampa Morning Tribune,* February 18, 1948.

86. Mormino, *Land of Sunshine,* 80; Robert N. Dow Jr., "Yesterday and the Day Before: 1913 to the Present," in *Oldest City,* 231–33.

87. Mormino, *Land of Sunshine,* 17–18, 282–84; "Cuban Pledges Fight to Death against Batista," *Tampa Daily Times,* November 28, 1955; Bretos, *Cuba and Florida,* 120, 122–23.

88. The study of modern Miami has become a cottage industry. Some of the best studies include María Cristina García, *Havana USA: Cuban Exiles and Cuban Americans in South Florida* (Berkeley: University of California Press, 1996); Alejandro Portes and Alex Stepick, *City on the Edge: The Transformation of Miami* (Berkeley: University of California Press, 1993); Raymond Mohl, "Maurice Ferré, Xavier Suarez, and the Ethnic Factor in Miami Politics," in *Spanish Pathways,* 302–27; Bretos, *Cuba and Florida,* 122–28.

89. "Martínez Is Not Florida's First Hispanic Governor," *Gainesville Sun,* November 9, 1986.

90. Andrew Huse, *The Columbia Restaurant: Celebrating a Century of History, Culture, and Cuisine* (Gainesville: University Press of Florida, 2009).

I

LA FLORIDA

First and Second Spanish Periods

Introduction

Three Hundred Years of La Florida

VIVIANA DÍAZ BALSERA

Two decades after the momentous encounter between two worlds in 1492, still unaware of the scope of the lands opened up by Christopher Columbus, Juan Ponce de León sailed from the town of San Germán in Puerto Rico in search of the island of Bimini. On Easter Sunday, March 27, 1513, somewhere between St. Augustine and Cabo Cañaveral, the explorer and conquistador from Valladolid imposed the name La Florida on the land, a Spanish name signifying both beauty and salvation. Authoritative sources such as Pietro Martire d'Anghiera and Antonio de Herrera y Tordesillas declare that Ponce de León believed that the graceful land held a water spring that defied the (fallen) natural order of old age and decay. But La Florida, the wondrous island and beatific challenger of mortality, soon turned out to be a hostile paradise where European permanence would be constantly rebuffed.

The first part of *La Florida: Five Hundred Years of Hispanic Presence* centers on the period when Florida was a possession of the Spanish Crown. The essays tell the stories of the dramatic entrance of La Florida into the historical record as the invaded territory of its native peoples; as a barren land imposing heavy blood tribute on those who attempted to conquer it; as a buffer zone of cultural encounters and difficult coexistences; as a haven for people looking for freedom; and as an international frontier where Spain, France, England, and then the young United States played out their bids for power—in short, Florida as a borderland theater of the heroic and destructive early modern thrust to produce an ever more linked world.

In "Charting Juan Ponce de León's 1513 Voyage to Florida: The Calusa Indians amid Latitudes of Controversy" Jerald T. Milanich tackles the long-standing debate over the precise location of Juan Ponce de León's landfall on the Atlantic coast of Florida. Because there are no extant firsthand accounts of the voyage, researchers have had to rely on Herrera y Tordesillas's *Historia general de los hechos de los Castillanos en las islas i tierra firme del Mar Oceano*, first published almost a hundred years after the expidition. However, another more contemporary document to the events is the map of Ottomanno Freducci, who is believed to have had firsthand information about Ponce de León's voyage to La Florida. Correlating these two main sources and the common geographical sites registered in both, Milanich masterfully reconstructs Ponce's trajectory along the Atlantic coast and southwest to the Keys, until he turned northward and encountered the Calusa in the Florida Gulf Coast region. The author then gives an overview of the 250-year contact between the Spaniards and the Calusa. The latter fiercely resisted the invaders until the late eighteenth century, when they were forced to seek refuge in Miami due to Creek Indian raids and then finally vanished from the historical record.

In "'Until the Land Was Understood': Spaniards Confront La Florida, 1500–1600" Paul E. Hoffman expertly and eloquently charts the first century of Spanish incursions into greater Florida and their reports about the economic potential of the territory and cultural practices of its inhabitants. Starting with Lucas Vázquez de Ayllón's account of his failed expedition in 1526, most reports from Spanish explorers concurred in envisioning the coastal lands as sterile and very poor. The area most likely to lend itself to Spanish settlement patterns in the Americas was the interior of the Carolinas. However, except for Pedro Menéndez de Avilés's coastal settlement in St. Augustine in 1565, all attempts to establish colonies failed. It would not be until the seventeenth century that some inroads were made into the peninsula's central ridge, with missionaries reaching the Apalachee in 1630. Ranches were created in north-central Florida in the mid-seventeenth century, suggesting that an agricultural economy powered by Native American labor would have been possible. But large-scale efforts along this line were not pursued because of pressure from the

English and the French and their client indigenous allies, who found these relatively defenseless ranches and missions attractive for looting.

Raquel Chang-Rodríguez's fascinating essay "On the Trail of Texts from Early Spanish Florida: Garcilaso's *La Florida del Inca* and Oré's *Relación de los mártires*" explores two towering chronicles in Florida historiography of the early modern period. *La Florida del Inca* treats Hernando de Soto's failed expedition to the land from 1539 to 1543. In her fine reading of this work, Chang-Rodríguez emphasizes how the Inca Garcilaso's detailed story about De Soto's expedition goes beyond a mere narration of facts, becoming a deep reflection about colonial ambition, cultural clashes, and international politics in the Spanish dominions of the Americas. Specific acts of savagery, cowardice, and bewildering desire from both Spaniards and Native Americans dim the light of humanity in *La Florida del Inca*. But soon after, other episodes attesting to bravery, intercultural recognition, and the intelligence of compassion, rekindle it anew. In his *Relación*, the Franciscan friar Luis Jerónimo de Oré explores a century of missionary activity in La Florida and the ordeals endured by the friars. Drawing from a wide array of sources and testimonies as well as from his own experiences of the land to write his account, Oré offers his readers information about navigation, the political struggles being played out in La Florida between the European superpowers, and the hardships of living in the Spanish colonial settlements. Chang-Rodríguez artfully brings these two chronicles together by emphasizing the Peruvian origin of the authors, how they met in Córdoba, Spain, and how each produced a fundamental text about La Florida. Weaving Cuzco, Córdoba, and La Florida together, Chang-Rodríguez deploys the vast transatlantic and transcontinental circuits that linked the subjects of the Spanish Crown who shaped the early modern history of the Americas and of Florida.

In a lively, powerful style, Amy Turner Bushnell's "A Land Renowned for War: Florida as a Maritime Marchland" depicts the three-centuries-long ordeal of the first permanent European settlement in North America. The assigned role of St. Augustine was to watch over the Crown's interests in the Gulf, the Caribbean, and the Atlantic, where European superpowers ruthlessly vied for their share of the New World pie. With unfertile soil surrounding the settlement, no gold or silver to lure colonists, and few indigenous populations available for producing agricultural goods for even a sustenance economy, North America's most ancient city was dependent on a royal *situado,* or yearly monetary allotment, which frequently arrived late and was never enough to sustain the population. In the seventeenth century, the *floridanos* tried to develop a trade economy with the Timucuan Indians, introducing cattle and planting wheat. Then the Crown undercut those efforts by withholding monies for gifts to the Indians. Yellow fever struck the colony; aggressions against Florida escalated during Queen Anne's War; St. Augustine was burnt down in 1702; and the Creeks, with the help of the English, raided the missions, pushing out the Apalachees. Taking this chain of misfortunes into account, it is no surprise that the only successful permanent Spanish settlement in the lands of North America was never a full-fledged city or town, but just a Spanish garrison. Bushnell persuasively argues that this was no failure of the inhabitants of St. Augustine, but rather a consequence of the specific role that they were appointed to assume and that they patiently fulfilled. The fact that St. Augustine managed to survive against all odds—including the little support it received from the Crown—is a testament to the fierce perseverance of its inhabitants.

In her compelling chapter "'Giving Liberty to All': Spanish Florida as a Black Sanctuary, 1673–1790" Jane Landers portrays the African experience in Florida during the first Spanish period as a story of resistance, strategic alliances, and will to be free. Because of a dire need for labor, and because unpopulated Spanish holdings were constantly challenged by both French and English powers, African slaves and freedmen became instrumental to the survival of Spanish settlement in Florida. Although allowing the exploitative institution of slavery, Spanish law and custom nonetheless had traditionally given slaves a legal persona and thus rights to hold property, purchase freedom, and even escape exceptionally abusive masters. These legal practices enabled Spaniards to lure African slaves from the English colonies into Florida with offers of less dismal living conditions. In a tactical move that served both Spanish interests and those of the Africans, who were considered chattel by the English, the Spaniards established a sanctuary policy under which runaway slaves from the English colonies would be given protection and the right to live in Spanish Florida if they became Catholic, swore loyalty to the Spanish king, and offered armed service to defend royal territories. Especially after the founding of Charles

Town in 1670, the Spaniards armed African freedmen and runaway slaves to form militias to resist English aggression. This was the origin of the town of Gracia Real de Santa Teresa de Mose, founded in 1738 two miles north of St. Augustine, as the first free African community in what is now the United States.

In the last essay of this section "The Experience of a Loss: Spain, Florida, and the United States (1783–1833)" Carmen de la Guardia Herrero recounts Spain's tortuous march toward the loss of its territories in North America during the fleeting second Spanish period from 1783 to 1819. Using personal correspondence and memorials to the Spanish kings from the main figures crafting Florida politics, De la Guardia gives us a detailed narrative of the intricate web of international political events, alliances, treachery, and diplomatic cultures that marked the way for Spain's forced cession of the peninsula. She takes as her point of departure the Paris Treaty of 1783 which reinstated Spanish control over Florida but failed to establish clear boundaries of the territory. De la Guardia then skillfully traces all the attempts and miscalculations of Spain as she tried to apply her outmoded ancien régime diplomacy based on rights of conquest to a courageous new world where republicanism was taking firm hold. As it asserted itself as a federation, the United States took advantage of Spain's vulnerability to the Napoleonic invasions, to the independence movements in Latin America, and to the unrelenting attacks and shifting alliances of the French and English who lusted after Florida. Unable to hold on to her continental colonies, an exhausted Spain finally rescinded all her claims to Florida to the United States of America in the Adams-Onís Treaty of 1819.

And so ended the Spanish period of La Florida. But the fragile Hispanic seed implanted by Ponce de León three centuries before as he pursued the chimera of Bimini would never stop bearing fruit in the land. Some stories of how this seed grew, developed, and shaped contemporary Florida's distinctive multicultural character, struggles, and imagination—at the edge of crucial challenges facing the United States as a nation today—are told in the second part of this book.

1

Charting Juan Ponce de León's 1513 Voyage to Florida

The Calusa Indians amid Latitudes of Controversy

JERALD T. MILANICH

Juan Ponce de León first made landfall on the east coast of Florida in 1513, though the exact location remains a debated topic. No firsthand narrative of the expedition exists, and the latitude and other information regarding the location of that first landfall—derived from a secondhand account of Ponce's voyage published nearly a century later—have been differently interpreted by researchers spanning several generations.[1] Almost everyone who has delved into the controversy, including myself, agrees that the recorded latitudes for both the Bahamas—through which Ponce sailed on the way to Florida from Puerto Rico—and his Florida exploration are erroneous and have to be "corrected" to interpret the voyage and landfall.

Comparing the latitudes for specific islands in the Bahamas and the Florida Keys with those recorded in the account of Ponce's voyage indicates that the correction factor is about one and one-half degrees of latitude south. For instance, the latitude given for La Yaguna Island in the Bahamas (modern Mariguana Island) is 24° N latitude, whereas the true latitude is 22°24' N latitude, and the latitude given for Guanahani Island (modern Walting Island, later called San Salvador) is 25°40' N latitude, while the true latitude is 24° N latitude. In other words, the latitudes we have for the voyage are all about one and a half degrees too far north, a distance of about ninety miles.[2]

Most researchers concur that after making landfall and spending about six days at anchor on the Florida Atlantic coast, Ponce's small fleet sailed northward for a day, then reversed course. Over several weeks Ponce's ships slowly made their way southward down the coast, encountering contrary currents along the way. After rounding the southern tip of Florida, Ponce's expedition took a westerly heading along the Florida Keys. Probably just west of modern Key West, Ponce's ships turned north into the Gulf of Mexico. Presumably the intent was to continue to explore what was thought to be a large island, one that Ponce had christened La Florida.[3]

Their northerly route brought the Spaniards to the southwest coast of Florida. There they would encounter the Calusa, Native Americans whose ancestors had inhabited that coastal region for at least several thousand years and who would continue to live in their traditional lands into the early eighteenth century.

The Calusa are the only identifiable American Indians who played a documented role in Ponce's 1513 reconnaissance of what is now the mainland of the United States. Information from the secondhand account of that voyage and archival materials from the sixteenth century allow us to pinpoint the location of the Calusa Indian town near where Ponce's ships anchored. Further, that location can be correlated with an archaeological site, an actual place.

Ponce and Early Sixteenth-Century Florida in Documents

The standard source of information regarding Juan Ponce's 1513 voyage to La Florida is the account assembled by Antonio de Herrera y Tordesillas and contained in his multivolume opus, *Historia general de los hechos de los Castillanos en las islas i tierra firme del Mar Oceano* (General History of the Deeds of the Castilians in the Islands and Mainland of the Ocean Sea), first published in 1601–15 in Madrid.[4] Herrera, appointed by Philip II of Spain to write a history of the Spanish conquest of the Indies, presumably had access to original materials pertinent to Ponce's Florida voyage. The present-day whereabouts of those documents is unknown, and historians and popular writers are forced to rely heavily on the sometimes vague Herrera account to try and map Ponce's route along the coasts of peninsular Florida. (It is, of course, the latitudes in the Herrera account that are off.)

Another primary document important in charting Juan Ponce's La Florida voyage is a world map drawn by the Italian cartographer Count Ottomanno Freducci, who was active from 1497 to 1539. The map seems to have been made shortly after Ponce's voyage, perhaps even the following year. Often referred to as the Freducci map, it portrays a portion of peninsular Florida as well as the adjacent Florida Keys, both in their correct geographical locations north of Cuba and westerly from the Bahamas.[5] On the map the Florida peninsula is labeled as an island and some of the Florida

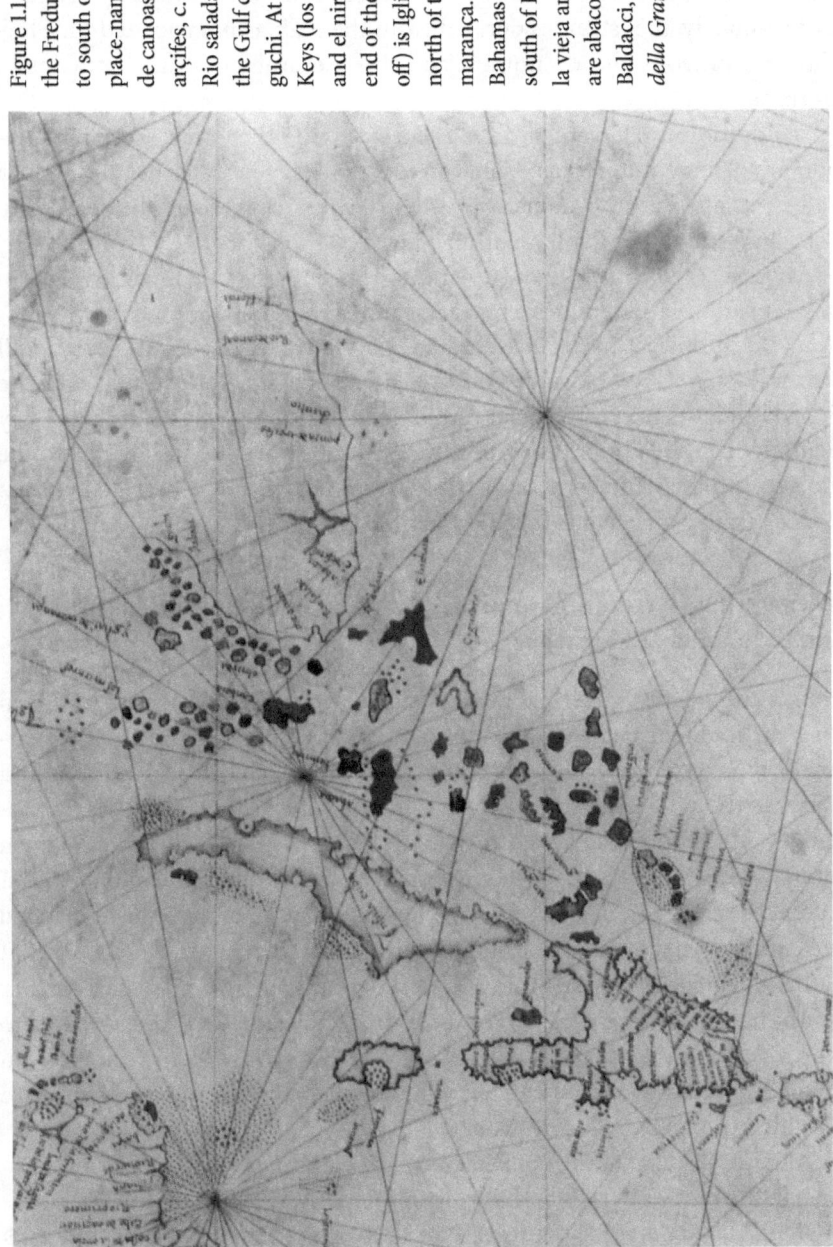

Figure 1.1. Florida depicted on the Freducci map. From north to south on the Atlantic coast, place-names are i. florda, Rio de canoas, chantio, ponta de arçifes, c. de setos, abacoa, Rio salada, and chequiche. On the Gulf coast are stababa and guchi. At the eastern end of the Keys (los martires) are canbeia and el nirda; off the western end of the Keys (partially cut off) is Iglias de tortugas, while north of the Keys is yglias de marança. Four places in the Bahamas are depicted east and south of Florida: east are y. de la vieja and c. luchaio; south are abacoa and beimini. (From Baldacci, *Atlante Colombiano della Grande Scoperta*)

place-names are the same as or very similar to ones in Herrera's Ponce narrative (see figure 1.1).

The assumption is that when drawing the map Freducci had access to navigation information recorded by Ponce's expedition, though this information seems to have been somewhat different from that used by Herrera. Unfortunately, the latitudes derived from the map as interpolated for Florida are erroneous and do nothing to solve the problem of the latitudes in Herrera.

In addition to Herrera and the Freducci map other sources of information are pertinent to interpreting the route of Ponce's ships around Florida and especially the encounter between the Calusa Indians and the Spaniards. Later in this chapter I will mention a few.

My goal is to draw a new generation of scholars to Ponce's voyage, in hopes of stimulating more archival research to find new sources of information. Questions yet to be answered are (1) Where did Ponce make landfall on the east coast of Florida? and (2) Did Ponce's 1513 encounter with the Florida Indians have an impact on them, or was the voyage simply the key that opened the Pandora's box of future colonization that so devastated the Florida Indians? In the case of the Calusa, it appears at first glance that Ponce's 1513 voyage had little or no lasting effect.

Interpreting Herrera and Freducci: Landfall, the Atlantic Coast, and the Straits of Florida

Ponce, the former governor of the Spanish colony of San Juan (modern Puerto Rico) received a royal contract in 1512 from Ferdinand II.[6] The contract gave Ponce three years to explore in search of Bimini, a land or island that was thought to lie somewhere in the Atlantic Ocean, north of the Bahamas. At the time of Ponce's voyage the Bahamas were known to Spanish interests, and it is possible that one or more unsanctioned (meaning without a contract from the Spanish Crown) Spanish voyagers might have reached the coast of what is now the southeastern United States before 1513. By that date knowledge of eastern Canada, and perhaps the Atlantic coast farther south, had been recorded by John Cabot, who had captained voyages to North America in 1497 and 1498–1500.[7] Cabot's voyages and rumors from Spanish sources about lands northwest and west of the Bahamas may have provided impetus for Ponce's voyage.

After leaving the harbor of San Germán on the southwest coast of Puerto Rico in the first week of March 1513 Juan Ponce's three ships sailed first to the town of Aguada on the northwest Puerto Rican coast. From there they took a northwest heading along the eastern side of the islands of the Bahamas (the Lucayos). The small fleet sailed past the Caicos Islands, then La Yaguna (modern Mariguana Island), Amaguayo (Plana Cays?), Manegua (Samana Cay?), and finally Guanahani, where Christopher Columbus made landfall in 1492 and which he named San Salvador. In his article "The Track of Ponce de Leon," Louis D. Scisco uses early sixteenth-century cartographic sources to equate the various islands of the Lucayos recorded in Herrera with modern place-names.

At the north end of the Bahamas Ponce's ships sailed past Great Abaco Island and that portion of the Little Bahama Bank to the north and west. If the ships continued on the same northwest heading, they would have made landfall on the Atlantic coast of Florida well north of Cape Canaveral. But Herrera states the expedition instead took a west-northwest track, which would have led to a landfall on the central Florida coast. But where? It is the site of Ponce's initial landing that remains a bone of contention among researchers and, again, a large part of the dispute revolves around interpreting the latitude of Ponce's landfall recorded in Herrera's account as 30°8′ N.

If we subtract a degree and a half from Herrera's 30°8′ N datum, we arrive at a latitude of 28°38′ N, the latitude of the southerly portion of the Mosquito River and not all that far south of the latitude of the large Indian shell mound known as Turtle Mound, which is in Canaveral National Seashore just north of Cape Canaveral. In 1513 the imposing shell mound would have been the tallest feature on the Atlantic coast of Florida. During the colonial period and later it was a landmark for sailors, one visible from ships at sea. Did Ponce make landfall near Turtle Mound? Maybe, maybe not.

Wherever landfall was made, Ponce's first sighting of the Florida coastline on April 2 was, of course, at the time of Easter Holy Week, the Feast of Flowers (Pascua Florida). According to Herrera, the religious holiday and the natural beauty of the land led Juan Ponce to name the land he saw La Florida.

Herrera's account is not totally clear, but it appears that about April 8 Ponce's ships went north along the coast for a day before reversing course and sailing just east of south down the coastline. They continued on that course until April 20 (nearly two weeks). There is no information on what may have transpired while the ships were at anchor between April 2 and April 8; perhaps they explored the land and took their horses ashore to relieve them from the sea journey. Likewise, Herrera's account provides no information about what transpired from April 9 to April 20 while Ponce's expedition was sailing south.

On April 20, however, the Spaniards saw Indian houses and anchored, though there was a strong current. Ponce and some of his men went ashore. A skirmish took place between the Spaniards and Indians, with people wounded on both sides. The next day the Spaniards went back ashore to collect firewood and water, again a minor skirmish occurred, and an Indian was taken to serve as a guide. Ponce left a stone cross at the place and named the stream La Cruz. It is likely the Indian village where Ponce's men went ashore and the place where they sought firewood and water were in a coastal inlet, rather than on the beach itself.

According to Herrera, Ponce's fleet then continued farther down the coast. The expedition apparently maintained at a slow pace, still battling the current. On May 8, a Sunday more than a month after first landfall, the ships finally passed what Herrera calls the "cabo de la Florida." Herrera records that the Spaniards also named the location the Cabo de Corriente (Cape of Currents), because the northward-flowing currents were very strong at that point. Possibly the cape was around Rivera Beach. Herrera notes that from the Punta de Arracifes (Point of Reefs, or Point of Shoals) to the north, but south of the landfall site, to the Cape of Currents the coast ran south-southeast. Presumably, the shoreline changed direction south of the Cape of Currents. Herrera also records that the Cape of Currents was at 28°15' N. (Riviera Beach is at 26°46' N, almost exactly one and one-half degrees south of Herrera's coordinates.) Because of the strong currents Ponce anchored his ships behind or south of the cape near an Indian village called Abaioa. Certainly the currents Herrera describes are the Florida Current, a part of the Gulf Stream system.[8]

The Freducci map shows both a "p. de arçifes" and a place named "abacoa." On the map "p. de arçifes" is next to a point on the peninsula coast off of which are markings that may indicate reefs or shoals. "Abacoa" is well to the south (but north of the place on the map labeled "chequiche," certainly the Indian town of Tequesta known to be located at the mouth of the Miami River).

I believe that Herrera's Punta de Arracifes, located south of Ponce's landfall, is Cape Canaveral. Later mariners were well aware of shoals off Cape Canaveral. The 1913 edition of the *United States Coast Pilot for the Atlantic Coast* describes those shoals as dangerous and as extending off the coast for thirteen miles to the north and northeast with depths of as little as eleven feet on the outer shoals.[9]

From the Cabo de Corrientes (Riviera Beach?) the expedition sailed farther south, finding two islands, one of which was christened Santa María and where they found water. (Herrera says they were at 27° N latitude; Elliott Key, at the northern end of the Florida Keys, is at 25°26' N.) After several

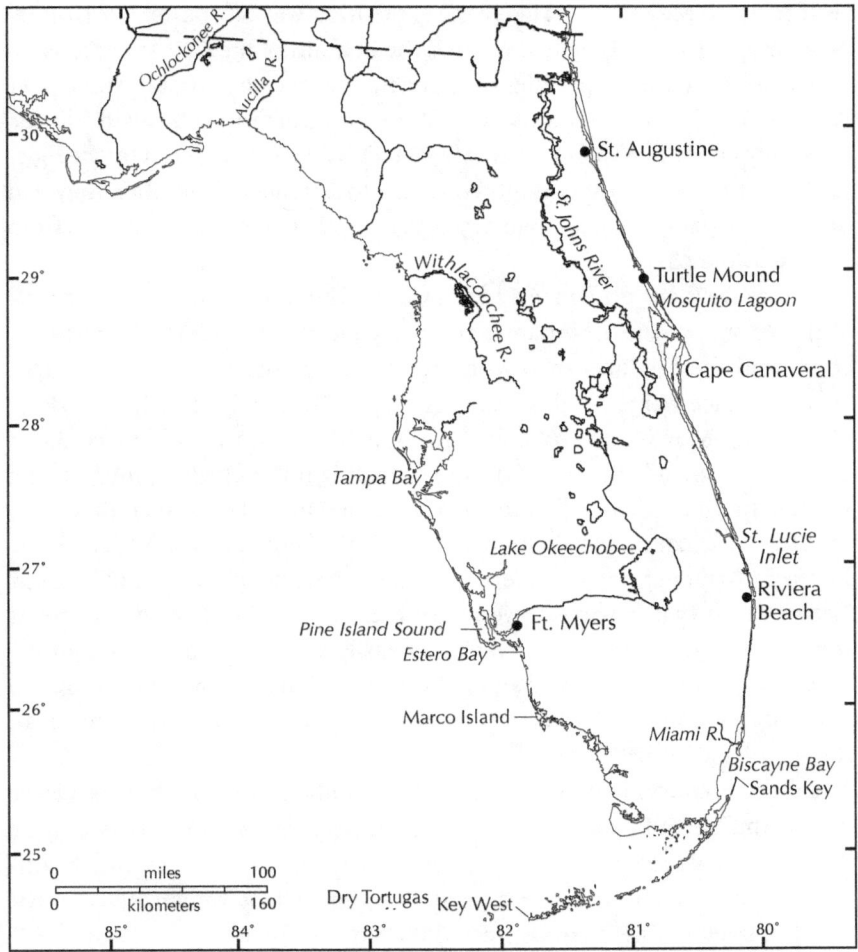

Figure 1.2. Modern locations mentioned in the text.

days (on Friday, May 13) they again set sail, running along sandbars and low islands. Across the shallows and islands there was open water and then the mainland. Certainly they were sailing off the Upper Florida Keys with either Biscayne Bay or Florida Bay (or both) in the distance. They named one of the keys Pola. For the next two days they sailed along the Keys, which they named Los Mártires (The Martyrs) because from a distance the islands looked like suffering men (men walking hunched over?). Herrera says these keys were at 26°15' (Marathon, in the central Florida Keys, is at 24°42' N; the one and one-half degree error seems pretty consistent). Reaching the west end of the keys (Key West) Ponce then sailed north, reaching the Florida

Gulf coast on May 23. Most likely the expedition was off coastal Lee County near Sanibel Island. They had entered the domain of the Calusa Indians.

The journey from the Cabo de Corrientes down the coast to the Upper Keys, along the Lower Keys to Key West, and north to southwest Florida took only about two weeks, from May 8 to May 23. Unhindered by the Florida Current, the ships apparently were able to sail much faster than they had down the Atlantic coast, a journey that had taken about four weeks (from April 9 to May 8).

Before we focus on Ponce and the Calusa Indians let's take another look at the voyage down the Atlantic coast, trying to correlate the Herrera account and the Freducci map with modern coastal geography. The northernmost place-name on the Freducci map is "i. [insula] flor[i]da" (Island of Florida). Moving down (south) the Atlantic coast the next place-name is "Rio de canoas" (River of Canoes), which is not mentioned in Herrera. Farther south is "chantio," probably the same name as Cautio contained in the Herrera account. Just south of chantio is the "ponta de arçifes," the same Punta de Arracifes noted in Herrera, which I have suggested could be Cape Canaveral. If that is correct, we might believe that the River of Canoes is Mosquito Lagoon, an inland waterway easily accessible to the dugout canoes of the Indians who lived along the lagoon. Today the Mosquito Lagoon is within the Canaveral National Seashore. Chantio could be the name of an Indian village in that locality.[10]

On the Freducci map well south of the "ponta de arçifes" there is a large inlet with three intersecting rivers emptying into the Atlantic. They may be the junction of the North and South Forks of the St. Lucie River, which converge to form the St. Lucie that today flows east to the Indian River.[11] That location may be where Ponce erected the stone cross.

South of the inlet on the Freducci map is the "c[abo] de setos." In medieval Spanish *setos* meant "poles, fence, or enclosure," suggesting Cabo de Setos may be "Cape of Fish Weirs." South of that cape is the place named "abacoa," the native village Herrera calls Abaioa, near where the expedition anchored in the lee of the cape, perhaps near Riviera Beach. Is there a place on the coast north of Riviera Beach where the Indians may have built fish weirs? One candidate is at Jupiter Inlet; another is at the north end of the Lake Worth lagoon, which is just north of Riviera Beach. That twenty-one-mile-long lagoon would have been a good place for weirs intended to trap fish when the tide went out.

Southward from Cabo de Setos the Freducci map shows two places on the southeast Florida coast. The first is "Rio salado," literally "Salt River." That place may be the North Bay portion of Biscayne Bay, the inland waterway north of the mouth of the Miami River. The second place is Chequiche (Tequesta), known from other accounts to be a native village at the mouth of the Miami River. Calling the same place Chequescha, Herrera intimates that Juan Ponce's expedition reached that town on its return voyage (to Puerto Rico) after leaving southwest Florida and the Calusa Indians. The dates in the Herrera account suggest Ponce's small fleet spent two weeks traveling between the Upper Keys and the Bahamas on the return voyage. Some of that time could have been spent at Tequesta.

The mouth of the Miami River once was marked by extensive shell middens, ample evidence of centuries of Indian towns, and it was a place well known to Spaniards in the sixteenth century (and later). The geographer Juan López de Velasco described that setting in his 1575 *Geographía y descripción universal de las indias*: "At the very point of Tequesta there enters into the sea a freshwater river, which comes from the interior, and to all appearances runs from west to east. There are many fish and eels in it. Alongside it on the north side is the Indian settlement that is called Tequesta, from which the point takes its name."[12] Tequesta is the only place on the Atlantic coast of Florida visited by Ponce in 1513 that can be definitely correlated with a specific location. Unfortunately there is no information on any encounters he may have had with the local Indians.

The Freducci map, like the Herrera account, also depicts the Florida Keys—"los mártires"—and names two of the islands: "canbeia" (the southernmost) and "el nirda." "Canbeia" is certainly the Achecambei of Herrera's account, an island in the Florida Keys west of the islands of Pola (also called Santa Pola by Herrera) and Santa María, where he says Ponce's fleet stopped on the return journey to Puerto Rico.

Among the Calusa Indians

According to Herrera's account, Ponce's ships arrived on the coast of southwest Florida on May 23. Though the location is not altogether clear, it may be that Ponce's ships were near Sanibel Island. Needing firewood and water and also to repair one ship, the Spaniards sailed southward then closer to shore near islands they could see. It is doubtful that they would have sailed into San Carlos Bay, because it is too shallow for the ships. Perhaps after moving closer to shore they were off Fort Myers Beach.

The Spaniards spent more than three weeks in the area, periodically engaging in minor skirmishes with the Indians. At one point the Calusa used bows and arrows to attack from canoes, some tied together as catamarans.

The Spaniards retaliated, taking women and men as prisoners and damaging canoes on shore. Fatalities were suffered on both sides.

Despite the fighting, both the Spaniards and the Calusa seem to have been interested in trading and learning more about one another. One native man understood some Spanish words, and it was believed he had come from Hispaniola or another island colonized by Spaniards. The Calusa told the Spaniards their chief had gold and that he was coming to trade, but this was apparently a ruse. Herrera says the chief's name was Carlos, a name also used by later Spaniards.

The three weeks Ponce spent within Calusa Indian territory was sufficient time for one or more of his ships to explore the Gulf coast north of the present-day Lee County area. That such a voyage took place is suggested by a notation on the 1519 map of the Gulf of Mexico coast (from Florida to Yucatan) drawn as a result of the Alvarez de Pineda expedition. Written on the map at about modern Apalachee Bay is "Juan Ponce discovered to this point."[13]

Deciding that it was time to return to San Juan, Ponce and his men set sail for the Caribbean. Apparently captive Indians told them about an island to the south, and they stopped at that place for water. A fierce fight with the local Indians took place. According to Herrera, the Spaniards named the island Matança because many Indians were killed there. That island might have been Marco Island, where there was a freshwater source near the southern end that later sailors knew of.[14] On the Freducci map this island is identified as "yglias de marança."

Taking leave of the Florida coast, Ponce's ships next sailed southwest and reached the Dry Tortugas, which they named Las Tortugas because of the large number of sea turtles they took for food; these islands also appear on the Freducci map ("Iglias de tortugas"). Next the fleet took a southern heading, which brought the Spaniards to a landfall on the north coast of western Cuba on June 29. On July 1, the ships turned north, reaching the Florida Keys two days later.

According to Herrera, the expedition moved east then north, passing by Tequesta at the mouth of the Miami River, then sailing back to the Bahamas, reaching them on July 14. The Spaniards must have been exploring the Keys and the southeast Florida coast along the way, and perhaps they spent time at Tequesta. They also explored the Bahamas on the voyage back to San Juan.

Let's take a second look at Ponce and the Calusa Indians. The Freducci map records two place-names in southwest Florida north of the island of Matança. The northernmost is "guchi"; the other is "stababa." Both are

Calusa names known from other, post-Ponce Spanish sources, though neither is mentioned in Herrera.

Guchi (also Juchi) was a Calusa town in the general San Carlos Bay/Pine Island Sound area. There is no shortage of possible archaeological sites on islands in that locality. Some sites are quite large, and all are characterized by extensive shell middens and mounds constructed of shell. We might guess that Guchi was south of Charlotte Harbor and away from the mouth of the Caloosahatchee River, because neither the river nor the harbor are mentioned in Herrera or depicted on the Freducci map.

The name Juchi appears in the writings of Hernando d'Escalante Fontaneda, who was shipwrecked in South Florida in the 1540s when he was a teenager and lived among the Calusa Indians until he was rescued by Pedro Menéndez de Avilés, the founder of St. Augustine.[15] Fontaneda wrote a memoir and other notes about South Florida and the native residents. In his writings, Fontaneda listed Juchi as one of the many Calusa towns that was subject to Carlos, the Calusa chief.[16]

The second name on the Freducci map—Stababa—was the Calusa name for the major town located on a small island, Mound Key, in Estero Bay. This is the same Calusa town that the Spaniards sometimes called Calos, which served as the capital of the Calusa Indians in the sixteenth and seventeenth centuries (and likely earlier as well). Ponce's ships must have anchored somewhere near Stababa, probably off Fort Myers Beach. Mound Key, with its shell middens and mounds and other shell works (and canals) today is a marvelous archaeological site. The entire key is covered with remains left by the Calusa Indians. In 1513 Stababa must have been a town to behold.

In his writings Fontaneda refers to the town as Estantapaca.[17] In 1575 López de Velasco described the place, calling it Escampaba:

> The Bay of Carlos, which is called Escampaba in the language of the Indians, for a cacique of that name, who later called himself Carlos out of a devotion for the Emperor, appears to be the same one that is called, of Juan Ponce, because he landed in it during the year of [1513] . . . , where he lost his people and where the Indians gave him wounds from which he died. It is at 26 ½ plus degrees (*esta en 26 grados y ½ largos?*). [It actually is at 26°24' N latitude; the Ponce-era errors in latitude had been corrected.] Its entrance [Big Carlos Pass] is very narrow and full of shoals as a consequence of which only boats (*barcos*) [small boats] are able to enter. Within it is spacious, about four or five leagues in circumference, although all subject to flooding. There is a little island [Mound Key] in the middle that has a circumference

of about half a league, with other little islets around it. On this (island) Cacique Carlos had his headquarters and presently his successors have it there (as well).[18]

Father Juan Rogel, a Jesuit missionary who lived among the Calusa, wrote a letter in 1568 in which he used the same name, Escampaba, to refer to the "kingdom of Carlos."[19] There is no doubt that the "stababa" of the Freducci map refers to the Calusa Indian capital, near which Juan Ponce's expedition anchored in 1513.

Mound Key is only one of a number of extraordinary Calusa-related shell work archaeological sites along the coast of modern Lee County and extending northward into the Charlotte Harbor vicinity and southward into Collier County. The size, number, and nature of those archaeological sites, nearly all of which feature large shell works, did not escape the notice of the Spaniards who traveled to that coast in the early sixteenth century. In a navigation guide (*Espejo*) compiled in the early sixteenth century by the Spanish cosmographer Alonso de Chaves, the region is referred to as the Costa de Caracoles (Coast of Shells).[20] One wonders if the name Costa de Caracoles might not be the basis for the name of La Costa Island, on which there are major shell mounds.[21]

Aftermath

Juan Ponce did not immediately follow up on his 1513 voyage, despite Ferdinand II granting a second contract in September 1514 that gave him permission to colonize Florida and "Beniny." But in February 1521, perhaps stimulated by the stories of wealth found by Hernán Cortés in New Spain (Mexico) and by the voyages of other Spaniards to the Gulf coast of Florida that threatened his rights to future colonization, Ponce decided to act. He penned a letter to Charles V, then his sovereign, informing him that he planned to return to Florida to explore further and establish a colony.[22]

Between 1513 and 1521 at least one other Spanish expedition voyaged to the Calusa coast. Francisco Hernández de Córdoba stopped in Calusa territory to search for water while sailing to Cuba from Yucatan. Significantly, Hernández de Córdoba's pilot was Antón de Alaminos, who had been Ponce's chief pilot in 1513. It is possible that Alaminos was searching for the *aguada* on or near the island of Matança (Marco Island?) where Ponce had been on his voyage in 1513.[23]

Ponce's 1521 voyage began on about February 20 when he departed Puerto Rico with two ships carrying two hundred men; priests; fifty horses;

livestock, including cows, sheep, and goats; as well as seed for planting crops. His intent apparently was to return to the Calusa. But the expedition turned out to be a colossal failure. The meager accounts of the 1521 venture agree that a major land battle was fought with native warriors, resulting in large numbers of fatalities on both sides (one secondhand account, quoted in Davis, says "not less than eighty" of Ponce's men were killed; another account says the number of Indians slain was more than twice the number of Spaniards killed). Juan Ponce himself was wounded with an arrow in his thigh. The expedition retreated to Cuba, where Ponce died of his wound.

The Calusa Indians after Ponce

Following Ponce's failed 1521 expedition, other Spaniards intent on exploring the Gulf coast by sea and by land seem to have deliberately avoided Calusa territory. The land expeditions of Pánfilo de Narváez (1528) and Hernando de Soto (1539) went ashore north of southwest Florida at Tampa Bay, and Tristán de Luna y Arellano's 1559 colonization venture was centered far to the north on Pensacola Bay.

After ousting the short-lived French settlement of Fort Caroline near the mouth of the St. Johns River in 1565 and establishing the town of St. Augustine (and a second town, Santa Elena, on the coast of South Carolina in spring 1566), Pedro Menéndez de Avilés decided that he needed the Calusa Indians as allies, part of a master plan to protect shipping lanes and secure Florida's coasts against other European powers.

In February 1566 Menéndez sailed to the Calusa Indian capital on Mound Key off southwest Florida. He and two hundred of his men marched into the town with weapons drawn and harquebus match cords lit, accompanied by banners, fifers, drummers, three trumpeters, a harpist, a violinist, and a dwarf who sang and danced, all intended to impress the Calusa.[24]

Menéndez sent a second expedition to the Calusa town later the same year for the purpose of placing a small garrison and mission station there. The Spanish outpost was christened San Antonio. In March 1567 Menéndez returned to the Calusa Indians a third time, bringing Father Juan Rogel, the aforementioned Jesuit missionary, who was to continue the task of bringing the Calusa to Catholicism and making them loyal subjects of the Spanish Crown.

But like the other mission outposts Menéndez established along the coast of Florida during that period, San Antonio was soon abandoned by the Spanish. The Spanish soldiers who manned the garrison clashed with the Calusa, leading to numerous problems. By mid-1568 there no longer was a Spanish presence among the Calusa Indians. For a century and a third the Calusa would continue to live as they always had, outside the realm of Spanish colonization.

Even though they were relatively isolated, the Calusa could not escape the ravages of colonization. The same epidemics that decimated the mission Indians of northern Florida and coastal Georgia also made inroads among the Calusa. By the end of the seventeenth century their numbers had fallen from about twenty thousand people in 1492 to two thousand. Some Calusa Indians also took advantage of new trading and economic opportunities, and in 1688 are recorded as having traveled to Cuba.

Near the end of the seventeenth century the colonial powers of Spanish St. Augustine again decided to send Catholic missionary friars to attempt to convert the Calusa to Christianity and bring them into Spain's Florida colony. The demise of so many of the mission Indians in northern Florida had left the Spaniards with a greatly diminished Native American labor force to work in support of the colony. It was thought the Calusa, if Christianized, could be coerced to toil in support of the colony.

In 1697 Franciscan friars arrived at Calos, the same town where Juan Ponce had been in 1513. But the Calusa were no more willing to submit to the Spaniards than they had been in 1513, 1521, or the 1560s. The mission attempt failed spectacularly and the Franciscans literally were sent packing. Spanish documents record that the Calusa ridiculed the priests, throwing mud, soot, and excrement on them when they tried to preach. Some of the Calusa hecklers even "turned around and showed them [the priests] their buttocks."[25] The friars fled down the coast in canoes, hoping to make it to Cuba. Along the way they were harassed, their canoes were tipped, and their supplies and clothes were taken. The naked friars, nearly dead, made it to Matecumbe Key in the Florida Keys, where they were rescued by a Spanish ship.[26]

Having thwarted the plans of St. Augustine officials, the Calusa were not so successful in countering a new threat, raids by Indians from the north who were armed with guns and against whom the Calusa and other South Florida Indians had little defense. Prior to 1704 the chain of Franciscan missions that stretched across northern Florida west from St. Augustine had served as a buffer against marauding Indians from Georgia, Alabama, and the Carolinas. But with the destruction of those missions, many of which had been protected by small outposts of Spanish soldiers, the entire peninsula was open to Indian raiders bent on causing general mayhem and capturing Florida Indians to sell as slaves to Carolinian colonists. The southern

Florida inhabitants, including some Calusa, fled to the Miami area or to the Keys to escape. Others were able to reach Cuba, where many died of disease.

After the Yamasee War, fought in South Carolina between Carolinian colonists and Yamasee Indians in 1715, the intensity of the raids lessened for a short time, only to begin again as armed Indians from Georgia and Alabama staged their own raids on the Calusa and their neighbors, the remnants of whom were pushed farther south. Over the next several decades the Calusa took a beating; some escaped to Cuba where again many died of disease; others lived in refugee villages in southernmost Florida.

Recognizing that the raids were severe enough to threaten Spain's hold on Florida, Spanish officials in Cuba laid plans for a mission settlement at the mouth of the Miami River at Tequesta, the same place Juan Ponce had visited in 1513. Such a settlement, it was thought, could provide defensive protection against the raiders, protecting Cuban fishing interests in the Florida Keys. In July 1743 the governor of Cuba wrote to the king, informing him of the plan. By that date two Jesuits, Fathers Joseph María Monaco and Joseph Xavier Alaña, had sailed from Havana to Tequesta. There they found 180 refugee Indians living in five large houses. Many of the men spoke Spanish as a result of having worked for Cuban fishermen. The Jesuits reported that among the refugees were Keys Indians, Calusa, and Boca Ratones (probably Tequesta Indians). Farther inland were another one hundred refugees made up of Mayaimies, Santaluces, and Mayacas, all southern Florida Indians. At Tequesta a church was built and christened Santa María de Loreto. Recognizing the precarious position of their mission, the missionary priests suggested to Cuban officials that a fort be placed there and manned with Spanish soldiers.[27]

Cuban authorities, however, decided that the cost of maintaining a mission and constructing and manning a fort was too steep. The Jesuits soon left for Havana and Santa María de Loreto passed into history, leaving the refugee Calusa and other Indians behind. By 1750 these and perhaps other surviving southern Florida Indians had relocated to the Keys, probably all to Key West. On May 17, 1760, Creek Indians raided the refugees in Key West, burning their houses, boats, canoes, and fisheries. In a final evacuation slightly more than sixty Indians were taken to Cuba and resettled.[28] The Florida Calusa Indians, among whom Juan Ponce de León had landed two and a half centuries earlier, were gone. Several years later Spain would relinquish its La Florida colony to Great Britain, and the Spaniards who had followed Ponce de León would likewise be gone.

Notes

1. One of the first scholarly studies in the United States to bring public attention to the documentation regarding Ponce's 1513 voyage is the article by Louis D. Scisco, "The Track of Ponce de Leon in 1513," *Bulletin of the American Geographical Society* 45 (1913): 721–35. Also frequently cited is T. Frederick Davis's 1935 article "History of Juan Ponce de Leon's Voyages to Florida: Source Records," *Florida Historical Quarterly* 14 (1935): 3–70. More recent studies include Robert Henderson Fuson, *Juan Ponce de León and the Spanish Discovery of Puerto Rico and Florida* (Blacksburg, VA: McDonald and Woodward, 2000); Edward W. Lawson, *The Discovery of Florida and Its Discoverer Juan Ponce de León* (St. Augustine, FL: E. W. Lawson, 1946); Samuel Eliot Morison, *The European Discovery of America, the Southern Voyages* (New York: Oxford University Press, 1974), 499–516; Douglas T. Peck, *Ponce de León and the Discovery of Florida: The Man, the Myth, and the Truth* (n.p.: Pogo Press, 1993); and Robert S. Weddle, *Spanish Sea, the Gulf of Mexico in North American Discovery, 1500–1685* (College Station: Texas A&M University Press, 1985), 38–53.

2. The latitudes from Ponce's 1513 voyage are recorded in Antonio de Herrera's narrative. An identification and correlation of the Ponce-era islands with modern islands can be found in Scisco, "Track of Ponce de Leon in 1513," 723–25. Scisco was among the first researchers, if not the first, to document the erroneous latitudes in Herrera.

3. Florida, as opposed to La Florida, refers to the modern state. La Florida eventually was used by the Spaniards to refer to all the lands north and east of New Spain, a huge area that encompassed modern Florida. Within only a handful of years following Ponce's 1513 voyage, other Spaniards sailing the Gulf and Atlantic coasts of Florida had determined that Florida was not an island but a part of a larger landmass.

4. Herrera's book is often referred to as *Las décadas* (The Decades), because of the chronological way it is organized. The account of Ponce's 1513 voyage is contained in the first volume, decade I, book IX, chapters X and XI, with some information on La Florida in the beginning of XII; those portions of the three chapters dealing with La Florida are numbered 311–316 (but pp. 312–19 are misnumbered as 302–9; the correct pagination resumes on page 320).

5. The Freducci map has not escaped the notice of historians and geographers. An early study of the map, apparently authored only several years after it came to light in a Florence, Italy, archive, is Eugenio Casanova, *La carta nautica di Conte di Ottomanno Freducci d'Ancona conservata nel R. Archivio di stato Firenze illustrata da Eugenio Casanova* (Firenze: G. Carnesecchi e figli, 1894). The map also was used in Scisco, "Track of Ponce de Leon in 1513." More than a half century ago the Florida significance of the map was further noted in two articles by David O. True: "The Freducci Map of 1514–1515, What It Discloses of Early Florida History," *Tequesta* 4 (November 1944): 50–55; and "Some Early Maps Relating to Florida," *Imago Mundi* 11 (1955): 79–80. In the *Tequesta* article (p. 50) True notes that the map was reproduced in Italian, German, and French sources as early as 1892. A more recent study of the Florida portion of the map as it pertains to Juan Ponce's 1513 voyage is Jerald T. Milanich and Nara B. Milanich, "Revisiting the Freducci Map: A Depiction of Juan Ponce de León's 1513 Florida Voyage?" *Florida Historical Quarterly* 74 (1996): 319–28. In conjunction with the Columbian Quincentenary an image of the Freducci map was published in the elephantine volume by Osvaldo Baldacci, *Atlante Colombiano della Grande Scoperta* (Rome: Libreria dello Stato, 1992), 123–26.

6. A translation of the royal contract awarded Ponce, the original of which is in the Archivo de Indias, is contained in Davis, "History of Juan Ponce de Leon's Voyages to Florida," 9–14.

7. Astute readers may be asking themselves, what is this about a Cabot voyage in 1498–1500? One of the more intriguing endeavors to surface in the last few years is the ongoing attempts to reconstruct the deliberately destroyed research of the late Alwyn Ruddock. Her work may have uncovered information about Cabot's third voyage (his second ended quickly and never reached North America). Ruddock's research apparently uncovered evidence that on his third voyage (from which it previously was thought he never returned) Cabot reached the Outer Banks and then sailed southward along the Atlantic coast of North America into the Caribbean and to the northern coast of Venezuela. He then returned to England. If this proves true, history may have to credit Cabot with the "discovery" of Florida. See Evan T. Jones, "Alwyn Ruddock: 'John Cabot and the Discovery of America,'" *Historical Research* 81 (2008): 224–54.

8. See http://oceancurrents.rsmas.miami.edu/atlantic/florida.html.

9. In the U.S. Coast Pilot pamphlet *Section D, Cape Henry to Key West* (Washington, DC: Government Printing Office, 1913), issued by the U.S. Coast and Geodetic Survey, the Canaveral shoals are the only ones noted on Florida's Atlantic coast (my clarifications are in brackets):

> Between Winyah Bay [South Carolina] and St. Johns River the shore is very broken, the harbors, inlets, and sounds being in many cases but little over 10 miles apart. This part of the coast has shoals which extend off from 3 to 8 miles. Cape Hatteras, Cape Lookout, Cape Fear, Cape Romain, and Cape Canaveral are distinguished for the distance to which dangerous shoals extend seaward from them. These shoals are generally sand, shifting to some extent with every heavy gale; with the strong currents which are found at times, they form the greatest danger for the navigator while passing along this coast. (p. 19)

And,

> Broken ground and shoals extend 13 miles northward and northeastward from Cape Canaveral, terminating in Hetzel and Ohio Shoals, which have depths of 11 and 19 feet, respectively. . . . The least depths found on the inner shoals range from 9 to 16 feet, the shoals are subject to some change in position and depth, and only small, light-draft craft can easily pass inside the outer shoals. In a heavy sea the shoals are marked by breakers, but with a smooth sea there is nothing to indicate them except the buoys marking Hetzel and Ohio Shoals and Cape Canaveral lighthouse. (p. 114)

10. In his book *Indians of Central and South Florida 1513–1763* (Gainesville: University Press of Florida, 2003), 85, John H. Hann provides the following information on Turtle Mound, translated from Álvar Mexía's 1605 "rutter for the coast from St. Augustine south to Ays" (the territory of the Ays, or Ais, Indians was south of Turtle Mound; that of the Surruque Indians was north): "That river continued toward the southeast entirely within the mangroves" passing "by the foot of the *buhio* that is called of Surruque, which is a hillock (*mogote*) of oyster shells and small bushes." The river spoken of would be Mosquito Lagoon. *Buhio* is a Caribbean, likely Arawakan, Indian word picked up by the Spaniards;

a *buhio* was a thatched structure whether a small hut, a family dwelling, or something as large as a council house that could seat several hundred people.

11. The name St. Lucie comes from the Spanish fort established on the coast on December 13, 1565. The fort was manned by Spanish soldiers who had deserted an outpost established by Pedro Menéndez de Avilés in the main village of the Ais Indians thought to be south of the St. Sebastian River in modern Indian River County. The deserters, who mutinied when their supplies ran out, were making their way down the Atlantic coast when they were found by loyal soldiers, probably at St. Lucie Inlet, and persuaded to go to the new fort that was six leagues farther south on an inlet. Eugene Lyon believes the fort possibly could have been at Jupiter Inlet This information is based on an undated report by Lyon: "Additional Material on the Origin of the Name 'Santa Elena.'" A copy of the typescript Lyons report is catalogued in the University of Florida's P. K. Yonge Library of Florida History. In other words, the modern St. Lucie Inlet, presumably named for the sixteenth-century fort, may not be where that fort was located.

12. Quoted in John H. Hann, *Missions to the Calusa* (Gainesville: University Press of Florida, 1991), 314. This quote is from a much longer, informative description of the coasts of Florida and other information written by López de Velasco, a translation of which can be found in Hann, *Missions to the Calusa*, 308–15.

13. Robert S. Weddle, *Spanish Sea, the Gulf of Mexico in North American Discovery, 1500–1685* (College Station: Texas A&M University Press, 1985), 95–108. Also see Paul E. Hoffman, *A New Andalucia and a Way to the Orient: The American Southeast during the Sixteenth Century* (Baton Rouge: Louisiana State University Press, 1990), 88.

14. Early maps show an *aguada* (watering place) in the Caxambas Ridge near the southern end of Marco Island. Local people and archaeologists who have worked on Marco Island have told me there is still a perched freshwater pond there. That may be the *aguada* listed in the Chaves *Espejo* at "25⅔ grados"; see Paulino Castañeda, Mariano Cuesta, and Pilar Hernández, *Transcripción, estudio y notas del "Espejo de navegantes" de Alonso Chaves* (Madrid: Instituto de Historia y Cultura Naval, 1983), 367. Roberts Bay, on the south end of Marco Island west of a portion of the ridge, is at 25°55' N. *Matança* can be translated as "carnage" or "slaughter."

15. Hann, *Missions to the Calusa*, 301. The information is contained in a letter from Pedro Menéndez de Avilés to the king dated October 20, 1566. Also see Eugene Lyon, *The Enterprise of Florida* (Gainesville: University of Florida Press, 1976), 147–50.

16. See Fontaneda's account in David O. True, ed., *Memoir of D. d'Escalante Fontaneda Respecting Florida, Written in Spain, about the Year 1575* (Coral Gables, FL: Glade House, 1945), 30, 51; also see John E. Worth, "Fontaneda Revisited: Five Descriptions of Sixteenth-Century Florida," *Florida Historical Quarterly* (January 1995): 342, 349.

17. Worth, "Fontaneda Revisited," 342, 348.

18. Hann, *Missions to the Calusa*, 311–12. In the translated quotation Hann's comments are in parentheses; mine are in brackets.

19. Father Juan Rogel in Hann, *Missions to the Calusa*, 237.

20. Castañeda, Cuesta, and Hernández, *Transcripción, estudio y notas del "Espejo de navegantes."* Navigational information, including latitudes, for the coasts of Florida is in chapter 13 (364–71). The Costa de Caracoles is on p. 366.

21. Numerous archaeological and historical sources contain information on the Calusa Indians and their pre-Columbian ancestors (as well as listing additional sources

of information). Some of these are John H. Hann's *Missions to the Calusa* and *Indians of Central and South Florida 1513–1763*; Darcie A. MacMahon and William H. Marquardt, *The Calusa and Their Legacy: South Florida People and Their Environments* (Gainesville: University Press of Florida, 1994); several books by Jerald T. Milanich: *Archaeology of Precolumbian Florida* (Gainesville: University Press of Florida, 1994); *Florida Indians and the Invasion from Europe* (Gainesville: University Press of Florida, 1995); *Florida's Indians from Ancient Times to the Present* (Gainesville: University Press of Florida, 1998); and *Laboring in the Fields of the Lord, Spanish Missions and Southeastern Indians* (Gainesville: University Press of Florida, 2006); and Jeremy D. Stahl, "An Ethnohistory of South Florida, 1500–1575" (master's thesis, University of Florida, 1986). Specific information on the archaeology of Mound Key can be found in Clifford M. Lewis, "The Calusa," in *Tacachale, Essays on the Indians of Florida and Southeast Georgia during the Historic Period*, ed. Jerald T. Milanich and Samuel Proctor (Gainesville: University of Florida Press and Florida Museum of Natural History, 1978), 19–49; Corbett McP. Torrence, Samuel Chapman, and William H. Marquardt, "Topographic Mapping and Archaeological Reconnaissance of Mound Key State Archaeological Site (8LL2), Estero Bay, Florida," Report submitted to Koreshan Unity Alliance by Florida Museum of Natural History (Gainesville, 1994), available online at http://koreshan.mwweb.org/virtual_exhibit/vex3/20101105%20torrence%20et%20al%201994.pdf; Ryan J. Wheeler, *Treasure of the Calusa: The Johnson/Willcox Collection from Mound Key, Florida* (Tallahassee, FL: Rose Printing, 2000). For more sources on the archaeology of the Calusa Indians and their pre-Columbian ancestors see Florida Museum of Natural History, "South Florida Archaeology and Ethnography," http://www.flmnh.ufl.edu/sflarch/publications.htm.

22. In his letter to Charles V, Ponce wrote that he intended to explore the coast of Florida to see if it was an island or if it connected with Mexico. By 1521 other Spaniards had established that Florida was a peninsula, not an island. Translations of documents and accounts pertinent to the second voyage are in Davis, "History of Juan Ponce de León's Voyages to Florida," 51–62. They include the royal contract awarded to Ponce in 1514; his letter to the Crown; and short relations from Herrera's *Historia general* (decade III, book I, chapter XIV, 30–31) and Gonzalo Fernández de Oviedo y Valdés, *Historia general y natural de las Indias, islas y tierra-firme del Mar Océano* (Madrid, 1853), vol. II, part II, book XXXVI, chapter I, 622–23.

23. Hann, *Indians of Central and South Florida*, 12.

24. Information on Pedro Menéndez and other Spaniards among the Calusa Indians in the late 1560s can be found in Hann, *Missions to the Calusa*, 219–321; Lyon, *Enterprise of Florida*; Lyon, "Pedro Menéndez's Strategic Plan for the Florida Peninsula," *Florida Historical Quarterly* 67, no. 1 (1988): 1–14; Gonzalo Solís de Merás, *Pedro Menéndez de Avilés. Adelantado, Governor and Captain-General of Florida*, trans. Jeannette Thurber Connor (Gainesville: University of Florida Press, 1964); and Stahl, *Ethnohistory of South Florida*.

25. Hann, *Missions to the Calusa*, 198.

26. John Hann's archival research (*Missions to the Calusa*, 3–216) brought attention to the Franciscan mission among the Calusa Indians, which was largely unknown previously. In the *Missions* volume and in *Indians of Central and Southern Florida*, 178–86, there are translations of documents and other information relative to the last years of the Calusa Indians. Building on Hann's work and conducting archival research in Cuba and elsewhere, John Worth has been further investigating the Calusa in the late seventeenth and

eighteenth centuries, including in Cuba; see his notes in two newsletters, "Tracking the Calusa Overseas," *Friends of the Randell Research Center Newsletter* 1 (December 2002), 1, and "Cuban Parish Records Reveal Immigrant Calusa Indians," *Friends of the Randell Research Center Newsletter* 2 (December 2003): 1, and his working paper "The Evacuation of South Florida, 1704–1760" (paper presented at the 60th Southeastern Archaeological Conference, Charlotte, NC, November 13, 2003). The latter is available online at http://www.uwf.edu/jworth/WorthSEAC2003Calusa.pdf. Hann and Worth are my sources for most of the information related here on the Calusa during the late seventeenth century into the mid-1800s.

27. The story of Santa María de Loreto, including pertinent documents, can be found in William C. Sturtevant, "The Last of the South Florida Aborigines," in *Tacachale*, ed. Milanich and Proctor, 141–62; and in Hann, *Missions to the Calusa*, 399–431.

28. Worth, "Evacuation of South Florida," 9.

2

"Until the Land Was Understood"
Spaniards Confront La Florida, 1500–1600

PAUL E. HOFFMAN

Writing some years after the failure of Licenciado Lucas Vázquez de Ayllón's 1526 colony (San Miguel de Gualdape) on the coast of what is today Georgia, the royal chronicler of the Indies, Gonzalo Fernández de Oviedo, recalled that while most of the colony's survivors had nothing good to say about its site or their experience "some [of the survivors] liked the shape (*la forma*) of the region they had seen and said that, doing what was requisite for settling in that place, and with enough foods to last until the land was understood, [settlement] would not be a bad thing, because the climate (*temple*) there was better suited for Spaniards."[1] What exactly does this statement mean? The colonists, after all, had spent at least two months on the southeastern coast of North America, surely enough time to become somewhat familiar with the resources of the area where they had been. Too, they had sailed from Hispaniola with the knowledge of the interior that Ayllón and a Native American he called Francisco El Chicorano had spread at the Spanish Court in 1523. However, Francisco's flight shortly after the expedition landed had cut off any possibility of his guiding them to the interior "kingdom" he had described. In short, the statement suggests that these survivors (or Oviedo) realized that neither their experiences nor Francisco's reports were adequate bases for the founding of a successful colony. The "secrets of the land" had still to be discovered. But before we consider what the secrets were and how they were discovered, it is worthwhile to unpack Oviedo's statement.

The first part of the statement—"doing what was requisite"—reflects Oviedo's moralizing comment that men like Ayllón, a judge who lacked military experience, were ill suited to undertake conquests and his somewhat more charitable observation that different preparations needed to be made for "great undertakings" in northern areas where the "people are more ferocious and the land is colder" than in the southern areas already subjugated. The second phrase—and "with enough foods"—reflected the colony's history, which was one of hunger even when surrounded by abundant natural foods.[2]

The final comment about the climate being better suited for Spaniards reflected not only the experience of late summer and early fall on the Carolina and Georgia coasts—including the passage of an early cold front—but also prevailing notions about climatic zones that derived from Ptolemy, the great Greek cosmographer. Ptolemy had observed that "all animals and all plants likewise, have a similarity under the same kind of climate or under similar weather conditions; that is, when under the same parallels [latitudinal bands], or when situated at the same distance from either pole."[3] This idea was one that Ayllón had used when propagandizing the discoveries his agent had made in 1521. He claimed, falsely, that they had been at the "height of the same degrees and identical parallels as Vandalian Spain"—that is Andalucía, which lies within Ptolemy's tenth "parallel," or climatic band (between 36° and 38°35' N). In fact, the slaving voyage of 1521 that gave rise to Ayllón's colonial venture had gotten no farther north than 33°30' N.[4] It is likely that the survivors who told Oviedo they thought the new land had possibilities understood that its climate, while closer to that of Spain than was true of the Caribbean islands, did not match what Ptolemy suggested should be the case. San Miguel de Gualdape was, after all, in the "parallel" just below the one that Ayllón had proclaimed.

Modern scholarship has proposed several locations for Ayllón's colony, all but one of them on the coastal strand of sandy barrier islands, back bays and marshes, river mouths, and the sandy eastern margins of the mainland.[5] The strand has abundant sources of proteins, especially fish and shellfish, but because of its acidic, sandy soils, it is a poor place to grow maize or other carbohydrates. Edible roots and acorns (from which a meal can be made) do exist in small quantities, but local knowledge is required to identify them.

Oviedo's account of the colony confirms this picture. He says that the colonists at San Miguel found abundant fish and shellfish (probably in tidal channels in adjoining marshes), berries of several types, wild grapevines, and various birds and small mammals. Conspicuously absent from his account is any reference to native agriculture. And since according to the modern calendar it was early October when the colony was created,[6] planting maize, European cereal grains, or (possibly) manioc was out of the question. The expedition's supplies of carbohydrates—wheat flour, and perhaps cornmeal and *casabe* (cassava) bread—mostly had been lost with the wreck of its largest ship approaching land farther north. A search for Native American stores of food quickly developed, with the predictable result: the local Native Americans turned hostile. Hunger and then disease began to kill.[7] Faced with uncertain prospects of resupply from the Antilles, most of the surviving colonists were willing enough to abandon the enterprise following Ayllón's death on October 18 (October 27 by the modern calendar).

Farther south, Juan Ponce de León had encountered a similar ecology along the east coast of peninsular Florida in 1513, although he did not attempt to create a colony. Like Ayllón's settlers, he encountered relatively small, widely spaced, and hostile Native American settlements, mostly on the mainland at or near river mouths.[8] On the west coast, Ponce had skirmishes with the Calusa in both 1513 and, fatally, in 1521, perhaps in the vicinity of Mound Key, but more likely a bit farther south, in the general area of the Ten Thousand Islands of southwestern Florida. The ecology there is quite different from that of the east coast barrier islands and back bays but just as limiting for Europeans because the area's natural resources require local knowledge for maximum exploitation.[9]

Ponce's voyage of 1513 to the lower west coast of the peninsula was followed in 1519 by a voyage usually attributed to Alonso Alvarez de Pineda but actually led by Diego de Camargo along the Gulf coast at least as far west as Vermillion Bay, Louisiana.[10] It also returned a negative image of the land, although the expedition's full report has not come to light. What we know about what Camargo found is in the contract between his employer, Francisco de Garay, governor of Jamaica, and the Crown. After the briefest of references to the voyage and the chart and sailing directions it generated, the contract says that "among other low, sterile land that they [Camargo and his crew] discovered, they touched the land of Florida that Juan Ponce de León discovered."[11]

Writing in about 1540, Alonso de Santa Cruz, one of the cosmographers of the House of Trade (Casa de la Contratación) at Seville, recorded what was by then the more common opinion; that is, that the east coast of what is now the United States from peninsular Florida to the Penobscot River had "many islands . . . all deserted and of little benefit [*provecho*], which were seen and discovered by the Licenciado Ayllón."[12]

Four expeditions, four reports, all agreeing circa 1540 that coastal La Florida, and perhaps the entire region, was apparently little populated, generally "low and sterile" and, consequently, "of little benefit" for the Spanish Empire. Or *was it* little populated and of little potential benefit? There was, after all, Ayllón's tale of a king ruling a farming population that lived "politically" in the interior.[13] That story lived on in Peter Martyr's *Decades*, published in

1530,[14] and was resurrected in Francisco López de Gómara's *History of the Indies* (1552) in what I have elsewhere called the Chicora Legend.[15]

Clearly, neither southern Florida nor the lower east coast of North America were unpopulated. Ponce de León had met hostile native peoples in Florida in 1513 at St. Lucie Inlet, Biscayne Bay, and the lower west coast. As for the rest of the Gulf coast, what we have of Camargo's record of his voyage is silent on population until the narrative reaches the coast of New Spain.[16] This silence about the west coast of Florida and the Gulf coast does not mean he did not see Native Americans, just that the reports we have do not mention them. On the Atlantic coast, Ayllón's explorers of 1525 found four different linguistic groups between the Cape of the Cross—the now-eroded headland of Anastasia Island by St. Augustine—and Delaware Bay. Ayllón himself attempted to settle near the Native American population at Sapelo Sound, Georgia, and listed the names of eighteen Indian groups in the general vicinity of the Santee River in his contract with the Crown.[17] The bottom line was that none of these coastal groups seemed to be very large and none gave evidence of being part of a large empire such as the Spaniards had found in New Spain (Mexico) and would shortly find in Peru. Still, Ayllón's tale of an interior "king" whose sway might have reached the coast offered some hope of large agricultural populations that could be added to the Spanish Empire.

In its gross details, this picture of La Florida circa 1540 was accurate. The ecology of the Southeast and, more particularly, the Florida peninsula, as well as Native American subsistence technologies, dictated that relatively small populations would be distributed as indicated. The various terraces of the coastal plain are covered with acidic sands of low fertility, interrupted here and there by the higher ground of hammocks. Rivers crossing the plain have often extensive, if flash-flood-prone bottomlands and marginal swamps. Frequent lightning-caused fires and underlying hardpans formerly maintained a pine subclimax forest—the famous pine barrens and pine flatwoods—over most of the coastal terraces, while hardwood forests dominated the riverine bottomlands. In many areas, coastal marshes partially fill the bays between the mainland and barrier islands. Native Americas took advantage of the combination of the rich maritime resources of those marshes, the agricultural potential of hammocks and riverine terraces that did not normally flood, and the hunting-and-gathering possibilities of the flatwoods and slopes, or ecotones, between terraces.[18] In Georgia, Sapelo Sound and the mouths of the various rivers that feed into the sounds behind the barrier islands offer this combination. In peninsular Florida, the mouth and much of the lower St. Johns River, Charlotte Harbor, Tampa Bay, and to a lesser degree the Jupiter Inlet and Miami areas, offered particularly favorable environments. As Ponce de León and Ayllón's explorers found, these few favorable areas supported multiple villages of several hundred persons each, sometimes organized into larger political units classified by anthropologists as paramount chiefdoms. The agricultural, and hence demographic, potential of such places was, however, limited given Native American agricultural techniques.

The piedmont inland from the coasts of the Carolinas, Georgia, Alabama, and Mississippi, as well as the Madison, Tallahassee, and Mariana highlands of northern Florida, consist of rolling hills covered with soils of varied composition and color. More fertile than the coastal sands, they support mixed forests of oaks, hickories, and pines. The slopes have been credited with supporting up to thirty-five species of trees per acre, along with a large variety of other edible and seemingly medicinal plants. Faunal life is also more abundant, although not all species are food.[19]

In some respects a continuation of the piedmont, Florida's central ridge is made up of two basic types of soils, both of which are moist to well drained and of moderate fertility. Pines and various species of scrub oaks are the natural forest cover, but other types of oaks and hardwoods occur where conditions are favorable. Rivers and streams drain away from the ridge and in a few areas create small floodplains that were especially useful for digging-stick agricultural methods. Native Americans sited their villages near ecotones, sources of freshwater, and areas of relatively fertile soil. Farther north, they favored piedmont riverine terraces for agriculture and the adjacent uplands for village sites and for hunting and gathering. Throughout the Southeast, trade, often over very long distances, supplied flint and chert for projectile points and cutting tools, as well as more exotic items such as copper, freshwater pearls, and Ayllón's "terrestrial gems"—almost certainly the quartz crystals found west of modern Charlotte, North Carolina.[20]

Such were the secrets of the land and the reasons for them. The story of Spanish exploration and colonization after 1530 and before circa 1650 is one of the discovery of the details of this picture and of trying and failing to move Spanish settlement into the interior of the Carolinas region that Ayllón's tale had pointed to as an area that would better fit what had become the Spanish pattern of conquest; that is, the subjugation of large, centrally governed agricultural populations. Only after circa 1610 did Spanish missionaries establish a presence on the central Florida ridge, and only after 1630 did they reach Apalachee's better soils and large population. They never established a lasting presence in the Piedmont. Nor did the small Spanish garrison at San Luís de Apalache in the late seventeenth century ever become the nucleus for an expanding Spanish settlement.

The first intentional scouting of what lay inland was the Hernando de Soto expedition's epic exploration of the Southeast from 1539 to 1543.[21] A veteran of the conquests of Panama, Nicaragua, and Peru, De Soto knew that as a rule the larger and potentially richer Native American settlements did not lie on the coast. He also knew about Ayllón's failed colony and, by a stroke of good fortune, about Pánfilo de Narváez's accidental peregrination of 1528 up the west side of Florida's Central Ridge and then westward by boat along the coast as far as modern Texas. The Florida part of the journey indicated that some small Native American settlements had limited stores of maize, while the Gulf coast voyage indicated widely scattered, hostile Indian groups. De Soto also may have known about Ponce's misadventures.[22]

From these and perhaps other sources, De Soto constructed his plan to move inland and follow the maize fields and native societies until he found mineral resources or areas of large agricultural populations suitable for a traditional conquest.[23] This strategy was dictated as well by his contract with the Crown, which allowed three years of exploration before De Soto had to designate the two hundred leagues (about 620 miles) of coast that would define his colony.[24]

The survivors of De Soto's expedition reported the same largely negative impression of most of La Florida that the earlier coastal expeditions had formed, although they confirmed Ayllón's report of large populations in the interior. The towns on the western side of Florida's Central Ridge and on its northern uplands, except for Anhaica and Apalache (modern Tallahassee), had proven disappointing, with only small supplies of food and no mineral wealth. The landing site, likely on Tampa Bay, seemed, in Rodrigo Rangel's words "sterile, as in truth the coast is reputed to be."[25] The Gentleman from Elvas said that peninsular Florida was "a lean land and most of it covered with rough pine groves, low and very swampy and in places having lofty dense forests, where the hostile Indians wandered so that no one could find them."[26] Only two places, Cofitachequi near modern Camden, South Carolina, and Coosa, in the ridge and valley terrain south of modern Chattanooga, were remembered by the survivors of the expedition as suitable for Spanish settlement.[27] The Spaniards had visited many other chiefdoms of varied size and agricultural abundance, but none were so promising as those two places.

Coosa's reputation did not survive the Tristán de Luna expedition of 1559–62. A scouting party of two hundred men sent to Coosa from the expedition's inland base at Nanipacana on the lower Alabama River initially reported that while the land between the coast and Coosa would be difficult to convert to Spanish farms and ranches because the Native Americans had cleared very little of the heavy forest covering it, Coosa itself was as well supplied with food as the De Soto survivors had remembered. That report was, however, quickly overridden by mutinous colonists anxious to return to New Spain. To justify the abandonment, the officers sent a mounted party to Coosa with *instructions* to report on "the insufficiency of the country" and withdraw the men already there.[28] This mutiny sparked by dashed hopes of an easy life proved to be the prelude to the colony's failure, which international events accelerated.

Luna's expedition broke up not just because of its well-known loss of supplies to a tropical storm not long after arrival on the sandy shores of Pensacola Bay and the subsequent hardships, but also because Philip II ordered part of the party to go to the Point of Santa Elena on the Atlantic coast at 32° N to prevent a reported Franco-Scots attempt to settle there and thus tap into the riches that might lie in the interior. Angel de Villafañe, who replaced Luna as the governor of the struggling colony at Pensacola, carried out that mission, but he and his men later claimed that on the Atlantic coast below 35° N "there is no land where settlement can be made nor a port suitable for it, nor native people who could be congregated nor joined to the Christian doctrine . . . nor in all that we have seen is found gold or silver or a good disposition of land for settlement which would serve and benefit Your Majesty." There was, they concluded, no danger of a successful French settlement. Better prospects might lie north of 35° N but exploration and settlement of that area should be undertaken from Spain, not New Spain.[29]

That Franco-Scots expedition never sailed, but Frenchman Jean Ribault did in 1562, and left men at Port Royal Sound, just north of the Point of Santa Elena and, by his own telling, near "Chicore"—Ayllón's Chicora. Reports of that French outpost and of the René de Laudonnière expedition to follow up on it, set in motion what became Pedro Menéndez de Avilés's successful settlements at St. Augustine and Santa Elena (Parris Island, South Carolina).[30] Both were sited on the coast in locations whose low-fertility soils yielded limited harvests of maize, keeping the colonies dependent on imported foods or such tribute in maize as might be extracted from nearby Native Americans. Moreover, the Spanish settlement occurred at a time when La Niña was common in the Pacific Ocean and producing repeated episodes of below-normal rainfall over the southeastern coast of North America. This weather pattern further reduced crop yields.[31]

Although in time the Spaniards found they could grow various Old

World fruits and vegetables and limited crops of maize in the sands of St. Augustine and Santa Elena, their general experience there was often nearly as grim as the Jesuit Juan Baptista de Segura's 1570 complaint that the three hundred leagues (about 950 miles) of La Florida that he had seen were "one long pile of sand" and "the most miserable land ever discovered by man."[32] That is, neither southwest Florida, where the Jesuits had had a mission, nor the coastal plain south of Chesapeake Bay could easily become the site of prospering colonies. The interior was another matter, as Ayllón's tales and De Soto's experience had suggested.

Menéndez de Avilés evidently knew of De Soto's Cofitachequi. When Philip II sent Menéndez nearly 1,500 soldiers under Sancho de Archiniega in 1566[33] (because of fears of a French return), he needed to spread them out among Native American towns so that they could be fed. Consequently, he sent Captain Juan Pardo and Sergeant Hernando Moyano de Morales along trails to the northwest of Santa Elena to see the countryside, obtain the agreement of the caciques (chiefs) to gather and hold a maize tribute for possible Spanish use, and report in detail on the resources they found.[34]

Pardo made two expeditions into the interior, carefully recording the Native American villages he found, the gifts he gave to the caciques, and their oaths of obedience to the Spanish Crown. The results were Spanish forts at Joara (near modern Morganton, North Carolina) and Olamico (an unknown location farther east in North Carolina), several written accounts of the expedition, and Notary Juan de la Vandera's very detailed description of the soils, clay that could be used for pottery and roof tiles, and how well maize and grapevines grew at every point along a route that reached almost as far as Coosa.[35] In combination, the various reports told of large populations, one or two paramount chiefdoms with mound-oriented ceremonial centers, and land that was just as fertile as De Soto's men had remembered.[36] The forts, and Pardo's agreements with the caciques of the Wateree River valley route to them, could have been the basis for the land grant and marquisate that the Crown had promised Menéndez, but Native Americans attacked and destroyed the interior forts in the spring of 1568 just as orders were received to return Pardo's surviving men to Spain.[37]

Menéndez never had another opportunity to bring those inland Native Americans under direct Spanish control. He did not live long enough, nor likely would he have had financial or human resources enough, to carve out that piedmont estate and settlement. The absence of tractable Native Americans in the interior and mineral resources to attract would-be settlers further restricted what he could have accomplished. Too, his activities in La Florida were in a period when the Crown no longer allowed either the enslavement or the forced labor of Native Americans, although as commoners they were expected to earn and pay a monetary tribute. And behind those restrictions was the constant threat that the French might begin trading for sarsaparilla with the coastal Indians, or even attempt a new colony, unlikely as that might have been for a nation in the midst of its Wars of Religion. The strategic imperative to guard the exit to the Bahama Channel that had led Philip II to send and partially fund Menéndez meant that Spanish settlement continued to be confined to the coastal plain, the part of La Florida that was least able to support agriculture. And as Menéndez also discovered, the poor pasturage, insect pests, and animal and human predators in that area also made cattle raising difficult.[38]

In the years after Menéndez's death, his two small towns were consolidated at St. Augustine (1587) and only a few expeditions crossed the coastal plain of Georgia to the foot of the piedmont.[39] The legend of *los diamantes* (the diamonds)—Pardo's quartz crystals—lived on, and there is some indication of growing Spanish–Native American trade that included the slowly emerging confederacy known to us as the Creek nation.[40] And, briefly, in the years 1645–51, Governor Benito Ruiz de Salazar Ballecilla developed a ranch and wheat farm near the village of Asile on the fringes of Apalachee. It proved that Spanish-style agriculture, with Native American labor, could be developed on the better soils of the peninsula. But after his death, the Franciscans and the cacique of Asile broke up the enterprise. They replaced it with small-scale food and peltry exports to Havana.[41] Other ranches developed after about 1650, and especially in the 1680s, as continued declines in mission populations in north-central Florida (near modern Gainesville) left old fields open to become pastures.[42] In the 1680s, the development of small-scale extractive industries such as naval stores and suggestions that others like cotton weaving might be possible suggest what might have been accomplished had the remaining Native Americans and Spaniards not been driven from the land by the Creek-English attacks of 1702–13.[43]

In sum, by 1600 Spaniards had discovered the physical and human "secrets of the land" but could not capitalize on them. La Florida of the explorers, conquerors, settlers, and missionaries was not "deserted and useless" as Santa Cruz had proclaimed, but nor was it an easy place to establish a colony. The physical geography that restricted Native American settlement also restricted the Spaniards, the more so because their model of colonization was to superimpose themselves on indigenous populations, extracting subsistence and livelihoods from their agricultural and other labors. A relative lack of exploitable natural resources, except good soils in the interior, and of incentives to attempt settlement inland (as distinct from missions), dominance of office and opportunities by a few families,[44] and the imperatives of Imperial policy toward Native Americans and the guarding of the strategic Bahama Channel further restricted what Spaniards could do to assert control over the peoples they found in La Florida or to take advantage of its natural resources. And those economic and sociopolitical restrictions, ultimately, were also among the "secrets of the land" that doomed Spanish Florida to be almost a footnote to the story of Anglophone America.

Notes

1. Gonzalo Fernández de Oviedo, *Historia general y natural de las indias,* 4 vols. (Madrid: Imprenta de la Real Academia de la Historia, 1851–55), 3:630 (bk. 37, chap. 2), translated in part in Paul E. Hoffman, *A New Andalucia and a Way to the Orient: The American Southeast During the Sixteenth Century* (Baton Rouge: Louisiana State University Press, 1990), 83.

2. Oviedo, *Historia general,* 3:625 (bk. 37, prohemio), 3:632 (bk. 37, chap. 3), 3:631 (bk. 37, chap. 3).

3. Claudius Ptolemaeus, *Geography of Claudius Ptolemy,* trans and ed. by Edward Luther Stevenson (New York: New York Public Library, 1932), 31–32.

4. Hoffman, *New Andalucia,* 3–83, is an account of Ayllón's activities; for these specific facts see pp. 21 and 10, respectively. Ptolemy's bands were based on the lengths of the longest day as one went north from the Equator. Within the confines of the Mediterranean basin they made some sense but even there were arbitrary.

5. Martín Fernández de Navarrete, ed., *Colección de los viajes y descubrimientos que hicieron por mar los españoles desde fines del siglo XV,* 5 vols. (Madrid: Imprenta de la Real Academia de la Historia, 1925), 3:84, 3:86–87, argued for a location near Cape Lookout, even though he had access to almost all of the documentary material that is now used to propose different locations; Johann G. Kohl, *The Discovery of the East Coast of North America* (Portland, ME: Bailey and Noyes, 1869), 247, 396–401, places Gualdape at Cape Fear; John G. Shea, "Ancient Florida," in *Narrative and Critical History of the United States,* ed. Justin Winsor, 8 vols. (Boston: Houghton Mifflin, 1884–89), 2:239, claimed a location at or near Jamestown! Woodbury Lowery, *The Spanish Settlements within the Present Limits of the United States,* 2 vols. (New York: G. P. Putnam's Sons, 1901–11), 1:155, 165, 448–51, placed the colony on the Pee Dee River, near modern Georgetown, South Carolina; Paul Quattlebaum, *The Land Called Chicora: The Carolinas Under Spanish Rule with French Intrusions, 1520–1670* (Gainesville: University of Florida Press, 1956), 10–11, 21–23, 126–29, argued for the same location. However, Hoffman, *New Andalucia,* 317–21, after reviewing these and a few other theories against the documentary evidence concluded that it was at or near Sapelo Sound, Georgia (p. 321). Douglas T. Peck, "Lucas Vázquez de Ayllón's Doomed Colony of San Miguel de Gualdape," *Georgia Historical Quarterly* 85, no. 2 (Summer 2001): 193, has argued for a site at the mouth of the Savannah River. The arguments of Navarrete, Kohl, and Shea can be dismissed as a misreading of Oviedo's account (that the colony was north of the first landing site in 1526; he plainly says it was "west," meaning southwest). I do not find Lowery's, Quattlebaum's, or Peck's arguments convincing. Shea's location is the one not on the coastal strand.

6. Spain, like the rest of the western world, was still using the Julian calendar, which was then about ten days behind the solar year. The colony's name, San Miguel (St. Michael the Archangel), suggests a formal founding on September 29, which would be October 8 on our Gregorian calendar. The Gregorian calendar reform took place in Spain in 1584.

7. Oviedo, *Historia general*, 3:628–33; Hoffman, *New Andalucia*, 73–74. Manioc (cassava), a staple on Hispaniola, requires at least a year to produce a crop of roots that could be processed into *casabe* bread. For Native American subsistence strategies in this ecology, see Lewis H. Larson, *Aboriginal Subsistence Technology on the Southeastern Coastal Plain During the Late Prehistoric Period* (Gainesville: University Presses of Florida, 1980). He shows that the Indians not only exploited the maritime environment but also hunted and gathered in an annual round that took them into the interior, perhaps as far as the piedmont. Indians in the piedmont towns, dependent on agriculture for much of their subsistence, also employed hunting and gathering to supplement the maize and beans they grew.

8. Anthony Q. Devereux, *Juan Ponce de León, King Ferdinand, and the Fountain of Youth* (Spartanburg, SC: Reprint Co., 1993), 113–16, esp. 115; see also 123, 127.

9. Devereux, *Ponce de León*, 129–35.

10. Rolena Adorno and Patrick Charles Pautz, *Álvar Núñez Cabeza de Vaca: His Account, His Life, and the Expedition of Pánfilo de Narváez*, 3 vols. (Lincoln: University of Nebraska Press, 1999), 3:231–40, correct the traditional account that ascribes this voyage to Alonso Alvarez de Pineda.

11. "Cédula allowing Francisco de Garay to populate the province of Amichel . . . , Burgos, n.d., 1521," in Navarrete, *Colección de los viajes y descubrimientos*, 3:160 (my translation). Robert Weddle, *Spanish Sea: The Gulf of Mexico in North American Discovery, 1500–1685* (College Station: Texas A&M University Press, 1985), 100, conflates the cédula's description of the richness of Amichel, the land on the Pánuco River, with the entire coast. In other respects, Weddle's account is reliable, but see also Adorno and Pautz, *Cabeza de Vaca*, 3:231–40.

12. Alonso de Santa Cruz, *Islario general de todas las islas del mundo* . . . 2 vols. (Madrid: Patronato de Huérfanos de Intendencia e Intervención Militares, 1918), 1:441–42.

13. The term "politically" was derived from Aristotle's *Politics* and indicated rational self-rule. It was a buzzword at the time because Native Americans not living "politically" were considered uncivilized and thus fair game for conquest and deprivation of their natural property rights. For a discussion of the issues surrounding how the Spaniards were expected to treat the Native Americans while insisting on missionary activity and trade among them, see Lewis Hanke, *The Spanish Struggle for Justice in the Conquest of America* (Boston: Little, Brown, 1965).

14. Pietro Martire d'Anghiera, *Décadas del Nuevo Mundo*, ed. Edmundo O'Gorman, 2 vols. (Mexico City: José Porrúa e Hijos, 1964–65), 2:596–97 (decade 7, bk. 2)

15. Hoffman, *New Andalucia*, 3–21, 125–28, 136–39.

16. Weddle, *Spanish Sea*, 100, 104, corrects accounts that have Alvarez de Pineda (i.e., Camargo) entering the Mississippi.

17. The names were supplied by Francisco and other Native Americans, a classic example of how Spaniards (and other Europeans) depended on native informants for knowledge of areas they had not visited.

18. These ecotones provide variable moisture conditions, and as a result support a greater variety of floral and consequently faunal life than the areas below or above them.

19. Paul E. Hoffman, *Florida's Frontiers* (Bloomington: Indiana University Press, 2002), 6–12.

20. George F. Kunz, "History of Gems Found in North Carolina," *North Carolina Geological Survey Bulletin* 12 (1907): 29–35, notes the quartz crystal deposits along the Catawba River in Alexander, Burke, Catawba, Iredell, and Lincoln Counties. For the Pardo expedition's claiming of these mines see Charles Hudson, *The Juan Pardo Expeditions*, rev. ed. (Tuscaloosa: University of Alabama Press, 2005), 161–64, 189–90, 279–80.

21. See Charles Hudson, "The Historical Significance of the Soto Route," in Patricia Galloway, ed., *The Hernando de Soto Expedition: History, Historiography, and "Discovery" in the Southeast* (Lincoln: University of Nebraska Press, 1997), 320, fig. 3 (showing Hudson's map as of January 1996). Hudson has since modified portions of the route in North Carolina based on the excavation of Joara. See the preface in Hudson, *Juan Pardo Expeditions*. See also the afterword by David G. Moore, Robin A. Beck Jr., and Christopher B. Rodning in the same volume, 343–49. See also Robin A. Beck Jr., David G. Moore, and Christopher B. Rodning, "Identifying Fort San Juan: A Sixteenth-Century Spanish Occupation at the Berry Site, North Carolina," *Southeastern Archaeology* 25, no. 1 (2006): 65–77.

22. Hoffman, *New Andalucia*, 29–32; Andrés Reséndez, *A Land So Strange; The Epic Journey of Cabeza de Vaca* (New York: Basic Books, 2007), 91–132, is an accessible account of the Narváez expedition's journey. For more details see Adorno and Pautz, *Cabeza de Vaca*. Volume 1 is the text in transcription and translation; volumes 2 and 3 are commentary on various parts of the story and on the creation, reception, and historical context of the *Relación*. I do not agree with either Reséndez or Adorno and Pautz about why and how Narváez ended up on the west coast of Florida. See Paul E. Hoffman, "Narváez and Cabeza de Vaca in Florida," in Charles Hudson and Carmen Chaves Tesser, eds., *The Forgotten Centuries: Indians and Europeans in the American South, 1521–1704* (Athens: University of Georgia Press, 1994), 50–73.

23. Charles Hudson, *Knights of Spain, Warriors of the Sun, Hernando de Soto and the South's Ancient Chiefdoms* (Athens: University of Georgia Press, 1997), 468. The four sixteenth-century accounts of De Soto's adventure and a number of other documents and studies are in Lawrence A. Clayton, Vernon James Knight Jr., and Edward C. Moore, eds., *The De Soto Chronicles: The Expedition of Hernando de Soto to North America, 1539–1543*, 2 vols. (Tuscaloosa: University of Alabama Press, 1993); hereafter *De Soto Chronicles*. These volumes have been reprinted in paperback format.

24. Contract of April 20, 1537, in *De Soto Chronicles*, 1:360. The evident intention, based on Peruvian examples, was to fix the boundaries using latitudes, much as was done with the later English grants in North America.

25. Hoffman, *Florida's Frontiers*, 36–37; quotation from Rodrigo Rangel's account.

26. "The Account of the Gentleman from Elvas," trans. and ed. James Alexander Robertson with footnotes and updates to Robertson's notes by John H. Hann, in *De Soto Chronicles*, 1:78.

27. Hudson, *Knights of Spain*, 172, locates Cofitachequi at the Mulberry site at the junction of Pine Tree Creek and the Wateree River; Coosa's location and nature is in ibid.,

203-4. For a discussion of the paramount chiefdom of Coosa see David J. Hally, "The Chiefdom of Coosa," in Hudson and Tesser, *Forgotten Centuries*, 227-53.

28. Hoffman, *New Andalucia*, 144-59, 169-74, gives an account of the Luna expedition. Paul E. Hoffman, "Did Coosa Decline between 1541 and 1560?" *Florida Anthropologist* 50 (1997): 25-29, documents how the colonists revised the initial, favorable reports on Coosa to negative ones. For published documents see Herbert I. Priestley, trans. and ed., *The Luna Papers: Documents Relating to the Expedition of Don Tristán de Luna y Arellano for the Conquest of Florida in 1559-1561*, 2 vols.(De Land, FL: Florida State Historical Society, 1928).

29. Hoffman, *New Andalucia*, 174-81; first quotation on p. 176, second on pp. 180-81, both from a deposition at Mexico City, March 3, 1562.

30. Ibid., 205-30, for Ribault and Laudonnière. Eugene Lyon, *The Enterprise of Florida: Pedro Menéndez de Avilés and the Conquest of 1565-1568* (Gainesville: University Presses of Florida, 1976) is the now classic account of Menéndez's work.

31. Joëlle L. Gergis and Anthony M. Fowler, "A History of ENSO Events since AD 1525: Implications for Future Climate Change," *Climate Change* 92 (2009): 364, 371; David W. Stahle and Malcolm K. Cleaveland, "Rainfall Tables, AD 933-1985," computer printout in the collection of the author, courtesy of Drs. Stahle and Cleaveland. On droughts see also David W. Stahle, Malcolm K. Cleaveland, Dennis B. Blanton, Matthew D. Therrell, and David A. Gay, "The Lost Colony and Jamestown Drought," *Science* 280 (1998): 564-67; and Hoffman, *Florida's Frontiers*, passim.

32. Quoted in Nicholas P. Cushner, *Why Have You Come Here? The Jesuits and the First Evangelization of Native America* (New York: Oxford University Press, 2006), 47, 31, respectively.

33. Half of these soldiers were destined for temporary garrison duty in the Antilles. See Paul E. Hoffman, *The Spanish Crown and the Defense of the Caribbean, 1535-1585* (Baton Rouge: Louisiana State University Press, 1980), 140-45, esp. table 18, p. 144.

34. Hudson, *Juan Pardo Expeditions*, is the best account of the expedition and the Native American polities encountered. It incorporates the various reports and modern archaeological and ethnographic materials. For more detail on Archiniega see Lyon, *Enterprise of Florida*, 143, 147, 165-66.

35. "The Short Bandera Relation," in Hudson, *Juan Pardo Expeditions*, 297-304 (transcription and translation by Paul E. Hoffman). Moyano's Joara fort was abandoned in the face of Indian hostility and the withdrawal of the Archiniega reinforcements during 1568. When the garrison withdrew from Joara, a number of Native American women, reported in other Spanish documents as the wives and servants of the soldiers, left with it.

36. For example, "Martinez Relation," in Hudson, *Juan Pardo Expeditions*, 319-21, is an account sworn at Santa Elena, July 11, 1567, highlighting the agricultural potential of Joara as "good in itself for bread and wine and all sorts of herded animals . . . because it is a level land and has many sweet rivers and good groves" of trees and "much game, deer as well as hares and rabbits and hens and bears and lions."

37. Lyon, *Enterprise of Florida*, 51; Hudson, *Juan Pardo Expeditions*, 173-77.

38. Charles W. Arnade, "Cattle Raising in Spanish Florida, 1513-1763," *Agricultural History* 35, no. 3 (July 1961): 117-18; Hoffman, *Florida's Frontiers*, 61; Amy Turner Bushnell,

"The Menéndez Márquez Cattle Barony at La Chua and the Determinants of Economic Expansion in Seventeenth-Century Florida," *Florida Historical Quarterly* 56 (1978): 407–31.

39. John Worth, "Late Spanish Military Expeditions in the Interior Southeast, 1597–1628," in Hudson and Tesser, *Forgotten Centuries*, 104–22.

40. Vernon James Knight, "The Formation of the Creeks," in Hudson and Tesser, *Forgotten Centuries*, 373–92, and Patricia Galloway, "Confederacy as a Solution to Chiefdom Dissolution: Historical Evidence in the Choctaw Case," in ibid., 393–420. For indications of trade see Hoffman, *Florida's Frontiers*, 113, 140; and Gregory A. Waselkov, "Seventeenth-Century Trade in the Colonial Southeast," *Southeastern Archaeology* 8 (1989): 117–33.

41. Catherine S. Lawson, "Governor Salazar's Wheat Farm Project, 1645–1657," *Florida Historical Quarterly* 24 (1946): 196–200; John E. Worth, *Tihmucuan Chiefdoms of Spanish Florida*, 2 vols. (Gainesville: University Press of Florida, 1998), 1:203–8; Hoffman, *Florida's Frontiers*, 119–20 (Asile farm); 113, 170 (Havana trade).

42. The ranch at La Chua dates from the 1620s. Worth, *Timucuan Chiefdoms*, 1:199–203; see also n. 36, above.

43. Hoffman, *Florida's Frontiers*, 134; 136–37 (ranching; see also n. 38, above); 172–73 (other industries). For the attacks of 1702–13 see ibid., 174–81; and Worth, *Timucuan Chiefdoms*, 2:140–47 (which also discusses raids beginning in 1685).

44. See Amy Turner Bushnell, *The King's Coffer: Proprietors of the Spanish Florida Treasury, 1565–1702* (Gainesville: University Presses of Florida, 1981) for the story of the family that fought with governors for domination of the colony and its economic opportunities.

3

On the Trail of Texts from Early Spanish Florida

Garcilaso's *La Florida del Inca* and Oré's *Relación de los mártires*

RAQUEL CHANG-RODRÍGUEZ

After securing its power in Mexico (1521) and Cuzco (1534), the respective capitals of the Aztec and Inca Empires, Imperial Spain began to assert its influence in the vast territory that Juan Ponce de León had named La Florida (1513). The reorganization of the fleet system (1564)[1] attracted fresh interest to the area, since the convoy stopped in Havana and from there went along the eastern coast of La Florida before completing the Atlantic crossing. There were several reasons why the territory became increasingly important. In the wider context of European politics it was urgent to protect Spanish ships and cities in the Americas from the attacks of French, English, and Dutch pirates and corsairs, in order to ensure the safe passage of New World treasures back to Spanish ports. The successful exploitation of silver mines in Zacatecas (Viceroyalty of New Spain) motivated colonial administrators and explorers to seek a new land route through La Florida. They hoped that, once established, such a route would enable the transfer of Mexican silver to a convoy of ships waiting on the east coast of North America, thus avoiding the Caribbean Sea and its marauding pirates. The 1562 arrival in La Florida of French Protestants (Huguenots) rekindled the religious fervor of Catholic Spaniards and enraged Philip II, who ordered them evicted from the territory at any cost. Likewise, news of rich kingdoms in the center of the continent awakened interest in the territory and sustained the ambitions of those who were hoping to find another Peru or Mexico.

And, of course, the search for the best route to Asia was still ongoing. When Vasco Núñez de Balboa discovered the Mar del Sur (that is, Pacific, 1513), the need to find a maritime passage between the Atlantic and Pacific became urgent. Ferdinand Magellan achieved this feat in the circumnavigation of the earth completed by Juan Sebastián Elcano (1522), his second in command. Magellan discovered the strait that bears his name, but since that passage was far out of the way and extremely risky, explorations seeking an alternative route continued. There was much speculation about finding a new route to China by crossing the continental mass to the north or via a sea route. The most expert navigators were looking for the Strait of Anián, named for a province in China, Anan or Ania (Hainan's island?), mentioned by Marco Polo in his travelogue. Although the interior of the continent was almost unknown, particularly the distance between the ports of the Atlantic coast and those on the Pacific coast, the map of Juan Vespucci (1526) confirmed the contour of North America and demonstrated that La Florida was not an island.

In many ways the letters, *relaciones*, chronicles, and poetry written shortly after the incursions into the northern frontier of the Spanish Empire reflect the aforementioned interests. This is why they should be framed in a context of exploration and ambition, of religion and evangelization, of international politics and colonial violence. These documents are the principal testimonies of decades of contact in this vast zone, now part of the United States of America. In many cases, they offer the only information about ethnic groups that disappeared soon after the arrival of the Europeans. With uneven artistic merit, these writings reflect on human behavior in unusual circumstances, present the agency of Europeans as well as Indians, and show unique and horrific aspects of frontier life. The trail of texts documenting the Florida experience is as varied as it is large, and it touches upon exploration, religion, acculturation, and destruction of native societies.

It is worth pointing out some representative works of this singular literature. In the epistolary category, the most studied are the letters written by Pedro Menéndez de Avilés,[2] *adelantado* of La Florida and governor of Cuba. Among the chronicles, *La Florida del Inca* (1605) by the Peruvian Garcilaso de la Vega stands out. For its representation of a major rebellion, the *Relación de los mártires de la Florida* (ca. 1619)[3] by the Franciscan Luis Jerónimo de Oré, also from Peru, is of great interest; in the category of epic poetry, *La Florida* (ca. 1600) written by another Franciscan, Alonso Gregorio de Escobedo, is a unique literary and historical document.[4] To virtually walk La Florida's trails, I have selected two texts: the Inca Garcilaso's chronicle and Oré's *relación* (see figures 3.1 and 3.2).

The selection of these texts was not arbitrary. Because my research has centered on the colonial Andean world, I arrived in La Florida by following, on sea and land, through mountains and marshes, in Europe and America,

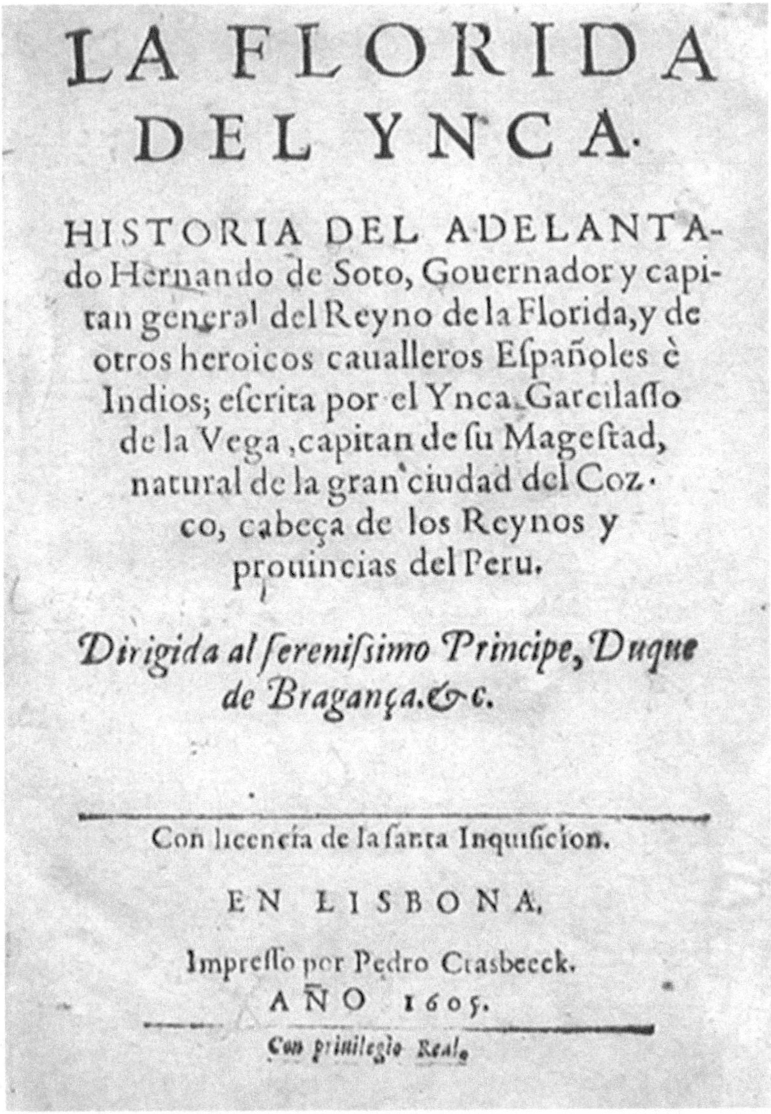

LA FLORIDA DEL YNCA.

HISTORIA DEL ADELANTA-
do Hernando de Soto, Gouernador y capitan general del Reyno de la Florida, y de
otros heroicos caualleros Españoles è
Indios; escrita por el Ynca Garcilasso
de la Vega, capitan de su Magestad,
natural de la gran ciudad del Coz-
co, cabeça de los Reynos y
prouincias del Peru.

*Dirigida al serenissimo Principe, Duque
de Bragança. &c.*

Con licencia de la santa Inquisicion.

EN LISBONA,

Impresso por Pedro Crasbeeck.
AÑO 1605.

Con priuilegio Real.

Figure 3.1. Title page of *La Florida del Inca*. (Courtesy of the Hispanic Society of America, New York)

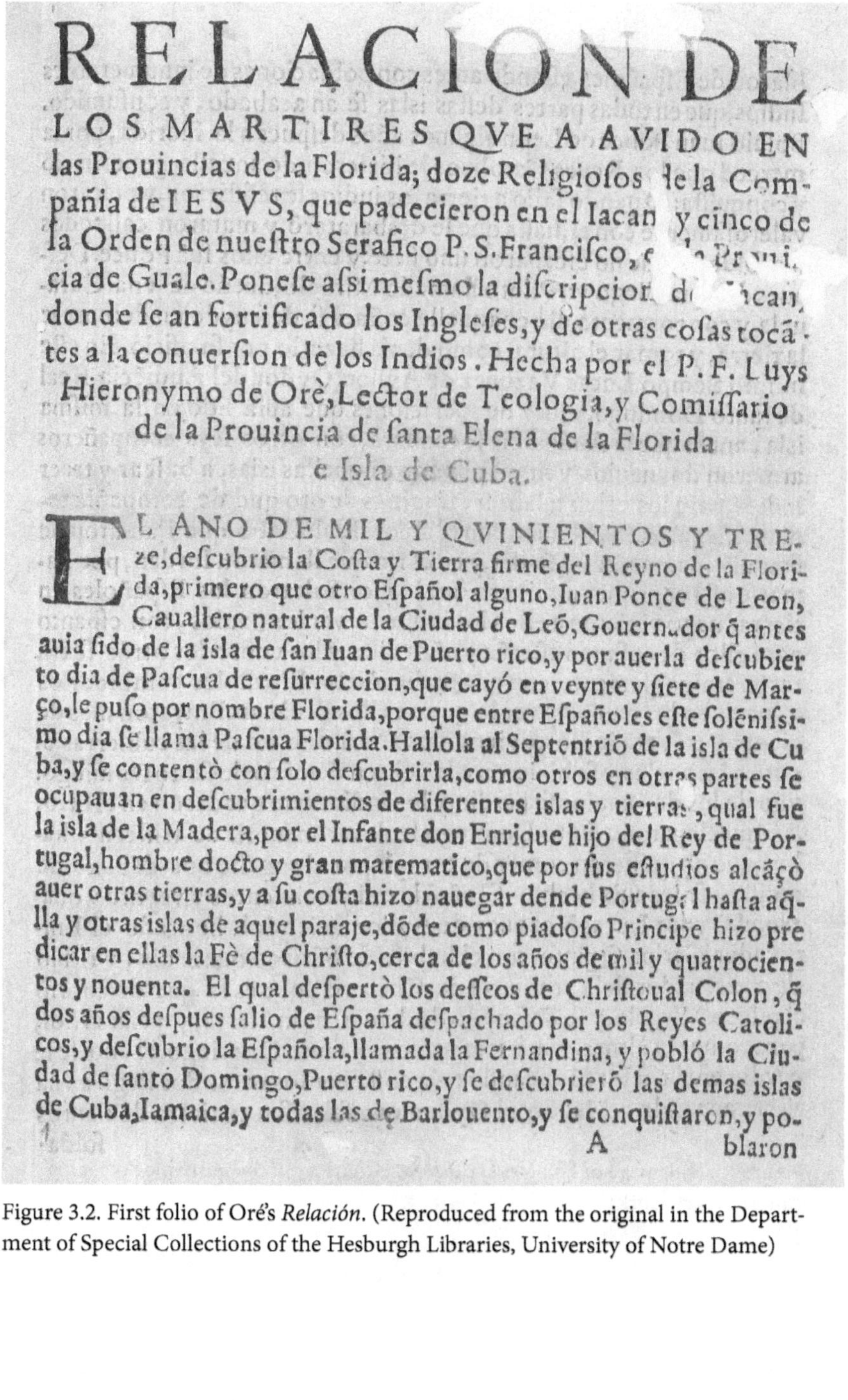

RELACION DE
LOS MARTIRES QVE A AVIDO EN
las Prouincias de la Florida; doze Religiosos de la Compañia de IESVS, que padecieron en el Iacan y cinco de la Orden de nuestro Serafico P. S. Francisco, e la Prouincia de Guale. Ponese assi mesmo la discripcion de Iacan, donde se an fortificado los Ingleses, y de otras cosas tocátes a la conuersion de los Indios. Hecha por el P. F. Luys Hieronymo de Orè, Lector de Teologia, y Comissario de la Prouincia de santa Elena de la Florida e Isla de Cuba.

EL ANO DE MIL Y QVINIENTOS Y TREze, descubrio la Costa y Tierra firme del Reyno de la Florida, primero que otro Español alguno, Iuan Ponce de Leon, Cauallero natural de la Ciudad de Leó, Gouernador q antes auia sido de la isla de san Iuan de Puerto rico, y por auerla descubierto dia de Pascua de resurreccion, que cayó en veynte y siete de Março, le puso por nombre Florida, porque entre Españoles este solenissimo dia se llama Pascua Florida. Hallola al Septentriõ de la isla de Cuba, y se contentò con solo descubrirla, como otros en otras partes se ocupauan en descubrimientos de diferentes islas y tierras, qual fue la isla de la Madera, por el Infante don Enrique hijo del Rey de Portugal, hombre docto y gran matematico, que por sus estudios alcaçò auer otras tierras, y a su costa hizo nauegar dende Portugal hasta aqlla y otras islas de aquel paraje, dõde como piadoso Principe hizo predicar en ellas la Fè de Christo, cerca de los años de mil y quatrocientos y nouenta. El qual despertò los desseos de Christoual Colon, q dos años despues salio de España despachado por los Reyes Catolicos, y descubrio la Española, llamada la Fernandina, y pobló la Ciudad de santo Domingo, Puerto rico, y se descubrierõ las demas islas de Cuba, Iamaica, y todas las de Barlouento, y se conquistaron, y poblaron

A

Figure 3.2. First folio of Oré's *Relación*. (Reproduced from the original in the Department of Special Collections of the Hesburgh Libraries, University of Notre Dame)

Figure 3.3. Hernando de Soto (ca. 1496–1542), engraving from *Retratos de los españoles ilustres con un epítome de sus vidas,* Madrid, 1791. (Courtesy of the Hispanic Society of America, New York)

the trail of two authors—Garcilaso and Oré—both born in the highlands of the viceroyalty of Peru. Bilingual in Quechua and Spanish, Garcilaso was the son of a Spanish conquistador and an Inca princess. He was born in Cuzco, traveled to Spain, established himself in Córdoba, studied the major texts of the period, and became the first great Spanish American writer. He penned *La Florida del Inca* (La Florida of the Inca), one of the central accounts of the failed 1539–43 expedition of Hernando de Soto (see figure 3.3).

Luis Jerónimo de Oré was born in Guamanga (Ayacucho). Son of a wealthy *encomendero* family, he entered the Franciscan order when he was very young, was educated in Cuzco and Lima, learned Latin, and spoke several indigenous languages (including Quechua and Aymara). He traveled to Spain as a representative of his order; recruited missionaries for the Franciscan outposts in America; visited La Florida on two occasions (1614 and 1616);[5] and wrote poetry, manuals and dictionaries for the religious instruction of the native population, and a *Relación* detailing his North American experience. Later he was appointed bishop of La Imperial (Concepción, Chile), where he died.[6]

While Oré visited La Florida twice, Garcilaso was a virtual traveler who knew the colony only by listening to others and reading about it. The two met in Córdoba (1612) and exchanged ideas about missionary work in La Florida and events related to Peru, their homeland. Both wrote with passion and conviction on the need to defend La Florida, preserve it for the Spanish Crown, and spread the Catholic faith in the territory. The meeting in Córdoba—recorded by Garcilaso in the second part of *Royal Commentaries*, also known as *General History of Peru* (1617)—underscores the importance of La Florida and reveals aspects of the interests and personalities of the authors.

Meeting of the Inca Garcilaso and Oré in Córdoba (1612)

As is well known, soon after receiving a family inheritance, Inca Garcilaso settled in Córdoba. It was in this Andalusian city where Oré, whom Garcilaso called a "gran teólogo" (great theologian), visited him. Oré was on his way to Cádiz to meet twenty-four missionaries he had recruited to catechize in La Florida, and then to travel with them to Seville, and perhaps accompany them onto La Florida:

> Este religioso, Fray Luis Jerónimo de Oré, iva dende Madrid a Cáliz [sic] con orden de sus superiores y del Consejo Real de las Indias para despachar dos dozenas de religiosos, o ir él con ellos, a los reinos de la Florida, a la predicación del Santo Evangelio a aquellos gentiles. No iva certificado si iría con los religiosos o si bolvería haviéndolos despachado. (This clergyman, Friar Luis Jerónimo de Oré, was going from Madrid to Cádiz on orders of his superiors and of the Royal Council of the Indies, to dispatch two dozen missionaries, or to go with them to the kingdoms of La Florida to preach the holy gospel to those pagans. It was not certified if he would go with the clergymen or if he would return after dispatching them.) (*General History*, vol. 3, book 7, chap. 30, 182)[7]

Oré wanted to meet the chronicler and discuss *La Florida del Inca*, a work that he obviously had read and was certain would be useful to the new missionaries. Garcilaso donated seven books to his compatriot: three copies of *La Florida del Inca* and four of *Royal Commentaries*. He also wished Oré success in his missionary endeavors: "La Divina Majestad se sirva de ayudarles en esta demanda, para que aquellos idólatras salgan del abismo de sus tinieblas" (May the Divine Majesty help you in this task in order that those idolaters leave the depth of their darkness) (*General History*, vol. 3, book 7, chap. 30, 182).

In the end Oré did not travel to La Florida with the missionaries he had recruited. Recognizing Oré's success, the Crown and the Royal Council of the Indies charged him with recruiting additional missionaries, this time for catechizing the native population in Venezuela. Following that assignment the Franciscans sent him to compile information about Francisco Solano's (1549–1610) early days in Andalusia, as the order was preparing to present his case for beatification in Rome. Oré did not travel to La Florida until 1614, when he was assigned to inspect the Franciscan missions of that territory and its convents in Havana. This was a brief trip, and there is little mention of it in the *Relación*. Afterwards Oré returned to Havana, where he spent two and a half years:

> Y [Oré] visitó la dicha provincia,[8] consolando a todos los religiosos y juntándolos a capítulo en la ciudad de San Agustín. Y dejando ordenadas y bien compuestas las cosas tocantes a la conversión de los naturales, se volvió a La Habana proveyendo en aquel convento de religiosos necesarios para predicar a los españoles y acudir a las demás cosas de aquella ciudad. Y [h]abiendo estado dos años y medio en el gobierno de esta provincia, le vinieron nuevas patentes y orden del prelado general para volver a visitar la provincia y juntar los guardianes y definidores y celebrar capítulo y sacar provincial y guardianes para todos los conventos de la provincia y para La Habana e isla de Cuba.

> (And [Oré] visited said province [Santa Elena], consoling all the religious and gathering them together for a meeting [*capítulo*] in the city of St. Augustine. And leaving in an orderly and well-constituted fashion all matters dealing with the conversion of the natives, [he] returned to Havana, providing in that convent the necessary clergymen to preach to the Spaniards and attend to other matters in that city. And after spending two and a half years governing this province, new instructions and orders came to him from the prelate general to

return and visit the province [Santa Elena] and gather all guardians and ministers [*definidores*] and to convene a meeting and elect a provincial and guardians for all convents in the province and for Havana and the island of Cuba) (*Relación*, chap. 11, 29v).[9]

Following these orders, Oré returned to San Agustín, arriving on November 6, 1616, after a risky sea voyage of more than twenty-five days. Shortly thereafter, accompanied by three friars, he started his visitations to the missions on foot and by canoe.

Garcilaso's chronicle is a product of reading various tracts (by Coles and Carmona), but primarily of interviews with Gonzalo Silvestre, veteran of La Florida and Peru, whom he called "mi autor" (my author) (*La Florida*, book 2, part 1, chap. 27, 114). In contrast, in addition to mining documentary sources, Oré shaped his *Relación* based on his Florida experience.

I propose that the texts that derived from what Garcilaso read and heard and from what Oré read and lived through show the importance of the region within the Spanish imperial project, the speed with which news of America arrived in Europe, and the links between the viceroyalty of Peru and La Florida; that is, between North and South America. Regarding the arrival of news from La Florida in Spain, the literary critic José Durand has proposed that Garcilaso began the first draft of *La Florida del Inca* immediately after Frenchman Dominique de Gorgues attacked the Spanish fort of San Mateo at St. Augustine (1567).[10] As we know, the ambitions of England and France substantially affected the vast La Florida territory, first with the arrival of the French Huguenots Jean Ribault and René de Laudonnière and, later (1567), with the punitive expedition led by Dominique de Gorgues who, allied with the Timucua chief Saturiba, attacked San Mateo (the former Fort Caroline) and killed all the Spaniards, including Jesuit missionaries.

La Florida del Inca

In 1590 Inca Garcilaso published a translation of León Hebreo's *Dialogues of Love*; in his dedication to King Philip II, he reveals that he had already drafted his major chronicles, *La Florida del Inca* and *Royal Commentaries*. In 1588, the year England defeated the "invincible" Spanish Armada, Garcilaso began regular interviews with his principal informant, Gonzalo Silvestre, a veteran of Hernando de Soto's expedition who later went to Peru and finally settled in Las Posadas, Andalusia, a village close to where Garcilaso lived. In 1591, while in Córdoba, Garcilaso received *Peregrinaciones*, a brief account written by Alonso de Carmona, another soldier in Hernando de Soto's expedition. Later, in a print shop in Córdoba, Garcilaso tells us he found "media comida de ratones" (half eaten by mice) the account of La Florida by Juan de Coles, another participant in De Soto's expedition.[11]

A meticulous historian, Garcilaso consulted various sources. For example, he read Álvar Núñez Cabeza de Vaca's *Relación* not in its first edition (Zamora, 1542), but in the second edition republished as *La relación y comentarios* (Valladolid, 1555).[12] Cabeza de Vaca's *Relación* tells the saga of Pánfilo de Narváez's ill-fated expedition to La Florida. After being shipwrecked off La Florida the author and three companions trekked along the North American Gulf coast to reach New Spain (1527–36).[13] Garcilaso cross-checked the accounts of Hernando de Soto's failed expedition against the later accounts of Coles and Carmona and completed his first draft by 1592. When the printing was delayed, he again revised the manuscript in 1602. It was finally published in Lisbon in 1605[14] as *La Florida/del Ynca./Historia del adelanta/do Hernando de Soto, Gouernador y capi/tan general del Reyno de La Florida, y de/otros heroicos caualleros Españoles é/Indios; escrita por el Ynca Garcilasso/de la Vega, capitan de Su Magestad,/natural de la gran ciudad del Coz/co, cabeça de los Reynos y/prouincias del Peru* ('The Florida/ of the Inca/history of the adelantado/Hernando de Soto, governor and cap/tain general of the kingdom of La Florida,/and of other heroic Spanish gentlemen and/Indians; written by the Inca Garcilaso/de la Vega, captain of his Majesty,/born in the great city of Cuz/co, capital of the Kingdoms and/ provinces of Peru).

With this long title Garcilaso underscores his Andean and American identity, his allegiance to Spain, and his concern for La Florida's affairs. The chronicle quickly became one of the principal narratives of Hernando de Soto's expedition to these vast lands.[15] It behooves us to ask why *La Florida del Inca* stands out and what distinguishes it from other accounts of De Soto's expedition.

Garcilaso proposes the conquest and colonization of La Florida by Spain with the aim of evangelizing the Native Americans: "digo que, para trabajar y haberla escrito [*La Florida del Inca*], no me movió otro fin sino el deseo de que por aquella tierra tan larga y ancha se extienda la religión cristiana; que ni pretendo ni espero por este largo afán mercedes temporales" (I say that, in working and having written [*La Florida del Inca*] I was not moved by any objective other than the desire to spread the Christian faith in such a large and vast land; from which (deed), I neither pretend nor aspire to any material rewards) (Proemio, 8–9).[16] In contrast to other accounts of De Soto's expedition, Garcilaso not only describes events; he presents an objective, then expands on and develops it. This strategy allows him to reinterpret facts and go beyond the failure of the expedition or the announced missionary agenda. His incorporation of anecdotes and statements, seemingly isolated from the central story, shows his effort to illuminate events in their entirety, revealing their different aspects and noting their impact on diverse subjects and geographies. Thus Hernando de Soto appears as a valiant and seasoned conqueror; through representations of minor incidents, however, we also see him as a passionate and ambitious person whose likes and dislikes brought him and his men to ruin. Garcilaso underscores the daring deeds of the conquistadores but also their greed. In doing so he questions their conduct and also how the imperial agenda is carried out. At the same time, the chronicler ties the failure of evangelization to these misdeeds by pointing out how the conquistadores' bad examples deter the native population from accepting the Christian gospel.

Garcilaso's main contribution is his representation of the native *floridanos*. Presenting the Indians as capable subjects, he compares them favorably with the Europeans. Thus, the lady of Cofachiqui, a paramount *cacica* of a region now in the state of South Carolina, is portrayed as an illustrious and crafty diplomat who, through her manners and communication abilities, earns the respect and admiration of the members of De Soto's expedition (book 3, chaps. 10–11). Garcilaso vehemently denies that the Indians are cannibals (book 1, chap. 4, 19). In a key passage he explains why he views them as gentlemen: "Este nombre caballero en los indios parece improprio porque no tuvieron caballos, de los cuales se dedujo el nombre, mas, porque en España se entiende por los nobles, y entre indios los hubo nobilísimos, se podrá también decir por ellos" (To use the name *caballero* to describe the Indians appears improper because they did not have horses, from which the name originated, but because in Spain it also refers to noblemen, and among the Indians there were many extremely noble ones, it [caballeros] can also be said of them] (book 2, part 1, chap. 1, 47).

In line with ideas popularized in the early modern period, Garcilaso judges individuals not by their lineage but by their conduct. Behavior supersedes national and ethnic origin and becomes the paramount measure for judging a person. The author does not miss any opportunity to heighten the agency of the natives, even in the most difficult circumstances. This is why, as the Spanish are retreating to Mexico in their ships, a native shouts from the banks of the Mississippi: "Si nosotros tuviéramos canoas grandes como vosotros—quiso decir navíos—os siguiéramos hasta vuestra tierra y la ganáramos, que también somos hombres como vosotros" (If we had big canoes like you do—he meant ships—we would follow you to your land and take it for ourselves, because we too are men like you) (book 6, chap. 10, 414).

In the last chapter of *La Florida del Inca* (book 6, chap. 22), the author offers a catalogue of the martyrs of La Florida. In this ending the reader can discern how a Janus-faced conclusion is imposed. Like a telescope that brings distant and blurry events closer, Garcilaso uses Gonzalo Silvestre's meeting with seven Florida Indians in the Andalusian countryside to illuminate his story and the history of the region by placing the incident in a wider context. When Silvestre, De Soto's former companion, identifies himself and asks the Indians where they are from, they answer: "'¿Dejando vosotros esas provincias [de La Florida] tan mal paradas como las dejasteis queréis que os demos nuevas de ellas?' . . . 'De mejor gana le diéramos sendos flechazos que las nuevas que nos pide.'" (After you left those provinces [of La Florida] in such a deplorable state as you did, do you want to hear news of these lands? . . . It is better for us to use our arrows against you than to give the news you ask of us) (book 6, chap. 22, 447). By means of this episode the chronicler shows in a more personal way the tragic consequences of the conquest and the audacity of the *caballeros floridanos*, even as captives. From a unique perspective, he thus problematizes the history of the region by indissolubly linking Europe with North and South America.

Relación de los mártires que ha habido en La Florida

Let us now turn to Oré's *Relación*. This *relación* has been studied mainly because it offers details of the Guale revolt of 1597[17] and the martyrdom of Jesuit and Franciscan missionaries, making important contributions to our knowledge of the area and of the global character of Spanish colonialism. The analysis of Oré's *Relación* reveals how events in La Florida resonate in the "carrera de Indias." We can listen to the voice, though often tenuous, of a Franciscan Creole who, as we have seen, visited his compatriot Inca Garcilaso, seeking information about La Florida and hoping to share it with missionaries bound for the region. Unlike Garcilaso's chronicle, which concentrates on Hernando de Soto's expedition, Oré's *Relación* reviews more than a century of La Florida's history (1513–1616). To compose it the author gathered information from eyewitnesses, ship's logs, historical sources, and reports to the Crown, all colored by his own experiences in Peru and La Florida. The *Relación* contains nautical details, miraculous feats, kidnappings, and opinions of other Franciscans. If *La Florida del Inca* is notable for its glowing descriptions of the natives, the *Relación* stands out for the many sources it incorporates and the longer time span it covers, albeit that some events are merely mentioned or presented in overview.

The account opens with the 1513 arrival of Juan Ponce de León in La Florida. Oré comments on Ponce de León's second expedition and his return to Havana, where he died from wounds inflicted by the arrows of Florida natives.[18] The *Relación* also introduces specific incidents that show the rivalries of European powers and their imperial ambitions in America. For example, it explains how, on instructions from the Spanish sovereign, the governor of Cuba ordered the removal of a pillar bearing the French coat of arms. This pillar indicated that the explorer Jean Ribault had taken possession of the area for the king of France. But it turned out that the French explorer had erected two pillars and the Spanish party found only one of them in the area of Port Royal (South Carolina).[19] This pillar was transported to Madrid while the other one (in the area of the St. Johns River) remained intact. The *Relación* concludes with the 1616 meeting of the Franciscan chapter in San Buenaventura de Guadalquini. They met in San Buenaventura, not San Agustín, because food for the natives and friars was less costly there and also because Franciscan representatives from the Timucua and Guale territories could travel there with greater ease (by canoe) (33v). This decision underscores the high cost of living in a border town and the transportation difficulties prevalent in La Florida, a theme Oré reiterates throughout the *Relación*. At the meeting, Francisco de Pareja (ca. 1570–1628), an expert in the Timucua language well known for his bilingual catechisms, was elected provincial of Santa Elena de La Florida, the new Franciscan province in America inaugurated in 1612.

Among the reports of navigation and exploration, the one in chapter 6 (rendered to Crown officials by Juan Menéndez Marqués) is pertinent for its precision regarding nautical details from the bay of Santa María del Jacán (Chesapeake Bay) and the San Pedro River (Potomac). It also confirms the fluidity of the northern frontier of La Florida, the impunity with which piracy was carried out in the Caribbean, and the constant exchanges between the Caribbean islands and the continent. In addition, it reveals Oré's opinion of the English establishments in the area. He characterizes them as "ladronera[s]" (den[s] of thieves) and considers their destruction imperative (chap. 6, 13v). Oré complains bitterly about corsairs and pirates stationed in Chesapeake Bay and Bermuda. He stresses the impunity with which the enemies of Spain enriched themselves with contraband and then returned safely to England, thanks to hideouts in Chesapeake Bay and Bermuda: These enemies run "la costa de la isla de Cuba, Puerto Rico, Jamaica, Santo Domingo, hacen los robos que pueden sin [los españoles] poderlos castigar porque, con la presa de cueros de vaca, vino y lo demás que pueden pillar, vuelven a desembocar [en] el canal de Bahama, . . . Y se entran en una de estas dos guaridas [la bahía de Chesapeake o Bermuda] de donde vuelven a Inglaterra ricos con el pillaje que pudieron hacer" ([These enemies run] the coasts of the islands of Cuba, Puerto Rico, and Jamaica; they steal what they want and [the Spaniards] are unable to punish them, because with their loot of cowhides, wine, and the other items they are able to steal, they return to the Bahama Channel . . . and enter one of two hideouts [Chesapeake Bay or Bermuda] whence they return to England rich with the pillaging that they were able to do) (chap. 6, 14r).

In the American voyages of exploration, kidnapping Indians was a common practice through which the conquistadores hoped to learn rudiments of native languages as well as details of the local geography and economy. Many captives died of homesickness, rage, disease, or suicide committed to avoid the humiliation of imprisonment and slavery. A small number traveled to Spain and, if they were young and of high rank, in addition to receiving religious instruction, often were taught how to read and write. In other words, they were acculturated in order to serve as intermediaries between Spanish authorities and the indigenous population. On the other hand, priests frequently traveled with adolescents who assisted them in religious services and also learned native languages with ease, thus beginning a process of reverse acculturation.

The *Relación* offers examples of both ways of adopting new customs and languages. In chapter 3 we find perhaps the most notable case of Hispanic acculturation and later return to native ways, revealing the complexity of these exchanges. The young cacique don Luis de Velasco, apparently a speaker of Algonquin, was captured around 1561 shortly after the failed Tristán de Luna y Arellano expedition (1559–61). Baptized in Mexico, his godfather was Luis de Velasco y Ruiz de Alarcón, viceroy of New Spain (1550–64), hence his Christian name. He was taken to Spain, where he enjoyed the protection of the king while being raised following Spanish customs by Dominicans and Jesuits. The pious conduct of this young man inspired confidence among his mentors, who believed he had a genuine desire to spread the Christian gospel among his people. Therefore, he accompanied the Jesuits on their mission to Santa María del Jacán (Chesapeake Bay). After returning to his homeland with the friars, don Luis reverted to his native ways, abandoned Catholicism, and incited a massacre of the Jesuits. The only survivor was another young boy, Alonso de Lara, who was protected by other natives.[20]

As expected, the miracles in Oré's *Relación* indicate that the missionaries received divine help in punishing those who defied Christian teachings or rewarding those who accepted the new faith. For example, in Jacán we meet a native rummaging through the clothing of the Jesuit martyrs. Attempting to open a box of relics with his *macana* (wooden club), he raises his arms, breathes deeply, and falls dead on the spot. Prospective looters who witness this event run away, and the relics are never desecrated (chap. 3, 5v.). Through the testimony of the Franciscan Martín Prieto we learn of another divine intervention when the friar attempted to convert a reluctant village. Its cacique, as a young man, had suffered greatly as a prisoner of Hernando de Soto and consequently forbade all contact with the Christians. When Friar Prieto met the cacique, the latter threw him out of the house. At that very moment a tropical storm developed, and the only edifice left standing was a church with its cross: "dio un trueno que todos cayeron en tierra con un viento tan grande que en el lugar y en el otro lugar, no quedó casa ni garita en [pie], ni [b]ohío ni cosa de edificio chico ni grande que [h]ubiese en los lugares. Quedó solo sin que cayese, por la misericordia de Dios nuestro señor, una cruz y una iglesia en que se [h]abían dicho algunas misas." (There was a thunderclap such that everyone fell to the ground, with such a strong wind that in this place and that, no house nor storehouse was left standing, nor hut [bohío] nor buildings large or small remained in either place. The only edifice still standing, thanks to the mercy of our Lord, was a cross and a church where several masses had been said) (chap. 10, 28r). Subsequently, the old cacique called for the friar, accepted Christianity, was baptized, and died the following day.

Oré also informs us that the converted natives were so zealous as to persecute others who had rejected Christianity. In these circumstances the missionaries became the protectors of the *hanopira,* or red men—in other words, of the *floridanos* who resisted the gospel and, as a sign that they remained true to their beliefs and culture, painted their bodies with red *bija* and black coals.[21] Oré takes advantage of the opportunity to compare this practice with native customs from the Peruvian jungle area: "en lo cual son semejantes estos de La Florida a los indios infieles y bárbaros que [h]ay en la otra banda de las cordilleras del Pirú. Y los unos y otros son flecheros, pero allá andan vestidos, o menos desnudos que los de acá, y estos se aventajan en ser más guerreros y que carecen del vicio de la embriaguez de que son notados los indios todos, así de la Nueva España como del Pirú" (in which those [natives] of La Florida are similar to the infidels and barbaric Indians on the other side of the Peruvian mountains. Both are archers, but there [in Peru], they wear more clothing, or are less naked than those from [La Florida]. But the latter are better because they are more warlike and they lack the vice of drunkenness that all Indians from Nueva España and Peru share) (chap. 6, 10r).

The observation about attire is notable because at the time nudity was associated with barbarism and otherness. Thus, when Father Ávila, another missionary, is kidnapped by *floridanos* who take away his habit, the narrator comments "quedé como indio en lo que toca a lo exterior" (I was left looking like an Indian because of my appearance) (chap. 8, 19v). As I have pointed out, Oré uses this passage to reinforce that the missionaries recognize the humanity of all natives and protect them, regardless of whether or not they accept the Christian gospel. He also underscores, surely following Garcilaso, the courage of the *floridanos* and exempts them from the vice of alcoholism associated with other native groups. In other passages, Oré stresses how closely the Christian natives of La Florida followed the teachings of the Church and points out their ability to rapidly learn to read and write and to teach others those skills. He takes advantage of these assertions to encourage Franciscan friars and colonial administrators to speed up the processes of colonization and catechization in the region.

Throughout the *Relación* there are references to Andean practices that parallel those in La Florida.[22] Among them one stands out. Oré reiterates how difficult missionary work is in La Florida on account of the tortuous trails and deep rivers that the Franciscans must traverse to reach the native population. In fact, one of the most personal passages of the *Relación* narrates these difficulties:

> los ríos caudalosos que por ser hondables no se pueden vadear ni tienen mas puente que un pino largo y grueso por donde pasaban los indios que me acompañaban, corriendo, como quien [h]abía perdido el miedo de aquellos pasos peligrosos, los cuales, confesándome primero, pasé en nombre de nuestro Señor y por la santa obediencia de mis prelados que me encomendaron esta visita y comisión (the largest rivers, because of their depth, are impossible to wade through, and they do not have any bridge other than a large and thick pine trunk which the Indians that accompanied me ran across, as if they had lost all fear of those dangerous crossings. After first making confession, I crossed in the name of our Lord and for the sake of holy obedience to my superiors who had charged me with this visit and commission) (chap. 11, 31r–v]).

To ease the difficulties he suggests establishing *reducciones* as was done in Peru under Viceroy Francisco de Toledo: "Que si los gobernadores quisiesen hacer reducciones de tres o cuatro lugares pequeños en uno, como se hicieron en las reducciones del Pirú por traza y resolución del virrey don Francisco de Toledo, serían los indios mejor enseñados y los ministros aliviados del excesivo trabajo que a[h]ora tienen" (That if the governors would wish to make reductions [*reducciones*] of three or four small villages into one, as was done with the *reducciones* in Peru, by order and resolution of the viceroy don Francisco de Toledo, the Indians would be better taught and the ministers relieved of the excessive work they now have) (chap. 10, 29r). As we may recall, the *reducción* system gathered the populations of small villages and isolated groups into new towns with, of course, more inhabitants. The purpose was to "civilize" the Indians, with the implication of imposing political authority, economic exploitation, and religious conversion on them. But the fact of the matter was that Church and Crown officials were unable to carry out missionary work or collect taxes if the natives were dispersed. In each new town the natives built a church and received religious instruction. The attending priest was paid with a portion of the taxes collected from the inhabitants (*indígenas reducidos*). Both Jesuits and Franciscans accepted and established *reducciones*. Perhaps the best known were those organized by the Jesuits in Guaraní-speaking areas of modern Paraguay.

The Andean *reducciones* had an extremely detrimental impact on the indigenous population. The system destroyed ancient communal labor practices and traditions; it forced the relocation of many individuals, increasing the number of *forastero* Indians with no attachment to old or new villages. With no place to go, they scavenged throughout the countryside. Since the Franciscan order accepted the *reducciones* as a means to advance missionary work, it is not surprising that Oré proposes their establishment in La Florida and that he praises Francisco de Toledo, the viceroy who instituted them in Peru. Thus, in the *Relación* Oré recommends replicating in La Florida a system that in the Andes contributed to dismantling traditional communities and accelerating colonization.

* * *

The examination of Garcilaso's chronicle and Oré's *Relación* reveals and underscores the colonial links between Peru and La Florida, South and North America, Europe and America. Hernando de Soto attempted to conquer and colonize La Florida with the gold and silver he received from the Inca Atahualpa's ransom. Garcilaso began his chronicle of De Soto's failed expedition to this land because in Montilla and Córdoba he heard about French incursions into La Florida and murders of Jesuits, first in San Mateo and later in Jacán. Gonzalo Silvestre, the key informant for *La Florida del Inca*, arrived in the territory with Hernando de Soto and later fought in Peru where he met Garcilaso de la Vega's father.

Luis Jerónimo de Oré came to seek his compatriot in Córdoba. He had read *La Florida del Inca* and wanted to converse with Garcilaso about La Florida in order to share this information with the missionaries traveling to that distant land. His *Relación* is a direct product of the time he spent in La Florida. As we have seen, it is punctuated with allusions and comparisons to Peru, his native land. He even proposes to implement in La Florida failed colonial measures imposed earlier in Peru.

La Florida del Inca stresses native agency and calls the Indians "caballeros" due to their conduct, valor, and ability to fight the Europeans. Even though this chronicle has been criticized for some historical inaccuracies, it forces us to reflect on several issues. It shows the shared humanity of Spaniards and Indians, as well as the devastating impact of colonialism in La Florida. For its part the *Relación* draws on a variety of documents and experiences to offer a more nuanced view of life on the Florida frontier. It underscores the intelligence of the natives, who quickly learn to read and write and assimilate Church teachings. It also underscores the dangers of living and catechizing on the Florida frontier, and the firm conviction of the friars who accepted that challenge. If in many instances Hispano-Indian relations in this early period were marked by cruelty, territorial ambitions characterized the policies of the principal European powers. From different vantage points, both texts show the impact of Spanish colonialism in North and South America and how interconnected were the deeds and people in both areas. If *La Florida del Inca*, in depicting De Soto's expedition, offers an epic vision of this early period that incorporates criticism of the conquistadores, the *Relación*, when representing the deeds of the soldiers and the friars in multiple contexts, portrays the human dimension of one hundred years of life in La Florida. Both lead us to the shared history of North and South America.

Notes

I am grateful to the Reed Foundation for its support of my research related to early Spanish La Florida. My gratitude to Sara Weber, Hesburgh Libraries of the University of Notre Dame, for her graciousness and assistance with queries related to Oré's *Relación*. Many thanks to Amy Turner Bushnell, Jerald T. Milanich, and Eugene Lyon for their guidance, and to Anne J. Cruz and Viviana Díaz Balsera for inviting me to participate in the symposium and including my essay in this volume.

1. In 1564 the Spanish fleet system (*sistema de flotas*) was reorganized with an obligatory stop in Havana.

2. See Pedro Menéndez de Avilés, *Cartas sobre la Florida (1555–1574)*, ed. Juan Carlos Mercado (Frankfurt and Madrid: Vervuert and Iberoamericana, 2002).

3. Since it was not republished until the twentieth century and the original lacks a title page, several dates of publication have been proposed. However, internal evidence in the *Relación* makes 1619 the most probable date. The suggestion of an earlier date (1604) could be attributed to information provided by Friar Diego de Córdoba Salinas in his *Crónica franciscana de las provincias del Perú*, ed. Lino G. Canedo (Washington, DC, and México, DF: Academy of American Franciscan History and Editorial Jus, 1957 [1651]). In fact, Córdoba mentions two possible dates of publication for the *Relación*, 1604 and 1607; he further indicates that the *Relación* was written in Latin and printed in Naples in 1651 (see pp. 342, 1016). Probably he confused the *Relación* with the *Manuale Peruanum*, printed in Naples and correctly described later in the chronicle (p. 1015). However, the latter work contains no reference to La Florida.

4. For a complete annotated edition, see Alexandra Sununu, "Estudio y edición anotada de *La Florida* de Alonso Gregorio de Escobedo, O.F.M.," 3 vols. (PhD diss., Graduate Center, City University of New York, 1993); also see her article "Escobedo y su poema, *La Florida*," *Boletín de la Academia Norteamericana de la Lengua Española* 8 (1992), 37–49.

5. On orders from the king, the Royal Council of the Indies, and Franciscan Commissary-General of the Indies Juan de Vivanco, Oré visited La Florida and the convents in Cuba (commission signed June 12, 1614); after this initial visit, he remained in Havana. Two and a half years later Oré was again ordered to visit the Franciscan missions in La Florida and convene a meeting of the provincial chapter there (see Oré, *Relación*, chap. 11). Oré mentions the following Franciscan missions: St. Augustine, San Antonio de Enacape, Avino, San Francisco de Potano, Apalo, San Martín de Timucua, Santa Cruz de Tarihica, San Juan de Guacara, Teleco, and Cofa in Florida; Santa Isabel de Utinahica in Florida or Georgia; and San Buenaventura de Guadalquini and San José de Zápala in Georgia; see Maynard Geiger, *Biographical Dictionary of the Franciscans in Spanish Florida and Cuba, 1528–1841* (Paterson, NJ: St. Anthony Guild Press, 1940), 124.

6. For more details of Oré's biography, see Córdoba Salinas, *Crónica franciscana*; José Toribio Polo, "Luis Jerónimo de Oré," *Revista Histórica* (Lima) 2 (1907): 75–91; Julián Heras, "Bio-bibliografía de fray Luis Jerónimo de Oré, 1554–1630," *Revista Histórica* (Lima) 29 (1966): 173–92; Federico Richter, *Fr. Luis Jerónimo de Oré, O.F.M., Obispo de Concepción* (Santiago de Chile: Archivo Franciscano, 1990); Rocío de los Reyes Ramírez, "Fray Jerónimo de Oré, Obispo de Concepción en Chile," *Actas del III Congreso Internacional sobre los franciscanos en el Nuevo Mundo (siglo XVII) La Rábida, 18–23 de septiembre de 1989* (Madrid: Deimos, 1990) 1099–1114; Luis Enrique Tord, "Luis Jerónimo de Oré y el *Symbolo Catholico Indiano*." In *Luis Jerónimo de Oré, Symbolo Catholico Indiano*, ed. Antonine Tibesar, facsimile edition with studies by Luis Enrique Tord and Noble David Cook (Lima: Australis, 1992 [1598]), 15–34; Noble David Cook, "Luis Jerónimo de Oré: una aproximación," in Oré, *Symbolo Catholico Indiano*, 35–63; Cook, "Beyond the *Martyrs of Florida*: The Versatile Career of Luis Gerónimo de Oré," *Florida Historical Quarterly* 71, no. 2 (1992): 169–87; Cook, "Viviendo en las márgenes del imperio: Luis Jerónimo de Oré y la exploración del otro," *Histórica* (Lima) 32, no. 1 (2008): 11–38, available at http://www.scribd.com/doc/61753838/Viviendo-en-la168:597-609.s-margenes-del-imperio-Luis-Jeronimo-de-Ore-y-la-exploracion-del-Otro-Por-Noble-David-Cook; Xavier Pello, "Los

últimos días de Luis Jerónimo de Oré (1554-1630): un nuevo documento biográfico," *Bulletin de l'Institut Français d'Études Andines* (Lima) 29, no. 2 (2000), 161–71; Giuliana Miranda Larco, "Misiones y catequesis en el Perú del XVI: fray Luis Jerónimo de Oré (1554-1630), el *Symbolo catholico indiano* y *El rituale seu manuale peruanum*," *Allpanchis* 69 (2008), 14–82.

7. Quotations from *General History of Peru* (1617), also known as the second part of *Royal Commentaries*, are from Inca Garcilaso de la Vega, *Historia general del Perú*, ed. Ángel Rosenblat, 3 vols. (Buenos Aires: Emecé, 1944). Translations are mine.

8. The reference is to the Franciscan Provincia de Santa Elena, established in 1612; it included missions and convents in La Florida and Cuba. Regarding the Franciscan missions in the area see Jerald T. Milanich, *Laboring in the Fields of the Lord: Spanish Missions and Southeastern Indians* (Gainesville: University Press of Florida, 2006 [1999]).

9. All quotations from Oré's *Relación* are from my forthcoming revised and modernized edition of Luis Jerónimo Oré, *Relación de los mártires que [h]a [h]abido en las provincias de La Florida*. [ca. 1619] (Lima: Fondo Editorial, Pontificia Universidad Católica del Perú). My edition is based on a copy from the original printing at the Hesburgh Libraries of the University of Notre Dame. I indicate the chapter and folio of this printing.

10. José Durand, "Las enigmáticas fuentes de *La Florida del Inca*," *Cuadernos Hispanoamericanos* 168 (1963), 597–609. Aurelio Miró Quesada also suspected this historical link. See Miró Quesada, prologue to *La Florida del Inca* (México, DF: Fondo de Cultura Económica, 1956), xlviii–xlix.

11. At that time Garcilaso was writing a genealogical tract, *Relación de la descendencia de Garci Pérez de Vargas*. He finished it by 1596 and initially planned to include it in *La Florida del Inca*, but later changed his mind.

12. This edition included Cabeza de Vaca's account of his governorship in the Río de la Plata territories (1541–45), as told by his secretary, Pero Hernández.

13. In the eighteenth century Andrés González de Barcia republished the 1555 edition as "Naufragios de Álvar Núñez Cabeza de Vaca, y relación de la jornada que hizo a la Florida con el adelantado Pánfilo de Narváez (1731)," in vol. 1 of *Historiadores primitivos de las Indias Occidentales* (Madrid, 1749). Thereafter "Naufragios" became its popular title.

14. See Aurelio Miró Quesada, prologue to Garcilaso, *La Florida del Inca*, ed. Emma Susana Speratti Piñero (México, DF: Fondo de Cultura Económica, 1956 [1605]), liv.

15. For other accounts of the expedition see Luis Hernández de Biedma (the "factor," or purveyor, of the expedition), *Relación del suceso de la jornada que hizo Hernando de Soto, y de la calidad de la tierra por donde anduvo* (1544; printed 1857); "the Gentleman from Elvas" *Relaçam verdadeira dos trabalhos q'ho Gouernador don Fernando de Souto e certos fidalgos portugueses passaron no descobrimento da prouincia da Frolida* (Evora, 1557) (Garcilaso did not have access to this edition); and the account of the official chronicler Gonzalo Fernández de Oviedo based on the diary of Rodrigo Rangel (De Soto's secretary) included in *Historia general y natural de las Indias* (book 17, chaps. 21–28). Also see Eugene Lyon, "The Précis of the *Relación* of Fray Sebastián de Cañete and Other Soto Narratives," in Raquel Chang-Rodríguez, ed., *Beyond Books and Borders: Garcilaso de la Vega and "La Florida del Inca"* (Lewisburg, PA: Bucknell University Press, 2006), 91–99.

16. Quotations from *La Florida del Inca* are from Emma Susana Speratti Piñero's edition. I indicate in parentheses the book, chapter, and page number. Translations are mine.

17. For a recent re-evaluation of the causes of the rebellion, see J. Michael Francis and Kathleen M. Kole, *Murder and Martyrdom in Spanish Florida: Don Juan and the Guale Uprising of 1597,* Anthropological Papers of the American Museum of Natural History no. 201 (New York: American Museum of Natural History), 95. Available at http://digital library.amnh.org/dspace.

18. Oré also mentions the expeditions of Lucas Vázquez de Ayllón, Francisco Vázquez de Coronado, Pánfilo de Narváez, Hernando de Soto, and Luis Cáncer de Barbastro.

19. These events happened in 1564. The captain in charge left the Havana harbor in the frigate *Nuestra Señora de la Concepción* on May 12, 1564; he destroyed Charlesfort; found the pillar, transported it to his frigate, and sent it to Spain, as indicated in a report dated July 9, 1564. See Paul E. Hoffmann, *A New Andalucia and a Way to the Orient: The American Southeast during the Sixteenth Century,* 2nd ed. (Baton Rouge: Louisiana State University Press, 2004), 212–15.

20. The Inca Garcilaso offers a different version of events in *La Florida del Inca* (book 6, chap. 22), drawn from Jaime Bartolomé Martínez, a former Florida soldier later transferred to Potosí. See Amy Turner Bushnell, "A Requiem for Lesser Conquerors: Honor and Oblivion on a Maritime Periphery," in *Beyond Books and Borders,* 66–74.

21. With regard to Oré's ideas about the abilities of the natives and how evangelization should be carried out, see his *Símbolo católico indiano.*

22. For example, the author compares the *macana* (wooden club) with the *champi* (or *chambi*) of the Inca armies (chap. 7, 7v).

4

A Land Renowned for War

Florida as a Maritime Marchland

AMY TURNER BUSHNELL

I

As colonies went, Spanish Florida was not especially large. Potentially, it had all of Atlantic North America for a claim, and the whole Southeast for a sphere of influence, but its *ecumene* was confined to the upper third of the Florida peninsula plus parts of present-day Alabama and Georgia: the mission provinces of Timucua, Apalache, and Guale. You and I know that whatever progress the seventeenth-century colony makes toward becoming self-sufficient will be undone during Queen Anne's War, when slave raiders overrun the mission provinces, and that even mission-resistant South Florida will be picked clean as a whistle. We know that by the mid-eighteenth century the Indians who met Pedro Menéndez will have vanished—some as victims of epidemics, some enslaved, and some as pilgrims in search of a better land, leaving behind them enough old fields and feral cattle to attract bands of Creeks and turn them into Seminoles. We know, moreover, that the Spanish themselves will eventually move out, twice: in 1764, after the colony is ceded to the British, and again in 1821, after the United States has shown that, when runaway slaves are at stake, it is no respecter of Spanish borders, nor Indian ones.

Knowing all this, why should we care about a colony that left no constituency to vote as a bloc and no adobe mission ruins to bring in tourist dollars?[1] What is the point of studying Florida's many-layered Hispanic heritage? Nothing less than a revindication of Florida's Hispanic past. Spanish Florida was not a failure.[2] Notwithstanding its low settler population, the colony survived, doing what it was designed to do, for two and a half centuries, longer than many a country. True, there was a twenty-year British period, and toward the end of the American Revolution some five thousand British Loyalists with over eight thousand slaves washed in and out of the peninsula, leaving behind them empty shacks, lines of discarded belongings along the seashore, and hundreds of self-freed slaves. But the Spanish returned to Florida, and throughout the Napoleonic Wars, when whole kingdoms were being shaken from their moorings, they held fast.

Elsewhere, demography was everything. Why is French still spoken in Québec? Because after the Seven Years' War there were too many French Canadians for the English to expel. The population of Spanish Florida did not increase like that of New France for a good reason: Florida was "a land renowned for war." Its presidio was positioned, not to support itself and grow into a colony of settlement, but to monitor a strategic seaway. The garrison was a deficit enterprise maintained at royal expense. Its annual subsidy, the *situado*, was a charge against defense funds, like the subsidies to maritime presidios in Cuba, Chile, and the Philippines.[3]

Florida was no remote, landlocked colony like New Mexico, where seventeenth-century settlers expected to fend for themselves.[4] It was integral to the worlds of the Atlantic, the Caribbean, and the Gulf and could not be extricated from any of them without damage to Spain's vital defense system. St. Augustine, with its exhausted soils and its poor harbor, was a naval base. The king supported a presidio there beside the Gulf Stream, not because the Crown had money to burn on ships and soldiers, but because Spain's seaborne enemies—the French, the English, the Dutch, and a swash of buccaneers—were circling like sharks around the empire's ports and seaways, seeking places to unload their stolen goods, if not to plant colonies of their own. Queen Anne's War would bring the loss of Florida's mission provinces, but not of its maritime presidio, which in the eighteenth century would continue to receive the king's coin and to be reinforced. So let's take a closer look at Spain's seaborne enemies and at St. Augustine, the base too important to be closed.

II

In 1562, Philip II of Spain came to a decision. For half a century, Spain's every attempt to establish a foothold north of New Spain had been thwarted. With appalling loss of life, one expedition after another had been defeated by a combination of storms, food shortages, disease, defective intelligence, hostile natives, inadequate financing, and inept leadership. No more approaches should be made via the Gulf coast, the king resolved.[5] Instead, he would concentrate on keeping the Atlantic coast out of enemy hands.

In the first year of France's Wars of Religion, the French began to reconnoiter and build forts on the Atlantic coast of Florida, much as they had ten years earlier on the coast of Brazil.[6] This challenge Philip the Prudent could not ignore. His chosen champion, the Asturian Pedro Menéndez de Avilés, first cleared the coast of Jean de Ribault and his forces, then in fulfillment of his three-year contract of *adelantamiento*, founded three municipalities (St. Augustine, San Mateo, and Santa Elena), introduced Jesuits, and sent expeditions over mountains, up rivers, and along coasts to discover the "secrets of the land."[7] Like many another lord of the marches, the *adelantado* claimed more than he could explore and explored more than he and his heirs could conquer and settle. Disappointingly, Florida revealed no silver or gold, no waterway to the Orient, and no assignable reserves of labor. Settlers without a sponsor chose to go elsewhere, leaving Menéndez's unfinished conquest in the hands of missionaries and career soldiers.

Founded with *gente de guerra* detached from an armada, the Florida garrison was commanded like an armada by a captain general.[8] But St. Augustine was little more than a coastguard station along the route of the treasure fleet. Its harbor, guarded by a perilous sandbar, offered the huge galleons no haven; after a storm, the governor could only send out the presidio's boats and *gente de mar* to look for shipwrecks, rescue survivors, and salvage cargoes before the Indians got to them. Indians would barter with anybody, and corsairs continued to visit the coast in defiance of Spain's claims.

The English had had some hopes of trading with the Spanish Indies peacefully, but Elizabeth I could not resist schemes that cost her little, such as hijacking Ribault's relief expedition in 1563, or allowing William Grenville to plant a colony at Roanoke in 1585, near the old site of the Florida Jesuits' short-lived mission to Axacán.[9] During the queen's long reign, English pirates, fortified by the anti-Catholic propaganda coming out of Amsterdam, made ever bolder incursions into the Spanish Main. In 1572, three English ships put out landing parties to attack St. Augustine. Pedro Menéndez was present to help drive them off only because his ship had been wrecked on Florida's hostile Wild Coast and he had managed to fight his way back to the presidio.[10]

The French, for their part, continued to trade in Guale. In 1577, the vessel *Le Prince*, with a cousin of Catherine de Medici on board, ran aground near Santa Elena. Governor Pedro Menéndez Márquez, the adelantado's nephew, succeeded in recovering most of the hundred castaways, whom he executed as the king commanded, without allowing the seamen to turn coat or the gentlemen to raise ransom. In 1580, the same governor outmaneuvered and sank another French ship, under Captain Gil de Marseilles, in the mouth of the St. Johns River. An account of that naval encounter has survived, written up like a medieval *romancero*.[11]

Sir Francis Drake's 1586 attack on St. Augustine, which led the Spanish to close their base in Santa Elena, was the tail end of a corsairing voyage that had included attacks on Havana and Cartagena. Elizabeth's aid to the rebellious Dutch and her execution of Mary Stuart provoked Philip II to launch an armada to chastise his former sister-in-law. But Philip was the one chastised. A storm destroyed the "Invincible Armada," and in the same year five silver-laden ships were wrecked on the Florida coast. Deliveries to Florida were disrupted for the next ten years, and the price of supplies rose precipitously.[12] But the *floridanos* tightened their belts and stayed on. Menéndez Márquez, summoned to be captain general of the silver fleet, reportedly saved a part of it from French pirates in 1590 and all of it in 1591, while the Florida coastguard rescued 578 shipwrecked Spaniards between 1589 and 1602 alone.[13]

III

After fires and a hurricane destroyed St. Augustine in 1598, some questioned whether the presidio should be there at all, and the king ordered an inquiry. Not one to wait around for instructions, Governor Gonzalo Méndez de Canzo rebuilt the town in its present location, with water on three sides. Nothing remains of that St. Augustine except the grid pattern of the streets, but in 1600 the settlement had a church, a Franciscan convent, a small hospital, a market, a gristmill, 120 houses, and a population of some seven hundred.[14] The biggest problem that the residents faced was provisioning. The rations for a garrison could not feed a whole town, even when they arrived promptly and in an edible state. Farmers barely grew enough to feed their own families. Allied Indians failed to see why they should support everyone, although once when the town was flooded with castaways, the neophytes at Nombre de Dios mission contributed some maize.[15]

These eastern Timucuans were the Franciscans' first converts; the Jesuits had shaken the dust of Florida from their boots after the martyrdoms at Axacán and the death of the *adelantado*. The French continued to visit Guale for cargoes of sassafras and deerskins. Although the testimony taken after the Guale Uprising of 1597 was silent about French involvement, Treasurer Juan Menéndez Márquez I informed the Crown that for the six years of the rebellion, French ships had been a familiar sight in Guale waters, and some of them had left factors to collect the next season's cargo.[16]

Ordered to investigate the presidio's viability, Governor of Cuba Pedro de Valdés sent his son Fernando to take testimony, but the inquiry was overtaken by events.[17] Five English ships pursued and captured the ship taking Florida governor Pedro de Ybarra to that colony in 1603. Put ashore on the Cuban coast, Ybarra walked to Havana, borrowed a shirt and a frigate from Governor Valdés, and continued to his post. The visit of Bishop Juan de las Cabezas Altamirano to Florida the same year was delayed by a fleet of thirty enemy ships. When the bishop finally reached St. Augustine, he found that Governor Ybarra had captured a French ship and twenty-one corsairs. The bishop, the governor, and a special Inquisition examiner reconciled all but one of them to the Church, and after their executions were carried out, gave them Christian burial.[18]

Still the corsairs came, under a confusing variety of banners. When Captain Juan Fernández de Ecija captured a ship in the Savannah River, the governor recorded it as "Anglo-French." Rumors of foreign settlement, like rumors of enemy fleets, flew from port to port, and some of them turned out to be true. The English founded two colonies in 1607: Virginia and Bermuda. Father Jerónimo de Oré, a visitor from Peru, thought that with three galleons and one thousand men Spain could easily wipe out both fledgling colonies, killing two birds with one stone. As a result, instead of withdrawing the presidio from St. Augustine, the Crown raised the number of its *plazas* to three hundred, filled them with reinforcements, and ordered Governor Ybarra to make regular reports on what the English were up to in the Chesapeake.[19] The Crown also asked him for a report on the number of foreigners on the payroll: three Frenchmen, five Germans, two Flemish, and thanks to the union of Spain and Portugal in 1580, thirty-two Portuguese, many of them mariners.[20]

Elsewhere in the Americas, the era of the High Conquest was over, and the Crown was turning to a policy of pacification intended to curb the military's enthusiasm for private conquests and reduce them to protecting missions and missionaries. In Florida, pacification was mostly honored in the breach. There, conversion was only one of the four agreements making up the colonial compact, the others being exclusive trade, military alliance, and vassalage, ratified by an exchange of gifts.[21] Florida chiefs did not agree to become allies until the Spaniards had proven themselves powerful, and the most convincing demonstration of power was a conquest. Governor Juan Treviño Guillamas made central and western Florida safe for Christianity with a gunboat. In that boat, built on one of the Gulf coast rivers, Captain Juan Rodríguez y Cartaya ranged the Gulf, attacking the foes of Spain's allies. The Tocobaga scattered to other rivers, taking their canoes with them, and the chief of the Calusa sent word that he wanted no more war with Christians.[22] Eastern Timucua was on a different course. The town of San Juan del Puerto at the mouth of the St. Johns River rebelled in 1617 under its *cacica*, whom the governor captured and hanged, condemning her followers to hard labor at El Morro, the great fort that commands Havana's harbor.[23]

A cluster of shipwrecks in 1622 brought Spanish salvors to Matecumbe Key. Their trading contacts with the Indians of the Gulf coast, and the recent doubling of the garrison, made it possible to think about expanding into western Timucua and beyond. When the Spanish moved into Apalache in the 1630s it was not so much for religious reasons as to have a new source of food and labor and to keep the Dutch and English from trading or settling there. The threat was real. A Puritan colony on Providence Island off the coast of Nicaragua, founded in 1630, the same year as Massachusetts Bay, lasted for eleven years.[24]

The Eighty Years' War that would bring the United Provinces their independence from Spain did not register in the New World until 1621, when the Dutch West India Company was formed after the Twelve Years' Truce, but the Dutch more than made up for their late entry and regularly cast anchor in Florida waters. When the corsair Piet Heyn captured the silver fleet in the Cuban harbor of Matanzas in 1628, St. Augustine lost two years' worth of supplies and subsidies.[25]

While it was not easy to develop the economy in a land renowned for war, *floridanos* did what they could. When they ran short of iron tools, Governor Diego de Rebolledo melted down an anchor, some mortars, and a few old gun barrels to make the implements that Indians of the south coast wanted in exchange for their ambergris. Soldiers traded their muskets and even their clothes. In the 1620s, Governor Juan de Salinas managed to introduce cattle. Governor Benito Ruiz de Salazar Vallecilla planted a wheat farm on the border between Apalache and Timucua, and imported millstones and a miller. A regular trade in agricultural products developed between the Apalache outpost of San Marcos and Havana, where the silver fleets rendezvoused and were provisioned.[26] The Franciscans invested their profits in adorning mission churches and underwriting the travel expenses of more friars.[27]

But the Crown was letting its end down. Half of the time between 1624 and 1645, the *gasto de indios*, or fund for gifts to Indians, was either reduced or not released at all.[28] Between 1637 and 1643, the royal treasury in Mexico City fell farther and farther behind on the *situado,* and in 1638 the king himself sequestered it entirely.[29] The cause was the fiscal burden of the Thirty

Years' War, compounded in 1640 by revolts in Catalonia and Portugal. But as the Indians saw it, the king had reneged on his promises, and the compact was void. In the unfinished conversion of Apalache, the non-Christian chiefs expressed their dissatisfaction in 1647 by killing three friars and the deputy governor and his family.[30] The colonial economy received a further setback in 1650 when yellow fever or typhus came to St. Augustine from San Juan de Ulúa by way of Havana, where it had wiped out a third of the population. This was the "putrid fever" to which Spaniards had little resistance, and many *floridanos* succumbed. It was followed in 1654 by epidemics of smallpox and the plague, which decimated the colony's African slaves and the indigenous population alike. In 1647 there had been thirty-five thousand baptized Indians; a mission list in 1655 showed only twenty-six thousand.[31]

Oliver Cromwell's Western Design, which followed the Lord Protector's attack on Catholic Ireland, was meant to bring the fear of God to Caribbean Catholics, but the English recruits were unused to tropical diseases and many of them died. Failing to take Santo Domingo, the Penn-Venables fleet descended on Spanish Town in 1655, found the place deserted, and demobilized its troops to live or die as God willed. An English settlement in Jamaica was a more serious threat than an English Virginia, Bermuda, or New England, because Jamaica, in the heart of the Caribbean, was made for privateers. In 1656, Governor Rebolledo called on the chiefs of the Florida provinces to reinforce St. Augustine against the attack that he expected, ordering some of them to bring enough maize to ration themselves and others to hand over their firearms.[32] More accustomed to giving orders themselves, the chiefs of western Timucua rose in revolt. After 150 years of contact with European and African diseases, the Timucuans did not have the strength to mount a serious threat, but during the "Great Rebellion" they abandoned their towns to wander from place to place, and many of them left for the north. When peace was restored, the governor resettled the remnants at intervals along the trans-peninsular road to provision the council houses, transport supplies, and operate ferries.[33]

As the governor had predicted, Jamaican pirates did infest the seaways. One of them, Robert Searles, sacked St. Augustine in 1668, killing people in the streets and carrying off everyone who struck him as non-Spanish, meaning nonwhite. Searles did not destroy the town, which to *floridanos* meant that he planned to come back and occupy it. In response, the Council of the Indies raised the garrison strength by another ninety-three soldiers and ordered the Mexico City treasury to release the funds to build a stone fort. In 1670, Charles II of Restoration England challenged Spain by encouraging Barbadians to plant a colony on the Atlantic coast halfway between

Virginia and Florida. One of the Menéndez clan, Accountant Juan Menéndez Márquez II, went up to destroy the little settlement of Charles Town, but a storm drove his small fleet out to sea, and before he could return, peace had been declared between England and Spain. Carolina was there to stay, and St. Augustine was on the defensive.[34]

IV

The long reign of the other Charles II, last of the Spanish Habsburgs, was a time of despair and decline in Spain. Not so in Florida, where his reign coincided with the building of the Castillo de San Marcos. Hundreds of Indians were summoned from the provinces to work on the building, in addition to the three hundred who came in shifts to grow maize for the soldiers. The supply network was strained, prices rose, and *floridanos* were given a rare opportunity to show their aptitude for business. Governor Manuel de Cendoya speculated with the building fund and fixed a monopoly on maize. The Menéndez Márquez brothers, with connections at the treasury, kept the presidio in beef. Several families bought slaves. Governor Pablo de Hita Salazar conveyed land titles and granted lands, some to his own children. Indian chiefs leased their towns' old fields. Even the soldiers made money, moonlighting at their secondary trades.[35]

Dismayingly, the indigenous population continued to fall. A census of the provinces in 1675 showed only eleven thousand Indians subject to the king, and four-fifths of those were in Apalache, two hundred miles by land from St. Augustine. Timucua had never recovered from its mid-century rebellion, and Guale was in the midst of a thirty-year decline that would turn it into a no-man's-land by 1685.[36] The deputy governor of Apalache traveled to Madrid and obtained an increased export quota for Florida products. He proposed Apalache as an outpost for explorations and settlement on the Gulf, and soon there was a new fort in the port of San Marcos. Depopulated central Florida became an exporter of ranch products, especially the large ranch of La Chua, with the Suwannee River as its recognized outport.[37]

Florida was now worth raiding not only for its artillery and the silver in its coffers, but for its cattle, and buccaneers put it on their itineraries. In summer, no part of the peninsula was safe. St. Augustine occasionally had news of the pirates' plans from a Dutch merchant, Philip Frederic of New York, whose little seventeen-tun sloop could enter the harbor. Thanks to Frederic's warning and the ammunition that he supplied on credit, the town was prepared for Michel de Grammont when he landed on Anastasia

Island in 1683, and was able to capture one of his galliots. When Grammont returned a few years later, Spanish privateers pursued him north, stopping along the way to wipe out the Scots settlement of Stuartstown below Charles Town.[38]

Most of the time between 1667 and 1697, Spain was at war with the France of Louis XIV. During the War of the League of Augsburg, England, Spain, and the Netherlands were even allies, although on a maritime marchland a peace against local interests was difficult to maintain. People in St. Augustine believed that Charles Town harbored pirates, and vice versa. Harassed beyond endurance, the Guales retreated, island by island, nearer to the Spanish capital. More dangerous than the pirates were the backcountry gunrunners who supplied Carolina's allies with firearms in exchange for deerskins and Indian slaves.[39] Work continued on the shellstone Castillo de San Marcos over a twenty-five-year period as funds became available—a gauge of the perceived level of threat. The last block of the structure was laid in 1695, but completing it had not been easy. The *situado* for 1690 did not reach St. Augustine until 1695. Meanwhile, the laborers burned lime and quarried coquina for other construction, including some government buildings, private homes, and a seawall that took ten years to build and cost three-fourths as much as the castillo itself.[40]

Settler population had increased very slowly during the seventeenth century. In 1695, St. Augustine had only one thousand inhabitants. Quaker merchant Jonathan Dickinson, who passed through town in 1696 with his family, white and black, observed that most of the houses looked old and that half of them, standing far apart in their little orchards, were unoccupied—evidence that most economic activities were conducted elsewhere.[41] Dickinson's journal reveals that his party, shipwrecked on the Wild Coast 230 miles below St. Augustine, feared to tell the Indians who they were; English vessels had been kidnapping divers on that coast for years.[42] South Florida was never reduced to Spanish control. Its contacts were with traders and fishermen from Cuba or the Bahamas, and in 1763 Cuban authorities would argue that the Keys were not part of Florida at all.[43]

In the 1680s, the French of Canada, already established in the Illinois country and trading down to the Arkansas River, began to push farther south. René-Robert Cavelier, Sieur de La Salle, descended the Mississippi River to its mouth and left a handful of settlers on the Texas coast. News of his expedition galvanized Spain into founding missions in East Texas and establishing a military presence on the Gulf.[44] Mexican savant Carlos de Sigüenza y Góngora produced the engineering reports for a 1693 expedition to Pensacola Bay, and in November 1698, the Spanish planted a garrison there, barely preempting the French, who would fortify Biloxi two months later.[45]

The death of Charles the Bewitched in 1700 threw Europe into turmoil, for the Spanish House of Habsburg expired with him. His will left Spain and the Spanish Empire to a Bourbon prince who was the grandson of Louis XIV. The small outposts of French Mobile and Spanish Pensacola now came to each other's aid in times of necessity, but the Family Compact spelled disaster for Florida, for it gave Carolina an excuse to attack its neighbor with no holds barred.

In the Southeast, Queen Anne's War began with raids and escalated to invasions. Early in 1702, Captain Anthony Dodsworth and a force of Creeks routed eight hundred Apalache under Captain Francisco Romo de Uriza in the Battle of Pedernales. Later that year, Colonel James Moore invaded eastern Florida with an amphibious force of militia and Yamasee. Part of his army paddled up the St. Johns in canoes, destroying Indian settlements along the way, then marched overland to St. Augustine to meet the rest of his forces, which had come down the coast from Charles Town in boats. The Spanish took refuge inside their new stone fort, driving their cattle into the dry moat. The invaders looted the town, then set up their positions to besiege the castillo. After some ineffectual bombardment back and forth, both sides sent off for reinforcements, the English to Jamaica and the Spanish to Havana, Pensacola, and Mobile. Troops from Cuba were the first to arrive, green and seasick. Unable to get out of the blockaded harbor, Moore set fire to the town and retreated by land. Only some twenty of the less important houses escaped. The siege took a further toll in the epidemic of smallpox that followed it. Moore had left St. Augustine in ruins, but in Charles Town, his expedition was termed a failure because his backers lost money.[46]

No one imagined that the Florida-Carolina War was over. Florida Governor José de Zúñiga y Cerda sent orders for every town to build a stockade. The next winter, Moore redeemed himself in the eyes of his countrymen by leading one thousand Creek warriors against Apalache. They devastated the province, carrying their captives back to Carolina to be sold as slaves and relocating the three towns that had surrendered with terms to places where they could act as burdeners for the Indian trade.[47] Refugees from Apalache scattered in all directions, one band going first to Pensacola, then Mobile, another band fleeing first to Potano, then St. Augustine.[48] The mission provinces of the seventeenth century disappeared; the interior became the haunt of bandits and slave raiders; and Indians of the Wild Coast who preferred a foraging life and spoke languages no priest could understand took refuge under the guns of the fort.[49]

V

In a land renowned for war, where empires met like tectonic plates, a normal Spanish colony, complete with settlers, peasant labor, tributaries, and an array of exports, was untenable. St. Augustine was something else, a naval base on a maritime marchland, and it would remain at its post as long as the king desired.

Notes

1. On the mistaking of nineteenth-century Georgia sugar mills for missions, see Amy Turner Bushnell, *Situado and Sabana: Spain's Support System for the Presidio and Mission Provinces of Florida*. American Museum of Natural History Anthropological Papers, no. 74 (Washington, DC: Smithsonian Institution Press, 1994), 24.

2. For examples of the persistent theme of failure, see Charles W. Arnade, "The Failure of Spanish Florida," *The Americas* 16 (1960): 271–81; Charlton W. Tebeau, *A History of Florida* (Coral Gables, FL: University of Miami Press, 1971), 29–56; Robert Allen Matter, *Pre-Seminole Florida: Spanish Soldiers, Friars, and Indian Missions, 1513–1763* (New York: Garland Press, 1990), 154; and Daniel S. Murphree, *Constructing Floridians: Natives and Europeans in the Colonial Floridas, 1513–1783* (Gainesville: University Press of Florida, 2006), 51–71.

3. Bushnell, *Situado and Sabana*, 43–48.

4. David J. Weber, *The Spanish Frontier in North America* (New Haven: Yale University Press, 1992), 87–91, 122–33.

5. Paul E. Hoffman, *Florida's Frontiers* (Bloomington: Indiana University Press, 2002), 20–44.

6. John T. McGrath, "France in America: A Reevaluation of the Evidence" (PhD diss., Boston University, 1994).

7. Eugene Lyon, *The Enterprise of Florida: Pedro Menéndez de Avilés and the Spanish Conquest of 1565–1568* (Gainesville: University Presses of Florida, 1976), see contract on pp. 213–19; Paul E. Hoffman, *A New Andalucia and a Way to the Orient: The American Southeast during the Sixteenth Century* (Baton Rouge: Louisiana State University Press, 1990), 205–50; Charles M. Hudson, *The Juan Pardo Expeditions: Exploration of the Carolinas and Tennessee, 1566–1568* (Washington, DC: Smithsonian Institution Press, 1990).

8. Paul E. Hoffman, *The Spanish Crown and the Defense of the Caribbean, 1535–1585: Precedent, Patrimonialism, and Royal Parsimony* (Baton Rouge: Louisiana State University Press, 1980), 39–48.

9. Hoffman, *A New Andalucia and a Way to the Orient*, 205–30, 294–307.

10. "Report of the Adelantado, Pedro Menéndez, on the Damage and Murders Caused by the Coast Indians of Florida, Madrid, 1573, 1574," in *Colonial Records of Spanish Florida*,

vol. 1, *Letters and Reports of Governors and Secular Persons, 1570–1577*, trans. and ed. Jeannette Thurber Connor (DeLand: Florida State Historical Society, 1925), 31–81.

11. Mary Ross, "French Intrusions and Indian Uprisings in Georgia and South Carolina (1577–1580)," *Georgia Historical Quarterly* 7, no. 3 (1923): 251–81; idem, "The French on the Savannah 1605," *Georgia Historical Quarterly* 8, no. 3 (1924): 167–94; Bushnell, *Situado and Sabana*, 62–63; idem, "A Requiem for Lesser Conquerors: Honor and Oblivion on a Maritime Periphery," in *Beyond Books and Borders: Garcilaso de la Vega and* La Florida del Inca, ed. Raquel Chang-Rodríguez (Lewisburg, PA: Bucknell University Press, 2006), 66–74, especially 69–70.

12. Amy Bushnell, *The King's Coffer: Proprietors of the Spanish Florida Treasury, 1565–1702* (Gainesville: University Presses of Florida, 1981), 24–26.

13. María Menéndez de Posada, widow of Juan Menéndez Márquez I, Petition to the Crown, Madrid, November 23, 1629, Archivo General de Indias, ramo Gobierno: Audiencia de Santo Domingo, legajo 6, documento 42 (hereinafter SD 6/42); Governor Gonzalo Méndez de Canzo, Informe to the Crown about dismantling the presidio, St. Augustine, September 22, 1602, SD 224.

14. Governor Gonzalo Méndez de Canzo, Informe to the Crown about dismantling the presidio, St. Augustine, September 22, 1602, SD 224; Kathleen A. Deagan, *America's Ancient City: Spanish St. Augustine, 1565–1763* (New York: Garland Press, 1991).

15. Bushnell, *Situado and Sabana*, 120.

16. J. Michael Francis and Kathleen M. Kole, *Murder and Martyrdom in Spanish Florida: Don Juan and the Guale Uprising of 1597*. Anthropological Papers of the American Museum of Natural History, no. 95 (Washington, DC: Smithsonian Institution Press, 2011); Juan Menéndez Márquez I to the Crown, St. Augustine, April 21, 1603, SD 232/27.

17. Charles W. Arnade, *Florida on Trial, 1593–1602* (Coral Gables: University of Miami Press, 1959), 6–7.

18. Bushnell, *King's Coffer*, 96; idem, *Situado and Sabana*, 68–69.

19. Hoffman, *Florida's Frontiers*, 94, 98, 114.

20. Governor Pedro de Ybarra to the Crown, Report on the foreigners, St. Augustine, August 1, 1607, SD 224/83.

21. Amy Turner Bushnell, "Spain's Conquest by Contract: Pacification and the Mission System in Eastern North America," in *The World Turned Upside Down: The State of Eighteenth-Century American Studies at the Beginning of the Twenty-First Century*, ed. Michael V. Kennedy and William G. Shade (Bethlehem, PA: Lehigh University Press, 2001), 289–320.

22. Bushnell, "Requiem for Lesser Conquerors."

23. Bushnell, *Situado and Sabana*. 119, 165.

24. Bushnell, *Situado and Sabana*, 125–27; Karen Ordahl Kupperman, *Providence Island, 1630–1641: The Other Puritan Colony* (New York: Cambridge University Press, 1993).

25. Bushnell, *Situado and Sabana*, 45; Hoffman, *Florida's Frontiers*, 112, 114. For "enemigos olandeses" see Francisca Ramírez, Petition to the Crown, St. Augustine, April 23, 1624, SD 232/88.

26. Bushnell, *King's Coffer*, 93–94; idem, "The Menéndez Márquez Barony of La Chua and the Determinants of Economic Expansion in Seventeenth-Century Florida," *Florida Historical Quarterly* 56 (April 1978): 407–31; idem, *Situado and Sabana*, 78–79, 112, 125–29.

27. Miguel Abengojar, Madrid, July 3, 1681, SD 226/79; Cristóbal de Viso, commissary general of the Indies, to don Francisco de Altamira y Angulo, July 14, 1682, SD 235/117.

28. Amy Turner Bushnell, "'Gastos de Indios': The Crown and the Chiefdom-Presidio Compact in Florida," in *El Gran Norte Mexicano: Indios, misioneros y pobladores entre el mito y la historia*, ed. Salvador Bernabéu Albert (Seville: Consejo Superior de Investigaciones Científicas, 2009), 137–63.

29. Hoffman, *Florida's Frontiers*, 118–19.

30. John H. Hann, *Apalachee: The Land between the Rivers* (Gainesville: University Presses of Florida, 1988), 15–16, 19.

31. Hoffman, *Florida's Frontiers*, 109–10, 126, 128, 147.

32. John H. Hann, *A History of the Timucua Indians and Missions* (Gainesville: University Press of Florida, 1996), 204–5, 213–14, 221; Fray Juan Gómez de Engraba to Fray Francisco Martínez, Havana to Seville, April 4, 1657, SD 225.

33. John E. Worth, *Timucuan Chiefdoms of Spanish Florida*, vol. 2: *Resistance and Destruction* (Gainesville: University Press of Florida, 1998).

34. Bushnell, *Situado and Sabana*, 136–38.

35. Bushnell, *Situado and Sabana*, 85, 136–42; Luis R. Arana and Albert C. Manucy, *The Building of the Castillo de San Marcos* (New York: Eastern National Park & Monument Association for Castillo de San Marcos National Monument, 1977); Amy Turner Bushnell, "Royal *Cédulas* and the Power of Local Custom: The Great Controversy of the Florida Granaries," in *They Came to El Llano Estacado: An Anthology of Essays Presented at "The Franciscan Presence in the Borderlands of North America,"* comp. and ed. Félix D. Almaráz Jr. (San Antonio: Diocese of Amarillo, 2006), 197–222.

36. Bushnell, *Situado and Sabana*, 144–45; John E. Worth, "Overview: The Retreat of Guale and Mocama, 1655–1685," in *The Struggle for the Georgia Coast: An Eighteenth-Century Spanish Retrospective on Guale and Mocama*, American Museum of Natural History Anthropological Papers, no. 75 (Washington, DC: Smithsonian Institution Press, 1995), 9–55.

37. Amy Turner Bushnell, "How to Fight a Pirate: Provincials, Royalists, and the Raiding of San Marcos de Apalache," in *Pirates, Jack Tar, and Memory: New Directions in American Maritime History*, ed. Paul A. Gilje and William Pencak (Mystic, CT: Mystic Seaport, 2007), 11–25; idem, "The Menéndez Márquez Barony of La Chua."

38. Bushnell, *Situado and Sabana*, 161–62, 166–68.

39. Paul Kelton, *Epidemics and Enslavement: Biological Catastrophe in the Native Southeast, 1492–1715* (Lincoln: University of Nebraska Press, 2007), 101–59.

40. Verne E. Chatelain, *The Defenses of Spanish Florida, 1565 to 1763*, Publication 511 (Washington, DC: Carnegie Institution of Washington 1941), 79, 161 n. 25.

41. *Jonathan Dickinson's Journal, or, God's Protecting Providence. Being the Narrative of a Journey from Port Royal in Jamaica to Philadelphia between August 23, 1696, and April 1, 1697*, ed. Evangeline Walker Andrews and Charles McLean Andrews, with an introduction by Leonard W. Labaree (Stuart, FL: Valentine Books, 1975).

42. Amy Turner Bushnell, "Escape of the Nickaleers: European-Indian Relations on the Wild Coast of Florida in 1696, from Jonathan Dickinson's Journal," in *Coastal Encounters: The Transformation of the Gulf South in the Eighteenth Century*, ed. Richmond Brown (Lincoln: University of Nebraska Press, 2007), 31–58.

43. John H. Hann, *Missions to the Calusa* (Gainesville: University of Florida Press, 1991); idem, *Indians of Central and South Florida, 1513–1763* (Gainesville: University Press of Florida, 2003), 59, 186.

44. Kathleen DuVal, *The Native Ground: Indians and Colonists in the Heart of the Continent* (Philadelphia: University of Pennsylvania Press, 2006); Robert S. Weddle, *Wilderness Manhunt: The Spanish Search for La Salle* (Austin: University of Texas Press, 1973); Weber, *Spanish Frontier in North America*, 148–65.

45. Judith Ann Bense, *Presidio Santa María de Galve: A Struggle for Survival in Colonial Spanish Pensacola* (Gainesville: University Press of Florida, 2003).

46. Charles W. Arnade, *The Siege of St. Augustine in 1702* (Gainesville: University of Florida Press, 1959); Hoffman, *Florida's Frontiers*, 175–76.

47. Bushnell, *Situado and Sabana*, 171–72, 178–80; Kelton, *Epidemics and Enslavement*, 182–84; Hoffman, *Florida's Frontiers*, 176–80.

48. Amy Turner Bushnell, "Patricio de Hinachuba: Defender of the Word of God, the Crown of the King, and the Little Children of Ivitachuco," *American Indian Culture and Research Journal* 3 (July 1979): 1–21.

49. Amy Turner Bushnell, "The Sacramental Imperative: Catholic Ritual and Indian Sedentism in the Provinces of Florida," in *Columbian Consequences*, vol. 2., *Archaeology and History of the Spanish Borderlands East*, ed. David Hurst Thomas (Washington, DC: Smithsonian Institution Press, 1990), 475–90.

5

"Giving Liberty to All"

Spanish Florida as a Black Sanctuary, 1673–1790

JANE LANDERS

The patterns of African life in La Florida had their institutional and customary origins in medieval Spain. Sub-Saharan Africans accompanied invading Muslim armies into Spain in AD 711, and long before Columbus discovered the so-called New World, Africans formed a significant element of the urban populations of southern Spain and Portugal.[1] While religious and ethnic prejudice was not absent, and hostility against minorities sometimes flared, cultural diversity had a long heritage in medieval Spain.[2] So did slavery. Spanish slave codes, based on Roman law, considered slavery as an accidental, and mutable, juridical condition into which people of any race might fall. Persons of many races and ethnicities who had been captured in "just wars," had been condemned, or had sold themselves into slavery shared the same legal status.[3] But enslaved persons were persons, not chattel, and as such, retained certain legal rights. They could hold and transfer property and purchase their freedom or that of relatives or friends.[4] Slaves could also use the law to escape an abusive owner and could earn freedom for meritorious service to the state. Medieval social and religious values also promoted charity toward "miserable classes" and encouraged Spanish owners to manumit favored slaves, often in their last testament.[5] The lenient attitude toward manumission created a free black class in Spain that filled accepted economic, social, and even low-level political roles.[6]

Free and enslaved Africans in early modern Seville congregated in the city's poorer ethnic enclaves, and in these black barrios city officials began to appoint free blacks as *mayorals* (stewards), whose function it was to maintain order, arbitrate disputes, and defend their charges in court, even against their masters. As Seville's black population grew ever more numerous, the

Catholic monarchs Isabella and Ferdinand named a royal servant, Juan de Valladolid, "of noble lineage among Negroes" to regulate the city's black community and be its "Chief and Judge."[7] This practice followed Reconquest patterns of governing subjugated peoples and foreshadowed the Spanish practice in the Americas of enacting dominion through "natural" leaders of alien communities, as took place in La Florida.

By the sixteenth century Africans were so numerous in southern Spain that one scholar compared early modern Seville to a chessboard with equal numbers of black and white pieces. In that city free and enslaved blacks worked as stevedores or in the city's public granary, slaughterhouse, gardens, and soap factories. They transported goods and people throughout the city and performed many other menial but useful services. Although excluded from Spanish guilds, Africans were artisans and petty merchants in the commercial districts and domestic servants in Spanish households. By that time many free Africans enjoyed the status of registered citizens, or *vecinos*. Though usually members of the lower classes they lived "decent" lives. Their less-fortunate fellows blended into the poor working and unemployed underclass known as the *gente de mal vivir*, becoming beggars, thieves, day laborers, street vendors, prostitutes, and boatmen.[8] In the multiracial and multiethnic barrios, miscegenation and common-law unions between Spaniards and Africans were common, and the lower classes entered into mixed-race marriages with apparently little stigma.[9] Like the patterns of congregation, black political autonomy, and religious incorporation, this social pattern would also be replicated in the New World.

Given their numbers and roles in Spanish port cities like Seville, and their generally depressed economic conditions, it is not surprising that both free and enslaved Africans hoped to improve their lots by crossing the Atlantic on the earliest voyages of exploration and conquest. With the Europeans they soon formed a specialized and limited pool of human resources circulating throughout the circum-Caribbean. Together African and European explorers faced extraordinary hardships and life-altering events and, later, helped create a new creole society in the Americas.

The first African explorer to Florida was Juan Garrido, a man of unknown West African origins. Garrido traveled to Lisbon sometime in the 1490s and then went on to Seville, whence he sailed for Hispaniola. In Hispaniola Garrido encountered other free blacks such as Juan González (Ponce) de León, an interpreter of the Taíno language, who had adopted his surname from his Spanish patron on the island. The two African adventurers took part in the "pacification" campaigns against the native populations who were then in revolt.[10] They may well have faced other Africans in these battles, for

Governor Nicolás de Ovando complained in 1503 that some of the island's first African slaves had already run away, thereafter to be known as *cimarrones*, and that they had found refuge among the Indian rebels. The alliance of revolting Indians and fugitive slaves haunted the Spaniards, who were a minority in Hispaniola and only tenuously held power.[11]

Despite these fears, however, Spaniards came to regard African slaves as indispensable to successful colonization of the Americas. In 1513 the Crown established the *asiento*, or contract system, whereby licensed contractors are estimated to have sent between 75,000 and 90,000 enslaved Africans to Spanish America by 1600, and approximately 350,000 by the end of the seventeenth century. Because contraband trade in slaves was endemic, those are probably conservative figures.[12]

Once the Indian wars on Hispaniola waned and settlement was well under way on that island, it became the base from which Spaniards launched new conquests—claiming Puerto Rico in 1508, Jamaica in 1509, Cuba in 1511, and Florida in 1513. Juan Garrido and Juan González joined Juan Ponce de León's expedition to explore and conquer Puerto Rico (San Juan de Boriquén) and both men settled there briefly to become gold miners.[13] Although Queen Isabella had forbidden the enslavement of her new Indian subjects, the alleged ferocity of the Carib, and their reputed cannibalism, led Queen Isabel to authorize "just war" against hostile indigenous groups, and Spaniards swept through the Caribbean islands then the mainland coasts in search of captives to sell into slavery.[14] From Puerto Rico Ponce de León led slave raids against the "Carib" on the islands of Santa Cruz, Guadalupe, and Dominica, and the Africans, Juan Garrido and Juan González Ponce de León, were among the raiders.[15] They also accompanied Ponce de León on his voyages to Florida in 1513 and 1521, where the hostile reception by the indigenes suggests Caribbean-based slavers had already preceded them.[16] Africans, thus, helped stake Spain's first claim to exclusive sovereignty over an area stretching north from the Florida Keys to Newfoundland and west to Mexico, a claim disputed by both the French and the English, who viewed effective occupation as the true measure of sovereignty.[17] To hold Florida, the Spaniards would have to populate it.

Five years after Ponce de León's death, and only five years after the first known American slave rebellion was crushed on Hispaniola, the prominent planter, jurist, and slaver Lucas Vásquez de Ayllón attempted to do just that at a site he called San Miguel de Gualdape near present-day Sapelo Sound, Georgia. Ayllón's expedition included some six hundred Spanish men, women, and children, as well as the first known contingent of African slaves brought to the present-day United States. As Paul Hoffman details, disease, starvation and mutiny undid Ayllón's new settlement, and as winter bore down, some slaves set fires and joined a native Guale rebellion, finally destroying Gualdape.[18] These first African rebels disappeared from history and presumably blended into the indigenous population, as many of their counterparts were already doing in Hispaniola, Puerto Rico, Jamaica, Cuba, and Mexico.[19]

Despite the slave arson at Gualdape, all subsequent expeditions to La Florida also incorporated Africans.[20] The explorations could not have succeeded without them. Pánfilo de Narváez landed approximately six hundred persons, with unknown numbers of Africans, somewhere near Tampa Bay in 1528, but that expedition, too, proved a disastrous failure, undone by hurricanes, supply losses, and separation of the forces. Among the four survivors who "came back from the dead" after eight years wandering along the Gulf coast and westward to the Pacific Ocean, was Estevan, the African slave of Andrés Dorantes, whose linguistic and healing talents greatly contributed to the group's survival.[21]

Drawing on lessons learned and fortunes won in Peru (where Africans also fought alongside Spaniards against the Incas), Hernando de Soto hoped to succeed in Florida where his predecessors had failed.[22] He outfitted ships in Spain and stopped in Cuba for additional supplies and personnel, including free and enslaved Africans and large numbers of native porters. In 1539 De Soto marched them all on a brutal and circuitous route through eleven modern states in the Southeast, along which many deserted. One enslaved African, Gómez, helped the captive *cacica* of Cofitachequi escape from Spanish control and return to her headquarters near present-day Camden, South Carolina, where he became her consort.[23] Other African slaves, and Spaniards too, from this expedition also "went over" to the natives. For the next three centuries the Indian nations of the vast territory of La Florida provided a potential refuge for enslaved Africans.[24]

Although enslaved Africans often tried to ally themselves with local Indians who might help them to escape, free Africans tended to remain with the Spaniards until the bitter end, hoping to earn their share of the expedition's fortunes. Among the free Africans in the De Soto force was Bernaldo, a caulker from Vizcaya and formerly the slave of one of De Soto's captains, Pedro Calderón. Bernaldo survived the many bloody Indian battles, severe hunger, killing marches, and finally a voyage down the Mississippi River in hastily constructed boats. After an epic voyage of over four years, during which the expeditionaries traversed six hundred miles and ten of the present-day United States, Bernaldo was among those who limped back to Mexico City "dressed only in animal skins."[25]

Finally, in 1565, Pedro Menéndez de Avilés succeeded in establishing the first permanent European settlement in the Americas at St. Augustine, Florida. As Florida's Spanish colonists and an unknown number of African slaves began the hard work of launching a new settlement, Menéndez made an exploratory tour of his new province. Among the Calusa nation to the south of St. Augustine, Menéndez encountered a mulatto named Luis. Hernando d'Escalante Fontaneda's memoir of his captivity among the Calusa described Luis as part owner of a richly laden vessel out of New Spain wrecked on the Florida coast a decade earlier. Fontaneda credited Luis's knowledge of the Ays language and customs with saving other Spanish shipwreck victims, including some of African descent, and also with uncovering a plot against Menéndez's life.[26] As required of a good Christian ruler, Menéndez ransomed eighteen Christians found in the southern villages, including Luis. The Calusa chief, Carlos, released five Spaniards, five *mestiza* women from Peru, and an unnamed black woman who returned to St. Augustine with Menéndez. Luis and at least one other African, Juanillo, became official interpreters of indigenous languages for the Spanish, as Africans often did in other areas of the Spanish Americas.[27] However, some of the prisoners Menéndez tried to free chose to stay among their captors, perhaps to avoid separation from families established with native spouses. These included a black woman and a mulatto who had lived among the Calusa since they were children and could hardly speak Spanish.[28] Knowledge of these mixed families may have inspired those slaves who according to Menéndez later ran to, and intermarried with, the Ays.[29]

The loss of any slaves was significant. Like other areas in the Spanish Caribbean, Florida suffered from early and dramatic Indian depopulation and a shortage of European manpower, and this demographic imperative created a demand for black labor.[30] Slaves were costly, averaging around two hundred pesos for a healthy worker through the sixteenth century, and demand commonly outstripped supply in many areas. Although Menéndez's charter allowed him to import five hundred African slaves to do the difficult labor required in settling a new colony, probably fewer than fifty slaves accompanied Florida's first settlers, and those slaves probably belonged to the most elite Floridians.[31]

A year after establishing St. Augustine, Menéndez established a second settlement, Santa Elena, in modern-day South Carolina, and he sent skilled African craftsmen from St. Augustine to help build fortifications there, at Spain's northernmost settlement. Africans thus were reintroduced among the Guale, who forty years earlier had risen against Ayllón.[32] Although Spanish sources do not comment on it, it seems likely the story of the earlier revolt at Gualdape and of the interracial alliances against the Spaniards would still have been known among the Guale and may well have been transmitted to the African laborers from St. Augustine. The new Spanish settlement among the Guale was no more successful than the first, however. Jesuit efforts to prohibit polygamy and to interfere in tribal successions angered the Guale, as did what they considered to be excessive demands for food and services. Finally, in 1576, the Guale revolted again. This major rebellion lasted more than four years and was defeated only after the Spaniards killed many natives and put nineteen towns, granaries, and fields to the torch. Whether black slaves seized this opportunity to again ally with the Guale is unknown, but a new group of black laborers who arrived from St. Augustine in 1583 to rebuild Santa Elena witnessed the aftermath of that tragedy.[33]

Because labor was always at a premium in Florida, Spanish authorities initiated a draft, or *repartimiento,* system that rotated hundreds of "Christianized" Guales, Timucuans, and Apalachees into St. Augustine to work. The result was catastrophic. Between 1613 and 1617 a series of "pests and contagions" devastated the native peoples of Florida. The same diseases that felled these groups must have also affected the black population, for by 1618 there were only eleven aged and infirm slaves left in St. Augustine, and Florida officials petitioned the Crown for replacements from Havana to cut and saw timber for fort and ship repairs. Another series of epidemics—typhus or yellow fever in 1649, smallpox in 1654, and measles in 1659—took a harsh toll on St. Augustine's limited population, killing many government officials and all the royal slaves.[34] In response, the Crown ordered Havana to send as many slaves as it could to Florida, "so that for lack of them, royal service does not cease ... considering the need existing in Florida for such blacks and the necessity of preserving (sovereignty in) that land."[35]

For the first century of its existence, Florida was "a society with slaves" rather than "a slave society," to use Ira Berlin's categorization, and its success was uncertain.[36] In the mid-seventeenth century, however, the colony's distress finally led the Crown to accede to major land grants and to the introduction of cattle, an economy in which Africans participated throughout the Americas. In 1645 Florida's governor established a wheat ranch in the lands of the Apalachee, near present-day Tallahassee, and in violation of a royal prohibition, he employed black slaves from Angola and a mulatto overseer named Francisco Galindo to supervise the free Indians working on the ranch.[37] Blacks and mestizos, some imported from New Spain, also served as ranch hands on vast new cattle estates in north central Florida, such as La Chua ranch, established around 1646 by the Menéndez Márquez family, near present-day Gainesville.[38] Such establishments diversified both Florida's population and its economy, and made the colony somewhat more self-sufficient, but much of the surplus production found its way to Havana, rather than St. Augustine. Moreover, the ranches' locations in the midst of Indian lands only increased native complaints against the Spaniards: the Apalachee rose in 1647 and the Timucuans in 1656.[39] These rebellions may have also encouraged slave participation or desertion, because subsequent documents refer to the need to hold slaves in "the royal fort [at St. Augustine] and with good security so that they may not flee, joined by some slaves that have been brought from Havana to be sold at this presidio as a form of exile because of their being delinquents and incorrigible."[40]

In response to increased piracy and foreign territorial encroachment in the "Spanish Lake," the Crown had belatedly embarked on a major effort to fortify its Caribbean ports. African masonry and metalworking skills eventually helped erect great stone forts at Havana, Santo Domingo, San Juan, Cartagena, Portobelo, Acapulco, and St. Augustine, as well as many minor constructions in lesser ports along the threatened coasts. The Spaniards launched the construction of St. Augustine's massive stone fort, the Castillo de San Marcos, in 1672.[41] Although the construction generated funds for the town, the project increased the labor and food demands on nearby Indians whose numbers had already been "thinned" by recurring epidemics of typhus, yellow fever, smallpox, measles, and unidentified epidemics. The governors had to import additional Indians from the western provinces of Timucua and Apalachee and Guale Indians from north coastal Florida and Georgia to augment the labor force. Convicts provided another source of labor—among them blacks and mulattoes. From Havana the Crown also sent some of its royal slaves skilled in stonecutting. The polyglot laborers lived and worked in close proximity to one another in St. Augustine.[42]

To further protect its American holdings, the Crown also required all residents of the Spanish colonies to form militias to defend themselves in case of attack. Free and enslaved Africans supplemented such local Spanish forces across the Americas.[43] By the mid-seventeenth century free blacks and mulattoes were also serving throughout the circum-Caribbean in their own formally organized militias. A Central American roster from 1673 listed almost three thousand *pardos* (usually meaning mulattoes, but sometimes referring to non-Europeans of mixed ancestry) serving in infantry units throughout the isthmus.[44] Similar black units served in Hispaniola, Cuba, Mexico, Puerto Rico, and Cartagena.[45] Most of the black militias were formed by free black artisans and skilled workers. They were Catholics who lived as Spaniards and were integrated into their communities through powerful social institutions such as godparentage and patron-client networks. Leading useful and orderly lives they mirrored the early African communities of Spain and enjoyed the protections promised by Spanish law and custom.

Military service was one way for free blacks to prove themselves to their community and also advance themselves through occasional opportunities for plunder. Moreover, through the militias free blacks acquired titles and status, and eventually, in the eighteenth century, full corporate privileges, known as the military *fuero*, which included exemption from civil prosecution.[46] It is possible that militia units also functioned to reinforce relationships within the African community, as "natural" leaders rose to command and assumed responsibility for their men. In this way they were not unlike the military captains of Maroon communities or the leaders of slave revolts. Parish registers from St. Augustine show that African militia families commonly intermarried and served as godparents and marriage sponsors for one another. Church records also suggest that the double connection of family and military corporatism may have worked to move some men out of slavery. Their slave past was certainly not forgotten, but it was in a sense excused by appropriate behavior, valuable services, and the sponsorship of Africans whom the community already approved.

The service of African militiamen would become more critical after 1670, when after more than a century of Spanish settlement in Florida, Barbadian planters already hostile to Spain established an English colony at Charles Town "but ten days' journey" from St. Augustine. The English settlers were intent on establishing profitable plantations such as they had known in Barbados, and this would require the hard work of African slaves—many of them. Unlike Spanish slave laws, the slave codes English planters developed in the Caribbean and transplanted to Carolina considered slaves as chattel or moveable property, not unlike their cattle or furniture. These codes featured harsh regulation and minimal protections and strongly discouraged manumissions. Carolina slaves would soon learn the critical differences in the English and Spanish slave regimes.

Governor Juan Márquez Cabrera took on the task of trying to drive out the English "usurpers" who had taken up residence in Carolina, territory that Spain had claimed since 1513. He formed a company of free *pardo* (mulatto) and *moreno* (black) militiamen in St. Augustine in 1683, but other than their names, little is known about the forty-two men and six officers who composed this unit. Corporal Crispin de Tapia is known from other sources to have been a free mulatto who managed a store in St. Augustine.[47] It is testimony to his need that the governor would form such a unit because he and his predecessor had been complaining for years that the troops provided from New Spain in the 1670s were "sons of Negroes, *chinos* (of mixed race), and mulattoes," only good for work as cobblers, tailors, carpenters, blacksmiths, and cattle hands (precisely the kinds of occupations persons of African descent held throughout the Spanish Americas).[48] None of St. Augustine's black militiamen used an African nation for a surname, although several surnames indicate other origins—Catalan, Lima, Mexicano—and others shared surnames with some of the oldest families in Florida, including Menéndez, De Soto, Rutiner, and de Hita, which might indicate either possible patronage ties or that these men were formerly owned by those families.

The black militiamen were obviously acculturated and swore before God and the cross their willingness to serve the king. While their pledge may have been formulaic, it was also an effort to define their status as members of St. Augustine's religious and civil community, and as vassals of a king from whom they might expect protection or patronage in exchange for armed service. The same year it was organized St. Augustine's black militia helped successfully defend the city against the attack of the French pirate Michel, Sieur de Grammont (Agramón to the Spanish), who hit again in 1686 (this time with the black pirate Diego enlisted). Over the following years St. Augustine's black militia also became an effective offensive force for Spain.

In 1686 Florida's governor led a combined force of more than 153 Spaniards, Timucuan and Apalachee Indians, and members of the new black militia on raids against the new English plantations on Edisto Island, including that of Governor Joseph Morton. The Spanish raiding party killed some of the English settlers and stole thirteen of the governor's slaves before turning southward to burn down the Scottish settlement at Port Royal on their way home to St. Augustine.[49] The following year, Carolina captain William Dunlop made a failed attempt to recruit nearby Yamasee Indians for a counterattack on St. Augustine, and the repeated cross-currents of raids acquainted many blacks and native peoples with the routes to St. Augustine.

Not long after William Dunlop's foiled effort to attack St. Augustine, eight men, two women, and a nursing child escaped from Carolina to St. Augustine in a canoe and requested baptism into the "True Faith."[50] Perhaps they were the Spanish-speaking slaves captured by English corsairs at Vera Cruz and Campeche who had the year before asked a Guale man about escaping in canoes to St. Augustine.[51] Despite early uncertainty about the runaways' legal status, the Spaniards welcomed their labor and military services, so as required of a good Christian governor, Quiroga granted the petitioners safe haven. The governor saw to the runaways' Catholic instruction, baptism, and marriage, but he also made use of their skilled labor. The men became ironsmiths and laborers on the new Castillo de San Marcos and were paid one peso a day, the same wage paid to the indigenous laborers who worked beside them. The women became domestics in the governor's own household and earned half as much as the men.[52] When an agent from Carolina came to St. Augustine to reclaim the runaways the following year, the Spanish governor cited their religious conversion as a reason not to return them. Instead he offered to pay the Carolina slave owners their asking price for the group—1,600 pesos—as soon as St. Augustine's annual subsidy arrived. Satisfied with that promise, the agent returned to Charles Town empty-handed.[53]

The slaves' "telegraph" must have quickly reported the outcome of the negotiations, for soon other fugitives began arriving in St. Augustine. The Spaniards recorded new groups of runaways reaching St. Augustine in 1688, 1689, and 1690, and Carolina's new governor, James Colleton, complained to his Spanish counterpart that slaves ran "dayly to your towns." Unsure about how to handle the incoming refugees, St. Augustine officials repeatedly solicited Spain for guidance. Finally, on November 7, 1693, Charles II issued a royal proclamation "giving liberty to all . . . the men as well as the women . . . so that by their example and by my liberality others will do the same."[54] Hundreds did—risking all the dangers of the swamps and the patrollers and Indians hired to recapture them. The eight men and two women who risked their lives for freedom in 1687 were responsible for a major policy revision at the Spanish court that would shape the geopolitics of the Southeast and the Caribbean for years to come.[55]

Although the Spanish Crown emphasized religious and humane considerations for freeing the slaves, political and military motives were equally important, if not more so. In harboring the runaways and eventually settling them in their own town, Florida's governors were following a traditional Spanish policy of populating and holding territory threatened by foreign encroachment. But if the interests of Spain and Florida were served by this policy, so too were those of the ex-slaves. Spanish Florida offered them a refuge within which they could live free and maintain their families and in the highly politicized context of the day, they made creative use of Spanish institutions to improve the conditions of their freedom.[56]

The provocation inherent in the Spanish sanctuary policy increasingly threatened the Carolinians, who were trying to establish plantations in the new colony. Despite the institution of regulatory slave codes, ticket systems, and land and water patrols, Carolina slaves continued to run away—southward to Florida.⁵⁷ Not only did each runaway represent an economic loss but planters feared that the success of the few might inspire the many. By the beginning of the eighteenth century, blacks outnumbered whites in Carolina, and in that colony, as in all other slave systems, there were chronic fears of slave uprisings. Carolina slaves revolted in 1711 and 1714, and the following year many slaves joined the Yamasee War that almost eradicated the English colony.⁵⁸ After reinforcements from Virginia and North Carolina helped turn the tide, those defeated Yamasees and their black allies who managed to escape Carolina sought refuge among the Spaniards.⁵⁹

Peter Wood asserts that of all the Carolinians' conspiratorial concerns none seemed to worry them more after 1720 than St. Augustine. That year the townspeople of Charles Town uncovered a major slave conspiracy in which at least some of the participants "thought to get to Augustine." Fourteen got as far as Savannah before being captured and executed.⁶⁰ Still slaves continued to take the risk. In 1724, ten more runaways reached St. Augustine, assisted by English-speaking Yamasee Indians. According to their statement, they knew that the Spanish king had offered freedom for those seeking conversion and baptism.⁶¹

Initially at least, Governor Antonio de Benavides honored the 1693 edict freeing slaves of the English who converted. In 1725 he sent a delegation to Charles Town to negotiate boundary disputes and an agreement on the runaways. Following the precedent set by his predecessor in 1687, the governor offered to purchase the newly arrived fugitives for two hundred pesos apiece. Angry Carolina slave owners rejected the offer as insufficient, claimed that their property was worth much more, and demanded also to be compensated for the loss of the slaves' labor since they ran away.⁶² Governor Benavides wrote Spain to inquire whether the fugitives (who had entered Florida during a period of truce between England and Spain) were entitled to receive sanctuary, but no reply was immediately forthcoming and when the English threatened to reclaim their lost slaves by force, he sold the unlucky fugitives at public auction to the leading creditors of St. Augustine's treasury.⁶³ Although the governor gave the auction proceeds to the planters' envoy, the Carolinians charged that Benavides "Makes Merchandize of all our slaves, and ships them off to Havanah for his own Profit," and they were at least partially correct.⁶⁴

Undeterred, more Carolina slaves continued to flee to Florida. Thomas Elliott and other planters near Stono "had fourteen Slaves Runaway to St. Augustine" in 1726. The acting governor of Carolina, Arthur Middleton, complained to London that the Spaniards not only harbored their runaways but "They have found a New way of sending our own slaves against us, to Rob and Plunder us."[65] Some of the runaways were seasoned warriors who had fought with the Yamasee against the English, and some may have been warriors in their homelands. One of the most notable was the Mandinga man who upon his Catholic baptism took the name Francisco Menéndez. In 1726 Governor Benavides named Menéndez captain of St. Augustine's slave militia, and it is likely that he led the black forces among the raiders Benavides continued to send north to attack English settlements. Carolina's Governor Middleton claimed that "Six of our Runaway slaves and the rest Indians" in two canoes attacked near Pon Pon in the fall of 1727 and carried away white captives. Another account of the 1727 raid said that "Ten Negroes and fourteen Indians Commanded by those of their own Colour, without any Spaniards in company with them" had taken the action and that they had also brought back to St. Augustine one black man and a mulatto boy. That same year Spanish raiders and former Carolina runaways hit again at a plantation on the Edisto River and carried away another seven slaves.[66] Benavides sent another party of four dozen Yamasee northward and offered thirty pieces of eight for every English scalp and one hundred pieces "for every live Negro they should bring." Governor Benavides admired the military abilities of the runaways and recognized their diplomatic potential, but he did not free Menéndez and his fellow militiamen.[67]

The Spanish Crown also recognized that the service of the black militiamen was critical to holding the contested frontier and commended Menéndez's black militia for its bravery during Colonel James Palmer's retaliatory raid on St. Augustine in 1728. In 1733 the Crown reiterated its offer of freedom to Carolina runaways seeking religious sanctuary in Florida, but due to the local uncertainty about how to interpret the original decree, some, like Menéndez, remained enslaved.[68] Over the next five years Captain Menéndez led a determined campaign to make Florida's officials live up to the promises of the Spanish king, presenting petitions to the governors and to the auxiliary bishop of Cuba, who toured the province in 1735, but to no avail.[69] When Manuel de Montiano became the new governor of Florida in 1737, the group's fortunes changed. Captain Francisco Menéndez once more petitioned the new governor for freedom and listed thirty-one individuals unjustly enslaved, including some who had been shipped to Havana, and the names of the persons who claimed ownership over them. This time Captain Menéndez's petition was supported by another from his Yamasee ally Chief Jospo, who stated that he and the other Yamasee chiefs "commonly" made treaties with the slaves and that Captain Menéndez and three other escaped slaves had fought bravely for him for several years until they were ultimately defeated. Jospo related that when the Yamasee fled southward, their black allies joined them, hoping to receive in St. Augustine the Christian sanctuary promised by Spain.[70] War with England was expected at any moment, and the combined petitions of the African and Indian leaders must have made an impression on a governor in need of experienced fighters. After reviewing all relevant documentation and against the vehement protests of powerful owners, Governor Montiano granted unconditional freedom to all the fugitives from Carolina.[71] When the Crown reviewed Montiano's actions, it approved and ordered that not only all the blacks who had already come from Carolina "but all those who in the future come as fugitives from the English colonies" should be given prompt and full liberty in the name of the king. Further, so that there could be no further pretext for selling the runaways, the royal edict should be publicly posted.[72]

* * *

In 1738 the runaways from Carolina began new lives as freedmen and women on the Spanish frontier, establishing the new town of Gracia Real de Santa Teresa de Mose about two miles north of St. Augustine.[73] This became the first free black town legitimately constituted in what is today the United States, and in 1994 the site was declared a National Historic Landmark. The National Park Service also recognized Fort Mose as a National Underground Railroad site, one that predates its better-known Canadian counterpart by more than a century.[74] An interdisciplinary team directed by Kathleen Deagan of the Florida Museum of Natural History excavated this unique site, and the results of this research can now be seen at the Fort Mose Historic State Park Museum and on the website of the Florida Museum of Natural History. The local community has also created a Fort Mose Historical Society to promote awareness of this important site.[75]

Captain Francisco Menéndez, who had initiated the successful suit for freedom and who still led the black militia, also governed the new settlement, and Governor Montiano referred to the inhabitants of Mose as Menéndez's "subjects."[76] Governor Montiano clearly considered the benefits of a northern outpost against anticipated British attacks, and who better to serve as an advance warning system than grateful ex-slaves carrying Spanish arms? The freedmen apparently understood their expected role for, upon receiving the land, they vowed to be "the most cruel enemies of the English" and to risk their lives and spill their "last drop of blood in defense of the Great crown of Spain and the Holy Faith."[77] The new homesteaders were pragmatists, and their own interests were clearly served by fighting those who would return them to chattel slavery.

News regarding Spain's sanctuary policy in Florida and the existence of Fort Mose spread rapidly northward through the fledgling English colony of Georgia (where slavery was still prohibited) to the expanding plantations of South Carolina, where roughly thirty thousand blacks were tied to the arduous rice economy by the mid-1730s. Carolina planters complained that Spain's 1733 edict had been proclaimed publicly (as, in fact, it was), "by Beat of Drum round the Town of St. Augustine (where many Negroes belonging to English vessels that carried thither Supplies of provisions had the Opportunity of hearing it)."[78] They also alluded to secret measures taken by the Spaniards to disseminate their offer among the English slaves and frequently reported suspicious visitors from Spanish Florida. As the word spread, more slaves were emboldened to try for liberty.

On November 21, 1738, twenty-three men, women, and children escaped from Port Royal, Carolina, and made it safely to St. Augustine in a stolen launch. Governor Montiano promptly honored their request for sanctuary, and they joined their predecessors at Mose. Nineteen of the newcomers had belonged to Captain Caleb Davis, an English merchant who had been trading merchandise (and intelligence) in St. Augustine for years. Despite Davis's useful relationship with the Spaniards, Governor Montiano refused his attempt to reclaim his slaves the following month, and the frustrated Davis reported that his slaves laughed at his fruitless efforts to recover them.[79] Twelve years later Davis submitted a claim to the Spanish government for twenty-seven of his slaves "detained" by Montiano, whom he valued at 7,600 pesos, as well as for the launch in which they escaped and supplies they had taken with them.[80]

Each successful escape generated more attempts. In February 1739 Carolina authorities captured but released several runaways headed for St. Augustine. The following month four slaves and an Irish Catholic servant from Carolina made their escape to Florida on stolen horses. The English angrily reported that although the runaways had killed one man and wounded another, "They were received there [St. Augustine] with great honours, one of them had a Commission given to him, and a Coat faced with Velvet."[81] The same month, another group of envoys from Carolina traveled to St. Augustine to press for the return of the runaways. Governor Montiano was cordial but refused to comply, citing the royal edict of 1733 promising religious sanctuary. Carolina's governor, William Bull, wrote that the planters were very dissatisfied "to find their property now become so very precarious and uncertain." He added that Carolina's planters feared that "Negroes which were their chief support may in little time become their Enemies, if not their

Masters, and that this Government is unable to withstand or prevent it."[82] In April, frustrated members of the South Carolina Commons voted to offer bounties, even for adult scalps "with the two ears," to dissuade other slaves from trying to escape, and for added emphasis staged a public whipping and execution of two newly captured runaways.[83]

Despite the increasingly harsh measures taken against them, the enslaved still sought freedom, and the level of their own desperate violence escalated proportionally. In August, Don Diego Pablo, an Indian ally from Apalachee, sent word to Governor Montiano that the British had attempted to build a fort nearby but that the hundred black laborers had revolted, killed all the whites, and hamstrung their horses before escaping. Several days later some of the escaped blacks encountered the same Indians in the woods and asked directions to reach the Spaniards, presumably to ask for sanctuary.[84]

The following month, on September 9, 1739, a group of "Angolan" slaves revolted near Stono, South Carolina, where they killed more than twenty whites and sacked and burned homes before heading for St. Augustine.[85] Governor Bull quickly gathered a retaliatory force, which struck the rebels later that day when they stopped along the road for what the white pursuers viewed as a drunken dance, but which John Thornton identifies as a traditional feature of war in Central Africa. Kongo had long been a Catholic kingdom with many Portuguese speakers and Thornton contends, as did contemporary Carolinians, that the rebels could well have understood both the offer of Catholic protection and Spanish (a sister language to Portuguese), and that they based their flight plans on this knowledge. Those rebels who survived the first day's battle fought on for another week, moving southward toward St. Augustine, and Thornton attributes their success to possible training and service as soldiers in the eighteenth-century wars in the Kongo.[86] After a week's worth of fighting a larger white militia force finally caught and killed most of the surviving rebels; however, all reports say that some escaped this final battle. If any did make it to their destination, they would have been sheltered at Mose.[87]

Peter Wood argues that Stono led to a "heightened degree of white repression and a reduced amount of black autonomy" in South Carolina. Both factors would have made escape to St. Augustine even more worth the risk. An estimated 150 slaves rebelled near the Ashley River outside Charles Town in June 1740. Like the Stono rebels, they may have hoped to reach safety at St. Augustine. They chose a dangerous time for their escape since Carolina and Georgia were at that very moment joined in attacking Spanish Florida. It may have been that fact, however, that triggered the revolt. Carolinians captured fifty of the rebels and hung them at the rate of ten a day, but nothing is known of the fate of the other one hundred. Some may have reached Florida and joined their compatriots at Mose.[88]

Over the next decades the people of Mose adapted to Spanish religious and cultural expectations and battled English invaders and Indian raiders to defend their hard-won gains. The Mose militia fought bravely when General James Oglethorpe of Georgia invaded Florida in 1740, and when Francisco Menéndez wrote the king asking for appropriate rewards for his service, Florida's governor supported that petition. The following year Menéndez and others took to the seas as corsairs for Spain but after several successful expeditions Menéndez was taken prisoner, tortured, re-enslaved, and sold as a prize of war in the Bahamas. Other free sailors from Cuba faced similar fates in New York because the British presumption was that they were not white so they must be slaves. Remarking that Spain could not man its navies without people of color, Florida's governor went to great lengths to provide the British Admiralty courts with legal proofs of their free status and some were eventually freed. This may be what happened to Francisco Menéndez, who reappeared as the leader of Mose by 1752.

Truly an Atlantic creole, Menéndez had been enslaved and transported from West Africa to Carolina. After fighting for three years in the Yamasee War, he spoke Yamasee and English in addition to the African languages he already knew. In Florida he learned Spanish and wrote it beautifully. He may well have earlier been literate in Arabic. He sailed the Atlantic from Havana to Ocracoke Island and planned to travel to Spain to see the king and present his credentials. After a tumultuous life, Menéndez ended his days in Cuba at some seventy years of age. His seems an amazing story and yet it is only one of many recorded in the Spanish documents that relate this forgotten chapter in the history of African resistance in North America.[89]

Throughout the 1740s and 1750s enslaved people from South Carolina and Georgia made their way to freedom in Spanish Florida, where they became part of the Mose community. Male runaways outnumbered females, but despite the grave dangers involved, women continued to try for freedom. Runaway slave notices from colonial South Carolina papers describe some of them. Delia, who spoke very little English, took her "sucking child" and ran with Clarinda, whose English was good. They made good their escape in their owner's cypress canoe. Amoretta and Sarah joined three African men in their own successful escape.[90]

The escape hatch to Spanish Florida slammed shut in 1763, however, when the Treaty of Paris ceded Florida to Great Britain. Rather than be re-enslaved, the Mose community of about one hundred persons left Florida on a new southward passage—joining the Spanish exodus to Cuba, where they became homesteaders again on the Matanzas frontier.[91]

Notes

This essay is adapted from earlier essays, most notably "Gracia Real de Santa Teresa de Mose: A Free Black Town in Colonial Florida," *American Historical Review* 95 (February 1990): 9–30, and my earlier monograph, *Black Society in Spanish Florida* (Urbana: University of Illinois Press, 1999).

1. José Luis Cortés López, *Los orígenes de la esclavitud negra en España* (Madrid: Mundo Negro, 1986); William D. Phillips Jr., *Slavery from Roman Times to the Early Transatlantic Trade* (Minneapolis: University of Minnesota Press, 1985), 138–39, 155, 160–63; A. C. de M. Saunders, *A Social History of Black Slaves and Freedmen in Portugal, 1441–1555* (Cambridge: Cambridge University Press, 1982); Landers, *Black Society in Spanish Florida*, chap. 1.

2. David Nirenberg, *Communities of Violence: Persecution of Minorities in the Middle Ages* (Princeton: Princeton University Press, 1998); Lyle N. McAlister, *Spain and Portugal in the New World, 1492–1700* (Minneapolis: University of Minnesota Press, 1984), 43–45.

3. Cortés López, *Orígenes de la esclavitud*, 23–44, 121–32; Ruth Pike, *Traders and Aristocrats, Sevillian Society in the Sixteenth Century* (Ithaca: Cornell University Press, 1972), 170–92. Even Amerindians sometimes were sold as slaves in Seville, despite royal prohibitions against their enslavement. Alfonso Franco Silva, *Regesto documental sobre la esclavitud Sevillana (1453–1513)* (Seville: University of Seville, 1979).

4. McAlister, *Spain and Portugal*, 24–26; Cortés López, *Orígenes de la esclavitud*, 133–50.

5. Maureen Flynn, "Charitable Ritual in Late Medieval and Early Modern Spain," *Sixteenth-Century Journal* 16, no. 3 (1985): 1–30; Flynn, *Sacred Charity: Confraternities and Social Welfare in Spain, 1400–1700* (Ithaca: Cornell University Press, 1989).

6. Cortés López, *Orígenes de la esclavitud*, 151–76; Pike, *Aristocrats and Traders*, 188. For numerous examples of self-purchase or gratis manumission see Franco Silva, *Regesto documental*.

7. Pike, *Aristocrats and Traders*, 173–74.

8. Mary Elizabeth Perry, *Crime and Society in Early Modern Seville* (Hanover, NH: University Press of New England, 1980), 12–32; Pike, *Aristocrats and Traders*, 192–214.

9. Pike, *Aristocrats and Traders*, 29, 188.

10. Ricardo E. Alegría, *Juan Garrido, el conquistador negro en las Antillas, Florida, México y California, c. 1503–1540* (San Juan: Centro de Estudios Avanzados de Puerto Rico y El Caribe, 1990), 17, 20, 30. Alegría located other persons of African descent in the passenger lists and other unedited documents for Puerto Rico, including "Francisco Melgarejo, Negro servant of Jerónimo de Mendoza," "the Negro Antonio," "Juan, the Negro slave of Juan Martínez," "Piñon's wife, Negro," and "Gaspar, free Negro." On the wars in Hispaniola see Samuel M. Wilson, *Hispaniola: Caribbean Chiefdoms in the Age of Columbus* (Tuscaloosa: University of Alabama Press, 1990), 74–109.

11. Ovando recommended no more slaves be sent from Spain and charged that the Maroons were teaching the Indians "bad customs," a theme that would be reiterated many times in other areas of Hispanic conquest. Carlos Larrazábal Blanco, *Los negros y la*

esclavitud en Santo Domingo (Santo Domingo: Julio D. Postigo e Hijos, 1967), chaps. 5 and 6; José Juan Arrom and Manuel A. García Arévalo, *Cimarrón* (Santo Domingo: Fundación García Arevalo, 1986).

12. Phillips, *Slavery from Roman Times*, 184–94. Herbert Klein and others argue that the Atlantic plantation economies fundamentally altered Spanish slavery, stripping the slave of many medieval peninsular protections. See Herbert S. Klein, *African Slavery in Latin America and the Caribbean* (New York: Oxford University Press, 1986), 16–20.

13. Alegría, *Juan Garrido*, 17, 20, 30.

14. One African, Mejías, was said to have died defending the Indian *cacica*, Luisa, an ally of the Spaniards. At his death he had 210 pesos in gold, although his annual ranch salary was only 50 pesos, so Mejías, too, may have been involved in gold mining. Services of Francisco Mexía [sic], Contaduría 1072, Archivo General de Indias, Seville, Spain (hereafter AGI), cited in Jalil Sued Badillo, *La mujer indígena y su sociedad* (Hato Rey, Puerto Rico: Editorial Cultural, 1989), 59. Royal decrees of 1511 permitted the importation into Hispaniola of Indians from non-gold-bearing islands and the enslavement of the Carib. Franklin J. Franco, *Los negros, los mulatos, y la nación Dominicana* (Santo Domingo: Ediciones INTEC, 1976), 13.

15. McAlister, *Spain and Portugal*, 153–54; Alegría, *Juan Garrido*, 20, 27–36.

16. Peter Gerhard, "A Black Conquistador in Mexico," *Hispanic American Historical Review* 58 (1978): 451–59; Alegría, *Juan Garrido*, 114, 116, 119, 127–38. After Ponce de León's death, Garrido enlisted with Hernando Cortés and participated in the bloody battle to conquer Tenochtitlán. Garrido's rewards were land and paid positions, including doorman of the Mexico City *cabildo* and caretaker of one of the city's aqueducts. He also took up gold mining as he had in Puerto Rico. Several codices depict Garrido at the side of his new patron, Cortés, whom he joined on one final adventure in search of black Amazons in what came to be California.

17. Eugene Lyon, *The Enterprise of Florida: Pedro Menéndez de Avilés and the Spanish Conquest of 1565–1568* (Gainesville: University Presses of Florida, 1974), 1–10.

18. Paul Hoffman, *A New Andalucía and a Way to the Orient: The American Southeast during the Sixteenth Century* (Baton Rouge: Louisiana State University Press, 1990), 73–79.

19. Jane Landers, "*Cimarrón* and Citizen: African Ethnicity, Corporate Identity, and the Evolution of Free Black Towns in the Spanish Circum-Caribbean," in *Slaves, Subjects, and Subversives: Blacks in Colonial Latin America*, ed. Jane G. Landers and Barry M. Robinson (Albuquerque: University of New Mexico Press, 2006), 111–45; Landers, "Leadership and Authority in Maroon Settlements in Spanish America and Brazil," in *Africa and the Americas: Interconnections during the Slave Trade*, ed. José C. Curto and Renée Soulodre-La France (Trenton, NJ: Africa World Press, 2005), 173–84.

20. Landers, *Black Society in Spanish Florida*, chap. 1; Matthew Restall, "Black Conquistadores: Armed Africans in Early Spanish America," *The Americas* 57 (2000): 171–205.

21. The Indians of west Texas came to regard Estevan as a shaman and gave him a sacred gourd rattle, which he carried to his death in the southwestern expedition of Hernando Coronado. See Enrique Pupo-Walker, ed., *Castaways, The Narrative of Alvar Núñez Cabeza de Vaca* (Berkeley: University of California Press, 1993), 51, 56, 64–66, 104–5, 100, 111, 127. Herbert E. Bolton, *Coronado, Knight of Pueblos and Plains* (Albuquerque: University of New Mexico Press, 1990), 10–16; 25–35. The Indians at Piachi later told De Soto that when

the Narváez expedition was skirting the coast in homemade boats somewhere between Pensacola and Mobile, an unnamed Negro came ashore for water and was killed. See Cabeza de Vaca, *The Journey of Alvar Núñez Cabeza de Vaca*, trans. Fanny Bandelier (New York: AMS Press, 1973), 38–40.

22. Charles Hudson, *Knights of Spain, Warriors of the Sun: Hernando de Soto and the South's Ancient Chiefdoms* (Athens: University of Georgia Press, 1997).

23. Edward Gaylord Bourne, ed., *Narratives of the Career of Hernando de Soto* (New York: A. S. Barnes, 1904), 72.

24. The De Soto expedition left a black slave named Robles at Coosa because he was too ill to walk. He was described as a "very fine Christian and a good slave" and the chief promised to personally nurse him back to health. The Indians later told Spaniards from the Tristán de Luna expedition of 1560 that Robles lived another eleven or twelve years among them before finally dying. Garcilaso de la Vega, *The Florida of the Inca*, trans. John Varner and Jeannette Varner (Austin: University of Texas Press, 1951), 347. In September 1540 another black slave, Johan Biscayan, was left behind at Ulibahali (near present-day Rome, Georgia). He may have been trying to escape because his master, Johan Lobillo, later went back without permission to try to find him. Chester B. DePratter, Charles M. Hudson, and Marvin T. Smith, "The Hernando de Soto Expedition," in *Alabama and the Borderlands from Prehistory to Statehood*, ed. R. Reid Badger and Lawrence A. Clayton (Tuscaloosa: University of Alabama Press, 1985), 118–19.

25. Ignacio Avellaneda, *Los sobrevivientes de la Florida: The Survivors of the De Soto Expedition* (Gainesville: University Presses of Florida, 1990), 34, 17, 29, 34, 47, 56, 63. It is unknown if Bernaldo, like other survivors, succumbed to the lure of Peru, returned to Spain as his former master did, or remained in Mexico, where Africans like Juan Garrido and others carved out modest but free lives for themselves. Another free African, Luis Moreno, accompanied one of the chroniclers of the De Soto expedition, Luis Hernández de Biedma. Spaniards Baltasar de Gallegos and Juan de Añasco also took African slaves to Florida with them, some of whom survived with Bernaldo. Other De Soto explorers of African descent included Alonso de Pereda, Pedro de la Torre, and Juan Martín. See Antonio de Solar y Taboada and José de Rújula y Ochotorna, *El adelantado Hernando de Soto* (Badajoz: Ediciones Arqueros, 1929), 293, 305, 333. Pike, *Aristocrats and Traders*, 189. On the prominence of Africans in early Peru see Frederick Bowser, *The African Slave in Colonial Peru: 1524–1650* (Stanford, CA: Stanford University Press, 1974).

26. *Memoir of Do. d'Escalante Fontaneda Respecting Florida. Written in Spain, about the Year 1575*, trans. Buckingham Smith (Coral Gables, FL: Glades House, 1944).

27. Juanillo was a captive of Chief Saturiba and served as a Florida linguist until taken to Puerto Plata, Hispaniola, in 1567. Lista de la gente de guerra, Contaduría 941, AGI, reproduced in Eugene Lyon, *Enterprise of Florida*, 186.

28. The Jesuit missionary Father Juan Rogel complained that he could not trust the interpretive skills of the black woman and mulatto Menéndez found among the Calusa, saying they knew little Castilian because they had lived among the Indians since they were children. Betraying his prejudice, he added that they were not very intelligent because of their race. Father Juan Rogel to Father Didacus Avellaneda, November 1566 to January 1577, cited in John H. Hann, ed., *Missions to the Calusa* (Gainesville: University of Florida Press, 1991), 281.

29. The Ays nation provided refuge again in 1603 for seven black slaves from St. Augustine. Five were later recaptured but two others were said to have married Indians and were never retrieved. Verne E. Chatelain, *The Defenses of Spanish Florida, 1565–1763* (Washington, DC: n.p., 1941), 128.

30. Henry Dobyns, *Their Number Become Thinned: Native American Population Dynamics in Eastern North America* (Knoxville: University of Tennessee Press in cooperation with the Newberry Library Center for the History of the American Indian, 1983).

31. Eugene Lyon, *Richer Than We Thought: The Material Culture of Sixteenth-Century St. Augustine* (St. Augustine, FL: St. Augustine Historical Society). In the following decades Florida's soldiers began to petition the Crown to have their back salaries be paid in slave licenses, and it is clear that less elite colonists also desired slaves, although more for their profit potential than for the status slave ownership implied. Alférez Alonso Ordoñez to the Crown, February 20, 1577. Three days later the Council of the Indies recommended the same plan to the king; but it could not have been responding so quickly to Ordoñez's request; there must have been previous requests. See "Council of the Indies to King Philip II, February 23, 1577," in *Colonial Records of Spanish Florida*, ed. Jeanette Thurber Connor (DeLand: Florida State Historical Society, 1930), 120.

32. Connor, *Colonial Records of Spanish Florida*, 138.

33. After another serious revolt was brutally suppressed in 1597, the Guale settlements along coastal South Carolina and Georgia went into a long period of decline, and survivors were gradually relocated to barrier islands. In an all too common scenario, the remnants of many different villages were "reduced" to mission sites where they could more readily supply the Spaniards with food and labor. See David Hurst Thomas, ed., *Columbian Consequences*, vol. 2: *Archaeological and Historical Perspectives on the Spanish Borderlands East* (Washington, DC: Smithsonian Institution Press, 1990), 357–526; Bonnie McEwan, ed., *The Spanish Missions of La Florida* (Gainesville: University Press of Florida, 1993), 1–34.

34. Amy Turner Bushnell, "The Menéndez Márquez Cattle Barony at La Chua and the Determinants of Economic Expansion in Seventeenth-Century Florida," *Florida Historical Quarterly* 56 (April 1978): 419; Bushnell, *Situado and Sabana: Spain's Support System for the Presidio and Mission Provinces of Florida*, American Museum of Natural History Anthropological Papers, no. 74 (Washington, DC: Smithsonian Institution Press, 1994).

35. The order suggested Havana provide thirty men of working age and six women to cook and care for the men in illness, and noted that Florida's entire *situado* would not suffice if wages had to be paid for the unceasing labor of the slaves. Translation by the author. The king to Sancho de Alquía, Captain General of Cuba, April 9, 1618, Santo Domingo 225 (hereafter cited as SD), AGI. Florida's governor complained in 1624 that this order still had not been carried out, and he repeated the request for slaves from Havana. The Council of the Indies reprimanded Cuba's captain general and again ordered him to comply. Don Luis de Rojas y Borja to the king, May 7, 1624, and Order of the Council of the Indies, May 9, 1624, SD 225, AGI. In the first half of the seventeenth century blacks made up 45 percent of the population of Cuba, so scarcity was not the problem. Isabelo Macías Domínguez, *Cuba en la primera mitad del siglo XVII* (Seville: Escuela de Estudios Hispano-Americanos, 1978), 34.

36. Ira Berlin, *Many Thousands Gone: The First Two Centuries of Slavery in North*

America (Cambridge, MA: Belknap Press of Harvard University Press, 1998). See also Landers, *Black Society in Spanish Florida*.

37. Another mulatto supervisor at the same ranch was Juan de la Cruz, and at least one ranch hand, Ambrosio, is identified as Angolan. "Documentation Pertaining to the Asile Farm," manuscript translated and annotated by John H. Hann, on file at the San Luis Archaeological and Historical Site, Tallahassee, 4–5, 67; Bonnie G. McEwan, "Hispanic Life on the Seventeenth-Century Florida Frontier," in *Spanish Missions of La Florida*, 295–321.

38. Bushnell, "Menéndez Márquez Cattle Barony," 407–31; Lolita Gutiérrez Brockington found that 60–80 percent of the permanent ranch hands on Hernando Cortés's cattle ranches were black and mulatto slaves. See Brockington, *The Leverage of Labor: Managing the Cortés Haciendas in Tehuantepec, 1588–1688* (Durham: Duke University Press, 1989), 126–58, 171–72.

39. John H. Hann, *Apalachee: The Land between the Rivers* (Gainesville: University Press of Florida, 1988; John H. Hann, *A History of the Timucua Indians and Missions* (Gainesville: University Press of Florida, 1996); John W. Worth, *The Struggle for the Georgia Coast: An Eighteenth-Century Spanish Retrospective on Guale and Mocama* (New York: American Museum of Natural History, 1995), 13–15, 51, 69–70, 86, 123–24.

40. Petition of Juan Márquez Cabrera, September 28, 1686, cited in Worth, *Struggle for the Georgia Coast*, 159; see also Luis Arana, "Military Manpower in Florida, 1670–1703," "The Men of the Florida Garrison," and "Military Organization in Florida, 1671–1702," all in *The Military and Militia in Colonial Spanish America, St. Augustine, Florida* (St. Augustine: Department of Military Affairs, Florida National Guard, n.d.).

41. The same year another epidemic decimated the Indian laborers. Bushnell, *Situado and Sabana*, 136–42; Luis Rafael Arana and Albert Manucy, *The Building of* the *Castillo de San Marcos* (New York: Eastern National Park & Monument Association for Castillo de San Marcos National Monument, 1977).

42. Landers, *Black Society in Spanish Florida*.

43. "Información hecha por Diego de Mazariegos sobre la toma de La Habana por Jacques de Sores, 1555," Patronato 267, AGI, cited in César García del Pino and Licia Melis Cappa, *Documentos para la historia colonial de Cuba: siglos XVI, XVII, XVIII, XIX* (La Habana: Editorial de Ciencias Sociales, 1988), 8–40. Blacks helped Spanish militias defend Havana in 1555, Puerto Rico in 1557, Cartagena in 1560 and 1572, and Santo Domingo in 1583. They also served as defense forces on plantations and ranches, as coastal sentinels, and as sailors on locally organized patrol boats throughout the Caribbean. Irene Aloha Wright, *The Early History of Cuba* (New York: Macmillan, 1916), 315.

44. Stephen Weber, "Las compañías de milicia y la defensa del istmo centroamericano en el siglo XVII: el alistamiento general de 1673," *Mesoamérica* 14 (December 1987): 511–28.

45. Herbert S. Klein, "The Colored Militia of Cuba, 1568–1868," *Caribbean Studies* 6 (July 1966): 17–27; Allan J. Kuethe, "The Status of the Free Pardo in the Disciplined Militia of New Granada," *Journal of Negro History* 56 (April 1971): 105–15.

46. Lyle N. McAlister, *The "Fuero Militar" in New Spain, 1764–1800* (Gainesville: University of Florida Press, 1957).

47. Roster of Black and Mulatto Militia for St. Augustine, September 20, 1683, SD 266, AGI.

48. Luis Arana, "Military Manpower in Florida, 1670-1703," in *The Military and Militia in Colonial Spanish America* (St. Augustine, FL: Department of Military Affairs, Florida National Guard, n.d.).

49. J. G. Dunlop, "William Dunlop's Mission to St. Augustine in 1688," *South Carolina Historical and Genealogical Magazine* 34 (1933): 1-30. Two of the thirteen captured slaves escaped the Spaniards and returned to their English masters. Verner W. Crane, *The Southern Frontier, 1670-1732* (New York: W. W. Norton, 1981), 31-33; Worth, *Struggle for the Georgia Coast*, 146-71; "Edward Randolph to the Board of Trade, March 16, 1699," in *Records of the British Public Record Office Relating to South Carolina, 1663-1782*, ed. A. S. Salley (Atlanta, GA: Historical Commission of South Carolina, 1928-47), 4:88-95.

50. "William Dunlop's Mission to St. Augustine."

51. Deposition of Mateo, September 27, 1686, cited in Worth, *Struggle for the Georgia Coast*, 154-56.

52. Royal officials to the king, March 3, 1699, cited in Irene Wright, "Dispatches of Spanish Officials Bearing on the Free Negro Settlement of Gracia Real de Santa Teresa de Mose," *Journal of Negro History* 9 (1924): 151-52.

53. "William Dunlop's Mission to St. Augustine."

54. Royal edict, November 7, 1693, SD 58-1-26, Stetson Collection (hereafter cited as SC), P. K. Yonge Library of Florida History, Gainesville, FL (hereafter cited as PKY).

55. Despite the royal decree of 1693, in 1697 Governor Laureano de Torres y Ayala returned six newly arrived blacks and an Indian "to avoid conflicts and ruptures between the two governments." Joseph de Zúñiga to the king, October 10, 1699, SD 844, microfilm reel 15, PKY.

56. Landers, *Black Society*, 25.

57. Report of Governor Robert Johnson, January 12, 1719, cited in H. Roy Merrens, ed., *The Colonial South Carolina Scene: Contemporary Views, 1697-1774* (Columbia: University of South Carolina Press, 1977), 57-66.

58. Peter H. Wood, *Black Majority: Negroes in Colonial Carolina from 1670 through the Stono Rebellion* (New York: Knopf, 1974), 127-30; Frank W. Klingberg, ed., *The Carolina Chronicle of Dr. Francis Le Jau, 1706-1717*, University of California Publications in History 53 (Berkeley: University of California Press, 1956), 60-137.

59. Encouraged by the English, the Yamasee had earlier harried Spanish missions all along the lower southern coasts of Georgia and Florida. John H. Hann, "St. Augustine's Fallout from the Yamasee War," *Florida Historical Quarterly* 68 (October 1989): 180-200.

60. The following year Carolina enacted a new and harsher slave code. Wood, *Black Majority*, 298-99, 304.

61. Memorial of the Fugitives, 1724, SD 844, microfilm reel 15, PKY.

62. One of the Spanish delegates was the royal accountant, Don Francisco Menéndez Márquez, who was probably already by then the owner of the man who would be his namesake and the future leader of Florida's first free black town. Manuel Serrano y Sanz, ed., *Documentos históricos de la Florida y la Luisiana, siglos XVI al XVII* (Madrid: Biblioteca de los Americanistas, 1912), 252-60.

63. Antonio de Benavides to the king, November 11, 1725, cited in Wright, "Dispatches," 164-66; Consulta by the Council of the Indies, April 12, 1731, cited in Wright, "Dispatches," 166-72.

64. Accord, June 27, 1730, SD 844, microfilm reel 15, PKY.

65. June 13, 1728, BPRO Trans., XII, 61–67, cited in Wood, *Black Majority*, 305.

66. Later English visitors to St. Augustine recognized four former slaves taken from a plantation near Port Royal in 1726. Arthur Middleton, June 13, 1728, BPRO Trans., XIII, 61–67 and John Pearson, October 20, 1727, BPRO Trans., XIX, 127–28, cited in Wood, *Black Majority*, 305.

67. Wood, *Black Majority*, 305. Six years later Governor Benavides advocated sending the runaways north to foment rebellion in Carolina and paying them for English scalps, but the Council of the Indies in Spain rejected this plan. Antonio de Benavides to the king, April 27, 1733, SD 833, AGI.

68. The Crown actually issued two separate edicts in 1733. The first, on October 4, 1733, forbade any future compensation to the British, reiterated the royal offer of freedom, and specifically prohibited the sale of fugitives to private citizens (no doubt in response to the auction of 1729). The second, on October 29, 1733, commended the blacks for their bravery against the British in 1728, but also stipulated that they would be required to complete four years of royal service as an indenture prior to being freed. Royal edict, October 4, 1733, SD 58-1-24, SC, PKY; Royal edict, October 29, 1733, SD 58-1-24, SC, PKY.

69. Memorial of the Fugitives, included in Manuel de Montiano to the king, March 3, 1738, SD 844, microfilm reel 15, PKY.

70. Jospo added that a "heathen" Yamasee, Mad Dog, had betrayed Menéndez and the other black allies and sold them back into slavery, but Jospo did not hold him responsible. Rather, he blamed the Spaniards who, as Christians, should have known better. Memorial of Chief Jospo, included in Manuel de Montiano to the king, March 3, 1738.

71. Montiano's financially strapped predecessors had satisfied government debts to important citizens by giving them incoming fugitives as slaves. These prominent citizens requested reimbursement for their losses, but Montiano ruled that they had ignored the royal determination expressed in repeated decrees and, therefore, all deals were null and void and all slaves were free. Petition of Diego Espinosa and reply by Manuel de Montiano, May 5, 1738, SD 845, microfilm reel 16, PKY.

72. King to Manuel de Montiano, July 15, 1741, AGI 58-1-25, SC 5943, PKY.

73. The town's name was a composite of the old Indian place-name Mose; Gracia Real, a phrase indicating that the town was established with the king's permission; and the name of the town's patron saint, Teresa of Avila, who was also the patroness of Spain.

74. Fort Mose Historical Society, "African American Community of Freedom," 2012, http://www.fortmose.org/; National Park Service, "Aboard the Underground Railroad: Fort Mose Site," http://www.nps.gov/nr/travel/underground/fl2.htm (all accessed August 6, 2013).

75. Historical Archaeology at the Florida Museum of Natural History, "Fort Mose: America's Black Colonial Fortress of Freedom," http://www.flmnh.ufl.edu/histarch/mose.htm; Fort Mose Historical Society, "African American Community of Freedom."

76. Manuel de Montiano to the king, September 16, 1740, SD 2658, AGI.

77. Fugitive Negroes of the English plantations to the king, June 10, 1738, SD 844, microfilm reel 15, PKY.

78. J. H. Easterby, ed., *Journal of the Commons House of Assembly, May 18, 1741–July 10, 1742* (Columbia: Historical Commission of South Carolina, 1951), 83.

79. "Journal of William Stephens," in *Colonial Records of the State of Georgia*, comp. Allen D. Candler, ed. Lucien L. Knight (Atlanta, GA: C. P. Byrd, 1904-16),vol. 4, 358; Manuel de Montiano to Juan Francisco de Güemes y Horcasitas, February 16, 1739, SD 845, microfilm reel 16, PKY; Montiano to Güemes y Horcasitas, August 31, 1738, and January 3, 1739, "Siege of St. Augustine," in *Collections of the Georgia Historical Society*, vol. 7, part 1 (Savannah: Georgia Historical Society 1909), 7:27; "Journal of William Stephens," vol. 4, 357.

80. Claim of Captain Caleb Davis, September 17, 1751, SD 2584, AGI; Easterby, *Journal of the Commons House of Assembly, Nov. 10, 1736-June 7, 1739*, 595-97. There is no evidence that Davis ever recouped his losses.

81. Some of these men were "Cattel-hunters" belonging to Captain Macpherson, whose horses they stole. These men would have had opportunity to know the terrain. Although a large posse failed to recapture them, Indian allies of the English did kill one slave. "Account of the Negroe Insurrection," pp. 232-33, cited in Wood, *Black Majority*, 310-11.

82. Lt. Gov. Bull to the Duke of Newcastle, May 1739, BPRO Trans., XX, 40-41, cited in Wood, *Black Majority*, 311-12. Also see "Representation of President William Bull, May 25, 1739," in *Calendar of State Papers, Colonial Series, America and West Indies*, ed. K. G. Davies (London: Great Britain Public Record Office, 1969), 44:243-45.

83. Easterby, *Journal of the Commons House of Assembly, Nov. 10, 1736-June 7, 1739*, 680-81.

84. Manuel de Montiano to Juan Francisco de Güemes y Horcasitas, August 19, 1739, *Collections of the Georgia Historical Society*, 7:32.

85. Easterby, *Journal of the Commons House of Assembly, September 12, 1739-May 10, 1740*, 63-67. The most complete analysis of Stono is offered by Peter H. Wood in *Black Majority*. Also see Mark M. Smith, *Documenting and Interpreting a Southern Slave Revolt* (Columbia: University of South Carolina Press, 2005).

86. John K. Thornton, "African Dimensions of the Stono Rebellion," *American Historical Review* 96, no. 4 (1991): 1101-13. Thornton argues that the Stono rebels were probably not actually from Angola, but from the Kongo (which traders generically referred to as the Angola Coast). For more on Kongo war techniques see John K. Thornton, "African Soldiers in the Haitian Revolution," *Journal of Caribbean History* 25 (1991): 58-80.

87. "Extract of a Letter from South Carolina Dated October 2," *Gentleman's Magazine* (London), n.s. 10 (1740): 127-29, in *American Negro Slavery: A Documentary History*, ed. Michael Mullin (Columbia: University of South Carolina Press, 1976), 84-87.

88. Wood, *Black Majority*, 326; "Journal of William Stephens," 402-3.

89. Jane Landers, "The Atlantic Travels of Francisco Menéndez and His Free Black 'Subjects,'" in *Biography and the Black Atlantic*, ed. Lisa A. Lindsay and John Wood Sweet (Philadelphia: University of Pennsylvania Press, 2013).

90. Lathan A. Windley, comp., *Runaway Slave Advertisements: A Documentary History from the 1730s to 1790*, vol. 3 (Westport, CT: Greenwood Press, 1983). Also see Daniel E. Meaders, "South Carolina Fugitives as Viewed Through Local Colonial Newspapers with Emphasis on Runaway Notices, 1732-1801," *Journal of Negro History* 60 (April 1975): 288-317; Philip D. Morgan, "Colonial South Carolina Runaways: Their Significance for Slave Culture," *Slavery and Abolition* 6 (December 1985): 57-78.

91. Jane Landers, "An Eighteenth-Century Community in Exile: The Floridanos of Cuba," *New West Indian Guide* 70, nos. 1-2 (1996): 12-24.

6

The Experience of a Loss

Spain, Florida, and the United States (1783–1833)

CARMEN DE LA GUARDIA HERRERO

The borders of the Spanish Empire in North America were extremely difficult territories for the Catholic monarchy to govern. Regarded as the furthest limits of Spain's empire, these areas attracted more strategic than economic interest during the seventeenth and eighteenth centuries. From 1783 on, however, when the second period of Spanish control of the Floridas began, radical changes were implemented in the way these territories were both conceived and administered. In this paper, we focus on the second Spanish period in Florida and analyze the complex relations between Spain and the United States, as a way of coming to an understanding of the reasons for the Spanish loss of Florida.

"By Force of Arms"

The presence of Spain in Florida, and the way this presence was reflected in Spanish public opinion, was affected to a great extent by the vicissitudes of Spanish and American politics between 1783 and 1819. Broadly speaking, we can distinguish three different phases, which also corresponded to distinct perceptions of the Floridas in Spanish culture.

In the first phase—from 1783 to the fall of the Spanish secretary of state, the Count of Floridablanca, in 1792—Spanish actions in Florida were well planned and seemed feasible to implement. In political and also popular culture, the Floridas were an integral and important part of the Spanish Empire. From 1792 until the French occupied the Iberian Peninsula in 1808, however, Spanish policy was erratic and the position of the United States in North America began to be more clearly defined. The amount of information about the Floridas reaching Spanish public opinion gradually dwindled. In the third phase, from 1808 to the final loss of the Floridas in 1819, confusion and change were the norm. The United States could and did take advantage of the political chaos in Europe and started to occupy various enclaves in the Floridas. Spain was divided, at war, facing independence movements, subject to strict censorship imposed by an absolutist monarch, and conscious that Florida was losing its place in the cultural imaginary of the nation.

With a feeling close to euphoria, Spain welcomed the recovery of the Floridas, of other enclaves in South America, and of Menorca, as ratified by the Treaty of Paris in 1783. The Spanish secretary of state, the Count of Floridablanca, wrote to his king, Charles III, "Spain has not been granted such an advantageous concession in a peace treaty for more than two centuries."[1]

Spain did not appear to be concerned by the fact that the wording of the treaty did not clearly define the borders of Florida. This ambiguity, though, sowed the seeds for subsequent difficult relations between Spain and the United States in North America. From 1783 on there was significant disagreement between Spain and the former English colonies about the limits of the Floridas. The United States claimed the border was the 31st parallel—first on the grounds of a secret clause contained in the preliminary treaty between England and the United States signed in 1782 and later by the definitive treaty between the two countries concluded in 1783—whereas Spain considered that it was the 32nd parallel and that the Floridas extended as far as the Mississippi River. These early disagreements did not seem to concern His Catholic Majesty. The United States was not deemed a rival worthy of serious consideration.[2]

The Count of Floridablanca wrote, "The whole basis of the United States' [claim] . . . is taken from their treaty with England, where they agreed on the freedom of navigation of the Mississippi and arbitrarily determined the limits of the Floridas, but . . . it was then under the control of my arms, by right of conquest."[3] This was the first time in the eighteenth century that the argument of the Spanish right to the Floridas by conquest was employed. This traditional justification, a product of the diplomatic practices of the ancien régime, was one of the major difficulties in the negotiations between Spain and the republic of the United States, which, with good reason, had risen up against England under the banner of natural rights, rather than the traditional rights that had kept them bound to the mother country.

The importance Spain accorded to the recovered Floridas was reflected in its political cultural consciousness. In 1783, the territory of the Floridas appeared essential to the Spanish defense strategy.[4] In his various political memoirs the Count of Floridablanca explained the great advantages that possession of the Floridas meant for Spanish policy at the end of the eighteenth century. In *Su instrucción reservada* (1787), he devoted various points to "the two Floridas" and to Spain's complex relationship with the United States.[5] His *Memorial presentado al rey Carlos III y repetido a Carlos IV, renunciando a su ministerio* also devoted considerable space to the recovery of the Floridas in 1783 and their strategic and political importance for the Spanish Empire.[6] In addition, the subject of the Floridas formed a common thread in his political correspondence, where he issued instructions for how Spain had to act if its objectives with respect to the new and former Florida possessions were to be achieved.

Floridablanca wanted the Floridas both to help curtail American expansionism and to retain exclusive control of the Gulf of Mexico as the only means of keeping the United States and other powers away from the heart of the Spanish Empire, the viceroyalty of New Spain.[7] To contain the Americans in their persistent advance across North America, Floridablanca advocated creating a human buffer consisting of settlers loyal to His Catholic Majesty, as well as making pacts with the indigenous populations who lived on the borders of the empire.

However, despite the fact that Spain's interest in Florida was clearly evident between the years 1783 and 1792 and the policies designed to achieve her objectives were sound, their application was not possible. Although the officials who had spent years working on the Spanish frontier realized the dangers posed by incipient American expansionism and the change of regime in the United States from a confederation to a federation, the same was not true of the various Spanish ambassadors sent to North America.

After Counts Floridablanca and Aranda left the Secretary of State's office, neither their successors nor other diplomats were capable of comprehending the new values and the new American political system, and they failed to gauge the danger it posed for Spanish interests in the Americas. At the end of the eighteenth century, Spain remained wedded to the political values of the ancien régime. Although enlightened reforms brought rationalization to the imperial system, the justifications for Spain's policies were always replete with references to tradition and the past. In its early relations with the United States, the Catholic monarchy could never understand the republican values that imbued this young nation. Likewise, for the United States, the arguments and values put forward by the old Catholic European power were never considered valid or worthy.

Diego Gardoqui (1735–1798), the first Spanish chargé d'affaires in the United States, was a prime case in point.[8] Both his diplomatic practices and his perception of what was happening in the United States had a lot to do with the traditional values of the Spain of the ancien régime. Gardoqui was well acquainted with the former English colonies, since his family business, Gardoqui and Sons, had traded with them for years. Furthermore, Don Diego had dealt with many of the North American revolutionaries before he arrived in New York.[9]

In September 1784, when Floridablanca sent him to the United States to represent Spanish interests, Gardoqui epitomized the values of the ancien régime. When he found out that John Jay, whom he had met in Madrid, was the politician assigned to negotiate with him, Gardoqui proposed a strategy to Floridablanca to achieve Spain's diplomatic objectives: "the American Jay . . . demonstrates, through my continuous dealings with him, that he is a man motivated by interest, and that this passion is increased by his wife. Because . . . he likes her to be fussed over and even more for her to be plied with gifts. This woman, whom he loves blindly, dominates him and nothing is done without her knowledge, so that her decision is final . . . from which I conclude that with a little bit of guile in dealing with her and a few timely gifts, the friendship of both of them will be obtained."[10]

That Floridablanca valued the opinion of his new chargé d'affaires was obvious because the latter's sketch of John Jay, and particularly of his wife, Sarah Jay, led to the endowment of a special fund for "entertainment and gifts" for North American politicians and their families. In addition to the means by which his objectives were to be realized—through gifts (and bribes?)—Gardoqui received clear instructions from the Spanish secretary of state containing the principles of his mission. He was to negotiate a treaty between Spain and the United States to establish "the limits of our respective possessions" and to deprive the republic of navigation rights on the Mississippi. In exchange, Spain would offer the economic privileges proper to a "most favored nation."[11] It did not escape Spain's notice that the offer of a treaty would create disunity among the confederation of states. It was obvious that if the United States agreed to become party to a treaty, the mercantile states could increase their trade with Spain and her colonies, which would be attractive to them. Closing the Mississippi, however, effectively cut off the western and southern states. Thus discord was ensured.[12]

The diplomatic talks between Jay and Gardoqui were slow and difficult. The domestic situation in the United States appeared, in theory, to favor the ambitions of the European powers. The Continental Congress had sparse powers and the way it functioned was slow and complicated. The weakness of the United States against the diplomacy of the European powers was obvious to everyone. During the Jay-Gardoqui negotiations, this difficulty was clearly expressed in the offices with their respective authorities. Although this fragility was the reason why some members of the confederation, among them John Jay, were ready to give way and sign a treaty with Spain that would be difficult for all the states to accept, it was in the end also the reason why a treaty with the Bourbon power could not be concluded.

On August 3, 1786, Jay appeared before Congress to argue the need for the United States to give way and finalize a treaty with Spain to establish the limits of the Floridas, the conditions of trade between the two nations, and a resolution about navigation on the Mississippi. This, according to the secretary for foreign affairs, would have greater validity "than any they have formed or can form with any other nation. I am led to entertain this opinion from the influence which Spain may and will have both on our politics and in our commerce." For Jay, the articles that Spain was disposed to include would to some extent benefit the United States. "Most favored nation" status would considerably increase North American trade in Europe and Spanish America, and furthermore Spain committed herself to payment in kind, which would increase liquidity in the United States. The only disadvantages, according to Jay, were that Spain still refused free navigation of the Mississippi River and would not accede to the territorial pretensions of the United States. The Floridas would therefore maintain the borders established by Spain after 1783. Although these were two key points for the United States when the talks started, John Jay thought it necessary to give way. His arguments were various. Insisting that the Spanish were adamant on these sections of the treaty, he thought that the depopulation of the West would make navigating the great river unnecessary for another fifteen or twenty years. His proposal was clear: Without denying the right of the United States to free navigation of the Mississippi a clause could be inserted in the treaty requiring it to be reviewed once these years had passed, and in the meantime, the United States could concede the Spanish demand to close the lower reaches of the river to the North Americans. He firmly believed that if the United States pressed its claims, war with the Bourbon power was inevitable. His clearest argument for giving way to Spanish demands, though, was the political situation in the United States in 1786. John Jay stressed to Congress that the United States should be flexible

> at least until the American nation shall become more really and truly a nation than it is at present. For, *unblessed with an efficient government*, destitute of funds, and without public credit at home or abroad,

we should be obliged to wait in patience for better days, or plunge into an unpopular and dangerous war with very little prospect of terminating it by a peace either advantageous or glorious . . . the situation of the United States appears to me to be seriously delicate, and to call for the greatest circumspection in our conduct, both at home and abroad; nor, in my opinion, will this cease to be the case until a vigorous national government be formed, and public credit and confidence established.[13]

On August 10, Congress asked Jay to gather information from his archives about the exact limits that Spain demanded. Jay's reply to Congress on August 17, 1786, was ambiguous: "It is well known that Spain claims the two Floridas and contends that West Florida extends higher up the river Mississippi than is admitted by our Treaty with Britain, but how much higher *exactly* your Secretary is uninformed."[14]

If Jay considered that the weakness of the United States justified concessions in the treaty negotiation with Spain, the position of the Spanish representative was different. Diego Gardoqui believed that the political and economic difficulties of the new nation made it not easier to negotiate, but rather impossible to conclude a treaty. "The present state of Congress, whose authority has visibly declined through the absence of executive power, is an impediment to my assignment, and makes it open to suspicion, since not being able to rely on the energy of that body [the Congress] makes for less trust when working," wrote a demoralized Gardoqui to Floridablanca to justify the slowness of the negotiations, "because if one tries, one may reveal oneself without being certain of it turning out to be beneficial . . . every State is suspicious of its neighbor, is variable in its maxims, divided into internal parties and has no public or private credibility."[15] The Spanish chargé d'affaires seemed taken aback. He had used the established tricks of European diplomacy but the new American political system appeared to be beyond his grasp. The decision-making process in the United States was very strange to a representative of an absolute monarchy, as Spain was.[16]

The dispute in the American Congress between those parties ready to make concessions (the majority representing states in the North and East with clear commercial interests in Europe and the Americas) and those who were not (congressmen from states in the West and South that demanded navigation of the Mississippi) became increasingly heated. "The complex circumstances of this whole business disturbs me and keeps me awake many nights," Gardoqui wrote to Floridablanca. "The thought that if I were to receive His Majesty's orders, as I expect to shortly, to conclude the Treaty, and were to break down Jay further . . . there is still the concern that the Confederation may change this summer, and what we have agreed will not take place."[17]

The American historian Walter LaFeber wrote "nothing contributed more directly to the calling of the 1787 Constitutional Convention than did the spreading belief that under the Articles of Confederation Congress could not effectively and safely conduct foreign policy."[18] And indeed, the first call for reforming the Articles of Confederation was made at the Annapolis Convention of 1786 during the debate between Jay and the Congress over signing a treaty with Spain. The representatives were convened to reflect on the dire situation of North American trade due to the lack of treaties with other nations. The delegates were firmly resolved to meet again to amend the Articles of Confederation. In 1787, at the Constitutional Convention in Philadelphia, the reason there was little debate about diplomatic affairs was because of an overwhelming consensus that the mechanism ought to be changed. Almost everybody agreed that it was necessary to create a common government strong enough to be able to conduct international relations and be respected by other nations.[19] The new political model designed at the Constitutional Convention of 1787 established this. On October 17, 1788, John Jay informed Gardoqui that Congress was transferring all the reports about the signing of a treaty between Spain and the United States to the new federal government. Jay wrote to the Spanish minister: "the dispositions of His Catholic Majesty . . . will leave no presence for misrepresentations to the peculiar situation of our national government and not to any desire or disposition to postpone a business which is in the interest of both parties."[20]

His Catholic Majesty, however, greatly influenced by Gardoqui's perception of the political future of the United States, was convinced that the American nation did not pose any danger to Spain's possessions or policies in North America because the United States was immersed in insurmountable problems. It was an interpretation which, at the very least, underestimated the threat to the territorial interests of the Catholic monarchy in the Americas and the potential that the States represented once they became a federal republic.

When Gardoqui left New York in the summer of 1789 without having concluded a treaty and convinced that a difficult future awaited the United States, everyone at the court in Madrid believed his assessment. Floridablanca was so convinced of an American debacle that he did not even name a successor to Gardoqui. The ambassador's assistants, José de Jaúdenes y Nebot and Juan Ignacio de Viar, remained in the United States in charge of Spanish affairs.

Federation and Empires (1792–1808)

The political transformation of the United States from a confederation to a federation coincided with major political changes in various European countries that would alter the course of international relations. The United States was already poised to take advantage of events. From 1792 onwards, national and international problems caused Spain to neglect her policy in the Americas to a certain extent and, because the Floridas were situated on the frontier between the United States and the European empires, they underwent significant territorial and political changes.[21]

The death of Charles III in 1788 and the accession to power of the incompetent King Charles IV (1788–1808)—and from 1792 that of his favorite Manuel Godoy—together with the eruption of the French Revolution in 1789 brought about important changes in the alliances that had prevailed in Europe for a large part of the eighteenth century. Furthermore, in 1792, shortly after Charles IV ascended to the throne, the Count of Floridablanca was dismissed from his post as Spanish secretary of state, accused of disloyalty. His successor, the Count of Aranda, did not last long either. With the removal of politicians who had dominated the reign of Charles III, a particular way of doing politics in Spain came to an end. Neither Charles IV nor his favorite Manuel Godoy had the skills and political vision of their predecessors; in the ancien régime in Spain where the king had all the power, this reduced competence was critical.[22]

These changes in Spain's internal politics were accompanied by serious difficulties on the international stage. The outbreak of the French Revolution had a profound effect on European power relations. Throughout the eighteenth century, Spain had been France's greatest ally, and the Bourbon dynasties in the two nations had led to the Family Compact and a common foreign policy. Following the French Revolution, however, the Spanish international policy of close relations with France was no longer viable, especially after the execution of the Bourbon King Louis XVI in France in 1793. Spain and France soon became enemies.[23] In 1793, Spain joined England in opposing revolutionary France. The then U.S. secretary of state, John Quincy Adams, wrote to John Adams "as the citizens of a nation at a vast distance from the continent of Europe; of a nation whose happiness consists in a real independence, disconnected from all European interests and European politics, it is our duty to remain, the peaceable and silent, though sorrowful spectators of the sanguinary scene."[24] That neutrality with regard to the serious problems in Europe would bring material progress to the United States and the territorial growth that they desired.

The ceasing of armed conflict between England and Spain and the political rapprochement between the two nations put a stop to American expansionist plans, although the seeds of expansionism had now been sown. The United States would not cease in its endeavors until it had achieved a suitable treaty with prospects for territorial and political expansion. In 1792, Americans William Carmichael and the young William Short, chargé d'affaires in Paris, were appointed commissioners to sign a treaty with Spain. Their instructions, dated March 18, 1792, stated that they should ask Spain for the 31st parallel as the boundary, the free navigation of the Mississippi, and a port of deposit near the mouth of the river.[25]

Nevertheless, Spanish authorities' perception of the United States had not changed. In 1793, Spain's expert on U.S. affairs, Diego Gardoqui, now in Madrid, reiterated his view of the political situation in the United States. Short and Carmichael wrote to Jefferson from Madrid about Spain's negative impression of the federal republic and the difficulty this posed for negotiations: "he still sees them [the States] divided among themselves and without efficient government."[26]

An unexpected event coupled with the lack of skill of the then Prime Minister Manuel Godoy precipitated the negotiations, however. The news that John Jay had been sent to London to sign a treaty on behalf of the United States alarmed Godoy. An alliance between two nations with strong territorial presences in North America was obviously dangerous for Spanish interests in the Americas. The Spanish prime minister thought that the only way to stop England and her powerful navy would be to seek closer relations with the United States. Spain was now ready to negotiate a treaty and give ground. The United States—still not realizing how easy it would be to negotiate with Spain now that its ministers were seeking friendship—appointed a new ambassador to Madrid, Thomas Pinckney, to endow the enterprise with a greater air of gravity. In fact, the signing of the Jay Treaty between the United States and England in 1794 had increased the Spanish ministers' concern.[27] The article in the treaty where Britain recognized, as it had done in 1782, the right of the United States to navigate on the Mississippi was to Godoy a sign that the two nations were prepared to defend their presence on the great river jointly and with determination.[28]

While negotiations between Spain and the United States continued in Madrid, other significant changes took place in international alliances. The

Anglo-Spanish alliance came to an end in 1795. Spain, with the Peace of Basel, put an end to the War of the Convention and "betrayed" Britain by returning to its alliance with France (San Ildefonso, August 18, 1796). Though consistent with Spanish tradition in international relations, this meant that Spain now had to deal with the great power that Britain had become. Despite everything, the people of Madrid were delighted and took to the streets in jubilation. Charles IV bestowed a new title on his favorite: Manuel Godoy, Prince of the Peace.[29]

Spain's return to her policy of the old alliance with France also gave impetus to finalizing the treaty with the United States. Godoy and his aides argued that Spain needed a friendly nation in North America to contain likely British aggression. Once friendship between Britain and Spain had been broken off, nothing would prevent Britain's penetration through Mexico and the Antilles in search of markets and ports of exchange. Spain wanted to drive a wedge into the alliance signed by the two English-speaking countries—that is, the Jay Treaty—so as to move closer to, or at least neutralize, the United States.[30] William Short had already initiated negotiations when the new envoy, Thomas Pinckney, arrived in Madrid. In the Treaty of Friendship, Limits, and Navigation Between Spain and the United States, signed on October 27, 1795, in San Lorenzo de El Escorial, the Prince of the Peace not only conceded to the Americans the right to navigate on the Mississippi but also agreed to set the 31st parallel as the northern limit of Spanish possessions in America.[31] Moreover, it recognized the right of deposit in the port of New Orleans for citizens of the United States. Articles 15 and 16 granted freedom of trade and navigation between both countries, and listed licit merchandise and contraband. In the Treaty of San Lorenzo, or Pinckney's Treaty as the Treaty of Limits came to be known, Spain put an end to the well-designed and -negotiated policy of Charles III's reign.

Meanwhile, there was even more turmoil in Europe. Spain opted to maintain its alliance with France in spite of Napoleon coming to power in 1799. Napoleon despised the Bourbons, and Charles IV failed to see that the relationship between the two countries was not that of equals. Spain supported Napoleonic policy, but Napoleon did not protect the interests of a country that was now France's satellite. In 1800, the Second Treaty of San Ildefonso sealed the Franco-Spanish Alliance. In exchange, however, Spain had to return Louisiana, without establishing its limits, but also stipulated that Napoleon could not cede Louisiana to a third country. As a result of this treaty, Spain was obliged to follow Napoleon's policy of aggression not only in America but also in Europe, which set the scene for the Spanish navy being destroyed by Britain at the Battle of Trafalgar (1805).[32] The continuing confrontations between Spain and Britain further isolated Spanish America, and its northern limits in the Floridas, from the mother country. Lacking ships, with Britain dominating the Atlantic, and with the Americans trading with Spanish America, Spain was hard-pressed to maintain its presence in the New World.

Such important changes for the future of the Floridas were hardly mentioned in the Spanish press. Since the outbreak of the French Revolution, the Spanish monarchy had imposed strict censorship in both Spain and the Americas. In that year, 1789, the Count of Floridablanca banned all written propaganda from entering the country. He also ordered the inquisitor general to confiscate all books relating in any way to the American and French revolutions.[33] Fear of revolution and the processes of independence in the Americas colored everything. While repression was imposed on the peninsula and in the colonies, Spain's foreign policy continued to be erratic.

A crucial blow to the future of the Spanish presence in Florida was that after the retrocession of Louisiana to France, Napoleon broke his agreement with Spain and sold it to the United States on April 30, 1803. Because of his conflict with Britain, Napoleon was also in need of a rapprochement with the United States.[34] Spain declared, in accordance with the diplomatic principles in force, that the sale of Louisiana to the United States was illegal. Once more, in the turbulent world of the early nineteenth century, Spain failed to understand that legality was changing. "Great also was the violation of the pact of retrocession signed with Spain," Manuel Godoy wrote in his *Memorias*, "and low and contemptible the way it was violated, in the dark, treacherously ... to place dangerous neighbors on their borders."[35] The "dangerous neighbors" not only occupied Louisiana but went much farther. The United States contended that the Louisiana Purchase included most of West Florida.[36] Spain, with arguments based once again on their traditional rights—specifically the medieval Castilian right of conquest—claimed in turn that those territories had been conquered by Spain during the War of American Independence so they did not belong to Louisiana. In the treaties between Spain and France and between the latter and the United States, precise borders for Louisiana had never been fixed. After nearly forty years, the Spanish presence in Louisiana had come to an end.[37] Once again, Spanish interests in North America and in the heart of Mexico were teetering on the edge of collapse.

After the Treaty of San Lorenzo was signed in 1795, Spain finally sent a new ambassador to the United States. In 1796, Carlos Martínez de Irujo y Tacón (1763–1824) arrived in Philadelphia. He was a skillful diplomat and a cultured man. Deeply involved in American national politics, he despised the Federalists, especially President John Adams and Secretary of State Timothy Pickering, but he was a great friend of the Republicans.[38] After all, in 1798 he married Sally, the daughter of Thomas McKean, a signatory of the Declaration of Independence and the Articles of Confederation, governor of Pennsylvania, very close friend to Thomas Jefferson, and one of the most respected Republican politicians. Irujo took part in various debates published in U.S. newspapers, particularly the *Philadelphia Aurora*, in which he always defended Spain against the territorial expansion of the United States.[39] He also engaged in an acrimonious dispute with the Federalist William Cobbett, whom Irujo took to court. His fierce clashes with U.S. politicians caused the Adams administration, in 1800, to request that Godoy remove him from his post. Irujo did not want to leave the United States, though, and his contacts with illustrious Republicans came to his rescue. When Thomas Jefferson became president, he asked the Spanish government to retain Irujo in the United States.[40]

The two friends, however, would soon come into conflict. Irujo heatedly protested the sale of Louisiana to the United States and also vehemently defended the position that the Floridas should be kept intact. The arguments of President Jefferson and Ambassador Irujo had been diametrically opposed to each other since 1802 and were quite irreconcilable. As mentioned, Spain considered that France had violated the terms of the second Treaty of San Ildefonso by ceding the territory "to a third party." Arguing from the standpoint of the values that sustained prerevolutionary international law, Irujo stood alone. His opinion carried no weight. As President Jefferson commented in the Senate, the cession "would secure the territory under conditions which would ensure the secure exercise of U.S. rights."[41] The president expressed again his conviction that the United States had the natural right to expand across American territory.[42] With their points of departure so far apart—the natural right of expansion on the American side versus the defense of values framed in terms of traditional rights on the Spanish—negotiation was very difficult. In 1807, Irujo left his post and Valentín de Foronda, who until then had been the Spanish consul in Philadelphia (1801–7), became chargé d'affaires (1807–9).

Spain's problems, however, continued to increase. Much more serious for the beleaguered nation was the confrontation between the Spanish king, Charles IV (1788–1808) and his son Ferdinand VII in Aranjuez, which aided Napoleon's plans for expansion. When Napoleon invaded the Iberian Peninsula in 1808 the Spanish royal family moved to Bayonne. Ferdinand VII, Prince of Asturias, forced his father Charles IV to abdicate. Napoleon subsequently removed Ferdinand from the Spanish throne and made his brother, Joseph Bonaparte, the new king of Spain.[43]

The Loss of the Floridas (1808–1819)

The last period of Spain's presence in the Floridas was distressingly bleak. The Spanish War of Independence, the attempts to turn the Catholic monarchy into a constitutional regime, and the return of absolutism with Ferdinand VII were disastrous for the Spanish Empire. At a time when Atlantic republicanism was spreading, instability and war in the mother country facilitated the breakup of the empire. In addition, the power the United States acquired in this period of European confrontation spurred the republic on to achieve its territorial ambitions.[44]

Whereas Mexico and almost all of Spain's South and Central American territories obtained their independence, the northern limits of the Spanish Empire suffered a different fate. The United States wanted the Floridas as an integral part of the federal republic, especially after its acquisition of the immense territories of Louisiana. If every loss from the empire was painful for Spain, the way in which Florida was lost—ceded to another nation—was especially so.

The occupation of the Iberian Peninsula by Napoleon's troops in 1807 provoked not only a civil war but also an international conflict. The two parties were, on one side, France and supporters of Napoleon and his brother inside Spain—referred to as the *afrancesados*—and on the other, the Spanish "patriots" aided by Britain (1808–14). Spain was divided. One faction, supported by Britain, was at war with Napoleon while simultaneously undergoing a process of revolution. The result was the proclamation of the Constitution of 1812, which was both monarchical and liberal. The other faction was dominated by Napoleon, who had placed his brother Joseph on the throne. Part of Spain and the entire Hispanic world reacted strongly against the French invasion of the Iberian Peninsula. Faced with a power vacuum, both Spain and the Americas reacted similarly by organizing revolutionary committees, juntas. All the juntas were coordinated by the Junta Central located in Seville and, from 1810, by the Consejo de Regencia and the Cortes situated in Cádiz. This government remained allied to Britain and in opposition to the French throughout the Napoleonic Wars.[45]

Although in 1808 all the American and Iberian juntas pledged allegiance to the Spanish Crown, each one felt a right to autonomy. As Sisinio Pérez Garzón reminds us, the Junta Central in Seville defended "a republican form of government," and the other Andalusian juntas very clearly formulated the same idea: "all representation, authority and power are concentrated in the juntas."[46] The spread of republicanism was, as Rafael Rojas points out, the reason for the decline of Hispanic colonial discourse. "The dominions that Spain possesses in the Indies are not really colonies or trading posts like those of other nations but an essential and integral part of the monarchy," the Junta Central declared on January 22, 1809, acknowledging the autonomy and equality of the juntas on both sides of the Atlantic.[47] In 1810, as a result of the republican tradition of their leaders, the advance of Napoleon's troops, and the distance from Spain, some of these juntas began to seek independence. The first were those of Buenos Aires (which acted as an independent government from May 25, 1810), Caracas (1811), and Chile (1811).

These processes of independence and the Napoleonic Wars increased instability in the two Floridas. Everybody knew that this was the ideal time for the United States to pursue its expansionist aims. "I suppose the conquest of Spain will soon force a delicate question on you as to the Floridas and Cuba which will offer themselves to you," the former president Thomas Jefferson wrote optimistically to his successor and friend, James Madison, in 1809. "Napoleon will certainly give his consent without difficulty to our receiving the Floridas, and with some difficulty possibly Cuba."[48] But it was not necessary to wait for Napoleon to hand them over. In March 1812 a group of "patriots"—seventy Georgians and nine Floridians—proclaimed the Republic of East Florida with the military support of the United States. By March 17 they had taken the port of Fernandina, a town of about six hundred inhabitants, on Amelia Island. They seized the area of Santa María and San Juan and laid siege to St. Augustine. They thought the crisis in East Florida would encourage residents to rise up and welcome the "patriots" as liberators, but matters did not turn out that way. Florida split. Some Floridians supported the rebels, but many remained loyal to the Spanish monarchy and its constitutional process. In June 1812, the new Spanish governor, Sebastián Kinderlán, persuaded the Seminole to join the war against the "patriots" and North Americans. The latter had to retreat to the San Juan River. In March 1813, President Madison ordered the U.S. forces to abandon East Florida.[49]

In West Florida, the dispute between Spain and the United States affected the region west of the Perdido River, which the United States had reclaimed after the Louisiana Purchase. In July 1810, a rebellion broke out in Baton Rouge and its inhabitants declared it an independent state. Its flag was blue with a solitary silver star. They requested to be admitted to the Union as a state. The United States ignored this request but did authorize the occupation of the region as part of Louisiana. Almost all of West Florida was taken. In 1812, the lands west of the Pearl River were annexed to the state of Louisiana and the area between the Pearl and Perdido Rivers was included in the Mississippi Territory.[50]

The War of 1812 between the United States and Britain was an appropriate moment for confrontations in the Floridas. The Spanish faction that was fighting Napoleon was an ally of Britain. Given that the United States and Great Britain were at war, it was logical to expect attacks from the Spanish Floridas. So the United States launched preemptive invasions, one after another, although Spain retained Pensacola until 1821.[51]

While these events were occurring, the constitutional process in Cádiz was sweeping across the Hispanic world. Those territories of the Floridas that were still bound to the Spanish monarchy were thoroughly caught up in the process of change. On March 19, 1812, the new Spanish constitution came into being. In its first article, the Constitution of Cádiz proclaimed that the "Spanish nation is the union of all Spaniards in the two hemispheres." This was a new and difficult concept because it meant the transformation of a huge empire into one nation. To claim that the entire monarchy was one nation implied that all its constituent territories should be represented in the Cortes, which neither Britain nor revolutionary France had attempted.[52] It was a difficult measure to carry out. All those who were now citizens—(Spanish) Americans, Filipinos, and Spaniards—were to be represented in a single assembly. In any case, the constitution itself provided a solution. Article 22 of the 1812 Constitution excluded from citizenship all those "who had some trace of African blood in their veins." Natives and members of other castes were also excluded.[53] The territory of the monarchy, according to the Constitution of Cádiz, was to be divided into provinces with councils responsible for the provincial government. Again, the inequality between Europe and the Americas was obvious: in many cases, the American provinces were much larger than Spain itself.

Once the new constitution was approved, Spanish officials, in the middle of the war with Napoleon and facing wars of independence as well as foreign occupation, decided to comply with the new mandates. So, in October 1812 the governors of the Floridas announced the proclamation of the new Spanish constitution and their citizens took an oath to support it. As M. C. Mirow wrote, the Constitution of Cádiz "may be legitimately recognized as Florida's first written Constitution."[54] East and West Florida under the Constitution of Cádiz lost their provincial status and became *partidos* (districts) within the province of Havana. The governors of the two Floridas became *jefes políticos*, still under the *jefe superior político* in Havana. An election had to be held to choose a Florida *elector provincial* representing Pensacola and St. Augustine in Havana. The elector then had to vote in the election of four deputies who would represent Cuba and Florida in the Spanish Cortes. In 1813, Fernando Arredondo, a citizen from St. Augustine, was elected to participate in the electoral junta in Havana. The Cuban Gonzalo Herrera was elected as the deputy to the Spanish Cortes representing Cuba and the two Floridas. Constitutional town councils were organized in accordance with the constitution. Gerónimo Álvarez, a shopkeeper, was elected as the first constitutional mayor of St. Augustine.[55]

On August 14, 1812, a decree from the Spanish Cortes required that all plazas where the constitution had been proclaimed be renamed Plazas de la Constitución, and that a plaque be placed there commemorating the text of the constitution. In St. Augustine, as in many corners of the former Spanish monarchy, a pyramid built to commemorate the adoption of the Spanish constitution still survives.[56]

Spanish officials and now Floridian citizens were loyal to the constitution, and the two Spanish diplomats posted to the United States, Valentín de Foronda and Luis de Onís y González-Vara, carried out their duties impeccably. Both were convinced that the United States would never be a great nation because the various states would be permanently at loggerheads. It was impossible for Spaniards who had grown up with the structures of the ancien régime to gauge the strength of American republicanism.

Valentín de Foronda had already been the Spanish consul general in the United States for many years when he was appointed interim ambassador after Martínez de Irujo left the post in 1807. He was an extremely cultured man who left us, among many other works, an excellent text on the United States, in which we discover that Foronda—a member of the Philosophical Society of Philadelphia who corresponded with and admired Jefferson—was incapable of assessing the difficulties that lay in store for Spain in the Floridas through the inexorable advance of the United States.[57] In his *Apuntes ligeros sobre los Estados Unidos de la América Septentrional* Foronda, like all his predecessors, dwells on the failure awaiting the republic of the United States. "In this Country, there are many disparate matters, many Democrats, many Federalists, and a multitude of Sects: the Volcano of a Revolution cannot take long, therefore, to produce an eruption that will cover this extensive Country in Ashes and blood," he mistakenly declared in his text.[58] Nonetheless, Valentín de Foronda very much enjoyed the freedom of the press in Philadelphia, publishing pamphlets and other writings in the American newspapers. Accused of being an *afrancesado* by the Spanish and the Spanish American colony in Philadelphia, Foronda returned to Spain in 1809, despite passionately defending his innocence.

That year, the junta sent a new minister, Luis de Onís, to the United States with a difficult mission: to maintain the Spanish Empire intact and deter the United States from intervening in favor of the Spanish American independence movements. Onís was one of Spain's most prestigious diplomats and also a loyal member of the Spanish patriot faction.[59] At this point, the Spanish did indeed become very concerned about the support the United States was giving to independence movements throughout the Americas. Don Luis arrived at the port of New York on October 4, 1809, "after a horrendous voyage of forty-four days."[60] From there, he went to present his credentials to President James Madison, but the United States refused to recognize an envoy of the Junta Central. As a neutral country, the United States did not side with either the *afrancesados* or the Cádiz revolutionaries. These were years of nonexistent official dialogue between the two nations. Even so, the Junta asked Onís to stay in the United States. Only after 1815— when Napoleon had been defeated, Ferdinand VII restored to the throne, and Onís handed his credentials by the U.S. government—can one speak of a return to normal diplomatic relations.[61]

The entire period of Luis de Onís's posting in the United States was difficult. The United States never ceased giving indirect assistance to the independence movements nor making territorial demands in Florida. Agents looking out for the interests of the United States were deployed throughout the former Spanish Empire, and expeditions paid for by the United States headed south into New Spain.[62]

Spain was exhausted. Having just emerged from a brutal war on the Iberian Peninsula, the country was now at war with Central and South American revolutionaries who demanded independence, and the U.S. pressure continued, not only in East and West Florida but also along the border of New Spain. In 1817–19, the U.S. Army made repeated incursions into Spanish territory, claiming that they wanted to stop the Seminole Indians from raiding Georgia and the Spanish from offering a haven for American slaves. One of these incursions during the 1817–18 campaign led by Andrew Jackson, was known as the First Seminole War. The time had come for Spain to abandon the Floridas.[63]

The Treaty of Amity, Settlement, and Limits between the United States of America and His Catholic Majesty, or Adams-Onís Treaty, signed in 1819, begins as follows: "The President of the United States has furnished . . . John Quincy Adams, Secretary of State of the said United States; and His Catholic

Majesty has appointed the Most Excellent Lord Don Luis de Onís, González, López y Vara, Lord of the Town of Rayaces, Perpetual Regidor of the corporation of the city of Salamanca, Knight Grand Cross of the Royal American Order of Isabella."[64] This opening aptly sums up the immense distance between the political cultures of the United States and Ferdinand VII's Spain. The American secretary of state was a citizen, the Spanish ambassador a prominent subject of the Catholic king. The arguments used in the debate were equally disparate: the Spanish ones were based on traditional rights, those of the United States on the concept of natural rights. These differences between the two nations were at the root of their disagreements and difficulties in understanding each other, as played out especially in the Florida scenario.

The Adams-Onís Treaty ceded the Floridas to the United States and established a boundary with the Spanish province of Mexico that clearly made Texas a part of Mexico, thus ending the boundary conflict existing since the Louisiana Purchase. Spain also ceded to the United States her claim to the Oregon Country.[65]

A Time of Silence

Once Spain lost its colonies in the Americas, there was a long silence in Spanish political and cultural life. Ferdinand VII and his ministers never assimilated the fact that the Americas had become independent. Consequently, they neither came to terms with any of the peace treaties their officials signed with representatives of the various independence movements, nor did they recognize the new nations. This was a very different position from that of Britain with regard to its former colonies. As soon as the American Revolution ended in 1782, Great Britain recognized the independence of the United States. But Ferdinand VII did not ratify the Adams-Onís Treaty until several years later. His aim was to postpone recognizing the inevitable: the process of independence of Spanish America and the new situation of Spain in Florida.

During the Constitutional Triennium (1820–23), after Rafael del Riego's uprising, the Spanish liberals forced King Ferdinand VII to respect the 1812 Constitution. A liberal period had begun, and small advances were made in acknowledging the new reality. First, liberal Spain had the king ratify the Adams-Onís Treaty in 1821. Moreover, after briefly hoping that the restoration of the 1812 Constitution would make the American "rebels" capitulate, the Spanish liberals discussed the need to recognize Spanish America's independence.[66] Commissioners were sent to the Americas to inform themselves about the situation and offer solutions. Texts recommending recognition of independence were published and committees created in the Cortes to "propose what was most conducive to bringing an end in the best possible way to the dissensions that unfortunately afflict several countries in America."[67]

President Monroe's announcement to the U.S. Congress in 1822 recognizing the independence of America's "sister" nations triggered a formal rebuke of the United States, as well as Spanish culture again closing its mind to the reality of the cessions and the independence process. With liberal Spain humiliated, the country adopted the old absolutist position of not recognizing the secessions. The Spanish ambassador Joaquín Anduaga wrote to President Monroe in Washington: "Where is the evidence that these provinces will not rejoin Spain when so many of their inhabitants want to, and where is the right of the United States to declare that a rebellion without cause is legitimate?" The Spanish ambassador could not understand the U.S. attitude. Spain had been so generous that "it had even ceded the Floridas," while the United States by comparison appeared to the Spanish ambassador to be an avaricious nation.[68]

The return to absolutism under Ferdinand VII in 1823 made relations between Spain and the former American territories even worse. The suppression of newspapers and establishment of rigid censorship on publications kept Spain insulated from what was happening in the American territories that had been ceded to the United States or had become independent. It was not until the death of King Ferdinand VII in 1833 that the Spanish Crown tried to establish some kind of normalcy with the former territories. It was, however, a long and difficult process, not only for the Floridas, but for all the Americas after so many years of conflict and silence.

Conclusion

Ferdinand VII's death in 1833 marked the beginning of a slow and tortuous path to modernity for Spain. Except for Cuba and Puerto Rico, the Catholic monarchy had lost all its American colonies between 1809 and 1824. Anchored in stagnant absolutism and submerged in turmoil at home and abroad, Spain was blind to the expansionist forces of the federal republic of the United States and the eruption of independence movements across the Americas. Up to 1789, Spanish policy had been clear-sighted and effective, but after that, Spain's policies and actions were at best erratic. Spain had lost almost all of Spanish America to independence, and although it had ceded the Floridas in 1819, the cession treaty was not ratified until 1821 during the brief period when the liberals were in power. Absolutist Spain's lack of perception of this loss was merely one more indication of its inability to understand a world in state of flux. Secrecy, silence, and denial were useless weapons employed by the last absolute Spanish king when faced with one of the most dramatic events in the history of Spain. If the loss of Florida and almost all Spanish America radically shifted the future of the Spanish nation, the lack of recognition of the new American republics, the delay in ratifying treaties, and the emphasis on diplomatic and political practices linked to the ancien régime were among the reasons for Spain's isolation and difficult process of modernization in the first decades of the nineteenth century.

Notes

1. Conde de Floridablanca, "Memorial presentado al rey Carlos III y repetido a Carlos IV renunciando el ministerio," in *Obras originales del conde de Floridablanca y escritos referentes a su persona*, ed. Antonio Ferrer del Río (Madrid: Atlas, 1952), 318.

2. Arthur Preston Whitaker, *The Spanish-American Frontier, 1783–1795: The Westward Movement and the Spanish Retreat in the Mississippi Valley*, 2nd ed. (Lincoln: University of Nebraska Press, 1969), 9–12. The author gratefully acknowledges financial support for this research from the Instituto Universitario de Investigación en Estudios Norteamericanos Benjamin Franklin.

3. Conde de Floridablanca, "Instrucción reservada que la Junta de Estado, creada formalmente por decreto de este día, 8 de julio de 1787, deberá observar en todos los puntos y ramos encargados a su conocimiento y examen" in *Obras originales del conde de Floridablanca*, 228.

4. C. Alcázar Molina, *Los hombres del Despotismo Ilustrado en España. El conde de Floridablanca: Su vida y su obra* (Murcia: Instituto de Estudios Históricos de la Universidad de Murcia, 1934); J. Hernández Franco, *La gestión política y el pensamiento reformista del conde de Floridablanca* (Murcia: Universidad de Murcia, 1984).

5. Conde de Floridablanca, "Instrucción reservada que la Junta de Estado," 226–28 (points XCIX, C, CI, CII, CIII).

6. "Memorial presentado al rey Carlos III" in *Obras originales del conde de Floridablanca*, 317–20.

7. Juan Bosco Amores Corredano, "La capitanía general de Cuba y la defensa de la Luisiana y Florida ante el expansionismo norteamericano (1783–1789)," in *Actas del VII congreso internacional de Historia de América*, vol. 2, ed. José A. Armillas Vicente (Zaragoza: Diputación General de Aragón, 1998), 2:787–97; Pablo Tornero Tinajero, *Relaciones de dependencia entre Florida y Estados Unidos (1783–1820)* (Madrid: Ministerio de Asuntos Exteriores, 1976); David Weber, *The Spanish Frontier in North America* (New Haven and London: Yale University Press, 1992), 271–301. Gene Allen Smith and Sylvia Hilton, eds., *Nexus of Empire: Negotiating Loyalty and Identity in the Revolutionary Borderlands, 1760s–1820s* (Gainesville: University Press of Florida, 2011), 9–36.

8. Eric Beerman, *El bilbaíno Diego de Gardoqui: el primer embajador de España en los Estados Unidos (1784–1789)* (Bilbao: Instituto Vasco de las Artes y las Letras, 1991);

Francisco de Ygartua Landecho, *Diego de Gardoqui. Primer embajador de España en los Estados Unidos de Norteamérica* (Bilbao: Editorial Vizcaína, 1964); María Jesús Cava y Begoña Cava, *Diego María de Gardoqui. Un bilbaíno en la diplomacia del siglo XVIII* (Bilbao: Bizkaia Kutxa, 1992); Natividad Rueda, *La compañía comercial de Gardoqui e hijos, 1760-1800* (Vitoria: Servicio de Publicaciones del Gobierno Vasco, 1992); Enrique Fernández y Fernández, "Esbozo biográfico de un Ministro Ilustrado. Diego de Gardoqui y Arriquíbar (1735-1798)," *Hispania* 172 (1989): 713-30. Reyes Calderón, *Empresarios españoles en el proceso de independencia norteamericana: la Casa Gardoqui e hijos de Bilbao* (Madrid: Unión Editorial, 2004).

9. Carmen de la Guardia, "Hacia la creación de la República Federal. España y los Estados Unidos: 1783-1789," *Revista Complutense de Historia de América* 27 (2001): 35-67.

10. Miguel Gómez del Campillo, *Relaciones diplomáticas entre España y los Estados Unidos, según los documentos del Archivo Histórico Nacional* (Madrid: Consejo Superior de Investigaciones Científicas, 1944), 1:LII. From here on all the translations are mine. Bemis, *Pinckney's Treaty: America's Advantage from Europe's Distress, 1783-1800* (New Haven, CT: Yale University Press, 1960), 62. About John Jay see Richard B. Morris, *John Jay: The Making of a Revolutionary, Unpublished Papers 1745-1780* (New York: Harper and Row, 1975); and idem, *John Jay: The Winning of the Peace, Unpublished Papers, 1780-1784* (New York: Harper and Row, 1980).

11. "Instrucciones dadas a Diego de Gardoqui, 2 de oct. de 1784, minuta," legajo 3885, expediente 21, Archivo Histórico Nacional, Madrid (hereafter AHN).

12. John Jay, "Record of the correspondence between the honorable John Jay Esqr. Secretary of the United States and Sr. Don Diego de Gardoqui, Encargado de Negocios of his C. M. relative to the negotiations of a treaty between the said U.S. and his said C. M. together with their respective powers to negotiate and sundry acts and Proceedings of Congress on the Subject of the said negotiation," Letterbook, May 21, 1785-Oct. 4, 1789, Rare Book and Manuscript Library, Columbia University.

13. Ibid., emphasis mine.

14. Ibid.

15. AHN Estado, legajo 3893 bis.

16. "Instrucciones a don Diego Gardoqui," AHN Estado, leg. 3893, bis.

17. Ibid.

18. Walter LaFeber, "The Constitution and the United States Foreign Policy," *Journal of American History* 74 (1987): 697, as cited in B. Perkins, *The Cambridge History of American Foreign Relations*, vol. 1, *The Creation of a Republican Empire, 1776-1865* (New York: Cambridge University Press, 1995), 1:58. Fredrick W. Marks, *Independence on Trial: Foreign Affairs and the Making of the Constitution* (Baton Rouge: Louisiana State University Press, 1973).

19. Perkins, *Cambridge History of American Foreign Relations*, 1:58.

20. John Jay, Letterbook, May 21, 1785-Oct. 4, 1789. Rare Book and Manuscript Library, Columbia University.

21. José María Jover Zamora, *España en la política internacional. Siglos XVIII y XIX* (Madrid: Marcial Pons Historia, 1999).

22. Teofanes Egido López, *Carlos IV* (Madrid: Arlanza Ediciones, 2001); Enrique Martínez Ruiz, *La España de Carlos IV (1788-1808)* (Madrid: Arco Libros, 1999).

23. J. R. Aymes, *España y la Revolución francesa* (Barcelona: Crítica, 1989).

24. John Quincy Adams to John Adams, cited by Raymond Arthur Young, *La influencia de Godoy en el desarrollo de los Estados Unidos de América, a costa de Nueva España* (México, DF: Editorial Jus, 1968), 118.

25. French Ensor Chadwick, *The Relations of the United States and Spain* (New York: Russell and Russell, [1909] 1968), 36-37.

26. "Carmichael and Short to Secretary of State," in Chadwick, *Relations of the United States and Spain*, 36.

27. Samuel Flagg Bemis, *Jay's Treaty: A Study in Commerce and Diplomacy* (New Haven, CT: Yale University Press, 1965).

28. José A. Armillas Vicente, *El Mississippi frontera de España. España y Estados Unidos ante el Tratado de San Lorenzo* (Zaragoza: Institución Fernando el Católico-Universidad de Zaragoza, 1977); Arthur P. Whitaker, "Godoy's Knowledge of the Terms of Jay's Treaty," *American Historical Review* 34, no. 4 (1930): 804-10; Young, *Influencia de Godoy en el desarrollo*, 129.

29. Manuel Godoy, *Memorias*, Emilio La Parra and Isabel Larriera, eds. (Alicante: Publicaciones de la Universidad de Alicante, 2008); Emilio La Parra, *Manuel Godoy. La aventura del poder* (Barcelona: Tusquets, 2002).

30. Young, *Influencia de Godoy en el desarrollo*.

31. Arthur P. Whitaker, "New Light on the Treaty of San Lorenzo: An Essay in Historical Criticism," *Mississippi Valley Historical Review* 15, no. 4 (March 1929): 435-54.

32. Josep Fontana, *La época del liberalismo* (Barcelona: Crítica-Marcial Pons, 2007), 12-13.

33. Carlos Corona, *Revolución y reacción en el reinado de Carlos IV* (Madrid: Ediciones Rialp, 1957), 240-45; Richard Herr, *España y la revolución del siglo XVIII* (Madrid: Aguilar, 1988), 214-21.

34. Jerónimo Bécker, *Historia de las relaciones exteriores de España en el siglo XIX (Apuntes para una historia diplomática)* (Madrid: J. Ratés, 1924-26); Philip C. Brooks, "Spain's Farewell to Louisiana, 1803-1821," *Mississippi Valley Historical Review* 27, no. 1 (1940): 29-42; Arthur P. Whitaker, "The Retrocession of Louisiana in Spanish Policy," *American Historical Review* 39, no. 3 (1934): 454-76.

35. Godoy, *Memorias*, 894.

36. David Weber, *Spanish Frontier*, 291; Thomas Fleming, *The Louisiana Purchase* (Hoboken, NJ: John Wiley and Sons, 2003).

37. Paul E. Hoffman, *Luisiana* (Madrid: Mapfre, 1992), 297.

38. Gerald H. Clarfield, *Timothy Pickering and American Diplomacy, 1795-1800* (Columbia: University of Missouri Press, 1969).

39. Merle E. Simmons, *La revolución norteamericana en la independencia de Hispanoamérica* (Madrid: Mapfre, 1992).

40. Eric Beerman, "Spanish Envoy to the United States (1796-1809): Marques de Casa Irujo and His Philadelphia Wife Sally McKean," *The Americas* 37 (1981): 445-56.

41. Elizabeth Pugliesi, "International Law and the Louisiana Purchase Treaty," in *The Louisiana Purchase: A Historical and Geographical Encyclopedia* (Santa Barbara, CA: ABC-CLIO, 2002) 151-52.

42. Pugliesi, "International Law and the Louisiana Purchase Treaty," 151-52, 154-55.

43. Charles Esdaile, *La Guerra de Independencia: una nueva historia* (Barcelona: Crítica, 2003).

44. Manuel Fernández de Velasco, *Relaciones España–Estados Unidos y mutilaciones territoriales en Latinoamérica* (México, DF: Universidad Nacional Autónoma de México, 1982).

45. Miguel Artola, *Los afrancesados* (Madrid: Alianza, 2008). Jordi Canal and Manuel Chust, *España. Crisis imperial e independencia* (Madrid: Mapfre Taurus, 2010); Manuel Chust Calero, *1808. La eclosión juntera en el mundo hispano* (México: DCE–Colegio de México, 2007).

46. Sisinio Pérez Garzón, *Las Cortes de Cádiz. El nacimiento de la nación liberal (1808–1814)* (Madrid: Síntesis, 2007), 167–68.

47. Rafael Rojas, *Las repúblicas de aire. Utopía y desencanto en la revolución de Hispanoamérica* (Madrid: Taurus, 2009), 97.

48. Jefferson to Madison, April 19, 1809, in Thomas Jefferson, *The Works of Thomas Jefferson* (New York: Cosimo Books, 2009), 11:106.

49. J. C. A. Stagg, *Borderlines in Borderlands: James Madison and the Spanish American Frontier, 1776–1821* (New Haven and London: Yale University Press, 2009); James G. Cusick, *The Other War of 1812: The Patriot War and the American Invasion of Spanish East Florida* (Athens: University of Georgia Press, 2007); Rembert W. Patrick, *Florida Fiasco: Rampant Rebels on the Georgia-Florida Border, 1810–1815* (Athens: University of Georgia Press, 2010 [1954]).

50. Charles C. Griffin, *The United States and the Disruption of the Spanish Empire, 1810–1822* (New York: Octagon Books, 1974); Andrew F. McMichael, *Atlantic Loyalties: Americans in Spanish West Florida, 1785–1810* (Athens: University of Georgia Press, 2006); Isaac Joslin Cox, *The West Florida Controversy, 1798–1813: A Study in American Diplomacy* (Baltimore, MD: John Hopkins University Press, 1918).

51. Carlos M. Fernández Shaw, *Presencia española en los Estados Unidos* (Madrid: Ediciones de Cultura Hispánica, 1987), 260–68.

52. José María Portillo, *Crisis atlántica. Autonomía e independencia en la crisis de la Monarquía Hispánica* (Madrid: Fundación Carolina–Marcial Pons Historia, 2006).

53. Juan Francisco Fuentes Aragonés, "Las Cortes de Cádiz. Nación, soberanía y territorio," *Cuadernos de Historia Contemporánea* 32 (2010): 17. Miguel Artola, *Los orígenes de la España contemporánea* (Madrid: Centro de Estudios Políticos y Constitucionales, 2010).

54. M. C. Mirow, "The Constitution of Cádiz in Florida," *Florida Journal of International Law* 24, no. 2 (2012): 271–330.

55. Alejandro Quiroga Fernández de Soto, "Military Liberalism on the East Florida 'Frontier'": Implementation of the 1812 Constitution," *Florida Historical Quarterly* 79, no. 4 (2001): 441–68.

56. José Antonio Cubeñas Peluzzo, *Presencia española en la Florida desde el descubrimiento hasta el bicentenario* (Madrid: Ediciones de Cultura Hispánica, 1978), 53.

57. J. R. Spell, "An Illustrious Spaniard in Philadelphia, Valentin de Foronda," *Hispanic Review* 4, no. 2 (1936): 136–40.

58. José de Onís, "Valentin de Foronda's Memoir on the United States of North America, 1804," *The Americas* 4, no. 3 (1948): 351–87.

59. Fernández de Velasco, *Relaciones España–Estados Unidos*, 59–177.

60. Luis de Onís, *Memoria sobre las negociaciones entre España y los Estados Unidos de América que dieron lugar al tratado de 1819 con una noticia sobre la estadística de aquel país* (Madrid: Imprenta P. M. de Burgos, 1820).

61. Ibid., 2; Luis de Onís, *Observations on the Existing Differences between the Government of Spain and the United States* (Philadelphia: n.p., 1817). Fernández de Velasco, *Relaciones España–Estados Unidos*.

62. Jaime E. Rodríguez O., "The Emancipation of America," *American Historical Review* 105, no. 1 (2000): 131–52; Arthur P. Whitaker, *The United States and the Independence of Latin America (1800–1830)* (Baltimore, MD: Johns Hopkins University Press, 1941); Stagg, *Borderlines in Borderlands*, 131–32.

63. *Official correspondence between Don Luis de Onís minister from Spain to the United States of America and John Quincy Adams, Secretary of State in relation to The Floridas and the Boundaries of Louisiana with other matters in dispute between the two Governments* (London: Effichan Wilson, 1918).

64. *Tratado de Amistad, arreglo de diferencias y límites entre S. M. Católica y los Estados Unidos de América*, 1822, Available online from the Biblioteca Digital Hispánica of the Biblioteca Nacional de España at http://bdh-rd.bne.es/viewer.vm?id=0000123726&page=1.

65. Samuel Flagg Bemis, *John Quincy Adams and the Foundations of American Foreign Policy* (New York: Alfred A. Knopf, 1949); Philip Coolidge Brooks, *Diplomacy and the Borderlands: The Adams-Onís Treaty of 1819* (New York: Octagon Books, 1970).

66. Timothy E. Anna, *España y la independencia de América* (México: Fondo de Cultura Económica, 1986), 266. Melchor Fernández Almagro, *La emancipación de América y su reflejo en la conciencia española* (Madrid: Instituto de Estudios Políticos, 1944); Jaime Delgado, *La independencia de América en la prensa española* (Madrid: Seminario de Problemas Hispanoamericanos, 1949); Luis Miguel Enciso Recio, *La opinión pública española y la independencia de Hispanoamérica, 1819–1820* (Valladolid: Universidad de Valladolid, 1967); Emilio de la Cruz Hermosilla, *El periodismo y la emancipación de Hispanoamérica* (Cádiz: Quorum Editores, 1992).

67. Archivo del Congreso de Diputados (Madrid), legajo 22, no. 19, cited in Braz Augusto Aquino Brancato, "Las cortes españolas del 'trienio liberal' y la cuestión del reconocimiento de las independencias hispanoamericanas," *Anuario de Estudios Bolivarianos* 14 (2007): 41–55.

68. Archivo General de Indias, Estado, 90, cited by Anna, *España y la independencia*, 308; Jerónimo Bécker, *La independencia de América (su reconocimiento por España)* (Madrid: J. Ratés, 1922): 88–89.

II

POSTCOLONIAL AND CONTEMPORARY FLORIDA

Introduction

Florida in the Modern World

RACHEL A. MAY

Modern Hispanic Florida is often assumed to begin with the exodus of Cubans from the Island in the aftermath of Fidel Castro's revolution in 1959. Although the Cuban Revolution did substantially alter the demographic trajectory of Florida, the Hispanic history of Florida is much more profound and deeply rooted than this, as Gary Mormino reminds us in the volume introduction. Moreover, the modern, or "American," period of Florida does not begin neatly with a transition of power from Spain to the United States in 1821. Conflict and global intrigue marked this transition for decades. The "American period" begins before 1821, and Florida history continues to be marked by its Spanish past well into the twenty-first century.

Karen Racine's fascinating analysis of the Amelia Island controversy of 1817 illustrates the complicated geopolitical stage on which Florida's incorporation into the United States was achieved. As she eloquently explains, "the figures involved hailed from Spain, Cuba, Haiti, Puerto Rico, Colombia, Venezuela, Scotland, France, Italy, England, Upper Peru (now Bolivia), Río de la Plata (now Argentina), Mexico, and several U.S. states, including the Louisiana bayous. Coming as it did at the tail end of the Napoleonic Wars, as the Spanish Empire was entering its death throes and the United States and Great Britain were reaching an uneasy agreement over spheres of influence in North America and the Caribbean after the War of 1812, the Amelia Island affair encapsulates the entire spirit of the independence era in one fantastical, chimerical, inspiring, infuriating, and ultimately ambiguous action." This essay beautifully narrates the fascinating history of the little-known dispute that involved both government entities and rebel forces from Spain, Britain, the United States, Mexico, Spanish America, Cuba, and even Haiti. Racine argues that this conflict laid out the Atlantic dimensions of American revolutions. It also had an important role in shaping U.S. policy toward the region more than ten years before the Monroe Doctrine. Racine's account of this incident in fact sets the perfect context for all of modern Hispanic history in Florida, and places Florida's role as a modern transatlantic crossroads in perfect focus.

Richard L. Kagan's delightful essay about the Spanish craze in Florida at the turn of the twentieth century provides an important historical marker for the Hispanic heritage of Florida. At the end of the nineteenth century, so-called Spanish culture referred to both Spain and Spanish America. And Florida became a magnet for Spanish-influenced design and culture. And as such, Florida became the center of a trend toward a more multicultural understanding of American culture in the twentieth century. Kagan reminds us that "whatever the political differences between Spain and the United States, these were but superficial and temporary inasmuch as the culture, the language, and indeed the history of the two countries were deeply and profoundly intertwined. Much of this was pure invention, but it allowed Spanish style . . . to be understood as authentic, homegrown and thus quintessentially American."

Darién J. Davis paints a picture of pre-1959 Miami as a city already engaged in vibrant cultural and demographic exchange with Cuba, especially in the era between the end of World War II and 1958, when twenty thousand Cubans left the island for South Florida. These prerevolutionary Cubans joined an already vibrant Hispanic community in Miami (mostly Puerto Ricans) whose music and culture had already become popular among the general population by the middle of the twentieth century. He provides us with an original and textured analysis of the ways in which music and popular culture interacted with racial politics in the American South during the Jim Crow era (in the 1940s and 1950s), and how these complex cultural interactions influenced both migration patterns and the identities of Cubans and Cuban Americans in the twentieth century. He reminds us that before Fidel Castro marched triumphantly into Havana,

Cubans of many ethnic backgrounds had brought Afro-Cuban culture to Miami, despite the violent racism of the Jim Crow South. According to Davis, "the movement of Cuban culture across borders in the contentious period of the 1950s, despite the unequal treatment and movement of peoples, offers us insight into the history of Florida. It also highlights the importance of studying inequalities and cultural celebration to gain a greater understanding of the transmission of Afro-Caribbean cultural practices across national, ethnic, and racial divides."

Jorge Duany describes the changing face of contemporary Hispanic Florida in his essay on changing migration patterns—particularly of Puerto Rican immigrants—to Florida. He argues that new Hispanic immigration to Central Florida is quite distinct from earlier waves of Cubans who flocked to Miami in the 1960s and 1970s. The "Puerto Ricanization" of Florida reflects the trend toward diversification within the U.S. Latino population as a whole. Recent Puerto Rican immigrants into Florida, especially Central Florida, are both wealthier and more influential than their counterparts in previous generations. It remains to be seen how the more diverse "Latin" population in Florida will evolve, and exactly what influence it will have. But Duany does make it clear that this trend in Florida (and elsewhere) has enormous potential to transform this "minority" population economically, politically, and culturally.

Alex Stepick and Marcos Feldman make a compelling argument for the increasing importance of social class as a political category that has influenced the way we view race and ethnicity in Miami. Just as Duany describes the diversification of the Hispanic population of Florida, Stepick and Feldman note that the Hispanic population of metropolitan Miami has become increasingly diversified along the lines of class, race, and ethnicity. As the interests of wealthy white Anglos have merged with the interests of relatively wealthy (mostly white) Cubans, inequalities have increased between rich and poor and between white and nonwhite. The Hispanic population of Miami is increasingly diverse, and deeply rooted connections between people and place are becoming institutionalized in ways that are shaped by social class as much as or more than by race and ethnicity.

Susan Eckstein echoes the analysis of Stepick and Feldman in her examination of the shifting patterns of national political influence of

Florida's increasingly diverse Hispanic population. Eckstein argues that the influence of Miami's Cuban exile population has been most important during presidential election years, and that this influence is now waning as the ethnic and class identifications and political interests of Florida's Hispanics have become more complex and diverse. Eckstein concludes this volume by arguing that unless Cuban Americans embrace a more broadly "Hispanic" agenda, their influence will continue to diminish. She also notes that a younger generation of Cuban Americans from Florida already identifies with the larger Hispanic American community in Florida. They are in the best position to be politically influential in years to come.

This collection of essays provides a rich and fascinating depiction of modern Hispanic Florida. This is a history with surprising historical continuity. While the contributors to this volume hope to provide a profound and historically complex context within which to view Florida's Hispanic heritage, we also aspire to provide clear insight into how Hispanic Florida is evolving in the twenty-first century.

7

Fireworks over Fernandina
The Atlantic Dimension of the Amelia Island Episode, 1817

KAREN RACINE

For more than five years, a small swampy island near the Florida-Georgia border preoccupied the minds of politicians, pirates, and prospectors on three continents. Amelia Island, long ignored and left to its few residents, began to grow in significance during the complicated era of the Napoleonic Wars. It was a Spanish territory, but one with just as many English and Scottish residents, located at the southern frontier of the United States and acting as a gateway to the British Caribbean. French agents hoped to set up a Napoleonic confederation and eyed East Florida as a potential base for their machinations. Ultimately, though, it was Spanish American patriots' open attempt to set up an independent republic at Fernandina in 1817 that brought matters to a head and forced the rival governments to reveal the true depth of their ability (and perhaps more importantly, their willingness) to assert power in the Caribbean Basin area.

One could even argue that James Monroe's famous doctrine was shaped by his longstanding personal intervention and interest in East Florida during his time as secretary of state from 1811 to 1817. During that time, he repeatedly sought to undermine Spanish monarchical authority in the area, warned the British ambassador that he would brook no transfer of territory in the Floridas to another European power, and backed republican rebels who sought to spread the "American system" and bring the Floridas into their orbit. The fireworks these machinations generated were considerable and could be seen throughout the Atlantic world. The figures involved hailed from Spain, Cuba, Haiti, Puerto Rico, Colombia, Venezuela, Scotland, France, Italy, England, Upper Peru (now Bolivia), Río de la Plata (now Argentina), Mexico, and several U.S. states, including the Louisiana bayous.

Coming as it did at the tail end of the Napoleonic Wars, as the Spanish Empire was entering its death throes and the United States and Great Britain were reaching an uneasy agreement over spheres of influence in North America and the Caribbean after the War of 1812, the Amelia Island affair encapsulates the entire spirit of the independence era in one fantastical, chimerical, inspiring, infuriating, and ultimately ambiguous action.

To be sure, there had been conflicts and competition over the Floridas and the Gulf coast region dating back to the sixteenth century. Throughout the turbulent eighteenth century, and intensifying during the American Revolution, various European powers recognized the pivotal position that the Floridas would play in controlling access to resources, interior settlements, and exercise of political sovereignty in the region. As the French, British, Spanish, and eventually Americans variously invaded, seized, occupied, settled, traded, and exchanged control over portions of the territory, the Floridas themselves evolved into a distinctly creole space, one with a marked Atlantic quality in which political loyalties and personal friendships transcended boundaries of idiom, race, culture, or legal status. East Florida had been administered by the Spanish Crown through its agents in Cuba during the so-called First Spanish Period to 1763.[1] Nevertheless, its coastlines were regularly haunted by English, Scottish, Irish, French, Dutch, and a few Portuguese ships, along with other non-state-affiliated vessels of murky provenance. Many British-descended residents established powerful trading companies that remained even when political control was ceded to another country.[2]

Amelia Island itself is quite small, a little more than fifty square miles of flat terrain, lovely beaches, and marshy grasslands located along the continental shelf on the southernmost tip of the Carolina barrier islands.[3] It was originally identified by a French Huguenot, later claimed by Spanish governors based in the Caribbean, and eventually named for the daughter of Britain's King George II. Because of the concentration of missionary attention at nearby St. Augustine, and because it lacked obvious or easy riches to extract, Amelia Island was ignored for much of the colonial period. It did, however, become a way station for stray ships and smugglers, and periodic attempts were made to establish frontier mission-fortresses there in order to buttress claims to the territory. In 1686, Spain established a small fort called San Carlos, a move toward greater presence in the area that was tolerated only until 1702, when South Carolina governor James Moore, along with a motley assortment of British, Indian, and Caribbean troops, attacked and destroyed it.

For the rest of the century, East Florida bounced back and forth between the Atlantic powers. Spain held it for a time. Then, from 1763 to 1783, the British Crown took control and began to entrench its presence by offering generous land grants to settlers who would agree to go to the island.[4] In 1783, many of these Anglo families opted quite happily to remain where they were when Spain regained control of East Florida as part of the Atlantic powers' renegotiation of borders in the aftermath of the American Revolution.[5]

Tiny Amelia Island was not immune to the repercussions of the continental wars of the Napoleonic era. From 1806 to 1812, when the Americans' trade embargo was officially in force, smugglers used it as a depot from which to supply commercial goods, food, and war materiel to British fleets operating out of their Caribbean Islands.[6] Along with receiving valuable cargoes of wood, turpentine, cotton, rice, tar, and barrel staves, the ad hoc port also facilitated trade with at least nine slave ships that had come from Africa.[7] It seems the cosmopolitan and multiethnic residents of East Florida preferred to exist under a benign sort of autonomy within the Spanish imperial context rather than entertain any scheme to join the United States in some sort of formal union; it was better for business.[8] Andrew McMichael finds a similar "Atlantic loyalty" among residents of West Florida at the same time and notes a change only occurred in 1810 when a series of internal and external alignments caused the Anglo residents' calculation of benefits to shift and they declared independence from Spain (only to join the United States shortly afterward).[9] In East Florida, the town of Fernandina on Amelia Island was not officially established until 1811, but by then it had already reached a not-inconsiderable size of six hundred residents.

The Amelia Island episode of 1817 had its immediate roots in a previous attempt to revolutionize the region. During the fall of 1810, Washington politicians contemplated sending a mission to scout and potentially secure East Florida in the wake of the declaration of independence by English residents in Baton Rouge. General George Mathews, a Virginia planter and veteran of the Continental Army, was tapped to be its leader.[10] It was a localized scheme but one conceived clearly within an Atlantic context. On January 3, 1811, James Monroe took advantage of Spain's difficulties with its colonies-in-revolt to deliver a secret message to Congress in which he warned that the British had designs on the Floridas; because the Spanish government was incapable of dealing with that threat on top of its problems at home and throughout its tottering empire, Monroe asked for congressional approval to seek Spanish consent for the United States to occupy and defend the Floridas in its stead.

In fact, the request was part of a greater Atlantic vision. Monroe framed the issue in exactly the same terms he would use a decade later in the much more famous Monroe Doctrine. It was his determination, as set out in this note, that the United States could not tolerate any part of its neighborhood being transferred from Spain to the control of any other foreign power, by which Monroe meant, quite obviously, Great Britain. Monroe's not-so-gentle nudge worked and the skittish Congress, already operating in a climate of heightened tensions in the middle of the economic blockade, swiftly passed a joint resolution that included a secret act with a very cumbersome title: "An Act to enable the President of the United States, under certain contingencies, to take possession of the country lying east of the river Perdido, and south of the state of Georgia and the Mississippi territory, and for other purposes."[11] The act gave the president authorization to occupy the Floridas with the consent of the residents in order to protect their lives, liberty, and property, especially if threatened by a foreign power. He was granted $100,000 and access to the navy and armed forces, as required. It was noted that Fernandina was a nest of smugglers, pirates, and slavers whose presence could not be tolerated because they represented a real and ongoing threat to U.S. interests.[12] The actions contemplated here were deemed so explosive that a subsequent act was passed that banned any mention of them and forbade any publication or acknowledgment of their existence.[13] By January 26, events were already in train; George Mathews was on his way to Florida as a commissioner, taking along with him Colonel John McKee, an Alabama-born Indian agent with his own financial interests in territorial expansion.

Of course, it was hard to keep this sort of thing a secret. Spain had spies and sympathizers throughout the United States who kept it well informed about any official or unofficial business that might affect its interests. As volunteers streamed southward from Tennessee, Georgia, and South Carolina to form a self-styled "Patriots Group," there could be no doubt that something was happening. From St. Augustine, the center of Spanish operations in East Florida, a frustrated Commander Vicente Folch sent note after note to his superiors in Havana, warning them of the Americans' designs on the Floridas and pressing the urgency of the need to shore up the region's defenses.[14] Similarly, Spain's longtime agent in the United States, Luis de Onís, repeatedly and furiously protested to the government about the not-so-secret planned invasion of Amelia Island, which everyone knew was gathering across the Georgia border at St. Marys. He also worried about rumors that the French might have a similar scheme, which he warned would mean that the Spanish government would turn to Britain for help. These so-called

Napoleonic confederations indicate just how Atlanticized the fight for control over the Floridas had become.[15] In fact, news and speculation about the participants and outcome were being circulated as far away as London and Santiago de Chile.[16]

On November 2, 1811, James Monroe, who had assumed the office of secretary of state, sent a warning to British ambassador Augustus Foster in which he forcefully defended his government's right to protect its interests in terms that show his doctrine of the 1820s had been put into effect already. He asserted, "Situated as East Florida is, cut off from the other possessions and surrounded in a great measure by the territory of the United States, and having also an important bearing on their commerce, no other Power could think of taking possession of it, with other than hostile views to them. Nor could any other Power take possession of it without endangering their prosperity and best interests."[17]

In other words, Britain had no business involving itself in the affairs of Spain in the Americas and risked a showdown if it pressed the issue. And so, in short order, the officially unofficial East Florida Revolution went into effect using the strategy that had recently been successful in West Florida. Anglo residents banded together, declared independence from Spain, forged an autonomous representative body, then requested protection and even potential annexation from the United States.[18] George Mathews was not above stoking racialized fears to advance his cause, hinting that the Floridians should move quickly to choose sides before the British could mobilize black regiments from Jamaica and elsewhere in the Caribbean. He arranged for shots to be fired across the river at his troops in order to give him a pretext to invade in the name of establishing order. Amelia Island, with its capital at Fernandina, surrendered on March 17, 1812, and Mathews took control of the town the next day.[19] Luis de Onís hastily warned the viceroy of Mexico of this disturbing turn of events and begged him to help stamp out any hint of the spreading subversion.[20]

The Republic of East Florida did not last long, little more than a year, but it was a clear forerunner of the even more tense international episode that centered on the same island five years later.[21] Furthermore, it reveals the renegotiation of power taking place throughout the Atlantic world in the early nineteenth century, and it clearly shows that this decade of events in the Floridas was central to the formation of James Monroe's famous doctrine as a guiding foreign policy principle after the 1820s. The real fireworks over Fernandina came in 1817 when a Scottish filibuster lately in the service of the South American patriots arrived and established an independent stronghold with the intention of furthering the cause of liberty. Gregor MacGregor was a notorious and colorful character in his own right, yet he may have been a better governor and Atlantic visionary than his detractors have been willing to recognize.[22] At any rate, he was a relatively renowned soldier who had famously defeated the royalists at Juncal. He later safely extracted the remnants of the Aux Cayes expedition from Barcelona and Ocumare in 1816 as the royalists closed in, thereby saving many patriot lives and probably Bolívar's relationship with Pétion and the Haitians too.[23] MacGregor's early, hostile biographer Michael Rafter claims that he ultimately could not work with the "haughty" black officer Manuel Piar, and so decided to take up Juan Bautista Arismendi's suggestion that he go the United States and compile a force to launch an assault on the Floridas.[24] For reasons that remain murky still today, MacGregor split acrimoniously from the Liberator's side and headed to the United States, where Colombian Manuel Torres served as the unofficial procurement agent and de facto diplomat for the South American patriots.[25]

In an ironic parallel to the American patriots who had constituted themselves as an official body and sought to control East Florida in 1812, MacGregor also secured a commission from a self-appointed group calling themselves "the deputies of free America, resident in the United States of the North" to do the same thing. Meeting in Philadelphia on March 31, 1817, Lino de Clemente, Pedro Gual, and Martin Thompson signed a decree on behalf of the patriot governments of South America that authorized MacGregor to seize and hold the Floridas as part of a larger strategy of weakening the Spanish Empire by opening many fronts.[26] If the island were eventually to be ceded to the United States, MacGregor was instructed to request 1.5 million dollars which would, in turn, be handed over to the patriots to fund their war efforts.[27]

Confident that he had secured the legal niceties for such a venture, MacGregor proceeded to drum up interest in a settlement venture by advertising cheap land to prospective settlers at one dollar per acre, while being cagey about the actual destination.[28] He told friends and investors that he was headed for New Orleans and the former West Florida territories, but along the journey he feigned a need to stop in a south Georgia port for repairs and to take on supplies. In fact, he loaded up soldiers and arms that his Savannah merchant friends had secured for him and prepared to take Fernandina from Spain.

Just as the Mathews and Clarke expedition had been an open secret in 1812, so too did the Spaniards know full well what MacGregor was planning in 1817. Its chargé d'affaires in Charleston, a competent man called Antonio Argote, had sent warnings ahead to fortress commander Francisco Morales by the fastest horse possible.[29] Onís was nearly apoplectic with outrage and sent protest after protest to the U.S. government, which itself was unhappy with MacGregor's designs but was waiting to see if it could exploit the outcome down the line. Rumors circulated that MacGregor was actually part of a secret pact between Spain and the United States to act as a cover for the former to cede the Floridas to the latter without arousing British ire, but the intensity of Onís's lobbying against the expedition negates that possibility.[30] The Scottish adventurer had just seventy-eight recruits with him when he led the attack with the declaration, "I shall sleep either in hell or Amelia tonight!"[31] He forced Fernandina's surrender on June 29 by cleverly intimating that there were two thousand more men following just behind him.[32] Morales signed a capitulation later that afternoon while MacGregor raised a flag of his own devising that boasted a green cross of St. George upon a white background. Susan Fatio L'Engle recalled a friend of her father's describing the arrival of "the Carthaginians" into Fernandina. They were, he sneered, "[a] splendid army! Every man with a long green plume in his hat—*muy hermoso*." The plume later turned out to be fennel—a sham, just like MacGregor himself.[33]

The Republic of the Floridas lasted for just more than six months, an even shorter time than the American occupation of the island in 1812–13. Yet they were busy and surprisingly competent and idealistic months. MacGregor seems to have been quite sincere in his desire to create a fully functioning, free, and forward-thinking political entity. He was, like all quixotic founders of republics throughout the Atlantic world in the age of revolution, perennially short of cash but long on ambition. His immediate goal was to establish control and legitimacy over Fernandina, with a view to extending his territory over time. To that end, one of MacGregor's first two official proclamations as leader on June 30 prohibited looting. He also made it clear that Fernandina was conceived right from the start as a homeland for all who believed in liberty, that neither language nor national origin mattered. He and his men had arrived as liberators and friends:

> Peaceable inhabitants of Amelia! Do not apprehend any danger or oppression from the troops which are now in possession of your Island, either for your person, property or religion; however various the climes in which they may have received their birth, they are nevertheless your brethren and friends . . .

You who, ill-advised, have abandoned your homes, whatever may be the place of your birth, your political or religious opinions, return without delay and resume your wonted occupations . . .

Friends or enemies of our present state of emancipation, whoever you be, what I say unto you is the language of truth; it is the only language becoming a man of honour, and as such I swear to adhere religiously to the tenor of this proclamation.[34]

Rafter describes this speech as being "couched in such ridiculous terms of bombast and turgid verbosity, as have seldom been equalled and certainly never will be surpassed."[35] Eventually, MacGregor issued a medal to be pinned to all those who had shared in the struggle against Spanish tyranny. The front side bore the Latin inscription "Duce MacGregorio, libertas Floridarium" (MacGregor the leader liberates Florida) and on the obverse a line that immodestly echoed Caesar: "Amalia, Veni, Vidi, Vici" (Amalia, I came, I saw, I conquered).[36] MacGregor's high-minded, cosmopolitan ideals may have sat uncomfortably with the murky legality of the manner in which he came to power; nevertheless, this so-called Amelia Island affair was not appreciably different than other attempts to renegotiate power in the Americas at the same time. A Scottish adventurer was acting on behalf of South American patriots using U.S.-based recruits to seize control of Florida territory from Spain before French plotters or British negotiators beat them to it.

Where MacGregor went wrong was in assuming that the United States would remain neutral or benignly indifferent to his venture and that Fernandina's Anglo residents shared his multilingual, cross-cultural vision of a republic grounded in ideals not in mere commerce or material self-interest. Susan Fatio noted that her father and his Anglo-Spanish friends were not enthusiastic about the demand of Governor José Coppinger in St. Augustine that they rally to the Spanish cause and supply his troops with food and funds to oust the "Carthaginians."[37] Local resident Belton Kopp reported to John Quincy Adams that when MacGregor was in charge of Fernandina "everything went on more quietly than could have been expected" and that he improved the security situation with regard to the Indian raids to which Spanish neglect had left them dangerously exposed.[38] Although one American historian dismisses MacGregor's agenda as being concerned mainly with "profits rather than patriotism," it seems clear that the Scotsman's hatred of Spanish tyranny did on several occasions override any desire to make a quick sale. It was only after several weeks of dwindling supplies and threatened mutiny that MacGregor expanded access to Fernandina for smugglers and slavers.[39] His military force was small and undisciplined but felt enough loyalty to the man or their payments to behave decently enough in the first weeks.

If MacGregor's takeover of Fernandina had been accomplished with more pomp and puffery than battle and bloodshed, that did not mean that worse days were not ahead. From Havana, Alejandro Ramírez warned Governor Coppinger that he had better regroup and reassert Spanish control over Fernandina.[40] They had already been worried that the loss of Amelia Island might have significant spillover effects on both the tranquility of Cuba and the trade in slaves that kept its economy going.[41] To the royalists, fighting insubordination on several fronts, the issue was as much about preserving Spanish imperial honor as it was about the actual island domain itself. No challenge could go unanswered, no matter where or how small.

By July 1817, MacGregor had established the elements required to validate a claim to national status: a flag, a post office, a rudimentary tax regime, passports, civic honors, and an admiralty court, and he had begun to issue land grants and privateer patents.[42] He officially maintained a neutral stance while an assembly of local residents voted for their representatives then installed their new government with due pomp and ceremony. This start was all very promising. International press coverage was generally positive. His backers in Charleston made sure that favorable stories regularly appeared, like the one in the *Charleston Gazette* on July 12, 1817, praising General MacGregor's liberal conduct and telling readers that as "they are fighting in the holy cause of LIBERTY and INDEPENDENCE, all true Americans ought to wish them success."[43] The Washington-based *Daily National Intelligencer* stoked religious sectarianism and anti-Spanish sentiment when it praised MacGregor and his desire to remove the influence of "Machiavellian politicians and hypocritical priests among an ignorant people [who] will have no efficacy on the minds and masculine muscle of our citizens and deliverers of Florida."[44] In Great Britain, reports initially seemed bemused by the whole episode, rightly understanding that it seemed to be "connected with some design on Amelia Island" while wholly unsure as to who might ultimately benefit.[45] The *Examiner* noted approvingly that MacGregor had managed a revolution without bloodshed, and the *Royal Cornwall Gazette* reported he had a "considerable force" of five hundred. The *Liverpool Mercury* looked forward to Fernandina becoming an important depot for trade in the region and considered it to be a "beneficial change."[46] Yet there were dissenting opinions too. *Trewman's Exeter Flying Post* complained that he had become so desperate as to have been "seizing the negroes of the planters and openly exposing them for sale."[47] In Washington, DC, editors took the locally popular opinion that MacGregor's intrusion threatened what previously looked to be an inevitable Spanish cession of the Floridas to the United States. Thus MacGregor should be seen as nothing other than an unwelcome interloper in the region.[48] Ironically enough, this was the one thing on which both Spain and the United States could agree.

In fact, there were many more than three parties involved in the Amelia Island adventure. If Spain and the United States were the countries with the most immediate stake in the outcome of MacGregor's republic, patriot governments and conspirators in Mexico, Cuba, Haiti, Venezuela, Colombia, and the Río de la Plata region also took an active interest in what was happening there. In August 1817, the first printing press arrived at Fernandina, and it was a Bolivian, Vicente Pazos Kanki, who enthusiastically directed its operations, printed proclamations and government business, and briefly edited a newspaper after his arrival there in October.[49] Government agents throughout the Atlantic, from Cuba to Mexico to Britain to Brazil to the European continent, monitored events at Amelia that either fueled their own revolutionary actions or fed into pre-existing paranoia about the potential for rebellion. The Spanish intendant at Havana, for example, fed a steady stream of documents back to Spain outlining events in Florida and Louisiana and assessing the potential for slave rebellion at home, which he calculated was high and being made more likely by these events.[50]

The sweltering summer brought many deaths from tropical diseases and several defections of high-profile Anglo residents across the border to the American side in Georgia or to the Spanish royalist stronghold at St. Augustine. One contemporary estimate thought MacGregor might have been reduced to seventy or fewer men by mid-August.[51] Newspapers in the United States and Britain published contradictory reports; one claimed MacGregor had become a brutal tyrant bent on filling the colony with violent black troops from the Caribbean but the next day retracted that story and said it had received entirely different reports.[52] By late August, it was impossible to determine what was happening at Fernandina because of all the misinformation, disinformation, rumor, and rapidly changing events. Morale plummeted with the uncertainty about what was happening. The supply ships that sympathizers had promised to send MacGregor appeared, but without the badly needed provisions.[53] Coppinger and the Spanish forces successfully blocked supplies from the west and MacGregor's Charleston backers decided not to throw good money after bad and went silent as well. On the night of September 4, MacGregor and his Venezuelan wife abandoned the fort and took refuge on the *Morgiana*, a patriot ship lying off the coast; a few days later they unceremoniously sailed away. A hostile biographer saw this as a cowardly act, not befitting a British military officer, to flee to comfort "at a moment when the Spaniards were attacking his deceived and deserted followers."54 Former Pennsylvania congressman and veteran of the War of 1812 Jared Irwin was sworn in as his temporary replacement.

Confusion followed. It was not clear who was in charge or what might happen next. By September 15, however, a French privateer named Luis Aury who was in the service of Mexican and South American patriots had asserted control over the outpost at Amelia. Some say Aury had landed before MacGregor's departure; others say he arrived a few days later and quickly shoved Irwin and Ruggles Hubbard, MacGregor's lieutenants who had assumed interim control, aside.55 No matter what happened, the orientation and interests of the struggling Florida republic shifted with the arrival of Aury and his racially heterogeneous crew from their base at Galveston. As Pedro Gual later remembered it, this new phase was to be a "mercantile arrangement," a characterization that is certainly reflected in the increasingly hostile coverage of Fernandina as a haven for pirates and smugglers.56 It is true that Aury had fewer scruples, or perhaps was less politically savvy than MacGregor, so the economic basis of the self-declared republic mutated. After September, the number and speed of prize ship adjudications increased and the port's openness to slave ships and auctions expanded. Thanks to the watchful eye and aggressive lobbying of Onís and his wide network of consuls and spies, U.S. courts were being flooded with claims against captains sailing under Spanish American flags. Onís had been warning about the dangers of British designs on Florida for quite some time; now he could add the French and Mexicans to his growing list.

Onís was right to be concerned. The arrival of Aury and his troops further underscored the Atlantic nature of the Amelia Island experiment. If MacGregor had been a Scottish adventurer formerly in the service of the Venezuelans and Colombians, Aury was linked to the Mexican patriots and welcomed ships sailing under the Buenos Ayres flag, which typically were populated by U.S. and Caribbean crews. He was immediately joined at Amelia by several interesting Atlantic characters who arrived on board the ship *América Libre* from New York and Charleston under a Venezuelan flag. These adventurers included the Bolivian Vicente Pazos Kanki; the Venezuelan Pedro Gual; the Italian Agustín Codazzi; and two former Napoleonic officers, Auguste Gustave de Villaret and cavalry captain Maurice Persat. Newspaper accounts juxtaposed stories from revolutionary locales dotted around the Atlantic, thereby conflating the struggles for liberty that seemed to share not just ideals but also actual personnel. For example, a single page of the *Caledonian Mercury* reported on September 18 that MacGregor's forces were active, though embattled, in Florida; that Margarita Island in Venezuela had been retaken by royalists loyal to Spain; and that Francisco Javier Mina's small revolutionary force in Mexico seemed to be making progress.[57] Newspaper articles underlined a patriotic republican sweep throughout the Atlantic world, including the actions of the Polish liberal patriot Tadeusz Kósciuszko who was a friend and correspondent of Thomas Jefferson, and news of the revolt in Pernambuco, Brazil.[58]

With the arrival of the *América Libre* on October 4, the so-called American party headed by Irwin and Hubbard was sidelined. Aury instated Pedro Gual as the civil governor of the island republic but kept himself as military governor and commander of the garrison, though he took care to state that he remained subordinate to Gual and the civilians. Within a week, something grandiloquently called the Supreme Council of the Floridas set about drafting a set of laws and commercial policies for the little community. Their first task was to craft a decree designed to reassure residents of the neighboring state of Georgia that Amelia, despite its rhetorical commitment to liberty and freedom, was not going to allow itself to become a haven for runaway slaves. Accordingly, they set up a system that required blacks to possess formal work permits and mandated their arrest until such documents could be produced; it also established harsh penalties for any resident of Amelia who knowingly induced American slaves to flee to the island.[59] The situation had to be both complicated and uncomfortable, given that the majority of the troops in Amelia charged with its defense were now Aury's black Haitians, who themselves provoked a great deal of unease among Americans. The *Charleston Courier* started up a drumbeat of opposition, warning its readers about "those brigands who participated in the horrors of St. Domingo."[60] Clearly, the memory of the Haitian Revolution had not dissipated with time and fears of a similar slave revolt on the American continent probably played a greater role in turning U.S. public opinion against the Amelia Island republicans than previously thought. It surely did not help that Bolívar had received much material assistance from Alexandre Pétion in 1816, or that Commandant Persat himself left Florida and went to Aux Cayes, all the while toasting Napoleon and singing *La Marseillaise*.[61]

Aury and his motley group of French, Haitians, Spanish Americans, and Mexicans were not the only group to arrive at Fernandina that month. On October 25, a ship called the *Two Friends* arrived from England and twenty-four of its Scottish, Irish, and English recruits joined cause with the American party against the "foreigners." Commandant Persat later recalled that there was a great deal of animosity between the two factions; his memoirs document one skirmish with "the treasonous Americans" that resulted in cannon fire and a cry of "Vive la France, Death to the Americans!"[62] An English pamphleteer sneered that "the original intention of the enterprise had degenerated into a lawless community of pirates, [so] these unfortunate enthusiasts, too honourable to join such a fraternity, sailed again for Venezuela."[63] Indeed, outsiders far more commonly called Amelia under Aury and his men a haven for corsairs, pirates, brigands, and buccaneers than they had done when MacGregor was at its head, and the racial anxieties were much higher as well. As one historian notes, the *Baltimore Patriot and Mercantile Advertiser* shrieked that Aury had connections with General José Antonio Páez and that some of his troops were "led by A BLACK MAN."[64]

There was some truth to the charges. While occupied by Aury, Amelia Island did become a notorious depot for the disposition of ships taken as prizes at sea. One estimate holds that at least $500,000 worth of seized cargo was auctioned off in October and November alone. Harder to determine is the number of slaves who were landed at the port of Fernandina and smuggled across the Georgia border; one report claims an unreasonably high figure of two thousand people.[65] Nevertheless, newspaper accounts abounded with stories of fantastic wealth being generated at Amelia. The *Caledonian Mercury* reported to its readers that it had it on good authority from eyewitnesses that on one day alone, Fernandina's port had three Spanish prize ships caught by two insurgent privateers (the *Patriota* and *Congreso*), with cargo totaling 1,600 boxes of sugar, 20,000 pounds of cochineal, and $20,000 in coin. In Washington, the *Daily National Intelligencer* similarly reported that its informants had sent word of at least two prize ships and a slave ship from the African coast in port, and "large quantities of prize goods" waiting to be sold once a dispute between Aury and Irwin had been resolved.[66] Amelia Island was just the latest manifestation of Europeans' long fascination with the Floridas as a place of eternal youth and easy wealth. Yet the hints of faction and civil war, along with the uncertain legality of the proceedings there made others wary. On the Swedish island of St. Barthélemy, an English soldier who was on his way to join Bolívar's troops recounted the excitement when the patriots brought to port a spectacular Spanish brig they had captured and been ordered to take to Amelia Island to be adjudicated in the prize court but who had gotten nervous and brought it to Gustavia instead.[67]

To deal with the discipline problem which he knew could not go on for long without attracting attention from the governors of Georgia and South Carolina, and even the U.S. federal government, Aury imposed martial law on November 8.[68] A week later, he called a meeting of town notables and charged them with establishing a truce and a workable civic order. His close associates Pedro Gual and Vicente Pazos received the most votes, with Jared Irwin coming in a distant third.[69] He also established a newspaper, *El Telégrafo de las Floridas*, with Pazos as editor and publisher. Sadly the prospectus and few numbers of this periodical are now lost.[70] Gual's popularity, resulting from his fair-minded, conciliatory personality and his learned approach to governance, indicates that language and ethnicity were less central concerns than personal qualities for the polyglot and diverse citizenry of Amelia Island.[71] It was a small Atlantic crucible in which the experimental ideals of liberty and republicanism (and, to be fair, material spoils) were more important than the usual markers of national origin.

Indicating the degree to which Amelia Island and the Atlantic context of its revolution preoccupied James Monroe, who had by then been elected U.S. president, he explicitly dealt with the issue in his first address to the House Committee on Foreign Relations on December 2. One historian goes so far as to say that "the subject of Amelia Island was the main item of business for the House" for the month of December and notes that it seems to have been a foregone conclusion that the United States was going to oust Aury and take control of East Florida.[72] By December 15, Monroe had prepared and submitted a whole package of documents intended to overwhelm and silence his critics and present the need for an invasion on the grounds of both U.S. national security and a more general duty to protect its Spanish ally's claim to the colony. He claimed that the secret clause from 1811 had authorized him to send U.S. troops to protect the rights, property, and persons in areas of direct national concern, and also to uphold the threat to Spain's territorial possessions presented by mercenaries of unclear origin or loyalty. It was clear then, as it is now, that the decision to occupy East Florida had long been made and it really was just a matter of timing.

The patriots at Fernandina scrambled to respond and to prove that they were not brigands but rather legitimate republicans and heirs to the American revolutionary tradition. On December 9 their official printer Findley issued the *Report of the Committee Appointed to Frame the Plan of a Provisional Government for the Republic of Floridas*.[73] Pedro Gual was the chair of the committee, and Vicente Pazos and J. Murden were cosignatories. It is a straightforward and interesting document, quite typical of the era, and one that draws on ideas from a variety of Atlantic sources. Although the structures were similar to those of the U.S. government, some elements and nomenclature from British and Spanish models crept in too. The government should be democratic and republican, with three independent branches exerting equal authority: executive, legislative, and judicial. The military was clearly subordinated to the civilian authority, which was vested in a seven-member general assembly. Executive power was held by a governor, who had a lieutenant governor as second-in-line in case of emergency and two secretaries, one for state and treasury and one for army and navy. Provisions were made for a constitution to be drafted by a convention at the earliest possible opportunity, but it was made clear that the Floridas were to remain "FREE and INDEPENDENT from all allegiance to the KING of SPAIN, his HEIRS, and SUCCESSORS." Although some early twentieth-century historians considered Aury's proclamations to be cynical and "shrewdly played up for the benefit of the outside world," others have emphasized that he was a "first-rate privateer" with no real experience or aptitude for high-stakes international politics.[74] It does seem clear from the emphasis that Aury, Gual, and the others saw Spain as their most important enemy and that they were probably operating in an emotional context of wanting to guarantee benefits for their Spanish American brethren.[75]

They need not have bothered. Less than two weeks after this declaration was issued, the Republic of the Floridas was no more. U.S. forces arrived off the coast of Fernandina on December 22 and sent messages to Aury to turn over the fortress and prevent needless deaths. He did not debate for long, and two days later the Americans moved in unopposed. As had been the case with MacGregor, Aury too was defeated in the end by the threat of a superior force and the failure of his allies to send reinforcements. Persat remained with him until the end, describing him as a man of "ardent imagination and full of honorable ambition, always searching for glory in his exploits, not by attacking the Spanish merchant marine, but rather in attacking navy gunships." Aury's detractors claimed he was nothing better than a buccaneer, an "independent marauder, acting generally for himself alone."[76] There was and still is much speculation about the real motivation and diplomatic positioning behind the U.S. occupation of the Floridas, but the one thing that cannot be denied is that every government and patriot band made their calculations based on the shifting reality of a transatlantic matrix of power. One historian claims that Spanish minister of state José García de León y Pizarro favored a scheme to trade the Floridas to Great Britain in exchange for its backing in an expedition to retake Louisiana. Given Spain's jealousy toward all its colonial possessions in the post-Napoleonic years, that seems unlikely, although the minister's own memoirs do reflect a willingness to see Britain as a potential ally in the effort to constrain U.S. ambitions in the region.[77] If nothing else, the frequent, long, detailed position papers that Luis de Onís sent to Secretary of State John Quincy Adams all throughout the year 1817 and even more emphatically in the opening months of 1818 indicate that a sophisticated diplomatic dance was taking place.[78] Aury's designated agent Vicente Pazos Kanki spent several months in Washington, energetically attempting to make the case for legitimate Spanish American jurisdiction over the settlement at Fernandina; he argued for "the justice of our cause, and . . . that the occupation of Amelia by the patriots had been a real conquest, which transferred to them all designates acquired by a regular and declared war."[79] As Venezuelan historian Tulio Arends notes "as a simple dispute between Spain and its colonies, [Amelia Island] was easy to manage, but the diplomacy, international law, and the ambition of the United States for territorial expansion complicated it unnecessarily."[80]

The Amelia Island episode of 1817 was significant for many reasons. First, it clearly laid out the Atlantic dimensions of the revolutions in America. Government entities and rebel forces in Spain, Britain, the United States, Mexico, Spanish America, Cuba, and even Haiti all became consumed by the events taking place on this small island. A contemporary writer was not exaggerating when he described it as a "transaction which threatened to plunge the eastern and western hemispheres in an expensive and sanguinary war, from which circumstance this little spot, trifling and insignificant in itself, had obtained, in the history of the present period, an unexpected degree of importance and celebrity."[81] As a small but centrally located island with a serviceable port and a fair degree of de facto political autonomy, Amelia Island was a lucrative prize for the many Atlantic players who tried to claim it. Its role as a nexus between North and South America, at the point of intersection between Spain and its colonies in revolt, on the borders of Louisiana and an increasingly expansive United States makes the short-lived Republic of the Floridas a valuable lens through which to assess not just shifting political loyalties, but the personal connections that transcended language, ethnicity, national origin, and economic status. And, given James Monroe's intense interest in the Floridas for more than a decade before his famous doctrine was asserted, and even the language he used in arguments that spanned a decade, one must conclude that events on Amelia Island played a key role in framing his international policies as an assertion of American rights in an Atlantic context.

Notes

1. Joyce Elizabeth Harman, *Trade and Privateering in Spanish Florida, 1732–1763* (Tuscaloosa: University of Alabama Press, 2004); Lawrence H. Feldman, *The Last Days of British Saint Augustine, 1784–1785: A Spanish Census of the English Colony of East Florida*

(Baltimore, MD: Clearfield Co., 1998); Maynard Geiger, "The Settlement of the East Florida Spaniards in Cuba, 1763–1766," *Florida Historical Quarterly* 42, no. 3 (1964): 216–31; Geiger, "Politics and Property during the Transfer of Florida from Spanish to English Rule, 1763–1764," *Florida Historical Quarterly* 42, no. 1 (1963): 16–34.

2. William S. Coker, "Una compañía privilegiada: John Forbes en la Florida española durante la Guerra de 1812," *Revista de Indias* 40 (1980): 219–54; Janice Borton Miller, "The Struggle for Free Trade in East Florida and the Cédula of 1793," *Florida Historical Quarterly* 55, no. 1 (1976): 48–59; David H. White, "The Forbes Company in Spanish Florida, 1801–1806," *Florida Historical Quarterly* 52, no. 3 (1974): 274–85; John Coatsworth, "American Trade with European Colonies in the Caribbean and South America, 1790–1812," *William and Mary Quarterly* 24 (April 1967): 243–66.

3. G. William Nixon, *Amelia Island Plantation: The First Ten Years* (Fernandina Beach, FL: Arrington Gale for the Amelia Island Plantation Community Association, 1984), 3.

4. Nixon, *Amelia Island*, 7.

5. Andrew McMichael has discussed the fluid nature of citizenship in West Florida at this time in *Atlantic Loyalties: Americans in Spanish West Florida, 1785–1810* (Athens: University of Georgia Press, 2008), 33. Other recent treatments of this region include Thomas Chávez, *Spain and the Independence of the United States: An Intrinsic Gift* (Albuquerque: University of New Mexico Press, 2002); and James E. Lewis Jr., *The American Union and the Problem of Neighborhood: The United States and the Collapse of the Spanish Empire, 1783–1829* (Chapel Hill: University of North Carolina Press, 1998).

6. Christopher Ward, "The Commerce of East Florida during the Embargo, 1806–1812: The Role of Amelia Island," *Florida Historical Quarterly* 68, no. 2 (1989): 179.

7. Ibid., 171. One such report on slaves and Amelia Island can be found in John Francis Barrie to Spanish minister of state José García de León y Pizarro (Coruña, February 10, 1817), Archivo Histórico Nacional, Madrid, Estado, legajo 5560, exp. 33.

8. Rufus Kay Wyllys, "The East Florida Revolution of 1812–1814," *Hispanic American Historical Review* 9, no. 4 (1920): 423.

9. McMichael, *Atlantic Loyalties*, 149.

10. Isaac Joslin Cox, "The Border Missions of General George Mathews," *Mississippi Valley Historical Review* 12, no. 3 (December 1925): 310–12.

11. Paul Kruse, "A Secret Agent in East Florida: General George Mathews and the Patriot War," *Journal of Southern History* 18, no. 2 (1952), 195–96. See also J. C. A. Stagg, "George Mathews and John McKee: Revolutionizing East Florida, Mobile, and Pensacola in 1812," *Florida Historical Quarterly* 85, no. 3 (2007): 269–96; and Stagg, "James Madison and George Mathews: The East Florida Revolution of 1812 Reconsidered," *Diplomatic History* 30, no. 1 (2006): 23–55. The two authors disagree on the degree to which the U.S. government knew about and approved Mathews' actions in Florida. Kruse says Madison and Monroe were fully aware and approved of everything he did; Stagg argues forcefully that they did not and that Mathews was a rogue who acted independently.

12. Francis J. Stafford, "Illegal Importations: Enforcement of the Slave Trade Laws along the Florida Coast, 1810–1828," *Florida Historical Quarterly* 46 (October 1967): 126.

13. Wyllys, "East Florida Revolution," 420–21. The second act was dated March 2, 1811, and promulgated on April 20.

14. See the voluminous correspondence in U.S. Library of Congress, Manuscripts

Division, East Florida Records, "Letters to the Captain-General 1813–1817," microfilm, reels 12–14, and "Letters to and from the Intendant, 1811–1818," reels 22–23.

15. Cox, "Border Missions," 318; Guadalupe Jiménez Codinach, "La Confédération Napoléonnie. El desempeño de los conspiradores militares y las sociedades secretas en la independencia de México," *Historia Mexicana* 38, no. 1 (1988): 43.

16. Luis de Onís reported to the Señor Capitán-General de la Isla de Cuba (Philadelphia, June 3, 1811) that he had received an anonymous letter with a copy of a printed proclamation from Chile full of false rumors and malign intentions. Archivo Nacional, Santiago, Chile, Fondo Varios, vol. 692, pieza 3, f. 121.

17. Monroe, quoted in Wyllys, "East Florida Revolution," 425n.

18. McMichael, *Atlantic Loyalties*, 168, 173–74.

19. There are several book-length studies of these events. The best and most recent is J. C. A. Stagg, *Borderlines in Borderlands: James Madison and the Spanish-American Frontier, 1776–1821* (New Haven, CT: Yale University Press, 2009). See also James Cusick, *The Other War of 1812: The Patriot War and the American Invasion of Spanish East Florida* (Gainesville: University Press of Florida, 2003); Rembert Patrick, *Florida Fiasco: Rampant Rebels on the Georgia-Florida Border* (Athens: University of Georgia Press, 1954); and Joseph Burkholder Smith, *The Plot to Steal Florida: James Madison's Phony War* (New York: Arbor Books, 1983).

20. Onís to Excmo Sr. Virrey de México (Philadelphia, April 1, 1812) reprinted in Isidro Fabela, *Los precursores de la diplomacia mexicana* (Mexico City: Editorial Porrúa, 1971): 36–37.

21. David Bushnell, "The Florida Republic: An Overview" in *La República de las Floridas: Texts and Documents*, ed. David Bushnell (Mexico City: Pan-American Institute of Geography and History, 1986), 8.

22. MacGregor's reputation as a duplicitous blackguard is largely tied to his heartless recruitment of settlers for a nonexistent colony at Poyais in 1825 that left dozens dead and hundreds more completely destitute. David Sinclair, *Sir Gregor MacGregor and the Land That Never Was: The Extraordinary Story of the Most Audacious Fraud in History* (London: Review, 2003); and Matthew Brown, "Inca, Sailor, Soldier, King: Gregor MacGregor and the Early Nineteenth-Century Caribbean," *Bulletin of Latin American Research* 24, no. 1 (2005): 44–70; Tulio Arends, *Sir Gregor MacGregor: Un escocés tras la aventura en América* (Caracas: Monte Avila, 1988); Alfred Hasbrouck, "Gregor MacGregor and the Colonization of Poyais between 1820 and 1824," *Hispanic American Historical Review* 7 (1927): 438–59.

23. Stuart Allan, "Liberators: Some Remnants of Scottish Service in the Wars of Spanish South America, 1805–1826," *Review of Scottish Culture* 21 (2009): 24; Brown, "Inca, Sailor, Soldier, King," 50–51.

24. Michael Rafter, *Memoirs of Gregor M'Gregor, Comprising a Sketch of the Revolution in New Grenada and Venezuela, with . . . a Narrative of the Expeditions to Amelia Island, Porto Bello and Rio de la Hache* (London: J. J. Stockdale, 1820), 87–88.

25. Charles A. Bowman, "The Activities of Manuel Torres as Purchasing Agent, 1820–1821," *Hispanic American Historical Review* 48, no. 2 (1968): 234–46; and Bowman, "Manuel Torres in Philadelphia and the Recognition of Colombian Independence, 1821–1822," *Records of the American Catholic Historical Society of Philadelphia* 80 (March 1969): 17–38.

26. Bushnell, "Florida Republic," 9. Manuel Torres was present but did not sign. Gual used a proxy to sign for a Mexican delegate named Cornelio Ortiz Zárate.

27. Charles A. Bowman, "Vicente Pazos and the Amelia Island Affair, 1817," *Florida Historical Quarterly* 53, no. 3 (1973): 277.

28. Richard G. Lowe, "American Seizure of Amelia Island," *Florida Historical Quarterly* 45, no. 1 (1966): 19.

29. *State Papers and Publick Documents of the United States*, 3rd. ed. (Boston: Thomas B. Watt, 1819), 12:169–78.

30. Onís to Minister of State José García de León y Pizarro (Washington, May 17, 1817), Archivo General de Indias, Seville, Estado 88, n. 18.

31. Rafter, *Memoirs of Gregor M'Gregor*, 94.

32. L. David Norris, "Failure Unfolds: The Loss of Amelia Island" in Bushnell, *La República de las Floridas*, 19.

33. Susan Fatio L'Engle, *Notes of My Family and Recollections of My Early Life* (New York: Knickerbocker Press, 1888), 39–40.

34. "General M'Gregor's Proclamations" (Fernandina, June 30, 1817) in the (London) *Times*, Saturday, August 16, 1817. This proclamation, and a second one directed to the troops, were also signed by his secretary Joseph de Yribarren.

35. Rafter, *Memoirs of Gregor M'Gregor*, 96.

36. See description in C. Gresham, *General Gregor MacGregor and the 1817 Amelia Island Medal* (Pompano Park, FL: privately printed, 1992). The medal is rare and hard to find now, but its inscriptions are also described in Brown, "Inca, Sailor, Soldier, King," 48n.

37. L'Engle, *Notes of My Family*, 43.

38. Belton A. Kopp to the Hon. John Quincy Adams, Secretary of State (St. Marys, April 1, 1818), published as "The Patriot War, a Contemporaneous Letter," *Florida Historical Quarterly* 5, no. 3 (January 1927): 165–66.

39. Lowe, "American Seizure of Amelia Island," 19.

40. Norris, "Failure Unfolds," 22–23. His fuller study is available as "José Coppinger in East Florida, 1816–1821: A Man, a Province, and a Spanish Colonial Failure" (PhD diss., Southern Illinois University at Carbondale, 1981).

41. Amelia Island is explicitly identified as a central concern in the February 10, 1817, letter from John Francis Barrie to José García de León y Pizarro.

42. Bushnell, "Florida Republic," 12.

43. *Charleston Gazette*, July 12, 1817, quoted in Norris, "Failure Unfolds," 26.

44. *Daily National Intelligencer*, Saturday, July 19, 1817.

45. *Caledonian Mercury* (Edinburgh), Saturday, July 26, 1817.

46. *Examiner*, Sunday, August 10, 1817; *Royal Cornwall Gazette* (Saturday, August 2, 1817); *Liverpool Mercury*, Friday, August 1, 1817.

47. *Trewman's Exeter Flying Post*, Thursday, September 4, 1817.

48. *Daily National Intelligencer*, Friday, July 25, 1817.

49. Bowman, "Vicente Pazos and the Amelia Island Affair," 290; *Narrative of a Voyage to the Spanish Main, in the Ship "Two Friends"* (London: Printed for J. Miller, 1819), 16.

50. "El Yntendente de la Habana, sobre el favor que encuentran los Piratas en los Estados-unidos, y proyectos que se forman para alterar la tranquilidad de la Isla, con la horrible idea de sublevar los esclavos, 1817," Archivo Histórico Nacional, Estado, legajo 5560, exp. 6.

51. Norris, "Failure Unfolds," 25.

52. For example, in London the *Morning Post*, Tuesday, August 19, 1817, signaled its frustration with the widely varying reports coming from the Americas and assured its readers that the contradictions should be considered "of no importance."

53. Charles A. Bowman Jr., "Amelia Island and Vicente Pazos of Upper Peru," in Bushnell, *La República de las Floridas*, 45.

54. Rafter, *Memoirs of Gregor M'Gregor*, 107.

55. Harris Gaylord Warren says MacGregor left on Sept. 4; see *Their Sword Was Their Passport: A History of American Filibustering in the Mexican Revolution* (Port Washington, NY: Kennikat Press, 1943), 198n. Bowman disagrees and claims he left on Sept. 16; see "Amelia Island Affair," 278.

56. Bowman, "Amelia Island Affair," 278.

57. *Caledonian Mercury*, Thursday, September 18, 1817.

58. *Raleigh Register and North-Carolina Gazette*, Friday, October 31, 1817; *Richmond Enquirer*, Friday, December 30, 1817.

59. Bowman, "Amelia Island Affair," 282.

60. *Charleston Courier*, October 24, 1817, as quoted in Bushnell, "Florida Republic," 15.

61. Maurice Persat, *Mémoires du Commandant Persat, 1806 à 1844* (Paris: Plon-Nourrit, 1910), 25, 36.

62. *Mémoires du Commandant Persat*, 30–31.

63. Rafter, *Memoirs of Gregor M'Gregor*, 110.

64. Quoted in Edgardo Pérez Morales, *El gran diablo hecho barco. Corsarios, esclavos y revolución en Cartagena y el Gran Caribe* (Bucaramanga: Universidad Industrial de Santander, 2012), 191–94; emphasis in the original.

65. Bushnell, "Florida Republic," 15.

66. *Caledonian Mercury*, Saturday, November 1, 1817; *Daily National Intelligencer*, Monday, November 3, 1817.

67. James Hackett, *Narrative of the Expedition which Sailed from England in 1817, to Join the South American Patriots* (London: John Murray, 1818), 25–26.

68. *Morning Post*, Saturday, December 20, 1817. The decree of martial law was supposed to last for ten days, but likely was extended as unrest continued to prevail.

69. Bushnell, "Florida Republic," 16.

70. Douglas McMurtrie, "The Beginnings of Printing in Florida," *Florida Historical Quarterly* 23, no. 2 (1944): 63–96.

71. Harold A. Bierck, *Vida pública de Don Pedro Gual* (Caracas: Ministerio de Relaciones Exteriores, 1983), 91.

72. Lowe, "American Seizure of Amelia Island," 28–29.

73. Pedro Gual, Vicente Pazos, and J. Murden, *Report of the Committee Appointed to Frame the Plan of a Provisional Government for the Republic of Floridas* (Fernandina, 1817); McMurtrie ("Beginnings of Printing in Florida," 68) indicates that this report is the only surviving document printed at Fernandina during the press's short operation.

74. T. Frederick Davis, "MacGregor's Invasion of Florida, 1817," *Florida Historical Society Quarterly* 7, no. 1 (1928): 46; Gerald Poyo, "La República de las Floridas: The Mexican Connection" in Bushnell, *La República de las Floridas*, 38–39.

75. Their personal connections to insurgent groups in Mexico, northern South America, and Buenos Aires is well known. The Mexican viceroy kept himself well apprised of events throughout Louisiana and the Floridas, and enlisted agents who helped him undermine these "deranged projects" according to the rights set out in the Congress of Vienna. Juan Mariano Picornell to Juan Ruiz de Apodaca, Viceroy of Mexico (Pueblo Viejo, November 8, 1817) Archivo General de la Nación, Mexico City, Notas Diplomáticas, vol. 1, f. 493.

76. *Mémoires du Commandant Persat*, 33; Rafter, *Memoirs of Gregor M'Gregor*, 109.

77. Philip C. Brooks, "Spain's Farewell to Louisiana, 1803–1821," *Mississippi Valley Historical Review* 27, no. 1 (1940): 40; José García de León y Pizarro, *Memorias* (Madrid: Centro de Estudios Políticos y Constitucionales, 1998), 652–56, 661–68.

78. See, for example, the long letter to Adams in which Onís recounted the entire history of the Spanish claim to the Floridas and Louisiana (Washington, January 5, 1818) in *State Papers and Publick Documents*: 12:25–42.

79. Vicente Pazos Kanki, *The Exposition, Remonstrance, and Protest of Don Vicente Pazos, Commissioner on behalf of the Republican Agents established at Amelia Island in Florida* (Philadelphia: n.p., 1818), 27–28.

80. Tulio Arends, *La república de las Floridas 1817–1818*, (Caracas: Academia Nacional de la Historia, 1986), 119, my translation.

81. Rafter, *Memoirs of Gregor M'Gregor*, 113–14.

8

The Old World in the New

Florida Discovers the Arts of Spain, 1885–1930

RICHARD L. KAGAN

For many of my readers, especially natives of Florida, the subtitle of this essay may appear a bit odd as I presume that you have mostly been taught that it was Spain that discovered Florida. How then could Florida "discover" the arts of Spain? By discovery, however, I am not referring to the sighting of new lands or journeys through uncharted seas. Rather I am using the term metaphorically in the sense of learning about something new, or previously unknown. In this case the new is Florida's Spanish past, along with its art, architecture, and history, all of which the territory, following its acquisition by the United States in 1821, did its best to forget. Starting in the 1880s, this began to change. What had been foreign became a friend, and even more importantly, something that developers across the state deployed to attract northerners to visit, relax, and spend their money in the Sunshine State.

Before going further it is necessary to clarify the terminology. To begin with, by Spain, I am referring to Spanish culture in the broad sense of the term, as encompassing not only peninsular Spain but also what is today commonly referred to as Hispanic (or Latino) culture, with its origins in various parts of Hispanophone America. In the nineteenth century, however, Anglo-Americans regularly used *Spanish* to refer to the cultures of both Spain and Spanish America, and that is how I will use the term here.

These Americans also conceived of Spanish culture in racial terms. From their perspective, the Spanish race was decidedly different from, and indeed inferior to the Anglo-Saxon as it was composed of a complex cocktail of the various peoples—Celts, Romans, Visigoths, Arabs, and Berbers (the North African peoples traditionally and derogatorily referred to as Moors)—who had once made the Iberian Peninsula their home. Put all of these peoples into a shaker, and the Muslim component would predominate, so much so that Spaniards and their culture were often viewed as "Oriental." Spain, in short was essentially Andalusia, whereas Andalusia was reduced to the cities of Córdoba, Granada, and Seville and especially to those monuments—Córdoba's former Umayyad mosque, Granada's Alhambra, and the Giralda in Seville—that harked back to the era of al-Andalus and the seven centuries during which southern Spain was subject to Muslim rule.

As for Florida's discovery of Spain, I want to emphasize that Florida was by no means alone in its effort to integrate Spanish culture into its definition and understanding of itself. Rather it was part of a broader cultural phenomenon; call it a vogue or even a mania or what I have referred to elsewhere as the Spanish Craze.[1] Starting in the 1880s, this craze swept across much of the United States—initially in Florida and New York, then in California, New Mexico, and Texas, and subsequently in Chicago, Kansas City, and other parts of the Midwest. The craze gained momentum in the decade or so following the Spanish-American War of 1898, peaked in the early 1920s, then finally ran its course. This craze was not the country's only craze—at different times and places there were manias for things Egyptian, Japanese, Mexican, even Dutch.[2] But compared to these other crazes, the Spanish one was remarkable for its duration, geographical spread, and diversity to the extent that it found outlets in art and architecture as well as cinema, fashion, music, even food. In other words, there was not just one Spanish craze but many, none of which was exactly alike.

Why Spain? No simple or easy answer exists, as numerous factors—artistic, cultural, economic, and political—come into play, and it is difficult to weigh the importance of each. I begin with what I perceive was a shift in American attitudes toward both Spain and its culture, which began in the 1880s and continued through to the decade of the 1920s interrupted only briefly by the Spanish-American War of 1898. This shift was all the more remarkable given the weight and preponderance of the so-called Black Legend, that centuries-old, largely Protestant tradition of anti-Spanish beliefs that equated Spain with the horrors of the Inquisition, religious bigotry, despotic monarchy, and the ruthless slaughter of indigenous peoples throughout the Americas, together with a lengthy laundry list of other abominations and cruelties.[3] That image began to soften during the romantic era, when writers such as Washington Irving, himself an ardent Hispanophile and the author of popular books on Columbus and the Alhambra, imagined Spain as quintessentially and delightfully picturesque, a country equated with bullfighters, gypsy dancers, dashing caballeros, and other equally romantic types. Spain's economic backwardness was also part of its allure, and in general Americans who wrote about the country represented it as a place where visitors could catch a glimpse of what life in the Middle Ages was actually like.[4]

Starting in the 1870s, moreover, the allure of Spain also captured the attention of some of America's most prominent artists. One of the first was Samuel Coleman (1832–1920), a leading member of the Hudson River school whose views of the Alhambra and of Seville, first exhibited in New York in 1864, represented the sunny, as opposed to the somber side of Spain.[5] Mary Cassatt did the same as she fastened on to bullfighters, Seville's flowered balconies, and other picturesque facets of Spain, as did other artists such as Thomas Eakins, John Singer Sargent, and William Merritt Chase, all of whom took a particular fancy to Spain.[6]

The last quarter of the nineteenth century also marked the moment when a number of writers began to integrate Spain's history into that of the United States. One was the famed poet Walt Whitman (discussed later); another was Helen Hunt Jackson, whose wildly popular novel *Ramona* (1884) offered a wholly positive assessment of Spain's presence in North America; and then there was Charles F. Lummis (1859–1918), whose influential book *The Spanish Pioneers* (1893) claimed Spain's conquistadores and missionaries did as much, if not more, than the "Anglo-pioneers" to bring both civilization and religion to what later became the United States. Spain was given an additional boost at the Columbian International Exposition held in Chicago in 1893. There, in the legendary White City, visitors could marvel at statues and purchase commemorative coins honoring both Columbus and his Spanish patron, Queen Isabella I of Castile, visit a full-scale replica of the Franciscan monastery at La Rábida near Huelva where Columbus supposedly hatched his plans for a transoceanic voyage, climb abroad replicas of Columbus's ships, wander through a replica of the interior of Córdoba's mosque, and marvel at the gothic-style Spanish pavilion modeled after Valencia's merchant hall and filled with the work of Mariano Fortuny and other contemporary Spanish artists.[7] Spain and its culture subsequently reappeared—again in positive light—in a number of other expositions, most spectacularly at Buffalo's Pan-American Exposition of 1901, which featured a replica of Seville's Giralda, and at San Diego's Panama-California Exposition of 1915, a fair whose buildings were modeled after the baroque architecture of both Spain and Spanish America.[8]

By 1915, moreover, the Spanish Craze had already made important inroads into Florida, most notably in St. Augustine, arguably one of the places where America's discovery of Spain began. Nowadays St. Augustine unabashedly promotes its Spanish heritage to attract tourist dollars. Prior to the 1880s, however, what is today viewed as an asset was a liability, something the town's municipal government deliberately endeavored to forget as it struggled to transform what were regarded as the "ruinous buildings" of the "ancient" Spanish town into what Rufus King Sewall, an enterprising lawyer from Maine, described in 1848 as the "neat, attractive style of American village architecture."[9] As for the old Spanish fort of San Marcos, there was little to be done other than Anglicize its name (to Fort Marion) and hope that visitors would regard it, together with the town's old Spanish gate, as bordering on the "picturesque." Otherwise, what little was left of Spanish culture was considered an embarrassment. Shivaree and Carnival—St Augustine's equivalent of Philadelphia's Mummers Parade—were both viewed as "drunken revels" and "relics of popish superstition and Spanish practice [symbolized by the town's old cathedral], and in 1843, two years before Florida became a state, William Cullen Bryant happily reported that another old Spanish custom—the Holy Week celebration known as "shooting the Jews"—had disappeared along with the Minorcan families who had kept that tradition alive. Bryant also noted that St. Augustine "soon will part of [from] all that reminds the visitor of 'Spanish origin'—its narrow streets, its high garden walls of shell-rock and its overhanging balconies—all but its fine old fort of St. Mark—to look like any other American town in the Southern States."[10] Bryant was right. In the decades in which St. Augustine attempted to build its reputation as a winter retreat, it did so by building houses, cottages, and hotels in a purely American or at least English idiom. The first was Magnolia House—built in plantation style and opened circa 1848—followed by Hotel St. Augustine (1869) and the San Marco, erected in 1885 in Queen Anne style. The town, in short, was doing its best to bury its Spanish past.

But change was in the air. It began, not with an architect or a developer, but with a brace of lawyers—Thomas Buckingham Smith (1810-71) and George Fairbanks (1820-1901)—whose immersion in the maze of lawsuits and property disputes stemming from Spanish land titles issued prior to 1821 led both to learn Spanish and later to share an interest in Florida's Spanish past. Smith led the way when, in 1851, he published the first English-language translation of Alvar Núñez Cabeza de Vaca's peregrinations through Florida and the Southwest, followed by a translation of Hernando de Soto's account of his adventures in Florida. In the book's preface, Smith steered away from the Black Legend, presenting De Soto in heroic terms ("brave, prudent, kindly, magnanimous"), and Spaniards of his era as "refined, enlightened and humane as any in Europe."[11] Smith also set the stage for Fairbanks (figure 8.1), whose own histories of St. Augustine (1868) and

Figure 8.1. George R. Fairbanks. (Courtesy of the Fairbanks House)

of Florida (1871) lauded the early Spanish explorers, De Soto in particular, for their "nobility of spirit, compassion towards the natives, . . . and manly virtues." Fairbanks's histories are not much read today, but together with Smith he paved the way—first for Florida, then for the nation at large—for a wholesale re-evaluation of the contribution of Spain to the history and civilization of the United States.[12]

Meanwhile, in Florida, the state's discovery of Spain took another step forward on March 27, 1885, the day when the St. Augustine Historical Society reenacted Juan Ponce de León's landing in Florida with a bit of staged history (figure 8.2). Reports on this first Ponce de León festival are sketchy—even the date is disputed—but it entailed nothing short of a celebration of the city's Spanish past. Francis B. Genovar, a local politician (and cigar

Figure 8.2. Program from the Ponce de Leon Celebration, 1925. (Courtesy of the St. Augustine Historical Society)

manufacturer) of Minorcan extraction, played the role of the Spanish explorer; forty-six townspeople donned Spanish-period costumes; high mass was sung in the fort; and various locals mounted horses and carriages to stage what was termed a "Parada de los Coches y Caballos." Finally, Fairbanks himself delivered an oration on St. Augustine's early history. The text of this oration has not survived, but we do know that the audience that heard him sing the praises of Spanish St. Augustine included one Henry B. Flagler, the railroad magnate and developer who was soon to give St. Augustine the look of "Old Spain."[13]

The look in question began with the construction of the Ponce de León Hotel, which opened its doors in January 1888. In that massive hotel, now Flagler College, Flagler and his New York–based architect, Thomas Hastings, created what amounted to a pastiche of Old Spain: some entranceways were adorned with the Spanish word for welcome—"bienvenida"—etched into their lintels; others were flanked with roundels featuring old Spanish proverbs and shell designs meant to evoke the traditional pilgrimage route to Santiago de Compostela; and in the spectacular dining room, the ceiling was decorated with inscriptions celebrating the deeds of the conquistadores together with reproductions of the escutcheons of the cities and provinces of Spain.[14]

As for the building's overall design, there was little, with the possible exception of a red tile roof, that was distinctly Spanish. Indeed, its somewhat mongrel mixture of design elements has led one prominent historian of American architecture to describe the building as a prime example of "academic eclecticism."[15] On the other hand, when the hotel first opened, it was generally referred to as a mixture of Spanish and Moorish, a building that captured the spirit of Spain.

The idea of building a grand hotel in the Spanish style derived partly from the Villa Zorayda, a neo-Moorish fantasy house built by Frank W. Smith in St. Augustine in 1884;[16] partly from Thomas Hastings's desire to harmonize with "the romance of Spain" and what he imaginatively called "the spirit of old [meaning Spanish] Saint Augustine;" and partly from Flagler's personal fascination with Spanish history and literature. Flagler in fact once remarked that he wanted to do away with the "dark and forbidding" aspects of the Spanish character and use the hotel to capture the "bright side of the Spanish race." As for the name Ponce de León, he claimed that it derived from "the romantic quest" of this "redoubtable knight and discoverer."[17]

At the same time, Flagler compared the hotel to a "pleasure dome," and in doing so connected it to the nineteenth-century romantic view of Spain— think Washington Irving—as a land of Oriental luxury and delight. In the

1880s, moreover, what scholars call medievalism was all the rage, inasmuch as the Middle Ages were thought to embody many of the values—authenticity, honesty, integrity—that modern civilization had lost. Interest in that era led, in one direction, to countries—Spain among them—whose perceived backwardness supposedly ensured the preservation of those values; and in another, to paraphrase T. Jackson Lears, to homegrown "places of grace" that could offer vacationers some respite from their modern, workaday world.[18]

These linkages—Spain, romance, adventure, pleasure dome, luxury, escape—were central to the Ponce de León and by extension to the other two hotels, the Alcázar and Cordova (originally Casa Monica), associated with Flagler's St. Augustine (figure 8.3). Hotels, however, were not enough to create the illusion of the romance of Spain. Consequently, Flagler endeavored to persuade the town council to Hispanicize the names of St. Augustine's streets with an eye toward enhancing the town's Spanish atmosphere. He was only partly successful. The council agreed to rename Washington Street as Granada Street, Gregg Lane as Cadiz Street, Hospital Street as Aviles Street, and so on, but drew the line at allowing King Street to become Alameda.[19] On the other hand, year after year the council saw fit to invest in ever more elaborate Ponce de León celebrations, once again with an eye toward creating—and, of course, selling—the romance and other attractions attached to Old Spain.[20]

* * *

But would the rest of Florida follow suit? Tampa, for one, did not, at least not immediately, undoubtedly for reasons connected to the presence of large numbers of Cuban émigrés who were decidedly hostile to both Spaniards and Spain in the decade leading up to the Spanish-American War.[21] This hostility helps explain, at least in part, why Henry Plant, after having decided that Tampa needed a grand hotel to rival the Ponce de León, did something other than copy the Spanish style that his great rival Flagler employed. The Tampa Bay Hotel, opened in 1891, would also be a pleasure dome, but one inspired less by the Alhambra than the "stately palace" Kublai Khan had decreed.[22] The Tampa Bay, moreover, opened the door to alternate models of tourist architecture which, over time, ensured that the Spanish style Flagler had pioneered would not find much of a foothold on Florida's west coast. In Sarasota, for example, Venice was the chief point of reference, as Ca' d'Zan, John Ringling's mansion, readily attests; and in St. Petersburg the only major Spanish-style hotel was the Rolyat, built at the tail end of the Florida land boom of the 1920s and designed to resemble a Spanish walled town with a

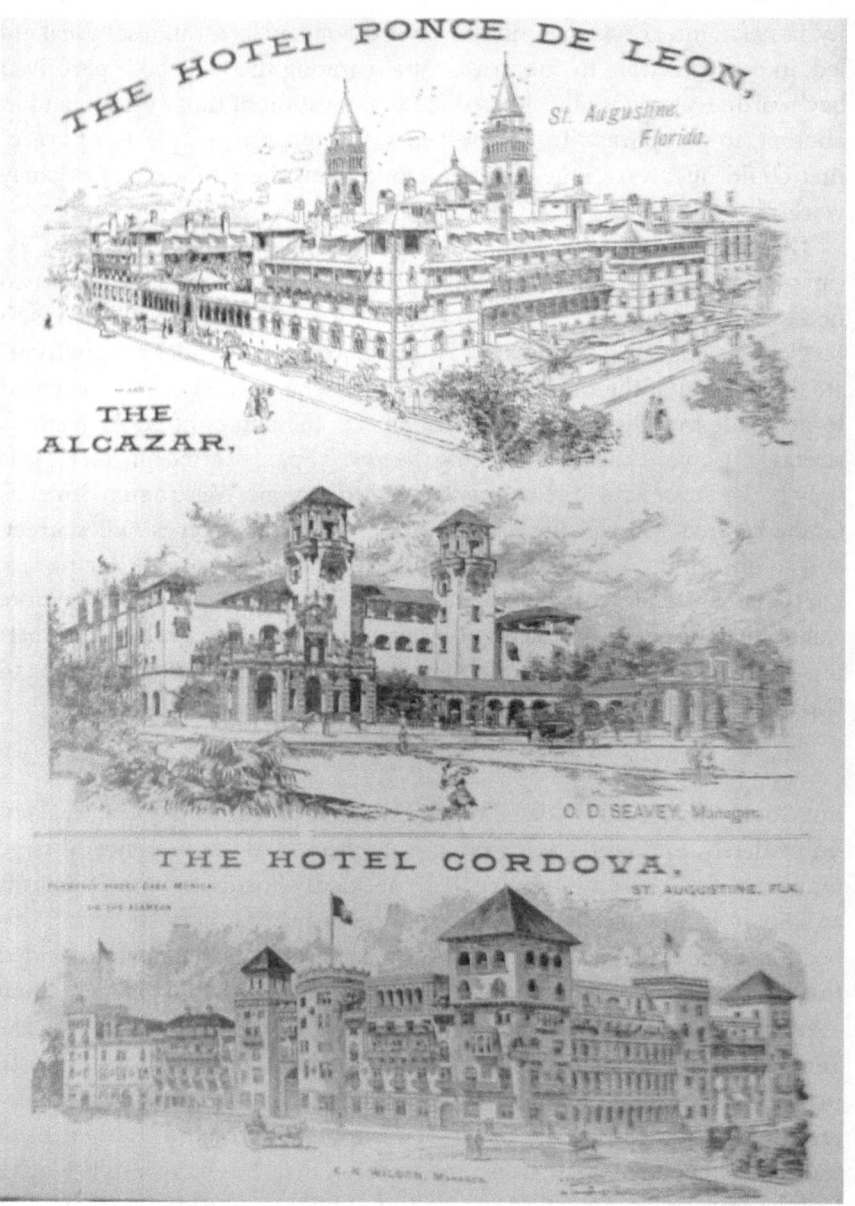

Figure 8.3. Flagler hotels in St. Augustine. (Courtesy of the St. Augustine Historical Society)

plaza mayor, a bridge modeled after one in Toledo, and an octagonal tower that was a replica of Seville's Torre de Oro.[23]

But if West Florida put up some resistance to the romance of Spain, other parts of the state rolled out the welcome mat—albeit not without a few wrinkles, as Coconut Grove's Villa Vizcaya, which was originally designed in Spanish style but abruptly changed to something more Italianate, attests.[24] There was another false start in the new resort town of Palm Beach, where Flagler, possibly to distance himself from the anti-Spanish propaganda that erupted in the run-up to the Spanish-American War, opted for a more sedate colonial style of architecture in his first hotels there (Royal Poinciana, Palm Beach Inn).

All this would change at the end of World War I, when Florida's land boom was just beginning and the Spanish Craze in New York, California, and other parts of the country was already in full swing. The postwar era marks the construction of Coral Gables, which was unabashedly modeled upon "such grand old Spanish cities as Cordova, Salamanca, Toledo and lovely old Seville." In the end Coral Gables became something of an architectural mishmash, with Moorish, Mediterranean, and Mexican, as well as Spanish, design elements, but what one of its developers described as the town's "fine old Spanish atmosphere" was reflected in the development's centerpiece, the Ritz Carlton Hotel, whose tower was a replica of Seville's Giralda. The same atmosphere manifested in the expansive entrance plaza to Coral Gables, dubbed the "Puerta de Sol;" street names that were largely Spanish; churches built in either mission or Spanish baroque style; fountains and statues dedicated to Hernando de Soto and other Spanish adventurers; and the emporium known as the Granada Shops, where the owners of newly constructed Spanish- and Mediterranean-style houses could find Spanish paintings, furniture, and antiques.[25]

There were more such shops in Palm Beach which, together with Boca Raton, became the epicenter of Florida's Spanish Craze. Much has already been written on the architectural and design history of these resorts, and there is no need to repeat it here, but what is arguably Spanish—or least Mediterranean—in both was largely the handiwork of the famed architect Addison Mizner (1872–1933). Born in California, educated first in Guatemala (where his father was the U.S. ambassador) and subsequently in Spain, where he studied for a time at the University of Salamanca, Mizner (figure 8.4) kept a detailed record of these and other travels in the form of sketches that he later organized into a series of albums currently preserved in the Four Arts Society of Palm Beach. These contain page after page of drawings of houses, gardens, and various architectural details, together with a

Figure 8.4. Addison Mizner, 1920. (Historical Society of Palm Beach County)

multitude of photographs, articles, and newspaper clippings, all of which testify to Mizner's interests in Spanish art, architecture, and design. The albums deserve detailed study, but it appears that Mizner used them as a kind of *aide memoire* and source of inspiration throughout his architectural career.

This career began in Southern California in the 1890s, where Mizner served as an apprentice to Willis Polk, an early proponent of mission-style architecture.[26] Mizner then moved to New York, where he befriended Stanford White, an architect known for his interest in Spanish culture and art, who was also responsible for the first Giralda-style tower constructed in the United States.[27]

While living in New York, Mizner designed his first "Spanish-style" house for a wealthy client on Long Island's north shore, and it was apparently this house that attracted the attention of Paris Singer, a wealthy socialite who had made Palm Beach his home. Singer soon invited Mizner to Palm Beach and commissioned him to construct the new Everglades Club in the Spanish style. That style quickly proved infectious, and starting with Mirasol (figure 8.5), built in 1919, Mizner designed a series of sumptuous private houses in a kind of hybrid Spanish-cum-Mediterranean style. He outfitted several with furniture, paintings, and other antiques that he himself purchased during several shopping sprees to Spain. The same Spanish-cum-Mediterranean style also appeared in the arcades and patios Mizner designed for Worth Avenue and through Mizner Industries, a workshop that provided his clients with pottery, tiles, grilles, and furniture of both Spanish and Mediterranean design, intended to harmonize with what he called Florida's "profoundly Spanish character." Mizner went one step further in Boca Raton which, though never fully realized, was envisioned as yet another Spanish town— with a Giralda; a grand hotel called the Castillo del Rey whose dining room was modeled after the refectory of a hospital Mizner had seen during one of his trips to Spain; an administrative building meant to replicate El Greco's house in Toledo; a mission-style town hall; a Spanish village; and for his own house, a mock Spanish castle, complete with drawbridge and moat.[28]

The collapse of Florida's land boom, starting in 1926, put most of these plans on hold, but by this point the Spanish-cum-Mediterranean style of architecture that Mizner had helped popularize was ubiquitous. The same

Figure 8.5. Mirasol postcard, 1923.

year, the architect Howard Major, in an important article as well as a book, expressed the view that the Spanish style "was totally at variance with our Anglo-Saxon temperament" and thus failed to express "American 'national character.'"[29] Major suggested the use instead of Greek revival, colonnaded colonial, or what he called British colonial (or West Indian–style) architecture.

What Major failed to recognize is that the Spanish Craze had opened Americans' eyes to the importance of Spanish culture in the United States, especially in places like Florida, where it connected with a history the country had either neglected or studiously attempted to forget. Historians like Smith and Fairbanks thought otherwise, as I have tried to suggest, but not nearly as eloquently as Walt Whitman who, writing in 1883, addressed the thorny issue of America's national identity in an essay published in Santa Fe in conjunction with a celebration marking what was mistakenly considered the 333rd anniversary of the foundation of that New Mexican town. Santa Fe authorities invited Whitman to visit New Mexico and present a commemorative address. Whitman—old, ailing, and residing in Camden, New Jersey—declined to make the cross-country trek, but because he was deeply concerned with the topic of America's "nationality," he sent in his place an essay, "The Spanish Element in Our Nationality," in which he explained that the Spaniard, just like the Englishman, was part of the "American identity." It read as follows:

> Character, literature, a society worthy the name, are yet to be establish'd. . . . To that composite American identity of the future, Spanish character will supply some of the most needed parts. No stock shows a grander historic retrospect—grander in religiousness and loyalty, or for patriotism, courage, decorum, gravity and honor. . . . It is time to realize—for it is certainly true—that there will not be found any more cruelty, tyranny, superstition, etc., in the *résumé* of past Spanish history than in the corresponding *résumé* of Anglo-Norman history. Nay, I think there will not be found so much.
>
> As to the Spanish stock of our Southwest, it is certain to me that we do begin to appreciate the splendor and sterling value of its race element. Who knows but that element, like the course of some subterranean river, dipping invisibly for a hundred or two years, is now to emerge in broadest flow and permanent action?[30]

The language is flowery, dare I say poetic, but the message crystal clear. Taking direct aim at nativists who identified America as Anglo-Saxon, Protestant, and white, Whitman linked Spain and its heritage to that of the United States. Soon other writers, such as the aforementioned Lummis, began to express similar sentiments. Despite the momentary upsurge in anti-Spanish sentiment leading up to the Spanish-American War, in the early twentieth century politicians in various parts of the country openly expressed similar sentiments, adding that Spain and America were essentially brethren in arms to the extent that they shared a common historic mission—that of converting the hemisphere's indigenous population to Christianity and thus furthering the cause of civilization itself.[31] Spain's soldiers and missionaries had initiated this campaign in the sixteenth century. The United States, the new standard bearer of the Americas, was now seeing it through to completion.

From this linkage emerged the idea that, whatever the political differences between Spain and the United States, these were but superficial and temporary inasmuch as the culture, the language, and indeed the history of two countries were deeply and profoundly intertwined. Much of this rhetoric was pure invention, but it allowed Spanish-style houses—and Spanish tiles, furniture, music, and dance—to be understood as authentic, homegrown, and thus quintessentially American in ways that other imported styles of architecture—whether British, Italian, Japanese, or French—were not. At the same time, what impressed many as the simplicity, honesty, and straightforward, workmanlike quality of the Spanish style was seen to reflect the values that had supposedly helped make America into the great power it was. From this perspective, Florida's discovery of Spain was but one phase in the story of Florida's discovery of itself.

Further Reading

Boone, M. Elizabeth. *Vistas de España: American Views of Art and Life in Spain, 1860–1914.* New Haven, CT: Yale University Press, 2009.

Braden, Susan R. *The Architecture of Leisure: The Florida Resort Hotels of Henry Flagler and Henry Plant.* Gainesville: University Press of Florida, 2002.

Hatton, Hap. *Tropical Splendor: An Architectural History of Florida.* New York: Alfred A Knopf, 1987.

Kagan, Richard L. "The *Spanish Craze* in the United States: Cultural Entitlement and the Appropriation of Spain's Cultural Patrimony, ca. 1890–ca. 1930." *Revista Complutense de Historia de America* 36 (2010): 37–58.

———. "The Spanish Turn: The Discovery of Spanish Art in the United States, 1887–1920." In *Collecting Spanish Art: Spain's Golden Age and America's Gilded Age,* ed. Inge Reist and José Luis Colomer, 3–23. Frick Collection Studies in the History of Art Collecting in America. State College: Penn State University Press, 2012.

Seebohm, Caroline. *Boca Rococo: How Addison Mizner Invented Florida's Gold Coast.* New York: Clarkson Potter, 2001.

Notes

1. See Richard L. Kagan, "The *Spanish Craze* in the United States: Cultural Entitlement and the Appropriation of Spain's Cultural Patrimony, ca. 1890–ca. 1930," *Revista Complutense de Historia de America* 36 (2010): 37–58.

2. For some of these "crazes," see Clay Lancaster, *The Japanese Influence in America* (New York: Walton H. Rawls, 1963); Annette Stott, *Holland Mania: The Unknown Dutch Period in American Art and Culture* (Woodstock, NY: Overlook Press, 1998); Scott Tafton, *Egypt Land: Race and Nineteenth-Century American Egyptomania* (Durham, NC: Duke University Press, 2004); Bob Brier, *Egyptomania: Our Three Thousand Year Obsession with the Land of the Pharaohs* (New York: Palgrave Macmillan, 2013); and Helen Delpar, *The Enormous Vogue for Things Mexican: Cultural Relations between the United States and Mexico, 1920–1935* (Tuscaloosa: University of Alabama Press, 1992).

3. For the Black Legend in the United States, the classic study, first published in 1971, is Phillip Wayne Powell, *Tree of Hate: Propaganda and Prejudices Affecting United States Relations with the Hispanic World* (Albuquerque: University of New Mexico Press, 2008).

4. For an introduction to Irving's romanticized view of Spain, see several of the essays included in *Spain in America: The Origins of Hispanism in the United States*, ed. Richard L. Kagan (Urbana: University of Illinois Press, 2002).

5. Cited in Henry T. Tuckerman, *Book of the Artists: America's Artistic Life* (New York: G. P. Putnam, 1867), 561.

6. For U.S. artists and Spain, see M. Elizabeth Boone, *Vistas de España: American Views of Art and Life in Spain, 1860–1914* (New Haven, CT, and London: Yale University Press, 2009), together with my essay, "The Spanish Turn: The Discovery of Spanish Art in the United States, 1887–1920," in *Collecting Spanish Art: Spain's Golden Age and America's Gilded Age*, ed. Inge Reist and José Luis Colomer, Frick Collection Studies in the History of Art Collecting in America (State College, PA: Penn State University Press, 2012), 3–23.

7. For an introduction to Spain's presence at this fair, see Judy Sund, "Columbus and Columbia in Chicago, 1893: Man of Genius Meets Generic Woman," *Art Bulletin* 75, no. 3 (1993): 443–46.

8. For an introduction to the San Diego fair, see Matthew F. Bokovoy, *San Diego's World Fairs and Southwestern Memory* (Albuquerque: University of New Mexico Press, 2005); and for that at Buffalo, see University of Buffalo, "Pan-American Exposition of 1901," http://library.buffalo.edu/pan-am/.

9. Rufus King Sewall, *Sketches of St. Augustine with a View to Its History and Advantages as a Resort for Invalids* (New York: G. P. Putnam, 1848), 11–12.

10. "Letters of William Cullen Bryant from Florida," *Florida Historical Society Quarterly* 14 no. 4 (1931), 262. See also Max Bloomfield, *Bloomfield's Illustrated Historical Guide: Embracing an Account of the Antiquities of St. Augustine, Florida* (St. Augustine: Max Bloomfield, 1885), 78.

11. *Narrative of the Career of Hernando de Soto . . .* , trans. Buckingham Smith (New York: Bradford Society, 1856), xxv–xxvi.

12. I refer here to George R. Fairbanks, *History and Antiquities of the City of St. Augustine, Florida, Founded AD 1565* (New York: C. B. Norton, 1858) and his *History of Florida from Its Discovery by Ponce de Leon, in 1512, to the Close of the Florida War, in 1842*

(Philadelphia: J. B. Lippincott, 1874). For more on Fairbanks see Arthur J. Lynch, *George Rainsford Fairbanks: A Man of Many Facets* (Los Altos, CA.: Shambles Press, 1999).

13. For a reprint of the account of this festival, originally published in the *St. Augustine Evening Record* on April 3, 1885, see *El Escribano* 5, no. 2 (April 1988): 4–5. For the celebration's influence on Flagler, see Sidney Martin, *Flagler's Florida: Henry Flagler, Visionary of the Gilded Age* (Lake Buena Vista, FL: Tailored Tours, 1949, 1998), 106.

14. The Ponce de León may be approached through Thomas Graham, "Flagler's Magnificent Hotel Ponce de Leon," *Florida Historical Quarterly* 54 (July 1975): 1–17; Rafael A. Crespo, "Florida's First Spanish Renaissance Revival" (PhD diss., Harvard University, 1987); and Susan R. Braden, *The Architecture of Leisure: The Florida Resort Hotels of Henry Flagler and Henry Plant* (Gainesville: University Press of Florida, 2002).

15. I refer to Mark Galernter, *A History of American Architecture: Buildings in Their Cultural Context* (Hanover, NH: University Press of New England, 1999), 199.

16. Smith noted that the design of the Villa Zorayda was in keeping with "the Spanish style of architecture"; see St. Augustine Historical Society, folder 18: F. W. Smith, clipping from *St. Augustine Record*, April 17, 1937. For Smith, see Susan L. Clarke, "Franklin W. Smith: St. Augustine's Concrete Pioneer" (MA thesis, Cooperstown Graduate Program, New York, 1990).

17. For Hastings's thoughts on the Ponce de León, see "Thomas Hastings: Architect of Famous Hotels in the Old City," *St. Augustine Record*, Monday, January 21, 1924, 1. For Flagler's interest in Spanish culture, see Julian Ralph, "Riviera, Our Town," *Harper's New Monthly Magazine* 86, no. 514 (March 1893): 489–510; and Edwin Lefevre, "Flagler and Florida," *Everybody's Magazine* 22 (February 1910): 168–88.

18. I refer to T. Jackson Lears, *No Place of Grace: Anti-modernism and the Transformation of American Culture, 1880–1920* (New York: Pantheon Books, 1981).

19. For these changes see Thomas Graham, "Henry Flagler's St. Augustine," *El Escribano* 40 (2003): 9.

20. For the program books and other materials relating to these festivals, see St. Augustine Historical Society, folder "Festivals: Ponce de León Celebration." These celebrations were held in 1885, 1889, 1890, 1901, 1907–10, 1913, 1923–27, and 1929–30. For the renaming of St. Augustine's streets, see "Excerpts from a Florida Diary," *El Escribano* 2, no. 1 (1965): 6–10; and Graham, "Henry Flagler's St. Augustine," 9.

21. For these anti-Spanish sentiments, see Gary R. Mormino and George E. Pozzetta, "The Cradle of Mutual Aid Immigrant Cooperative Societies in Ybor City," *Tampa Bay History* 7, no. 2 (1985): 36–58.

22. For this hotel, see Braden, *Architecture of Leisure*.

23. St. Petersburg's architecture may be approached through Raymond Arsensault, *St. Petersburg and the Florida Dream, 1888–1950* (Norfolk, VA: Donning Co., 1988); together with Hap Hatton, *Tropical Splendor: An Architectural History of Florida* (New York: Alfred A. Knopf, 1987); and Braden, *Architecture of Leisure*.

24. For Villa Vizcaya's design history, see Witold Rybczynski and Laurie Olin, *Vizcaya: An American Villa and Its Makers* (Philadelphia: University of Pennsylvania Press, 2007), 21–22.

25. For the design and planning of Coral Gables, see Hatton, *Tropical Splendor*, 60–63.

26. Donald W. Curl, *Mizner's Florida: American Resort Architecture* (Cambridge, MA: Architectural History Foundation and MIT Press, 1987).

27. I refer to the tower White designed for New York's Madison Square Garden in 1889. For this and White's interest in Spanish art, see my "Blame It on Washington Irving: New York's Discovery of the Art and Architecture of Spain," in *Nueva York: 1613–1945*, ed. Edward Sullivan (New York: New York Historical Society and Scala, 2010), 155–71.

28. On Boca Raton, see Caroline Seebohm, *Boca Rococo: How Addison Mizner Invented Florida's Gold Coast* (New York: Clarkson Potter, 2001).

29. Howard Major, "A Theory Relating to Spanish and Italian Houses in Florida," *Architectural Forum* 25 (August 1926): 97–120; and Major, *The Domestic Architecture of the Early American Republic: Greek Revival* (Philadelphia: J. P. Lippincott, 1926), 89.

30. Walt Whitman, "The Spanish Element in Our Nationality," in Whitman, *Complete Prose Works* (London and New York: D. Appleton, 1910): 388–89. The essay originally appeared in the *Philadelphia Press*, August 5, 1883. Available online at http://www.bartleby.com/229/5004.html.

31. The inauguration of the Christopher Columbus monument in Washington, DC, in 1908 occasioned a number of public addresses by politicians and other speakers echoing these themes. See, for example, "Address of the Hon. Joseph Scott of Los Angeles, California," delivered at the Christopher Columbus Memorial Celebration, Washington, DC, June 8, 1912," (I consulted the copy in the Archivo de Ministerios de Asuntos Exteriores, Madrid, Spain, Sección Histórica: Celebraciones); and Charles H. McCarthy, *Columbus and His Predecessors* (Philadelphia: John Joseph McVey, 1912).

9

Performing Diasporas, or *Cubanidad* Meets Jim Crow

Miami in a Period of Demographic Transition before the Cuban Revolution

DARIÉN J. DAVIS

According to the Pew Hispanic Research Center approximately six in ten Cubans (59 percent) in the United States are foreign born and more than 50 percent arrived in the United States in 1990 or later. The majority of Cubans in Florida certainly arrived after the 1959 Cuban Revolution. Thus, when Florida senator Marco Rubio speaks about his family fleeing oppression in Cuba, most Americans assume that his family members left Cuba after 1959. Yet many Cubans such as Marco Rubio Sr. and Oria García, the senator's parents, came to the United States during the 1950s when U.S.-backed military dictator Fulgencio Batista governed Cuba.[1] From the end of World War II to 1958, more than 20,000 Cubans immigrated to the United States, with more than half of that number coming between 1956 and 1958. Many of them settled in southern Florida and Miami, joining the approximately 20,000 Puerto Ricans, who made up 4 percent of the population, and a handful of other Latin Americans, compared to a black population of approximately 15 percent.[2]

Most scholars who have studied the Cuban presence in the United States prior to 1959 have focused on places such as New York City and Tampa, but few have studied Miami prior to the arrival of Cubans in the 1960s.[3] The Cuban diaspora transformed Miami in the 1960s in multiple ways, but demographic and cultural changes had already begun after the end of World War II as Miami developed and promoted itself as a tourist destination. This essay examines the impact of the movement of Cubans and Cuban popular music across national, racial, social, and linguistic lines in the late 1940s and throughout the 1950s prior to the massive wave of Cuban immigrants in the 1960s. Cubans of multiple ethnic backgrounds brought Afro-Cuban rhythms and idioms to Miami and elsewhere despite racial prejudice and discrimination. Ironically, American segregation ensured that white Cuban performers would play a more visible role than their black counterparts in the propagation of Afro-Cuban rhythms in the mainstream media. Afro-Cubans remained critical to the development and transformation of Cuban music in the United States, particularly through collaborations with African Americans and other Latinos in places like New York and Miami. In the developing tourist haven of Miami, musical venues celebrated Cuban rhythms, often in spite of segregation. Indeed, for many Cubans in the late 1950s, segregation represented an affront to Cuba's national celebration. To appreciate the complexities of the Afro-Cuban impact on Miami we have to understand the historical contradictions of Miami as a city at the crossroads of the Caribbean and a gateway to New York City; as a city of tourists, travelers, and immigrants and also a gateway to Havana; and as a segregated city that officially privileged whiteness but relied on black labor and entertainers (such as musical performers).

Cubanidad at the Crossroad of the Caribbean

The 1956 Pan American travel guide proclaimed that greater Miami, including Miami and Miami Beach, "have become the tourist center not only of Florida, but probably the entire nation."[4] Cubans in particular moved across the Straits from Havana to Key West and Miami (and often vice versa), taking with them rich cultural traditions that informed *cubanidad, cubanía,* or Cuban-ness, which they variously described with a number of competing but similar discourses, such as cultural *ajiaco, criollo* (creole), or *mulato*.[5] Despite the variations in the descriptions of the Cuban character, given the prolonged, significant, and direct African presence in Cuba from colonial times to the end of the nineteenth century, Afro-Cuban cultural traditions were ubiquitous and thus central to any recognition of *cubanidad* that took popular culture into consideration. Cubans traveling to Florida, whether black, white, *mulato*, Chinese, Jewish, or Lebanese knowingly or unknowingly participated in the transmission of *their* Afro-Cuban heritage. Nowhere is this more clearly seen than in the performance of Cuban music in Florida and elsewhere.

Before the mass immigration of the 1960s, Cuban culture left its mark on Miami's cultural landscape in subtle but important ways. The Cuban anthropologist Fernando Ortiz aptly described *transculturation* as the movement of people with their cultures relatively intact, but Ortiz does not account for elements of culture being carried by sojourners or transnational performers, the role of commercial institutions in promoting cultural forms, or the fact that foreigners may be capable of replicating and disseminating learned cultural practices with the aid of native collaborators. Prerevolutionary Latin American and Cuban immigrants, traveling performers, and the Miami tourist industry all collaborated to promote a distinct and exotic Hispanic Caribbean city in the midst of a decade that saw the slow dismantling of Jim Crow laws enforcing racial segregation.[6]

Prerevolutionary Miami serves as a rich laboratory for studying the arrival of early African-inflected Hispano-Caribbean musical and cultural traditions precisely because the 1950s was also an extraordinary time of transition from segregation and Jim Crow to a new racial paradigm. The contributions of diverse Cuban performers—from Desi Arnaz to Cachão, Machito, Mario Bauzá, Mongo Santamaría, and others such as Tito Puente—who played Cuban-inflected music prior to the Cuban Revolution give us insight into Caribbean transnational cultural practices beyond the local, regional, and national political discourses that tend to divide the island and reify racial, ethnic, or regional identities.[7]

Cuban music and performers came to Miami at a time when labor unions often prohibited foreigners from accepting certain jobs and racism disenfranchised blacks in both Florida and Cuba. Performers such as Graciela Bauzá, the sister of Latin jazz pioneer Mario Bauzá, claimed that in the early 1940s as "bad as things were in the United States, they were worse in Cuba," particularly for poor blacks.[8] Musician Israel "Cachão" López puts the racism in both countries in the 1950s into perspective:

> I came but not to play because there the unions and the racism were strong. The first was Aspiazú, afterwards Mario Bauzá and then Socarrás. I remember when I was in Miami in 1948, and I asked for a Coca-Cola in a bar. They did not refuse to serve me but when I returned the empty glass to them they threw it in the garbage and said "a black man drank here." In the hotels, we had to eat in the kitchens. We couldn't eat in the restaurant. In Cuba racism was also very strong. Blacks had to stroll around the perimeter of the parks, and whites inside them. A black man could not be a police official. There was a glass ceiling. Batista was the person who ended that.[9]

Cachão's experience highlights the transnational discrimination against people of African descent in both Cuba and the United States at a time when Latinos (or people of Hispanic origin, the term the U.S. census utilizes) represented less than 2 percent of the U.S. population. Moreover, Latino consciousness movements were only beginning to garner national attention. The League of United Latin American Citizens (LULAC), which focused on the plight of Mexican Americans, had won two landmark legal cases: the integration of California's Orange County public school system in 1945 and the landmark *Hernandez v. State of Texas*, challenging the fact that no Mexican American had ever been called to jury duty in Texas. Neither Florida nor Cubans figured prominently as a concern of the Latino civil rights movement despite the state's geographical place between North America and the Caribbean.[10]

In the 1950s most Afro-Cubans in the United States lived in the New York region. Afro-Cuban musicians and baseball players in the Negro Leagues were two of the most visible groups because they traveled and performed around the segregated United States, including to Florida. In Cuba, Afro-Cubans remained underrepresented in politics, business, and education. They were also absent from elite cultural circles, although ironically Afro-Cubans were represented in national government, starting with the country's *mulato* president and a number of statesmen. The 1940 Constitution outlawed racial discrimination, at least on paper. Cubans recognized if not revered Afro-Cuban artists and intellectuals such as Nicolás Guillén, Wilfredo Lam, and Rita Montaner. This contrasted with segregation in the U.S. South, which controlled movement and socialization by law. Segregation in Miami disenfranchised African Americans, discouraged Afro-Cubans from moving to Florida, and limited and infuriated many Cuban visitors. Indeed segregation was also problematic to many white Cubans, who often defied the laws (as did many American and Cuban business owners who did not always enforce the laws in their establishments).[11] There was also a strong current of anti-Semitism in Miami, which led to discrimination against the substantial Jewish population that had relocated to Miami after World War II. Many Jews in Miami had moved from places in the Caribbean such as Cuba and the Dominican Republic. There was also discrimination against temporary workers from the Bahamas, Jamaica, and Puerto Rico. These immigrants and workers built art deco Miami.

Political and economic turmoil in Cuba from the 1930s to 1959 also had a modest impact on demographic trends. Cuban exiles followed ex-president Mario Gabriel García Menocal to Miami Beach after he left Cuba in 1931, for example. Menocal's mansion on Collins Avenue served as a meeting place for many of the exiles. Cuban political protestors also made their way to Miami, including members of the Directorate of University Students (DEU) who regrouped in Miami in the early 1930s to advocate for the overthrow of General Machado. The flow continued in the 1940s and 1950s with well-known political exiles such as José Manuel Alemán, who served in the Ramón Grau San Martín government (1944–48). Alemán provided the money for Miami's baseball stadium, which was to be the most "significant ballpark built since Yankee Stadium."[12]

By the early 1950s, many of Havana's entertainment operations, which included hotels, casinos, and brothels, were run out of Miami. The AT&T Cable Company linked Cuba to the United States through telephone and telegraph, and the cruise liner the SS *Florida* linked Miami to Havana, carrying businessmen, travelers, and entertainers between the two countries. Cooperation between Miami and Havana occurred on many levels, including law enforcement. The Federal Bureau of Investigation office in Miami was also responsible for activities in Havana. In 1950, Lieutenant Sigfredo Díaz Biart, chief of the Cuban Bureau of Investigation, even visited Miami to observe the FBI's firearms training.[13] Miami was also home to Cuban publishers and music producers. The Editorial Cubano de la Música, for example, published a *guaracha* written by Roger Covington, an American student at the University of Miami.[14]

Miami hotels and apartment complexes also posted advertisements in Havana. White middle-class Americans flocked to Havana and white middle-class Cubans traveled to Miami, creating a corridor within which mutual exchange and cross-hybridization took place. While the majority of travelers were white, African Americans and Afro-Cubans were not entirely absent. Although American air carriers and ship lines did not formally enforce segregation, economic conditions did restrict African American and Afro-Cuban travel. Thus, while white travelers were the main gatekeepers and transporters of American and Cuban cultural products, they were influenced by blacks in both directions.[15]

Temporary visitors and tourists from Cuba were an important part of the pre-1959 Miami landscape, and the city was already acquiring a Caribbean if not Cuban air. Moreover, Cubans represented an important consumer market, and Miami businesses embarked upon a number of campaigns to make Cubans feel at home. According to Louis Pérez Jr., travel to Miami was also induced by budget summer rates, which made vacations in Miami more affordable and more attractive than similar vacations in Cuba.[16] At the same time Miami began to promote itself as a year-round exotic tropical tourist destination, and Cubans helped create that atmosphere. Hotels, theaters, nightclubs, and a host of other establishments hired Cuban artists and performers who came from the Caribbean as well as New York.[17]

As previously noted, earlier in the century New York had become a preferred destination for Cuban artists and performers. Immigrants found more opportunities in the Northeast and in New York City, which was much larger and more diverse than Miami, and they did not have to confront blatant segregation laws. As opportunities arose in Miami in the 1950s and 1960s, a New York–Miami travel corridor opened and performers took what John Roberts has called "the Latin Tinge" to Miami, joining other performers from Cuba and elsewhere in the Caribbean. Afro-Cuban–inspired rhythms such as the *son*, rumba, and mambo moved throughout the United States. This cultural influence came through the creative minds of Alberto Socorrás and Carlos Vidal Bolado in the 1930s, and Pérez Prado, Machito, Tito Rodríguez, and Tito Puente in the 1950s. These musical forms received greater attention when well-known American performers such as Cole Porter and Dizzy Gillespie adopted them. Ary Barroso and other Brazilians produced many of the Brazilian-Cuban fusions for the Carmen Miranda and Disney films of the 1940s and 1950s.[18] Dancers such as Amalia Aguilar highlighted the Afro-Cuban influences with performances entitled "Afro-Mood and Rumba."[19] The visibility of Afro-Cuban music crossed racial and cultural lines in the United States despite the social restrictions of Jim Crow.

Entertainment: The Cuban Musical Connection and Jim Crow

The Miami tourist industry exploited its connection to Cuba, maintained Spanish-speaking employees, cooked up Caribbean and Spanish cuisine, and made Caribbean and especially Cuban performers readily available in a number of venues throughout the 1940s and 1950s. Ironically, the appeal to Spanish-speaking Cubans and the creation of a Spanish-Caribbean atmosphere for tourists contrasted remarkably with the mood in the fashion and garment industries of the city. In those quarters, tensions between low-wage Puerto Rican workers and employers arose due to a lack of proper channels of communication, particularly because of language barriers between the almost exclusively English-speaking management and the Spanish-speaking labor force.[20]

Meanwhile, hotels hosted rumba nights with authentic Cuban bands. The University of Miami student composer Roger Covington performed his composition "Se Quema Mi Casa" at El Toreador Cabaret, an establishment that promoted itself as Spanish and Cuban. Miami nightclubs such as the Clover Club and the Olympia organized special Cuban reviews to attract tourists, helping to spur an employment boom for performers familiar with Cuban idioms.

Although unions gave preferential treatment to American-based performers, hotels like the Fontainebleau featured the Carlos Ramírez Orchestra from Havana. Other Cuban or Cuban-inspired bands with names such as the Latin American Orchestra, the Orchestra Sacasa, and Rafael y Sus Rumberos played at the Hotel Delmonico, the Miami Beach Blue Sail, and the Hotel Belmar, respectively. The famed Roney Plaza in Miami, which was demolished in 1968, featured Cuban groups including the Siboney Sextet, a rumba orchestra.[21]

Miami also attracted well-established Cuban stars such as Beny Moré and those who would become stars in the United States, such as Desi Arnaz. Incredibly, Afro-Cuban singer Beny Moré and his Afro-Cuban trombonist, arranger, and composer Generoso Jiménez were performing at Miami's Lido Hotel on the eve of the triumph of the Cuban Revolution, and both discussed whether or not to return to Cuba. They both did. Moré died a few years later in Havana while Generoso returned to the United States in 2003, participating in the proliferation of Cuban music with Gloria Estefan, a leading producer and promoter of Cuban and Cuban American music in contemporary Miami.[22] Desi Arnaz never returned to Cuba. Instead he became the most visible Cuban performer in the mainstream American media of the 1950s because of his pioneering role on the *I Love Lucy* show, which was often shot on location in Miami Beach.[23]

A Word on Desi Arnaz and Afro-Cuban Rhythms

The Santiago-born Arnaz arrived in Miami in 1933, the year of the Machadato, when rebels overthrew Cuban president Gerardo Machado. He was a guitarist, percussionist, and vocalist who gained experience in the Xavier Cugat Orchestra before creating the Desi Arnaz Band. Arnaz, a white Cuban from the predominantly Afro-Cuban city of Santiago, brought many of the Afro-Cuban popular rhythms to mainstream North American audiences. He played the congas relatively well, although he certainly was not a seasoned player or virtuoso. Arnaz promoted the conga line dance craze with his performances in movies such as *Cuban Pete* (1946), *Holiday in Havana* (1949), and *I Love Lucy* (1953).[24]

Arnaz's signature performance on the *I Love Lucy* show, also recorded in the short film *Desi Arnaz and His Orchestra,* was "Babalu" or "Babalu Ayé," first popularized for American audiences by Miguel Valdés, another "white" (non–Afro-Cuban) performer well versed in Afro-Cuban culture. As an ethnic performance, "Babalu" is even more remarkable when we remember that theaters and film sets were still largely segregated in the 1950s. Afro-Cuban rhythms were prevalent in many enclaves from theaters to dance halls to jazz clubs, and white and black musicians often played together, particularly in New York. But it was Desi Arnaz, a white Cuban, who was largely responsible for taking these rhythms into the mainstream. While black Cubans were clearly at a disadvantage because of segregation and discriminatory practices in the entertainment field, this was not a simple case of appropriation. Arnaz was certainly performing a watered-down, more secular version of the sacred rhythms of "Babalu Ayé," but the remnants of popular Afro-Cuban idioms were nonetheless there. Arnaz, like many Cuban immigrants, understood Afro-Cuban idioms as a part of *his* Cuban culture: the conga drums, the opening call, and the structure of the song with its slow escalating rhythm that often ended in epiphany or possession, as in the Santería ritual.

The lyrics, which Arnaz sang in Spanish to 1950s English-speaking audiences who probably did not understand them, simultaneously exposed and masked a racialized language in which Afro-Cuban influences were clearly present. Arnaz utilized Afro-Cuban (that is to say, Cuban) idioms, intonation, and improvisation into which he would insert onomatopoeic sounds or phrases such as "En Santiago se baile la conga" or engage in a call-response session with his band and finally as a narrator who calls for his "negra" (black woman or simply woman). When Arnaz performed the song, he would end with an extensive conga line dance. These were hardly mainstream American customs.

> Babalu
> Babalu ayé
> Babalu ayé
> Babalu
> Ta empezando lo velorio
> Que le hacemos a Babalu
> Dame diez y siete velas
> Pa ponerle en cruz.
> Y dame un cabo de tabaco mayenye
> Y un jarrito de aguardiente,
> Dame un poco de dinero mayenye
> Pa' que me dé la suerte.
>
> Quiere pedi
> Que mi negra me quiera
> Que tenga dinero

Y que no se muera
Av! Vo le quiero pedi a Babalu 'na negra [bembo][muy santa] como tú
   que no tenga otro negro
Pa' que no se fuera.
Anda [a caballo]

Babalu ayé!²⁵

Arnaz helped forge the Cuban connection and promote Miami as a Cuban destination but, as I have shown, he was not alone. The Ritz Plaza featured "rumba nights." The Atlantis Hotel featured the timbales player Raymond "Monchito" Muñoz and his eight-piece orchestra, while the Belmar featured Puerto Rican musician Juanito Sanabria, who arrived in Miami in 1955.²⁶ While Tony Negrett and His Authentic Cubans played at the Caribbean Hotel's Starlight Patio, Tito Rodriguez and the Mambo Devils performed at the Delano. In 1948 Pupi Campo headed to Miami Beach for a gig at the Saxony Hotel, which had opened the previous year.²⁷ In 1953 the William Morris agency booked the Puerto Rican Tito Puente to perform at the Casablanca Hotel. Puente's band was multinational, multicultural, and multiracial, and included the great percussionist Ramón "Mongo" Santamaría Rodríguez. While white Americans may have accepted Arnaz, albeit reluctantly at first, black Cubans such as Mongo Santamaría and Cachão faced overt racial discrimination, just as the great conga player Chano Pozo had experienced before them.²⁸ In 1950, Santamaría moved to New York, where he played with a number of jazz and popular musicians from John Coltrane to Pérez Prado. When he traveled to Miami to perform with Puente he was prohibited from sleeping in Miami Beach, and instead had to sleep downtown in the "Colored" neighborhood across the bay, where other black musicians from Sammy Davis Jr. to Nat "King" Cole, Billie Holiday, and Lena Horne stayed while performing in Miami Beach.²⁹

The Hispanic Presence in Overtown

While pre-1950s census data on Overtown, or Colored Town, are difficult to secure, most sources describe the neighborhood as predominantly black and multicultural, with residents who were primarily African American and black Caribbean from diverse islands, including the Bahamas and Cuba. Overtown would drastically change in the 1960s with the arrival of thousands of Cubans. The artificial social laws instituted by Jim Crow discriminated against all blacks, regardless of country of origin.

Cuban blacks were present in Overtown, though that presence has yet to be thoroughly studied or documented. The current urban renewal programs, anecdotal data from interviews, and census data have helped us understand Overtown's history as a cultural mecca that rivaled white-dominated Miami Beach, despite the many disadvantages of segregation. African-American and Latin performers performed in Miami Beach and Overtown, for example. We know, for example, that many African American and Latin American performers who played in Overtown often relied on Cubans and Puerto Ricans and to a lesser extent Dominicans and Mexicans.[30]

While the definitive cultural history of Overtown has yet to be written, it is clear that segregation posed a problem for some black and white Cubans in the late 1950s and early 1960s. Official racial segregation was an explicit affront to the official rhetoric of *cubanidad* if not to the way many Cubans lived, save members of the small Cuban elite. This is not to deny racism among white Cubans, but the American Jim Crow mandate of segregation meant that some Cuban friends, neighbors, and families had to be separated by race in ways that would be clearly unacceptable and antithetical to the way of life for most Cubans even before the 1959 revolution. Most musicians followed segregation laws, although not without considerable pain and discomfort. By the late 1950s, however, hotels and other entertainment establishments in Miami were inconsistent in their enforcement of the racial codes. Both performers and clients knew which establishments did versus did not practice segregation. Many early Cuban immigrants from Havana in the late 1950s and early 1960s expressed their opposition to the segregation laws by refusing to obey them in buses and public places, just as many performers began refusing to perform in segregated venues.[31]

Cuba-Miami in the early 1960s

The chaotic years of the early 1960s rapidly transformed Miami through the arrival of thousands of Cubans. Many scholars have documented this exile and migration, detailing the economic, political, and social change to the city in the post–Jim Crow era. Cuban musical and popular culture resurfaced in many ways. The roots that had already been planted in mass culture were strengthened with new Cuban fusions from the bugalú, cha-cha, and salsa to other hybrids such as the bossa nova, Motown, soul, and rhythm and blues. Over the following decades new Cuban American songs would emerge from Miami, for the first time produced by Miami-based companies. Like their traveling compatriots before them, the new Cuban and Cuban American generation continued to blend the old with the new, including Afro-Cuban rhythms and inflections, and African American and other Latin American styles and forms. Others returned to the old forms and styles, as many longtime musicians who had stayed in Cuba began to travel to and settle in Miami. These later Cuban transplants included Santamaría from New York and Cachão, Generoso Jiménez, and others from Havana.

The U.S.-imposed trade embargo, in force since 1962, stymied the movement and exchange of music between Havana and Miami, although the connection between Miami and New York would continue as many Cuban artists chose exile. Celia Cruz spearheaded another immigration wave of popular Cuban performers to the United States in the mid-1960s. New York–based Fania Records, founded in 1964, spearheaded another round of cross-hybridization and collaborations, playing no small part in the salsa craze of the 1960s and 1970s. Fania's sale to Miami-based Emusica and its transfer from New York to Miami in 2005 are emblematic of Miami's growth as the center of Cuban-inspired music since the 1950s.[32]

By the 1970s, some fourteen years after the revolution, musician and accordion player Emilio Estefan founded the Miami Latin Boys. The same year salsa performer Willy Chirino released his first professional album, entitled *One Man Alone*. Estefan and Chirino represented a generation of Cuban-born performers and producers who grew up in Miami in the shadow of the Cuban Revolution, which dispersed tens of thousands of Cubans to the Florida Peninsula and beyond. Like diasporic performers the world over, Chirino and Estefan would celebrate cultural idioms from their homeland while infusing new elements and influences from their adopted country, just as Cuban musicians did before the revolution. Despite the North American penchant for reifying identities, the post-1960s hybrid creations influenced by many diasporic traditions helped produce diverse Miami styles such as Chirino's Dominican-inspired merengues and the charanga sound of the duo Hansel and Raul, who left New York for Miami in 1980.[33] In that decade the Afro-pop sound of Estefan's Miami Sound Machine also became mainstream. Estefan and other Miami producers went on to promote and collaborate with the older generation of exiles as well as other Latin Americans just as Miami was becoming more Latin American than exclusively Cuban American. Meanwhile *son*, salsa, and Latin jazz continue to mingle with new musical idioms throughout Miami.[34]

Post–World War II and 1950s Miami represented a rich laboratory for studying the arrival of early African-inflected Hispanic-Caribbean musical and cultural traditions through the talents of black and white performers. Martin Luther King warned Floridians that political powers would pit two disenfranchised communities (Cuban immigrants and black African Americans) against each other. He urged the two communities to think of strategies to deal with these urban challenges. That white Cubans, African Americans, Afro-Cubans, and other Latin American performers played significant roles in promoting Afro-Cuban popular cultures indicates historical diasporic connections beyond the political discourses of identity politics. The movement of Cuban culture across borders in the contentious period of the 1950s, despite the unequal treatment and movement of peoples, offers us insight into the history of Florida. It also highlights the importance of studying inequalities *and* cultural celebration to gain a greater understanding of the transmission of Afro-Caribbean cultural practices across national, ethnic, and racial divides. To paraphrase José Martí, is it possible that Cuban music is more than black, more than white, and more than *mulato* yet nonetheless a celebration of Cuba's African roots?

Notes

1. Seth Motel and Eileen Patten, "Hispanics of Cuban Origin in the United States, 2010," Pew Research Hispanic Trends Project, http://www.pewhispanic.org/2012/06/27/hispanics-of-cuban-origin-in-the-united-states-2010/. Raymond A. Mohl, "On the Edge: Blacks and Hispanics in Metropolitan Miami since 1959," *Florida Historical Quarterly* 69, no. 1 (1990): 37–56. Batista and his second wife, Marta Fernández de Batista, had already forged Floridian roots when they moved to Daytona Beach in the 1940s.

2. The calculations come from Lisandro Pérez, "Cubans in the United States," *Annals of the American Academy of Political and Social Science* 487 (September 1986): 128. Figures from 1951 to 1958 refer to Cuban-born immigrants.

3. José Rivero Muñiz, "Los cubanos de Tampa," *Revista Bimestre Cubana* 74, no. 1 (1958): 5–140; Durward Long, "The Historical Beginnings of Ybor City and Modern Tampa," *Florida Historical Quarterly* 45, no. 1 (1966): 31–44; Louis A. Pérez Jr., "Cubans in Tampa: From Exiles to Immigrants, 1892–1901," *Florida Historical Quarterly* 56 (1978): 52–81.

4. Pan American World Airways, *New Horizons USA: The Guide to Travel in the United States* (New York: Simon and Schuster, 1956), 188.

5. Darién J. Davis, "Mulato o Criollo: Cultural Identity in Cuba, 1930–1960," in *Ethnicity, Race and Nationality in the Caribbean*, ed. Juan Manuel Carrión, 69–95 (Puerto Rico: Institute of Caribbean Studies, University of Puerto Rico, 1996). For an excellent piece on the Afro-Cuban presence in the diaspora and Afro-Cuban–African American dialogue, see Armando González Pérez, "Afro-Cuban Identity and the Theater of the Diaspora," in *Companion to U.S. Latino Literatures,* ed. Carlota Caulfield and Darién J. Davis, 88–100 (Rochester, NY: Boydell and Brewer, 2007).

6. Scott Yanow, *Afro-Cuban Jazz* (San Francisco: Miller Freeman Books, 2000), 10–11. See also the Montuno Cubano website dedicated to Cuban music http://www.montunocubano.com.

7. See Luis Tamargo's interview for *Latin Beat*, "Jesus Caunedo: The Musical Flights of a Tropical Crane" http://www.herencialatina.com/Jesus_Caunedo/English_Version.htm.

8. Graciela Bauzá, "Esto era tremendo," in *The Afro-Latin@ Reader: History and Culture in the United States*, ed. Miriam Jiménez Román and Juan Flores, 150–54 (Durham, NC: Duke University Press, 2010), quotation on 153.

9. "Cachão," interview transcript, October 19, 2011, http://cubadentro.blogspot.com; my translation.

10. The 2 percent figure comes from the U.S. Census Report, "Table 1. Race and Hispanic Origin, 1790 to 1990." While the census does not list any official figures for 1950, the 1940 (5 percent) sample pegs the Hispanic origin population at 1.4 percent. Even the 2 percent figure should be viewed with caution, as it did not account for blacks from Spanish-speaking countries. In addition, many whites with Latin American ancestry may not have officially identified themselves as Hispanic. For information on LULAC see Amy Waters Yarsinske, *All for One and One for All: A Celebration of 75 Years of History of the League of United Latin American Citizens (LULAC)* (Virginia Beach, VA: Donning Co., 2006).

11. Larry Harris, director, *Black and White in Exile* (Cutting Edge Entertainment, 1997).

12. Luisa Yañez, "Miami Stadium: Field of Broken Dreams," *Miami Herald*, May 11, 2007.

13. Federal Bureau of Investigation, Miami Division, "A Brief History," http://www.fbi.gov/miami/about-us/history-1; Michael L. Grace, "Social History: AT&T cable Linking the USA to Cuba during the 1950s . . . ," May 3, 2012, Cruising the Past website, http://cruiselinehistory.com/tag/cuba/.

14. "Student Composers Get 2 Chances," *Miami Hurricane*, April 28, 1950, p. 8. See also Rep. Charles C. Diggs Jr. to the president of Continental Airlines, May 12, 1955, in which Diggs asks Continental Airlines to cease segregation practices in the United States; available at http://airandspace.si.edu/exhibitions/america-by-air/online/objectsDetail.cfm?webID=308.p7.

15. Francis J. Sicius, "Cubans in Miami: An Historic Perspective," paper presented at the annual meeting of the Florida Historical Society, Miami, FL, May 13, 1988, available at the Cuban Information Archives, document 0016, http://cuban-exile.com/doc_001-025/doc0016.html. On travel between the two cities see Smithsonian National Air and Space Museum, "America by Air" online exhibition, http://airandspace.si.edu/exhibitions/gal102/americabyair/abaImage.cfm?webID=308.p7.

16. Louis A. Pérez Jr., *On Becoming Cuban: Identity, Nationality and Culture* (Chapel Hill and London: University of North Carolina Press, 1999), 432–46.

17. Pérez, *On Becoming Cuban*, 433.

18. John Roberts, *Latin Jazz: The First Fusions, 1880s to Today* (New York: Schirmer Trade Books, 1999), 85–114; Lisa M. Knauer, "The Politics of Afrocuban Cultural Expression in New York City," *Journal of Ethnic and Migration Studies* 25 (2008): 1257–81; Raúl A. Fernández, *From Afro-Cuban Rhythms to Latin Jazz* (Berkeley: University of California Press, 2006). For the Brazilian contribution, see Darién J. Davis, *White Face, Black Mask: Africaneity and the Early Social History of Popular Music in Brazil* (East Lansing: Michigan State University Press, 2008).

19. W. Merle Connell, director, *A Night at the Follies* (Excelsior Films, 1947).

20. Melanie Shell-Weiss, *Coming to Miami: A Social History* (Gainesville: University Press of Florida, 2009), 163.

21. Pérez, *On Becoming Cuban*, 432–44; "Student Composers Get 2 Chances"; "Cabaret Guide to Miami 1956," Cuban Information Archives document 0187, http://cuban-exile.com/doc_176-200/doc0187.html.

22. "Generoso Jiménez," interview, October 21, 2011, http://cubadentro.blogspot.com.

23. Louis A. Pérez, *On Becoming Cuban*, 346.

24. Coyne S. Sanders and Tom Gilbert, *Desilu: The Story of Lucille Ball and Desi Arnaz* (New York: William Morrow, 1994), 17, 28.

25. Margarita Lecuona wrote "Babalu" in 1941. See "Badass Babalu" video clips at http://www.youtube.com/watch?v=rAV3bOJaQuY; interestingly, when Arnaz sang the song in English the lyrics were significantly changed to avoid the Afro-Cuban references:

Babalu
Babalu aye
Babalu aye
Babalu
Jungle drums were madly beating,
In the glare of eerie lights;
While the natives kept repeating
Ancient jungle rites.
All at once the dusky warriors began to
Raise their arms to skies above
And a native then stepped forward to chant to his Voodoo Goddess of love.
Ah!
[CHORUS]
Great Babalu!
I'm so lost and forsaken.
Ah, great Babalu!
Bring back the love you've taken.
You can restore all the dreams that once were mine
If only you'll use some mystic sign.
Ah! Great Babalu!
Bring her back to me.
Ah!

26. "Orchestra leader John Sanabria dies in Puerto Rico," *Miami News*, Thursday, July 24, 1975.

27. Josephine Powell, *Tito Puente: When the Drums Are Dreaming* (New York: AuthorHouse, 2007), 153.

28. "Chano Pozo o la revolución de jazz," El Veraz, http://www.elveraz.com/articulo151.htm. César Miguel Rondón, *The Book of Salsa: A Chronicle of Urban Music from the Caribbean to New York City*, trans. Frances R. Aparicio with Jackie White (Chapel Hill: University of North Carolina Press, 2008), 1, 32–34.

29. Rondón, *Book of Salsa*, 85; see also Charles G. Gerard, *Music from Cuba: Mongo Santamaría, Chocolate Armenteros, and Other Stateside Cuban Musicians* (Westport, CT: Praeger, 2001).

30. Marvin Dunn, *Black Miami* (Miami: University of Florida Press, 1997), 151–57. The recent renovations include the reopening of the historic Lyric Theater and the creation of the Miami Black Archives (http://www.theblackarchives.org) and the Overtown Music Project (http://overtownmusicproject.org).

31. Harris, *Black and White in Exile*.

32. "The Return of Fania, the Record Company That Made Salsa Hot," *New York Times*, June 4, 2006.

33. Gerard, *Music from Cuba*, 71.

34. Celeste Fraser Delgado, "Jazz Returns to Overtown," *Miami New Times*, Thursday, June 22, 2000, http://www.miaminewtimes.com/2000-06-22/calendar/jazz-returns-to-overtown/.

10

Mickey Ricans?

The Recent Puerto Rican Diaspora to Florida

JORGE DUANY

After World War II, the exodus of Puerto Ricans was primarily directed to New York City and other cities of the U.S. Northeast. Since the 1960s, however, Puerto Ricans have widely scattered throughout the U.S. mainland. During the 1990s, Florida displaced New Jersey as home to the second largest concentration of stateside Puerto Ricans, a population that nearly doubled to almost half a million persons. By 2010 the census counted 847,550 residents of Puerto Rican origin in Florida.[1]

The growth of Florida's Puerto Rican population has been spectacular, from slightly more than 2 percent of all U.S. Puerto Ricans in 1960 to more than 18 percent in 2010. Puerto Ricans currently represent the second largest Latino group in Florida, after Cubans, and the most numerous in Central Florida, particularly in the Orlando-Kissimmee metropolitan area. In 2010, one out of five Latinos in Florida was Puerto Rican.

The "Puerto Ricanization" of Florida forms part of the growing diversification of the Latino population in the United States. It also signals the emergence of new ethnic categories among Puerto Rican immigrants beyond "Nuyorican"—the sobriquet used on the Island for Puerto Ricans born or raised in the United States—including "Floririan," "Orlando Rican," or even "Diasporican." Journalistic reports have humorously referred to Puerto Ricans in Orlando as "Mickey Ricans" because of their close association with the Walt Disney World Resort.[2] Such hybrid labels point to the significance of local contexts in shaping migrants' cultural identities and in distinguishing them from those based on the Island. At the same time, the differences between Puerto Ricans born on the Island versus the mainland raise emotionally charged issues such as who can claim to be Puerto Rican and how that claim can be legitimated culturally and politically.

The Puerto Rican diaspora in Florida, where Cubans have predominated among Latinos for decades, is fertile ground for rethinking cultural identities in the context of increasingly complex interethnic relations. Above all, it offers a unique opportunity to examine the extent to which a shared Latino affiliation is taking root among immigrants from Latin America. States and cities formerly dominated by a single group of Hispanic origin—such as Puerto Ricans in New York, Cubans in Miami, or Mexicans in Los Angeles—have received large influxes of people from other Latin American and Caribbean countries, such as Dominicans in New York, Nicaraguans in Miami, and Salvadorans in Los Angeles. Thus, each of these sites has experienced an increasing cosmopolitanism of their Latino populations. The crucial political question is whether the immigrants and their descendants will forge broader alliances with other Latinos, based on their geographic, historical, linguistic, and cultural affinities; assert their distinctive national origins and transnational connections to their home countries; or perhaps combine the two strategies.

Scholars have explored the growing "Latinization" of inner-city enclaves such as El Barrio (also known as Spanish Harlem) in Manhattan, the Corona section of Queens, the Humboldt Park and Pilsen neighborhoods of Chicago, and Little Havana in Miami.[3] In each of these neighborhoods, immigration from various Latin American countries (especially Mexico and the Dominican Republic in El Barrio, and Nicaragua and Colombia in Little Havana) has reconfigured national and transnational identities. Whether immigrants embrace a pan-ethnic affiliation, such as "Hispanic" or "Latino," is still contested terrain. In addition, few studies have examined the issue of Latinization of suburban areas in the United States.

This chapter examines recent Puerto Rican migration to Florida, especially the Orlando, Miami, and Tampa metropolitan areas. It focuses on the immigrants' settlement patterns, socioeconomic characteristics, racial self-classification, political incorporation, and cultural practices. I argue that the growing dispersal of the Puerto Rican diaspora away from its traditional concentrations in the U.S. Northeast and Midwest toward the Southeast and Southwest has long-term consequences for the migrants' cultural identities, as well as their socioeconomic progress. Puerto Rican communities in Orlando, Miami, and Tampa differ substantially from their counterparts in New York City, Chicago, and Philadelphia, not only in their socioeconomic origins and settlement patterns, but also in their modes of economic and political incorporation into the receiving society. The current Puerto Rican experience in Florida is largely unprecedented, especially in comparison with previous migrant waves from the Island to the U.S. mainland.

Changing Settlement Patterns

The geographic distribution of Puerto Ricans in the United States has shifted greatly over the last five decades (see table 10.1). Although Puerto Ricans still concentrate in the state of New York, their proportion decreased from nearly three-fourths of the total in 1960 to a little less than one-fourth in 2010. For the first time ever, the number of persons of Puerto Rican origin in New York declined (albeit slightly) during the 1990s. Still, New York has the largest number of Puerto Rican residents of any state in the U.S. mainland. Meanwhile, the proportion of Puerto Ricans has increased elsewhere, above

Table 10.1. Geographic distribution of the Puerto Rican population in the United States, by state, 1960–2010 (percentages in parentheses)

	1960	1970	1980	1990	2000	2010
California	28,108 (3.1)	50,929 (3.6)	93,038 (4.6)	126,417 (4.6)	140,570 (4.1)	189,945 (4.1)
Connecticut	15,247 (1.7)	37,603 (1.9)	88,361 (4.4)	146,842 (5.4)	194,443 (5.7)	252,972 (5.4)
Florida	19,535 (2.2)	28,166 (2.0)	94,775 (4.7)	247,010 (9.1)	482,027 (14.2)	847,550 (18.3)
Illinois	36,081 (4.0)	87,477 (6.1)	129,165 (6.4)	146,059 (5.4)	157,851 (4.6)	182,989 (3.9)
Massachusetts	5,217 (0.6)	23,332 (1.6)	76,450 (3.8)	151,193 (5.5)	199,207 (5.8)	266,125 (5.7)
New Jersey	55,351 (6.2)	138,896 (9.7)	243,540 (12.1)	320,133 (11.7)	366,788 (10.8)	434,092 (9.4)
New York	642,622 (72.0)	916,608 (64.1)	986,389 (49.0)	1,086,601 (39.8)	1,050,293 (30.8)	1,070,558 (23.1)
Ohio	13,940 (1.6)	20,272 (1.4)	32,442 (1.6)	45,853 (1.7)	66,269 (1.9)	94,965 (2.0)
Pennsylvania	21,206 (2.4)	44,263 (3.1)	91,802 (4.6)	148,988 (5.5)	228,557 (6.7)	366,082 (7.9)
Texas	6,050 (0.7)	6,333 (0.4)	22,938 (1.1)	42,981 (1.6)	69,504 (2.0)	130,576 (2.8)
Other states	49,156 (5.5)	75,517 (5.3)	155,045 (7.7)	265,677 (9.7)	450,669 (13.2)	787,862 (17.0)
Total	892,513 (100.0)	1,429,396 (100.0)	2,013,945 (100.0)	2,727,754 (100.0)	3,406,178 (100.0)	4,623,716 (100.0)

Sources: U.S. Census Bureau, *American FactFinder*; *Census of Population and Housing*.

Table 10.2. Puerto Rican–origin population in Florida, by county, 2010

County	Number of Persons	As Percentage of Puerto Ricans in Florida	As Percentage of All Latinos in County	As Percentage of All Residents in County
Orange	149,457	17.6	47.5	13.0
Miami-Dade	92,358	10.9	5.7	3.7
Hillsborough	91,476	10.8	29.8	7.4
Broward	75,840	8.9	17.3	4.3
Osceola	72,986	8.6	59.8	27.2
Palm Beach	39,529	4.7	15.8	3.0
Polk	34,825	4.1	32.7	5.8
Seminole	34,378	4.1	47.4	8.1
Volusia	27,679	3.3	50.1	5.6
Lee	24,503	2.9	21.6	4.0
All other counties	204,519	24.1	—	—
Total	847,550	100.0	—	—

Source: U.S. Census Bureau, *American FactFinder*, 2010.

all in Florida. The states with the largest increases in their Puerto Rican populations include Pennsylvania, Massachusetts, Connecticut, and Texas.

Within Florida, Puerto Ricans have settled primarily in three regions. As table 10.2 displays, Puerto Ricans cluster in Central Florida, particularly in Orange, Osceola, Polk, and Seminole Counties. In 2010, the census counted 291,646 persons of Puerto Rican origin living in those four counties. Although Orange County had the largest number of Puerto Rican residents in the state, Osceola had the largest percentage. A secondary concentration is located in South Florida, composed of Miami-Dade, Broward, and Palm Beach Counties. According to the census, 207,727 Puerto Ricans were living there in 2010. A third Puerto Rican cluster is found around Tampa Bay, which includes Hillsborough, Pinellas, Pasco, and Hernando Counties, with 143,886 Puerto Rican residents in 2010. Puerto Ricans are the majority of the Latino population in Osceola and Volusia, and are the largest Latino group in Orange, Seminole, Hillsborough, and Duval Counties. As one journalist has noted, "the Puerto Ricans settled here [in Central Florida] rather than in South Florida because the latter was so heavily dominated by the Cuban community. The Puerto Ricans saw an opportunity to establish their identity in Central Florida."[4]

Florida's Orange County was by far the leading destination of Puerto Rican migrants during the first decade of the twenty-first century (figure 10.1). Moreover, six of the ten main destinations of Puerto Rican migrants

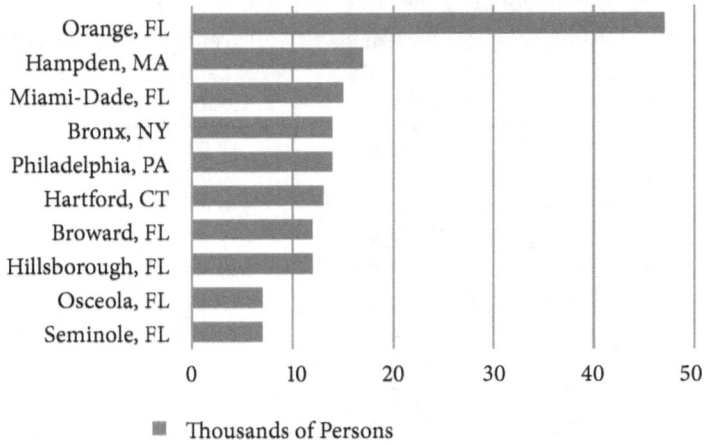

Figure 10.1. Main destinations of migrants from Puerto Rico to the United States, 2000–2009. (Source: U.S. Census Bureau, *American FactFinder*)

(Orange, Miami-Dade, Broward, Hillsborough, Osceola, and Seminole) are located in Florida. Between 2000 and 2009, 18.4 percent of all Puerto Ricans relocating from the Island moved to those counties. Thus, the recent Puerto Rican diaspora has been oriented primarily toward Central and South Florida.

Census data also document the restless circulation of people—the *vaivén*—between Puerto Rico and the United States, which I have analyzed elsewhere.[5] Many more Puerto Ricans are moving away from the Bronx and other traditional destinations (such as New York and Kings Counties in New York, and Cook County in Illinois, not shown in the figure) than from most places in Florida. Hence, not only are more Puerto Ricans leaving the Island for Florida than for other states, but more Puerto Ricans are leaving those other states and returning to the Island.

Florida now has three of the ten U.S. metropolitan areas with the largest Puerto Rican populations: Orlando-Kissimmee, Miami–Ft. Lauderdale–Pompano Beach, and Tampa–St. Petersburg–Clearwater (table 10.3). In 2010, Orlando-Kissimmee had the second largest concentration of Puerto Ricans in the United States after New York City. Moreover, Puerto Ricans are the largest Latino group in the Orlando and Tampa areas, and the second largest in Miami and Ft. Lauderdale (after Cubans). In Greater Orlando, almost 13 percent of all residents are Puerto Rican, a higher share of the total population than in the New York City metro area (about 6 percent).

Table 10.3. Top ten U.S. metropolitan areas for number of Puerto Rican residents, 2010

	Number of Puerto Ricans	As Percentage of Latinos	As Percentage of Total Population
New York–northern New Jersey–Long Island, NY-NJ-PA	1,177,430	27.2	6.2
Orlando-Kissimmee, FL	269,781	50.1	12.6
Philadelphia-Camden-Wilmington, PA-NJ-DE-MD	238,866	51.1	4.0
Miami–Ft. Lauderdale–Pompano Beach, FL	207,727	8.9	3.7
Chicago–Naperville–Joliet, IL-IN-WI	180,502	9.2	2.0
Tampa–St. Petersburg–Clearwater, FL	143,886	31.2	5.2
Boston-Cambridge-Quincy, MA-NH	115,087	28.0	2.5
Hartford–West Hartford–East Hartford, CT	102,911	68.1	8.5
Springfield, MA	87,798	82.4	12.7
New Haven–Milford, CT	77,578	59.8	9.0

Source: U.S. Census Bureau, *American FactFinder*, 2010.

As Tony Suárez, the second Puerto Rican elected to Florida's state legislature, quipped, "What Miami is to Cubans, Orlando soon will be to Puerto Ricans."[6] Since the 1990s, Orlando has become the new Puerto Rican mecca.

The Orlando-Kissimmee metropolitan area has four major Puerto Rican residential enclaves;[7] namely, the eastern section of the city of Orlando, the south central area of the city, Kissimmee (in Osceola County), and Poinciana (in Polk County). In 2010, Buenaventura Lakes in Osceola County, with 11,618 Puerto Rican residents, was the largest Puerto Rican neighborhood in Central Florida. The nearby Meadow Woods development in Orange County, with 8,974 Puerto Rican residents, was the second largest.[8] Such geographic concentrations occur primarily in suburban housing subdivisions with extremely high densities of Puerto Rican residents, ranging from 35 to 45 percent of all residents. The issue of residential segregation among

Puerto Ricans in Central Florida has attracted increasing attention from scholars.[9] Nonetheless, the physical and socioeconomic features of many Puerto Rican settlements in Florida are typical of middle-class suburban neighborhoods, departing from the inner-city barrios of New York and other northeastern states.

In short, much of the Puerto Rican population is on the move, both within the U.S. mainland and on the Island. As Florida has become the second most important location of stateside Puerto Ricans, several cities, notably Orlando, Miami, Tampa, and Ft. Lauderdale, have emerged as primary destinations for Puerto Rican migrants. Moreover, Puerto Ricans in Florida are highly concentrated in several counties; namely Orange, Osceola, Miami-Dade, Broward, and Hillsborough, and in some localities within those counties, such as Kissimmee in Osceola. The social, economic, political, and cultural consequences of such extreme geographic concentration have been documented among other Latino groups in the United States.[10]

Socioeconomic Profile

The existing literature on the socioeconomic background of Puerto Rican migrants to Florida provides a mixed portrait. Journalistic reports and census data suggest that many professionals and managers have relocated from the Island to Miami, Tampa, and Orlando (table 10.4). The Puerto Rican press has highlighted the "brain drain" of physicians, nurses, teachers, and engineers over the last decades.[11] Various reporters, planners, and scholars have depicted Puerto Ricans in Florida as predominantly middle class,

Table 10.4. Occupational distribution of Latinos in the Orlando-Kissimmee metropolitan area, by national origin, 2007–2009 (in percentages)

	Mexican	Puerto Rican	Cuban	Central American	South American
Management, professional, and related	9.4	23.0	27.2	16.3	22.6
Sales and office	10.3	32.0	26.3	20.4	30.3
Construction, extraction, maintenance, and repair	39.8	10.5	14.5	23.8	10.4
Production, transport, and material moving	10.3	11.7	10.0	12.9	12.5
Service	25.0	22.5	21.7	26.1	23.9
Farming, fishing, and forestry	5.1	0.2	0.4	0.5	0.2
Total	100.0	100.0	100.0	100.0	100.0

Source: U.S. Census Bureau, *American FactFinder*, 2010.

college educated, and suburban.[12] The 2010 census found that the median household income for Puerto Ricans in the Orlando-Kissimmee metropolitan area was $37,561. Fifty-three percent of Puerto Rican workers in the area were white-collar workers such as salespersons and managers. Contrary to popular reports, however, only 15 percent were college graduates.[13] As journalist Robert Friedman summed it up, "Puerto Ricans who have settled in and around the Orlando area are relatively well-off economically and have a higher educational level and a more thriving business community than earlier generations of Boricuas [Puerto Ricans] who settled mostly in the U.S. Northeast."[14]

According to another journalist, "the first wave of Puerto Ricans to settle here [in the Orlando area] were largely retirees attracted to the quiet, safer lifestyle portrayed in Central Florida at a time when the Island, and particularly San Juan, was experiencing a sharp increase in crime."[15] Studies conducted by the Puerto Rico Planning Board confirm that many people move from the Island for a host of noneconomic reasons, such as reuniting with family members and searching for a better quality of life, rather than simply finding a job or improving their salaries. This is particularly true for Island-born professionals who tend to relocate in Florida, California, and Texas.[16] In the early 1990s, for example, more than 40 percent of all graduates from medical schools in Puerto Rico were living in the United States; 18 percent of these were in Florida.[17]

Another index of the migrants' class selectivity is the growing number of Puerto Rican–owned businesses in South and Central Florida. According to the 2007 Survey of Business Owners, Puerto Ricans owned 24,150 businesses in the Miami–Ft. Lauderdale–Pompano Beach metropolitan area, and 6,738 in the Orlando-Kissimmee area. Most firms provided administrative and support services, professional services, transportation and warehousing, construction, retail trade, real estate, health care and social assistance, and other services.[18] Puerto Ricans dominate the Hispanic Chamber of Commerce of Metro Orlando, with more than one thousand members in 2005.[19] The economic boom of Puerto Ricans in Central Florida has attracted Island-based businesses, such as the Ana G. Méndez Educational Foundation, Banco Popular de Puerto Rico, Cooperativa de Seguros Múltiples, Empresas Fonalledas, Goya Foods, Martín's BBQ restaurant, *El Nuevo Día*, Plaza Gigante, Puerto Rican American Insurance Company (PRAICO), and R & G Crown.[20]

A 2001 survey of the members of PROFESA, the Puerto Rican Professional Association of South Florida, throws light on the socioeconomic profile of middle-class migrants in Miami.[21] At the time, two-thirds of members were relatively young (between twenty-five and forty-four years of age) and a similar proportion was born on the Island. On average, they had lived nineteen years in Puerto Rico and seventeen on the mainland. They had a high educational level: 33 percent had completed master's degrees. More than half earned more than $80,000 a year. Slightly more than one-fourth were professionals, especially accountants, attorneys, and physicians; and another fourth were executives, managers, and business owners. About a third was married to non–Puerto Ricans, largely Americans or Cubans. Eighty-four percent of the respondents spoke both Spanish and English at home. Eighty-seven percent traveled to the Island more than once a year. Although this survey was limited to a single voluntary association, its results suggest a highly mobile, bilingual, well-educated, and prosperous elite among Puerto Ricans in South Florida.

Nevertheless, many Puerto Rican migrants are service and blue-collar workers. Thousands toil at Orlando's tourist attractions, such as Walt Disney World, which actively recruits recent graduates and students from the University of Puerto Rico.[22] The majority of these recruits are young people looking for jobs and higher salaries abroad. Puerto Rican migration to Florida also draws on a large pool of disgruntled residents of the northern Rust Belt, attracted by better weather, economic opportunities, and lower costs of living in the southern Sunbelt of the United States.[23]

This wave of second- and third-generation Puerto Ricans from states like New York and Illinois is said to be of a lower class, less educated, and more likely to speak English than those coming from the Island. The relations between the two groups—that is, Islanders and so-called Nuyoricans—remain an important problem, both in Puerto Rico and abroad.[24] In Florida, as in other states, Puerto Rican communities are increasingly stratified by birthplace, language, class, race, and other factors.[25]

Analysis of 2010 census data confirms the socioeconomic differentiation between Puerto Ricans in Florida and in other states.[26] In 2010, Puerto Ricans in Florida had a much higher median household income ($41,198), than their counterparts in states like Massachusetts, Pennsylvania, and Connecticut, where Puerto Ricans had median incomes of $22,816, $26,966, and $31,486, respectively. Furthermore, Puerto Ricans in Florida had a relatively low poverty rate (18.3 percent). In Pennsylvania and Massachusetts, the poverty rates of Puerto Ricans hovered around 40 percent, more than twice that of Puerto Ricans in Florida. In New York, Puerto Ricans had a median household income of $33,436 and a poverty rate of 29 percent.

Despite the stronger economic standing of Puerto Ricans in Florida relative to other parts of the United States, their basic socioeconomic indicators suggest significant disadvantage vis-à-vis other ethnic groups in the state. In 2010, the median household income for Florida's entire population was $47,661, compared to $41,198 for Puerto Ricans. Among non-Hispanic whites, the corresponding figure was $52,316. The causes of this persistent income gap merit further attention.

Racial Identities

An intriguing question regarding Puerto Ricans in Florida is their racial composition. In the American Community Survey for 2006–10, 73.7 percent of Florida's Puerto Ricans classified themselves as white, the highest proportion of all states (figure 10.2). In contrast, 53.1 percent of Puerto Ricans in the entire United States said they were white in the 2010 census. Inversely, smaller proportions of Puerto Ricans in Florida than elsewhere said they were black (3.8 percent), some other race (17.7 percent), or two or more races (4.1 percent). In the United States, the corresponding figures for Puerto Ricans were 8.7 percent black, 27.8 percent some other race, and 8.7 percent two or more races. Such figures suggest that whites are overrepresented in the migrant flow to Florida, while blacks are underrepresented.

How can this racial self-classification pattern be interpreted? To begin, the higher class background of Puerto Rican migrants to Florida helps

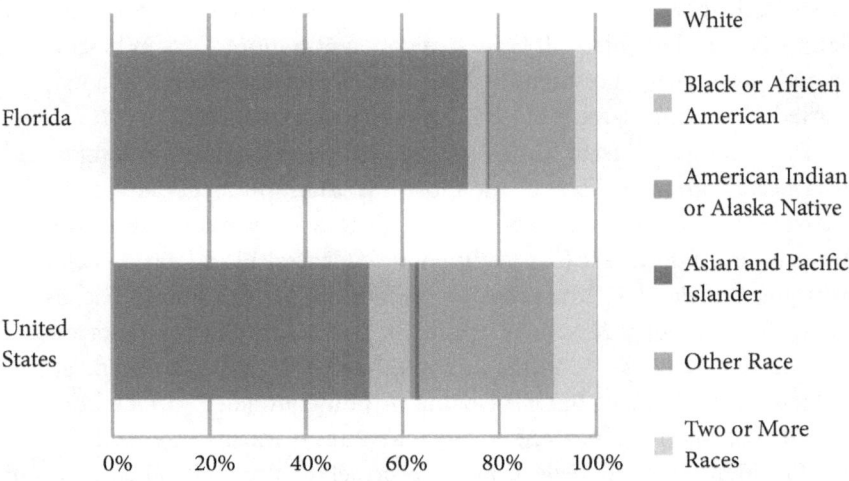

Figure 10.2. Racial self-classification of Puerto Ricans in Florida and the United States, 2006–10. (Sources: Shannon R. Ennis, Merarys Ríos Vargas, and Nora G. Albert, *The Hispanic Population of the United States: 2010*. Washington, DC: U.S. Census Bureau, 2011; U.S. Census Bureau, American FactFinder)

explain the larger percentage of persons of European background. Second, the preponderance of Island-born Puerto Ricans in Florida suggests that many still employ the racial categories prevalent in Puerto Rico, where most residents classify themselves as white. Third, Puerto Ricans living in southern states, such as Florida, may describe themselves as white to avoid the strong anti-black prejudice in that region. Finally, the presence of a large Latino population, especially of Cuban origin, which considers itself predominantly white, may skew the census results in favor of that racial category. In any case, the self-perception of most Puerto Ricans in Florida as white requires further reflection. Whether they are treated as white by other groups, such as non-Hispanic whites and blacks, as well as other Latinos, is another matter.

Political Incorporation

During the past decade, the mass media have frequently portrayed the Puerto Rican population in Florida as a "swing vote" that could decide local, state, and even presidential elections.[27] Journalists have paid much attention to the increasing strength of the Democratic Party in Central Florida, largely due to the backing of Puerto Ricans and other Latinos, in contrast to the predominantly Republican Cubans in South Florida. More than 70 percent of Puerto Rican voters in Florida supported Democratic candidate Al Gore in the 2000 presidential elections.[28] As Democratic Party consultant Jeffrey Farrow lamented, "If Gore had gotten 600 more votes in Florida, he would [have been] president."[29] Yet most of Florida's Puerto Ricans supported Republican governor Jeb Bush's reelection in 2002.

The expanding Puerto Rican electorate centered in Orlando, Tampa, and Miami has produced "one of the most important political battlegrounds" between Democrats and Republicans.[30] The 2004 presidential campaign targeted the Puerto Rican constituency in Central Florida as "crucial" to winning the election.[31] In 2004, 59 percent of Florida's Puerto Ricans favored Senator John Kerry for president, while 39 percent supported the reelection of George W. Bush. In 2008, Puerto Ricans and other Latinos helped elect President Barack Obama. A poll conducted in October 2012 found that nearly 61 percent of Florida's Puerto Ricans intended to vote for President Obama's reelection.[32] Nevertheless, the political activities of Puerto Ricans in Florida have not been well documented from a social scientific perspective.[33] This lack of information and analysis is intriguing because Puerto Ricans are the second largest Latino group in the United States (after Mexicans) and in Florida (after Cubans), and the largest in Orlando, which along with Miami is one of the main gateways for new immigrants from Latin America.

Most Puerto Ricans in the United States have traditionally voted for the Democratic Party. In Florida, where the Latino population is dominated by Cuban Republicans, the growing Puerto Rican presence could alter the state's electoral map. However, the Puerto Rican population boom has not yet translated into proportional political representation at local or state levels. At the time of this writing in February 2013, only four Puerto Ricans (Maurice Ferré in 1966, Tony Suárez in 1998, John Quiñones in 2004, and Darren Soto in 2007) had been elected to the Florida House of Representatives. Few have served on local school boards or county commissions. It is no wonder that Puerto Ricans have been touted as the "sleeping giant" of Florida politics, with "growing political clout."[34]

Regarding Puerto Rico's political status, Puerto Ricans in the United States are as sharply divided as their peers on the Island, although support for Puerto Rico becoming a state of the American union seems to be stronger in Florida than elsewhere. For instance, 55 percent of PROFESA's members preferred that political option in 2001.[35] A 2004 newspaper poll showed that 48 percent of Puerto Ricans in Central Florida favored the current Commonwealth status of the Island, while 42 percent supported its complete annexation as a state of the American union and 5 percent advocated independence.[36] These figures are similar to those for the Island's population.

However, the impact of stateside Puerto Ricans on Island politics remains limited. At this point, participation in Puerto Rican elections, referenda, and plebiscites is restricted to U.S. citizens residing on the Island (including naturalized U.S. citizens of non–Puerto Rican origin, such as Dominicans and Cubans). One of the key political challenges for the Puerto Rican diaspora is how to participate effectively in Puerto Rican affairs, including the thorny question of self-determination. So far, Puerto Ricans living in Florida and other U.S. states have been unable to vote on the Island's political future.

Cultural Practices

As already noted, the Puerto Rican diaspora to Florida is part of the increasing heterogeneity of the Latino population in that state as well as nationwide. Although Cubans still dominate the economic, political, and cultural landscape of Hispanic Florida, other groups—such as Puerto Ricans, Colombians, Nicaraguans, Mexicans, Venezuelans, and Dominicans—have increased their presence in the state. The growing mix of Latinos in Florida has multiple cultural consequences, of which I would like to single out five.

First, no group of Latin American origin can impose its own tastes, values, and practices, like Cubans did in Miami for several decades since 1960. Hence, Florida's popular culture may now be truly (pan) Latino for the first time. Language, music, food, sports, and religion are being Latinized insofar as groups of various Latin American origins are contributing to the Latino mosaic. For instance, the number and variety of public cultural events (such as parades and festivals) sponsored by Puerto Rican community organizations have multiplied in Orlando, Tampa, and Miami. Together with other Latino groups, Puerto Ricans are counterbalancing the earlier "Cubanization" of Florida.[37]

Second, the Spanish spoken in Central and South Florida is a mixture of various dialects of the Spanish language, not just those from Cuba and Puerto Rico, but also from other Caribbean, Central American, and South American countries. Differences in vocabulary, pronunciation, intonation, and other speech patterns may well be homogenized in the long run, but the Cuban "accent" can no longer be presumed to be the norm. Quarrels over the "correct" form of Spanish may intensify in the near future, as they have in Chicago between Mexicans and Puerto Ricans.[38] In New York City, various dialects of Spanish have converged as a result of the growing blend of Latin Americans of different national origins.[39]

Third, the demand for bilingual education and other public services for Spanish speakers in Florida has risen as a result of continuing immigration from Cuba, Puerto Rico, and other Latin American countries.[40] Some counties in Central Florida, such as Orange, Osceola, and Volusia, have received large influxes of immigrants, particularly from Puerto Rico and Mexico. In 2011, one of two public school students in Osceola and one of three students in Orange was Latino.[41] Unfortunately, Latino—especially Puerto Rican—students have higher school dropout rates than other groups.[42] One educational problem is that most children raised in Puerto Rico are not fluent in English when they arrive in Florida. In 2006–7, for example, 18.4 percent of the students with limited English proficiency in Orange County public schools were of Puerto Rican origin.[43] Hence, county officials have actively recruited Latino and bilingual teachers and staff members in an effort to reduce Latino dropout rates.[44]

Fourth, the degree of social interaction among different Latino groups will largely determine whether a new, hybrid identity emerges beyond their national origins. The incidence of Latino intermarriage in Miami, Orlando, and Tampa should be explored further, as it has been in New York City and other places. For instance, Puerto Ricans in the United States have a relatively high intermarriage rate with other ethnic and racial groups, especially Dominicans.[45] Puerto Ricans in Miami are more likely to marry Cubans than are their compatriots in Orlando. Is this simply a function of the size of each Latino community in each metropolitan area? Or does it also reflect other factors, like class and race selectivity and residential segregation, which affect intergroup relations? It is also important to ascertain whether the descendants of mixed marriages identify themselves with a specific nationality or simply as Latinos.

Finally, the rapid growth in Florida's Puerto Rican and Latino populations might heighten tensions with other groups, such as African Americans and non-Hispanic whites. Some sectors of the U.S. population feel uncomfortable with the public use of the Spanish language. Others are opposed to the expansion of the Catholic Church, to which most Latinos belong. Add to these culturally based frictions the competition in the labor and housing markets as well as for political power, and one can anticipate that interethnic relations between Latinos and other groups in Florida will be increasingly explosive. These ethnic rivalries have been well documented in Miami, with its impressive mix of Cubans, Latinos of other origins, non-Hispanic whites, African Americans, Jews, and Haitians.[46] How Puerto Ricans fit within this multiethnic picture awaits further documentation.

Conclusion

The settlement patterns of Puerto Ricans have changed drastically during the last five decades. Whereas New York had been the primary destination for Puerto Rican migrants during the 1940s and 1950s, Florida became their favorite location during the 1990s. The data presented in this chapter suggest that "Mickey Ricans" could follow a different path from other Puerto Rican diaspora communities. To begin, the class background of Puerto Ricans in Florida tends to be more favorable than that of earlier population flows from the Island. On average, Puerto Ricans in Florida have higher income, occupational, and educational levels than their counterparts in other states such as New York, Pennsylvania, and Massachusetts. Besides, Puerto Ricans in Florida describe themselves as white more often than those living anywhere else in the United States. Many of them have avoided living in poor inner-city neighborhoods and have resettled in suburban middle-class areas in the Orlando, Tampa, and Miami areas.

The recent Puerto Rican diaspora to Florida has a great economic, political, and cultural potential. Economically, Puerto Ricans have contributed their skills and capital to the local labor market, especially in the service sector. A thriving community of Puerto Rican entrepreneurs and professionals has emerged in South and Central Florida. Politically, Puerto Ricans are poised to influence both the Democratic and the Republican parties, as a key electoral bloc in a hotly disputed state. Culturally, Puerto Ricans are adding to Florida's ethnic, linguistic, and religious diversity. Despite the opposition of some established groups, the Puerto Rican and Latino populations in both Florida and the United States will continue to expand in the near future. It remains to be seen whether the host society will insist on culturally assimilating the immigrants, as it did with millions of people in the past, or will become increasingly multiethnic, multicultural, and multilingual.

Notes

I would like to acknowledge the substantial contributions of Félix V. Matos-Rodríguez, Gina M. Pérez, and Elizabeth M. Aranda to my work about Puerto Ricans in Florida. Patricia Silver has collaborated with me on several projects dealing with this topic. Ana Yolanda Ramos-Zayas, Luis Martínez-Fernández, and my brother Raúl Duany made useful observations and recommendations on earlier versions of this chapter. However, the views, analysis, and interpretation of the situation of Puerto Ricans in Florida contained herein are my responsibility. This chapter incorporates materials from a previously published monograph on Puerto Ricans in the Orlando area and an introduction to an edited volume on Puerto Rican Florida. See Jorge Duany and Félix V. Matos-Rodríguez, *Puerto Ricans in Orlando and Central Florida*, Policy Report 1, no. 1 (New York: Centro de Estudios Puertorriqueños, Hunter College, City University of New York, 2006); Jorge Duany and Patricia Silver, "The 'Puerto Ricanization' of Florida: Historical Background and Current Status," *CENTRO: Journal of the Center for Puerto Rican Studies* 22, no. 1 (2010): 4–31.

1. U.S. Census Bureau, *American FactFinder,* http://factfinder2.census.gov/faces/nav/jsf/pages/index.xhtml.

2. Simone Baribeau, "Puerto Ricans in Central Florida's Tourism Hub Are Driving Hispanic Growth," *Bloomberg News,* March 18, 2011, http://www.bloomberg.com/news/2011-03-18/puerto-ricans-in-florida-s-tourism-hub-drive-hispanic-growth.html.

3. Elizabeth M. Aranda, "Puerto Rican Migration and Settlement in South Florida: Ethnic Identities and Transnational Spaces," in *Caribbean Migration to Western Europe and the United States: Essays on Incorporation, Identity, and Citizenship,* ed. Ana Margarita Cervantes-Rodríguez, Ramón Grosfoguel, and Eric Mielants (Philadelphia: Temple University Press, 2009), 111–30; Elizabeth M. Aranda, Rosa Chang, and Elena Sabogal, "Racializing Miami: Immigrant Latinos and Colorblind Racism in the Global City," in *How the United States Racializes Latinos: White Hegemony and Its Consequences,* ed. José A. Cobas, Jorge Duany, and Joe R. Feagin (Boulder, CO: Paradigm, 2009), 149–65; Arlene Dávila, *Barrio Dreams: Puerto Ricans, Latinos, and the Neoliberal City* (Berkeley: University of California Press, 2004); Arlene Dávila and Agustín Laó-Montes, eds., *Mambo*

Montage: The Latinization of New York (New York: Columbia University Press, 2011); Nicholas De Genova and Ana Y. Ramos-Zayas, *Latino Crossings: Mexicans, Puerto Ricans, and the Politics of Race and Citizenship* (New York: Routledge, 2003); Gina M. Pérez, *The Near Northwest Side Story: Migration, Displacement, and Puerto Rican Families* (Berkeley: University of California Press, 2004); Patricia L. Price, "Cohering Culture on Calle Ocho: The Pause and Flow of *Latinidad*," *Globalisations* 4, no. 1 (2007): 81–92; Ana Y. Ramos-Zayas, *National Performances: The Politics of Race, Class, and Place in Puerto Rican Chicago* (Chicago: University of Chicago Press, 2003); Milagros Ricourt and Ruby Danta, *Hispanas de Queens: Latino Panethnicity in a New York City Neighborhood* (Ithaca, NY: Cornell University Press, 2003); Alex Stepick, Max Castro, Guillermo Grenier, and Marvin Dunn, *This Land Is Our Land: Immigrants and Power in Miami* (Berkeley: University of California Press, 2003).

4. Larry Lipman, "City Council Election Indication of Growing Hispanic Political Clout," *Cox News Campaign 2000 Archive*, May 28, 2000.

5. Jorge Duany, *The Puerto Rican Nation on the Move: Identities on the Island and in the United States* (Chapel Hill: University of North Carolina Press, 2002).

6. Robert Friedman, "Florida Now 2nd Most Populous P.R. State," *San Juan Star*, May 29, 2001, 6–7.

7. Kevin Archer and Kris Bezdecny, "Searching for a New Brand: Imagining a New Orlando," *Southeastern Geographer* 49, no. 2 (2009): 185–92; Ramón Luis Concepción Torres, "Puerto Rican Migration, Assimilation, and Settlement Patterns in the Orlando MSA" (master's thesis, Binghamton University, State University of New York, 2008); Luis Sánchez, *The New Puerto Rico? Identity, Hybridity, and Transnationalism within the Puerto Rican Diaspora in Orlando, Florida* (Saarbrücken, Germany: VDM Verlag Dr. Müller, 2009).

8. U.S. Census Bureau, *American FactFinder*, 2010.

9. See Carlos Vargas-Ramos, *Settlement Patterns and Residential Segregation of Puerto Ricans in the United States*, Policy Report 1, no. 2 (New York: Centro de Estudios Puertorriqueños, Hunter College, City University of New York, 2006); William Vélez and Giovani Burgos, "The Impact of Housing Segregation and Structural Factors on the Socioeconomic Performance of Puerto Ricans in the United States," *CENTRO: Journal of the Center for Puerto Rican Studies* 22, no. 1 (2010): 175–97; Jacqueline Villarrubia-Mendoza, "The Residential Segregation of Puerto Ricans in New York and Orlando," *Latino(a) Research Review* 6 (2007): 119–31; Villarrubia-Mendoza, "Characteristics of Puerto Rican Homeowners in Florida and Their Likelihood of Homeownership," *CENTRO: Journal of the Center for Puerto Rican Studies* 22, no. 1 (2010): 155–73.

10. See Patricia L. Price, Christopher Lukinbeal, Richard Gioioso, Daniel Arreola, Damián Fernández, Timothy Ready, and María de los Angeles Torres, "Placing Latino Civic Engagement," *Urban Geography* 32, no. 2 (2011): 179–207.

11. Ken Oliver-Méndez, "Welcome to Orlando, Puerto Rico," *Caribbean Business*, August 29, 2002, http://www.puertorico-herald.org/issues/2002/vol6n35/CBWelcome2Orlan PR-en.html; Aixa M. Pascual Amadeo, "La hemorragia que no cesa," *El Nuevo Día (A Fondo: Suplemento investigativo*, no. 3), May 17, 1994, 77; Daniel Rivera Vargas, "La invasión boricua en la NASA," *El Nuevo Día*, April 6, 2008, http://www.elnuevodia.com/Xstatic/endi/template/imprimir.aspx?id=388005&t=3.

12. Robert Friedman, "Stateside Puerto Ricans Fare Well, Study Says," *San Juan Star*,

March 26, 2002, 6; Luz H. Olmeda, "Aspectos socioeconómicos de la migración en el 1994–95," in Junta de Planificación de Puerto Rico, *Informe económico al gobernador, 1997* (San Juan: Junta de Planificación de Puerto Rico, 1998), 1–39; Francisco Rivera-Batiz and Carlos E. Santiago, *Puerto Ricans in the United States: A Changing Reality* (Washington, DC: National Puerto Rican Coalition, 1994); Francisco Rivera-Batiz and Carlos E. Santiago, *Island Paradox: Puerto Rico in the 1990s* (New York: Russell Sage Foundation, 1996).

13. U.S. Census Bureau, *American FactFinder*.

14. Friedman, "Stateside Puerto Ricans Fare Well," 6.

15. Lipman, "City Council Election."

16. "Migración de retorno en Puerto Rico," in Junta de Planificación de Puerto Rico, ed., *Informe económico al gobernador, 1999* (San Juan: Junta de Planificación de Puerto Rico, 2000), 1–16; Olmeda, "Aspectos socioeconómicos de la migración en el 1994–95."

17. Amadeo, "La hemorragia que no cesa."

18. U.S. Census Bureau, *American FactFinder*, 2007.

19. Friedman, "Stateside Puerto Ricans Fare Well;" Hispanic Chamber of Commerce of Metro Orlando website, "Hispanic Chamber of Commerce of Metro Orlando, 2012," http://hccmo.org; Walter Pacheco, "State Hispanic Chamber Conference Comes to Life," *El Sentinel* (Orlando), August 18, 2001.

20. Marvin Fonseca, "Crecen las empresas de origen boricua," *El Nuevo Día*, April 18, 2004, 8.

21. PROFESA (Puerto Rican Professional Association of South Florida), "Survey of Members," unpublished manuscript, 2001.

22. Juan Hernández Cruz, "La emigración puertorriqueña a Florida y el 'mundo maravilloso de Disney,'" *Diálogo* (University of Puerto Rico), August 2002, 29.

23. Bill Coats, "County's Hispanic Population Changes," *St. Petersburg Times*, May 23, 2001, http://www.sptimes.com/News/052301/news_pf/Census/County_s_Hispanic_pop.shtml; Lipman, "City Council Election."

24. See Erna Kerkhof, "Contested Belonging: Circular Migration and Puerto Rican Identity" (PhD diss., University of Utrecht, the Netherlands, 2000); José Lorenzo-Hernández, "The Nuyorican's Dilemma: Categorization of Returning Migrants in Puerto Rico," *International Migration Review* 33, no. 4 (1999): 988–1013; Pérez, *Near Northwest Side Story*; Ramos-Zayas, *National Performances*; Carlos Vargas-Ramos, "The Effect of Return Migration on Political Participation in Puerto Rico" (PhD diss., Columbia University, 2000).

25. Aranda, "Puerto Rican Migration and Settlement in South Florida"; Sánchez, *New Puerto Rico?*; Patricia Silver, "'Culture Is More Than Bingo and Salsa': Making *Puertorriqueñidad* in Central Florida," *CENTRO: Journal of the Center for Puerto Rican Studies* 31, no. 1 (2010): 57–83.

26. U.S. Census Bureau, *American FactFinder*.

27. José Delgado, "Voto puertorriqueño podría ser decisivo," *El Nuevo Día*, October 13, 2008, 46–47; Dahleen Glanton, "Hispanics Turn Florida into More of a Swing Vote," *Chicago Tribune*, November 20, 2000; "Puerto Rican Vote May Determine Presidential Election," *Puerto Rico Herald*, March 5, 2004, http://www.puertorico-herald.org/issues/2004/vol8n10/WashUpdate0810-en.html.

28. Ryan Lizza, "Orlando Dispatch," *New Republic Online*, November 6, 2000; Susan Milligan, "In Florida, Different Latino Group Now in Mix," *Puerto Rico Herald*, October 30, 2000, http://www.puertorico-herald.org/issues/vol4n44/DiftLatinos-en.html.

29. Cited in Robert Friedman, "P.R. Vote in Florida Seen as Crucial in '04," *San Juan Star*, March 15, 2004, 5.

30. Mark Silva, "Hispanic Democrats on the Rise," *Sun-Sentinel* (Broward–Palm Beach), July 6, 2001.

31. Friedman, "P.R. Vote in Florida Seen as Crucial in '04;" Ken Thomas, "Florida Hispanics Targeted During Upcoming Elections," *Havana Journal*, March 9, 2004.

32. Florida International University, "The Pulse of the Latino Voter: The U.S. and Florida," October 15, 2012, http://news.fiu.edu/wp-content/uploads/The-Pulse-of-the-Latino-Voter.pdf.

33. For an exception, see José A. Cruz, "Barriers to Political Participation of Puerto Ricans and Hispanics in Osceola County, Florida: 1991–2007," *CENTRO: Journal of the Center for Puerto Rican Studies* 22, no. 1 (2010): 243–85.

34. Lipman, "City Council Election"; Louise Story, "Hispanos de Osceola son como un gigante soñoliento," *El Sentinel*, August 11, 2001, http://www.orlandosentinel.com/elsentinel/comunidad/orl-span-elosceola081101.story?coll=elsent%2Dcomunidad%2Dheadlines.

35. PROFESA, "Survey of Members."

36. "Sobre el estatus de Puerto Rico," *El Nuevo Día*, October 18, 2004, 80.

37. See Thomas D. Boswell, *The Cubanization and Hispanicization of Metropolitan Miami* (Miami, FL: Cuban American National Council, 1995).

38. De Genova and Ramos-Zayas, *Latino Crossings*.

39. Ricardo Otheguy and Ana Celia Zentella, *Spanish in New York: Language Contact, Dialectal Leveling, and Structural Continuity* (New York: Oxford University Press, 2012).

40. Thomas D. Boswell, "Implications of Demographic Changes in Florida's Public School Population," in Sandra H. Fradd and Okhee Lee, eds., *Creating Florida's Multilingual Global Work Force: Educational Policies and Practices for Students Learning English as a New Language* (Tallahassee: Florida Department of Education, 1998), http://eric.ed.gov/?id=ED421854.

41. Florida Department of Education, *Membership in Florida's Public Schools, Fall 2011*, Education Information and Accountability Services, Data Report Series 2012-06D, December 2011, http://www.fldoe.org/eias/eiaspubs/word/pk12mbrshp1112.doc.

42. Walter Pacheco, "Hispanics Filling Up More Classrooms," *El Sentinel* (Orlando), August 11, 2001,; Leslie Postal and Tania de Luzuriaga, "Teaching English to Puerto Ricans Is Put to Test," *Orlando Sentinel*, April 26, 2004, http://articles.orlandosentinel.com/2004-04-26/news/0404260112_1_speak-english-rican-students-puerto-rico.

43. Michelle Snider, "Limited English Proficiency (LEP) Students and Their Teachers' Attitudes of the Learning Environment in Mathematics Classes" (EdD diss., University of Central Florida, 2007), 40.

44. María T. Padilla, "Hispanic Dropouts Trouble Educators," *Star-Telegram.com*, December 2, 1999.

45. Gabriel Aquino, "Puerto Rican Intermarriages: The Intersectionality of Race, Gender, Class, and Space" (PhD diss., University at Albany, State University of New York, 2011).

46. See Stepick et al., *This Land Is Our Land*.

11

Miami in the Twenty-First Century

Still on the Edge?

ALEX STEPICK AND MARCOS FELDMAN

In Tom Wolfe's 2012 book on Miami, one of his characters states, "In Miami, everybody hates everybody." As the rest of the book clarifies, "Everybody" in Miami is defined by race and ethnicity. Miami has historically been characterized and understood in terms of its ethnic and racial divisions, from the blacks and whites that built and founded the city to the early twenty-first-century mélange of blacks, whites, and Latinos, the last of whom are primarily immigrants from the Caribbean and Latin America. Portes and Stepick's *City on the Edge* argued that these divisions fundamentally explained the structure of Miami.[1]

In this chapter we argue that race and ethnicity remain fundamental, but class is increasingly important in Miami.[2] We argue that Cuban American and Anglo elites have coalesced and become increasingly interdependent in their ruling class formations, giving the impression of a thriving, Hispanic-American city. Yet, this *Latinized* city masks stubborn class divides in what is one of the most unequal metropolitan areas in the country. A majority of Miami's "black" and "brown" minorities remain entrenched in the burgeoning low-wage workforce that sustains the postindustrial urban economy. At the same time as Miami is a transient and increasingly diverse city, there are a growing number of institutions creating deeper and more rooted connections between people and place. We argue that this recent and growing institutionalization is shaped more by class than racial or ethnic solidarities, although the latter remain important. As we examine in this chapter, the nature of these deepening commitments to Miami is crucial for the future of a region in which, historically, everybody not only hates everybody else, but also is said to have come from somewhere else.[3]

Racial, Ethnic, and Class Structures

Miami was founded at the end of the nineteenth century by what are locally referred to as Anglos,[4] primarily from the Midwest, and was built by blacks, primarily from the Bahamas and the southern United States. In the second quarter of the twentieth century, Miami became an epicenter of U.S. Jewish life. In the early years, land covenants segregated them and they were excluded from the private clubs established by the white, overwhelmingly Protestant, elite. Land covenants largely evaporated after World War II, and the white elite gradually integrated successful Jews through the 1960s and 1970s. By the last quarter of the twentieth century, the term *Anglos* ironically—at least from the perspective of those who were not Jewish—included Jews.

The fundamental divide for most of the twentieth century was white versus black. As Miami is located in the South, from the city's founding to the civil rights movement in the mid-twentieth century, black-white segregation was legal and enforced by episodic violence by whites, particularly the Ku Klux Klan, against blacks.[5] Blacks remained politically oppressed and economically exploited, although segregation did permit a few blacks to establish businesses.[6] With the civil rights movement and legislation in the third quarter of the twentieth century, blacks both obtained the right to vote and assumed some positions of power and visibility in the public sector, which became the basis of a black middle class. Some blacks also owned land and became landlords over their fellow co-ethnics, which Connolly argues made them complicit in and supportive of segregation and its associated oppression,[7] although they had nowhere near the economic power of white businesspeople.

The 1960s arrival of Cuban exiles and subsequent establishment of Miami as the second city of Cuba initiated the transformation that has garnered the most attention. Newly arrived Cubans were not black nor were they accepted as white or Anglo. As Portes and Stepick describe, the Cuban presence altered the former dualistic society of whites and blacks to a tri-ethnic division of blacks, whites, and Hispanics.[8]

Since then, that general trend has continued, but also become more complex. In 1990, non-Hispanic whites composed nearly one-third of the population of Miami-Dade County, but by 2010 their share was less than half that (figure 11.1). The number and share of African Americans also declined. Within the overall black population, the share of Haitians nearly doubled while the percentage of African Americans and people from the West Indies (e.g., Bahamians, whose presence in Miami predates other Caribbean

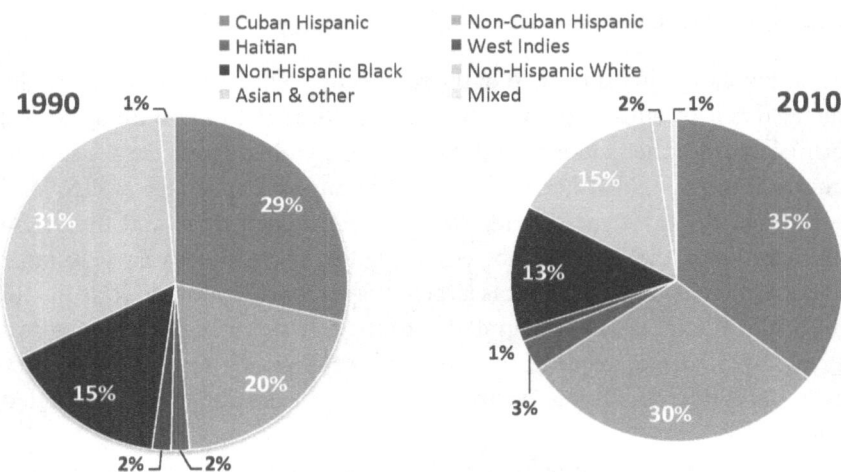

Figure 11.1. Race and ethnicity of Miami-Dade County Population, 1990 and 2010. (U.S. Census 1990 and American Community Survey 2010, from Integrated Public Use Microdata Series [IPUMS]: Version 5.0. Minneapolis: University of Minnesota, 2010)

populations) decreased. Hispanics, who already made up about half of the population in 1990, increased their share to 65 percent by 2010. This increase was fueled significantly by the decline in non-Hispanic whites along with the accelerating influx of non-Cuban Hispanics, whose share grew from 20 to 30 percent over the two decades. Central and South Americans such as Colombians, Hondurans, Nicaraguans, Venezuelans, and Dominicans increased their presence considerably.[9]

These racial and ethnic shifts have a distinct, seldom noted socioeconomic tint. Miami has also become one of the most economically unequal urban areas in the country. From the 1990s on Miami has had both the poorest of the poor and the richest of the rich. The City of Miami, which is the largest municipality within Miami-Dade County, has often ranked as the city with the highest poverty rate in the nation, while at the same time it has had one census tract, Fisher Island, with close to the highest average income in the nation. This bifurcation is not simply the rich getting richer and the poor getting poorer. Since the 1970s, middle-class native blacks and whites have been abandoning the area,[10] "pushed out" due to the dramatic and rapid transformation of the city caused by Cuban immigration and the devastation of Hurricane Andrew in 1992, which wrought damage on traditionally white neighborhoods in southern Dade County. At the same time as the overall number of non-Hispanic whites declined, they became increasingly concentrated in professional and managerial jobs and as entrepreneurs.[11]

Figure 11.2 compares income and ethnicity between 1990 and 2010, demonstrating how Miami-Dade County's population is significantly weighted toward the poor. Not only do the poor dominate, but ethnicity and race do not define poverty, which here is defined as a personal income of less than $20,000. Non-Hispanic blacks and non-Cuban Hispanics are more likely to be poor, but Cubans are not far behind, and there are even a significant number of poor non-Hispanic whites. The only notable changes among the poor between 1990 and 2010 were that the proportion of poor non-Cuban Hispanics declined from being the highest to being just below non-Hispanic blacks, and the proportion of poor non-Hispanic whites actually increased. In 1990 Cubans dominated the ranks of the poorest Miamians. As shown in Figure 11.3, by 2010 the share of poor non-Cuban Hispanics increased, although the absolute number of low-income Cubans increased the most.[12] Because of the huge influx of poor non-Cuban Hispanics, they surpassed Cubans in their share of the bottom income bracket. In addition, Caribbean blacks—particularly Haitians—have increased their share of Miami's low-income population. The most recent U.S. census inequality rankings based on the Gini coefficient, a statistical measure of the gap between rich and poor households, confirms the predominance of the poor. Miami-Dade

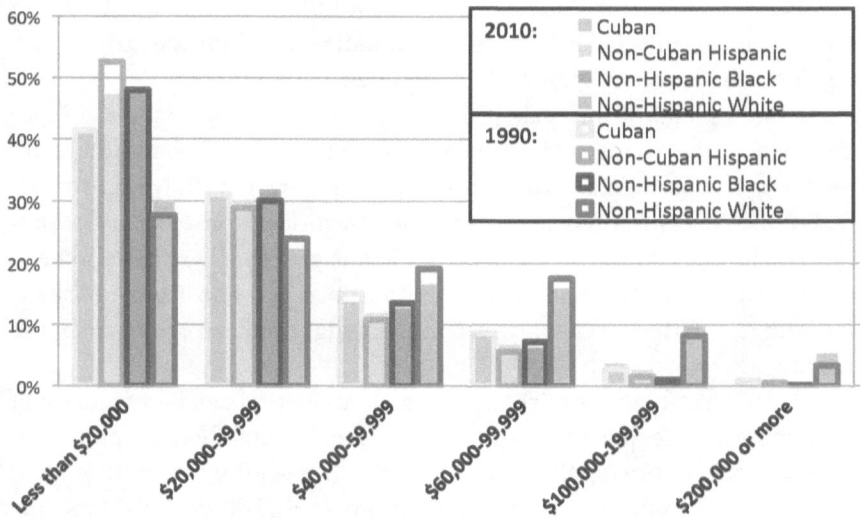

Figure 11.2. Share of racial/ethnic group by personal income bracket, 1990 and 2010. (IPUMS 2010)

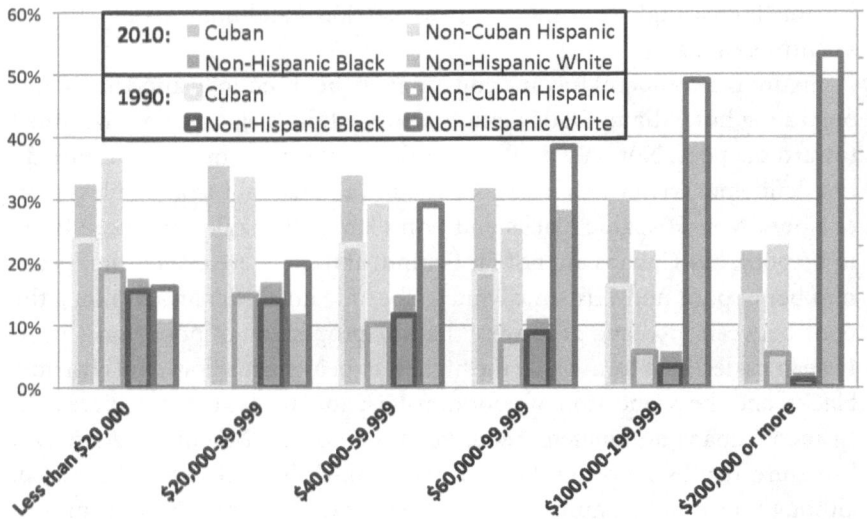

Figure 11.3. Share of personal income bracket by race/ethnicity, 1990 and 2010. (IPUMS 2010)

County is the second most unequal of the nation's twenty-five largest counties after New York.[13]

For purposes of this discussion the two income groups on the graph that cover $40,000 to $99,999 constitute the middle class, which is definitely not the majority in Miami-Dade County. This middle class was small in 1990 and became even smaller by 2010. The middle-class drop was driven by a decline in both non-Hispanic whites and non-Hispanic blacks.

At the top end of the scale in figure 11.2—specifically, incomes higher than $100,000—changes are a bit more difficult to see, because there are relatively few residents with high incomes. Figure 11.3, however, reveals the ethnic concentrations *within* income categories. Non-Hispanic whites overwhelmingly dominate the top two income groups. There has also been significant growth at the top among both Cuban and non-Cuban Hispanics, with non-Hispanic Cubans even moving slightly ahead of Cubans at the very top.

Figure 11.3 reflects the fairly balanced, or at least mixed, construction of all income levels below the top two. Given their general demographic presence, it is not surprising that Cubans are the largest group in most of these levels. The one exception, beyond the top two levels, is at the lowest income bracket. Among people earning less than $20,000, non-Cuban Hispanics are the largest group, followed by Cubans, another sign, albeit a negative one, of non-Cuban Hispanics' increasing presence in Miami. Contrary to some stereotypes, non-Hispanic blacks do not dominate among the poor. They are indeed disproportionately poor, but non-Hispanic blacks also constitute a substantial part of the middle-income groups, and in fact have increased their share of these groups between 1990 and 2010.

The changes among Cubans and other Hispanics are especially noteworthy, as stereotypes still often depict Cubans as disproportionately successful immigrants. The first wave of Cubans, the Golden Exiles, was disproportionately upper class and professional, as would be expected of those fleeing a socialist revolution.[14] As political violence spread in Colombia at the end of the twentieth century and after Hugo Chávez assumed control of Venezuela, elites from both countries settled in or established second residences in South Florida, joining other Latin American elite families who often keep their money in Florida banks and occasionally have homes there, too. By 2010, there were more non-Cuban Hispanics than Cubans at the top of the income distribution; that is, households with incomes of $200,000 or more.

Having so many Hispanics at the top of the income distribution distinguishes Miami. But, as the data show, this is not the whole story. The ethnic groups and Miami in general are strongly bifurcated by class. There are more poor Hispanics, both Cubans and non-Cubans, than there are rich or middle-income ones.

In short, at least as measured by income, the class structure in Miami is not marked by dramatic ethnic and racial differences at the bottom. The poor are both black and white, both Hispanic and non-Hispanic. All groups have large and growing concentrations among the poor, with the exception of non-Hispanic whites. Figure 11.3 reflects the general demographic growth of Hispanics in Miami, but it also reflects increasing Hispanic class inequality, as the greatest growth among both Cuban and non-Cuban Hispanics has been at the bottom and the top, not in the middle. Blacks, whites, and Hispanics are all found at the top of the income distribution, but non-Hispanic whites clearly dominate and Cubans are making visible inroads.

The Economic Base

The highly unequal class structure emerges not only from the flows of elite versus working-class immigrant Hispanics, but also from an economic base built on tourism, real estate, and trade, which has also become increasingly "localized" with the expansion of jobs in health, education, and human services. Miami, like much of the rest of Florida, has gone through more than a century of booms and busts tied primarily to real estate. The Atlantic coast first boomed in the wake of the railroad being laid south, eventually all the way to Key West.[15] Hurricanes and then the Great Depression caused a bust in Miami. The post–World War II decade saw another boom, followed by a lull in the late 1950s. Cuban refugees rejuvenated the economy until a late-1970s–early-1980s recession. This was followed by an initiation of gentrification first in Miami Beach and then in the periphery of downtown Miami, which boomed in the first decade of the 2000s before the bubble burst toward the end of that decade. This is a familiar story encapsulating the boom-and-bust cycles that characterize much of Florida.[16]

As others have argued, Florida, and Miami in particular, has grown not by manufacturing and producing things, but instead by creating images of a tropical lifestyle.[17] Manufacturing was never central to Miami's economy, and it has declined since its peak in the 1970s.[18] In fact, the largest manufacturing employer is Goodwill Industries, one of the few cases of recent expansion, an indicator of how feeble manufacturing is locally.

The economy instead revolves around the construction and servicing of the tropical lifestyle image. Construction skyrockets during the episodic booms. Meanwhile, compared to other cities, Miami's dominant jobs are low paying and concentrated in retail and services, in addition to transportation and real estate.[19] The industries with the most low-wage jobs—retail trade and personal services—constitute about one-quarter of all jobs, having added nearly 72,000 jobs since 1990. The largest employers are in the shrinking public sector, particularly education and public administration, including the school district and the various levels of government. In the private sector, health services are the largest employers, particularly the University of Miami, which has a major medical school and hospital, and Baptist Health System. These are followed by major supermarket chains (Publix and Winn-Dixie), American Airlines, and major telecommunications companies. Although Miami has only two Fortune 500 companies (World Fuel Services and Ryder),[20] it is home to the Latin American regional headquarters of many U.S. companies, as well as many foreign companies, particularly European and Latin American firms that conduct business throughout the Americas. Racial and ethnic trends, socioeconomic changes, and structural shifts in the local economy converge in the emerging processes of gentrification, which take a peculiar tone in Miami.

Reconquista Urbana: The Convergence of Ethnicity with Economics

While observers of Miami tend to focus on its Latin American and Caribbean connections, the other shift literally reshaping the city has taken place in real estate, the historic driver of the local economy and the source of the boom and bust of the first decade of the twenty-first century. After decades of suburbanization, in the 1990s investment began pouring back into central city neighborhoods such as South Beach, Brickell, and Coconut Grove.[21] Reinvestment and gentrification then spread to other central city neighborhoods near downtown: Edgewater, Wynwood, Little Havana, and the parts of Little Haiti that abut the wealthy Upper East Side neighborhoods all experienced a surge in rehabilitation and new construction, as well as new "upwardly mobile" residents (figure 11.4). After losing thousands of housing units in the 1980s, the central cities added slightly more than 1,500 housing units between 1990 and 2000.[22] By the 2000s, this trickle of housing became a flood. Between 2000 and 2010 the central cities added more than 43,000 housing units, accounting for nearly one-third of all housing units added countywide. These units have given a new upward thrust to downtown Miami and South Beach as skyscraping gray apartments and condominiums punctuate the blue sky.

Miami's gentrification reflects how the city is similar to yet different from other U.S. cities. As in other cities, a growing number of people are choosing to live in the city over the suburbs.[23] Also, as in some other cities, "cultural" policies promote redevelopment, although with a particular ethnic twist in Miami. Lobbied by Cuban American and African American officials, the City of Miami created the Calle Ocho and Little Haiti cultural districts along with the Wynwood Cafe District, which incentivize the establishment of bars, restaurants, and artistic venues.[24] Funders such as the Knight Foundation and the Miami Foundation (formerly Dade Community Foundation) have also aggressively supported the arts as part of a broader strategy of "place making," attracting young professionals, and cultivating young leaders in Miami.[25] As always, the boom emerges from a marketing image bonded with a specific place, but this is a new image of Miami. Not just sun and beaches, the new gentrification wave combines Miami's distinctive ethnic cast with art.

Compared to other cities, however, Miami's gentrification is international. Florida has led the nation in real estate sales to foreign buyers, comprising anywhere from one-quarter to one-third of such transactions nationally.[26] In 2012 the cities of Miami and Miami Beach accounted for nearly one-third of Florida's international sales, mostly to buyers from Latin America (particularly Brazilians and Venezuelans), the Caribbean, Canada, or Western Europe.

The prime movers, not just the consumers, of gentrification reveal the coalescence of class interests in spite of ethnic diversity and divisions. As already indicated, Cuban American and African American city officials

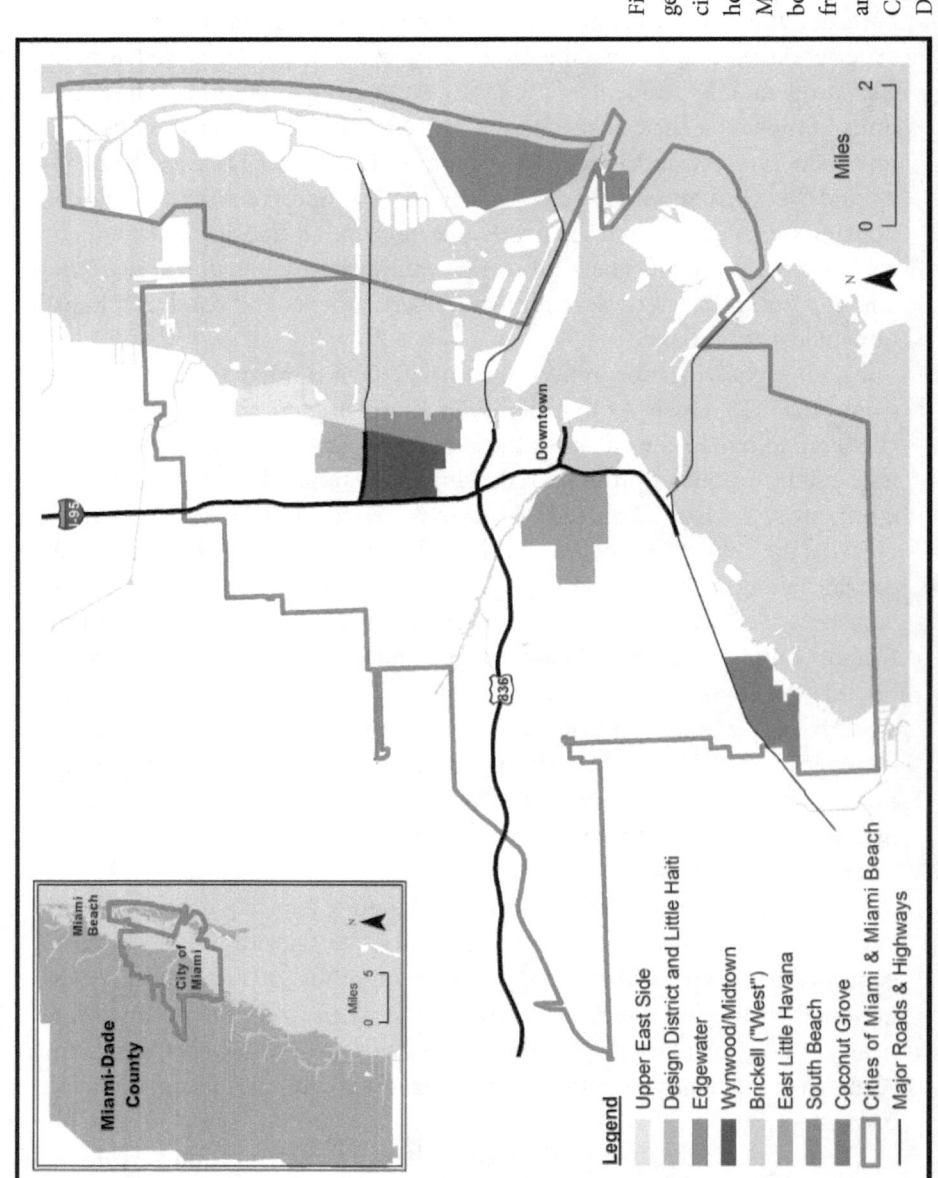

Figure 11.4. Map of gentrifying central city neighborhoods. (Map by Marcos Feldman; boundary files from City of Miami and Miami-Dade County Planning Departments)

promoted arts-associated development. The real estate developers of Miami's expanding inner city skyline are primarily non-Hispanic whites with New York connections and Cuban Americans based in Miami, such as "Condo King" Jorge Perez.[27] This ethnic contour of urban development is evident in a handful of major projects. Wynwood—a historically working-class area of Puerto Ricans, Dominicans, Central Americans, and U.S.-born and immigrant blacks—has been rebranded "Midtown Miami" on the north, through the development a major upscale commercial and residential complex by the same name, and the virtually overlapping Wynwood Art District and Café District on the south where garment manufacturing and warehousing is giving way to galleries, boutiques, and entertainment venues.

The growth of an internationally renowned art scene has created a unique "Miami Model" of arts entrepreneurship. The weeklong Art Basel Miami festival, which draws an estimated forty thousand people, was initiated in 2002 as a "sister exhibition" to the original festival held annually in Switzerland since 1970.[28] The Miami edition then expanded through satellite fairs, the largest of which (outside of Miami Beach) has been held since 2003 in the gentrifying Wynwood neighborhood, where the Wynwood Art District Association was created to promote the neighborhood to investors and consumers, and lobby for favorable local policies.[29] In addition to Wynwood, art scenes are expanding in Little Havana and Little Haiti, supported by philanthropic initiatives such as the Knight Arts Challenge. The "Miami Model," as it has been dubbed by collectors and critics,[30] refers to a significant institutional development in which art is collected and made accessible to the public by private collectors as opposed to public museums.[31] In Miami, many of these newly wealthy collectors made their money in real estate during the relatively recent political and economic ascendance of Miami and Miami Beach. As a result, while public museums have yet to amass collections, privately owned collections are exhibited to the public in warehouses largely clustered in Wynwood, where individual collectors can purchase or rent museum-like spaces. Moreover, such privately owned, de facto museums often focus on contemporary art,[32] since the market for "classics" is dominated by the world's most powerful public art institutions in New York, Paris, and other major art centers.[33]

The art scene is also an example of non-Hispanic whites and Latinos increasingly working together, although not without some tension. In 2004 voters approved a bond measure to finance the construction of a new public art museum at Miami's Bicentennial Park, soon to be renamed Museum Park, located downtown along the waterfront. Since then, promoters have struggled to raise money to acquire and expand a worthy collection, at least according to critics, many of whom rank among the Miami Model's major collectors.[34] In 2012 Jorge Perez, a Cuban American high-rise developer who started out by building affordable housing in Little Havana and has been central to gentrification in Brickell, gifted the new Miami Art Museum (MAM) $20 million in cash and $15 million in Latin American art, in exchange for the naming rights to the building, now the Perez Art Museum Miami (PAMM). In response, four board members—two Hispanic and two Anglo—resigned and one even took out a full-page ad in the *Miami Herald* to protest the name change. Despite some initial grumblings about the anti-Latin bias of Perez's critics (negated by the fact of opposition from prominent Latino collectors), the elites took issue because the building's name "would forever link it to the community that formed it," noting that "most city museums have the location front and center in the title."[35]

While less visible than the arts-based coalescence of Latino and non-Hispanic white elite interests, gentrification has also united environmentalists, who tend to be middle- and upper-income Whites, with the Latinos involved in urban redevelopment. The environmentalists are not greatly concerned with the arts or hip urban neighborhoods, but they do applaud infill urban development as an alternative to persistent suburban sprawl, which has threatened and shrunk the Everglades since Miami's founding.[36] Urban redevelopment has also been cited as a factor supporting the City of Miami's financial recovery from junk bond status in the late 1990s.[37]

The integration of Latinos into the previously Anglo-dominated local power structure was also visible in the 2012 Miami Leadership Summit, a three-part convening of "more than 70 top business and civic leaders."[38] The summit—the "brainchild" of the Cuban American president emeritus of Florida International University, Modesto Maidique—sought to help Miami overcome its social and spatial fragmentation, a frequently cited issue. The participants in the first summit were overwhelmingly male (77 percent) and disproportionately non-Hispanic white (48 percent). Among the 31 percent of participants who were Hispanic, more than one-quarter were non-Cubans. Cuban and Anglo American representatives were equally distributed among major industries, while non-Hispanic blacks, who represented about 15 percent of participants, were disproportionately concentrated in government and nonprofit organizations.[39]

In short, Miami's elite remains disproportionately dominated by Anglos, but it demonstrates an increasing integration of Latinos, who themselves are more diverse. Previously, Cubans were the local Latino power elite. Cubans remain the most significant ethnic group with power, but non-Cuban

Latinos are increasingly important. Blacks are visible, but with their base in the public sector, they have less power than the most significant Anglos and Latinos.

Emerging Class Politics

The history of Miami offers few positive examples of opposition to elite-promoted projects. During the three-quarters of a century in which segregation prevailed, elite whites had the backing of working-class whites to deny services and rights to the black population. Elite blacks also benefited from the status quo as poor blacks had no option but to rent ghetto housing owned by local elite blacks. In opposition to segregation, a few whites, primarily Jews, worked with African Americans to effect change.[40]

In the 1980s, a series of social convulsions shook Miami. First, in the spring of 1980 uncontrolled flows of Cubans began arriving in South Florida. Then, after the acquittal of a group of white policemen charged with shooting an unarmed black man, riots enveloped the largest black neighborhood, Liberty City. In the fall election, Miami-Dade County passed the nation's first English-only ordinance of the late twentieth century. These events thrust the Anglo elite into action. They urged the federal government to stop the flow from Cuba and make sure it never happened again. They mounted a campaign to aid local blacks, primarily through the promotion of entrepreneurial activities. Plus, they fretted over the delayed assimilation of Cubans who had yet to learn English and still seemed more obsessed with politics in Cuba than in Miami.

Cubans responded by becoming deeply involved in local politics and by the mid-1990s dominated local elections. Incidentally, they did so without learning fluent English or abandoning their passion for their homeland. Many in the Anglo elite responded by changing themselves rather than waiting for the immigrants to change. They took Spanish lessons and tutorials on Cuban culture, and championed Miami as the "capital of Latin America." These efforts combined to create the tripartite social structure described by Portes and Stepick in *City on the Edge,* in which Anglos, Cubans, and blacks shared the same geographic space but inhabited different social worlds.

Since that time, as we have argued, the Anglo and Cuban (now more broadly Latino/Hispanic) elites have begun the process of forming a unified power structure. We have also argued that the middle class has been shrinking. As for the working classes, they have progressed far less than the elites toward overcoming ethnic divisions, but there has been a discernible progressive trajectory.

From the end of the civil rights movement until the early 1990s, virtually all efforts aimed at remedying social inequities in Miami emanated from the local elites. For example, David Lawrence Jr., the publisher of the *Miami Herald* for ten years, established the Children's Trust, a dedicated source of funding for early childhood education and school readiness. He led campaigns in 2002 and again in 2008 in which Miami-Dade voters approved a half-mill (50¢ per $1,000) property tax increase to fund the Children's Trust. Lawrence embodies the turn among Anglo leaders toward incorporating Latinos into the power structure. When he became the *Miami Herald*'s publisher, he learned Spanish and hired a tutor to teach him the cultural nuances of the Cuban American community. Miami's Children's Trust exemplifies interethnic partnership among elites, as the successful appeals to voters have been attributed to comprehensive communications campaigns that were "broadly based, run in the country's three dominant languages—English, Spanish and Creole—and utterly nonpartisan."[41]

Other important social-service and advocacy institutions include Camillus House, founded in 1960 as a feeding program and eventually expanding into one of the nation's largest homeless assistance systems. Catalyst Miami (formerly the Human Services Coalition), founded in 1995, lobbies to protect government-funded services, promotes civic engagement, and serves as an important hub linking other groups and individuals, particularly social justice organizations. The boards of these organizations are composed primarily of prominent Anglos and Cubans, further reflecting a coalescence of the elite, but here in the service of the working classes and poor of all races and ethnicities.

Haitian refugees, with funding from national philanthropies and the support of the local Catholic Church, advocated for better treatment of Haitians. The ecumenical, church-based network People Acting for Community Together (PACT), which formed in 1988, has worked in low-income black and Hispanic neighborhoods. It has achieved a few victories, including code enforcement against crack houses, education initiatives aimed at the poor, and a sales tax for mass transit.

A few voices remained from the civil rights struggles, but most had been incorporated into social service organizations and were no longer fighting for social justice. There were virtually no social justice organizations working to directly alter local power relations. As has been described in greater detail elsewhere,[42] the labor movement, and particularly the Service Employees International Union (SEIU) Local 1199 Florida, was at the forefront of seeking to remedy this situation by working to "support and create organizations and networks capable of boosting union organizing drives and other working-class campaigns for social justice."⁴³ In 1997, leaders from the Central Labor Council, Human Services Coalition, Florida Legal Services, National Association for the Advancement of Colored People (NAACP), and other organizations formed the Community Coalition for a Living Wage (CCLW), which won a living wage ordinance in 1999. This victory stimulated other developments: the establishment of local chapters of the Association for Community Organizations for Reform Now (ACORN) and the Interfaith Committee for Worker Justice.⁴⁴

Since then, a variety of labor, neighborhood, and faith-based organizations working for social justice have blossomed in Miami.⁴⁵ In addition to prominent labor struggles, such as the Justice for Janitors strike at the University of Miami,⁴⁶ community organizations during the 2000s increasingly focused on challenging unequal urban development and demanding greater attention to the public infrastructures (education, transit, housing) used by working-class families.⁴⁷ In 1999, the Miami Workers Center (MWC) and the Power University for Social Change (Power U) were founded to address social injustices affecting inner-city neighborhoods. Power U, based in Overtown, has worked on issues of environmental justice and urban development in response to plans for and practices of downtown expansion into or affecting Overtown, including, most recently, the University of Miami's creation of a biotech facility on the edge of that inner-city neighborhood.

The MWC was created by activists who learned their trade in the labor movement, for a time with SEIU 1199 Florida. The MWC, headquartered in the predominantly African American area of Liberty City, founded two grassroots organizations that have focused on welfare, housing, and immigrants' rights: Low-Income Families Fighting Together (LIFFT), based in Liberty City, and Miami en Acción, which is organizing across several Hispanic neighborhoods. Although most of the center's work is based in these urban core areas, the MWC in recent years has broadened its scope to include campaigns oriented toward Florida state politics as well as accountability in recent federal stimulus spending. Its founding director moved on in 2009 to create Florida New Majority, which seeks to build a statewide coalition of activists and advocates.

In 1999, South Florida Jobs with Justice (SFJwJ) was created by the local chapter of the NAACP, the SEIU Healthcare Florida union, and other organizations. SFJwJ works to bring labor unions and community organizations together to achieve greater power. In 2001, the SEIU health-care union created United for Dignity for Immigrant Workers Rights to build stronger community ties and leadership among immigrant workers. In 2002, WeCount! was established to organize immigrant workers and families in southern Miami-Dade County, and the Florida Immigrant Coalition was formed to organize immigrants across the state.

Technical and research support organizations have emerged to complement these social justice organizations. Florida Legal Services has existed in the Miami area since the 1970s, but with the creation of new social justice organizations at the turn of the twenty-first century, it gained an organized constituency of organizations that it supported with litigation and legal advocacy. In 2004 the Research Institute on Social and Economic Policy (RISEP) was created as a university-based institute at Florida International University. RISEP conducts and publishes research on issues affecting low-income communities in order to support specific social justice campaigns and a broadly progressive policy agenda.

Some of these social justice infrastructure organizations began meeting on a regular basis in 2005 to discuss how to leverage the emerging political opportunities created by subsidized housing scandals and a critical shortage of affordable housing in order to address unequal urban development in Miami. Naming themselves the Community Benefits Coalition, they held monthly meetings for nearly four years; even though no formal, coalitional campaign emerged, the meetings facilitated the maintenance of a mutually supportive network that on key occasions collaborated to mobilize specific protest activities or advocacy. Since then, another alliance of labor, community, and research organizations won the countywide Wage Theft Ordinance, which established an office, funding, and processes for recuperating workers' unpaid wages.[48]

In 2003, several of the aforementioned organizations organized the ministerial meeting of the Root Cause Coalition against the Free Trade of the Americas. In 2007, the creator and main author of the Center for Pan-African Development, a "think tank ideological formation," launched Take Back the Land to assert homeless and low-income families' right to housing, most famously by creating a squatters settlement on land where squandered public housing funds were never spent. In 2011 SEIU 11 created 1Miami, a community organization meant to unite diverse neighborhoods and constituencies outside of the workplace.

In the second decade of the twenty-first century, several of these organizations, as well as new civic actors, have mobilized to defend their resources in the face of the combination of federal "bailouts" and austerity politics. During the first decade of the 2000s, Catalyst Miami and a number of labor unions mobilized in defense of welfare programs, and against the privatization of health-care and prison jobs. In 2011, people from a variety of racial, ethnic, and class backgrounds established the Occupy Miami encampment, modeled after Occupy Wall Street. The Miami version, however, occupied land in front of the downtown government center, as opposed to in the Brickell financial district, the Miami (and perhaps Latin American) equivalent of Wall Street. Young Cuban Americans' participation in the Occupy movement, associated with "anarchists and Marxist revolutionaries," prompted some local Cuban American leaders to call for an "Occupy Havana."[49]

None of these movements existed in the 1990s. They represent a rapidly growing array of working-class community and workplace institutions that reach across the racial and ethnic divides which seemed to have hardened in the early 1990s. But these nascent working-class institutions are still too young for us to reach any conclusions about their effects in helping to "root" Miamians to their place and to each other.

Conclusion

The decline of Miami's non-Hispanic white population that began in the 1970s continues, and Anglos are now the smallest of the region's three major racial/ethnic groups. At the same time, both the Hispanic and black populations are becoming increasingly heterogeneous as non-Cuban Hispanic and non-native black, particularly Haitian and West Indian, segments increase rapidly. Though ethnicity and race remain important, class is emerging as increasingly important in structuring Miami's social relations. As in the rest of the United States, the middle class in Miami has diminished, including the black middle class. The poor are increasingly non-Cuban Hispanics, and those at the top are a mix of whites, Cubans, and non-Cuban Hispanics, with a growing sprinkle of blacks. Interethnic coalitions are likely at both ends of the class hierarchy. Public- and private-sector Hispanics and private-sector Anglos, along with a few public-sector and nonprofit-sector blacks, have cooperated to promote the gentrification that has transformed a number of neighborhoods. Anglos and Hispanics, primarily in the private sector, also work together on the boards of nonprofits that address the needs of working-class and poor Miamians. Finally, grassroots organizations and coalitions of the poor have begun to emerge and achieve some victories that reach across ethnic communities.

Notes

1. Tom Wolfe, *Back to Blood* (New York: Little, Brown, 2012); Alejandro Portes and Alex Stepick, *City on the Edge: The Social Transformation of Miami* (Berkeley: University of California Press, 1993).

2. Although we refer loosely to Miami, sometimes we specifically mean the City of Miami, other times Miami-Dade County; generally we aim to examine conditions prevalent throughout Southeast Florida.

3. Alex Stepick, Guillermo Grenier, Max Castro, and Marvin Dunn, *This Land Is Our Land: Immigrants and Power in Miami* (Berkeley: University of California Press, 2003); Jan Nijman, *Miami: Mistress of the Americas* (Philadelphia: University of Pennsylvania Press, 2011).

4. The U.S. government uses the term *non-Hispanic white*. The adjective *non-Hispanic* is necessary because Cubans especially, but not uniquely among Hispanics, are likely to identify as white.

5. Marvin Dunn, *Black Miami in the Twentieth Century* (Gainesville: University Press of Florida, 1997); Nathan Connolly, "Timely Innovations: Planes, Trains and the 'Whites Only' Economy of a Pan-American City," special issue 2, *Urban History* 36 (2009): 243–61.

6. Nathan Connolly notes that the Anglo elite, with the assent of the black chamber of commerce, created a black police force to police black areas, with the idea to reduce conflict in the tourist-friendly city. Connolly, "Games of Chance: Jim Crow's Entrepreneurs Bet on 'Negro' Law-and-Order," in *What's Good for Business: Business and American Politics since World War II*, ed. K. Phillips-Fein and J. E. Zelizer (New York: Oxford University Press, 2012), 140–56.

7. Nathan Connolly, *A World More Concrete: Real Estate and the Remaking of Jim Crow South Florida* (Chicago: University of Chicago Press, 2014); Connolly, "By Eminent Domain: Race and Capital in the Building of an American South Florida" (PhD diss., University of Michigan, Ann Arbor, 2008).

8. Portes and Stepick, *City on the Edge*.

9. These five national groups grew by more than 136,000 between 1990 and 2010, compared to an increase of about 100,500 Cubans. U.S. census data likely underestimates the presence of non-Cuban Hispanics because they—particularly undocumented immigrants—are less likely to respond to the census.

10. See Ira Sheskin, "The Miami Ethnic Archipelago," *Florida Geographer* 26 (1992): 40–57. More recently, local observers have been concerned about the decline of young professionals. See Deborah Acosta, "Brain Drain?" *Miami Herald*, December 13, 2011; Brookings Institution, "Growing the Middle Class: Connecting All Miami-Dade Residents to Economic Opportunity" (Washington, DC: Brookings Institution Center on Urban and Metropolitan Policy, 2004).

11. The share of non-Hispanic whites in management and white-collar professional jobs increased by 10 percent while their share decreased for all other job sectors excepting a slight increase in services. While they became more concentrated in these occupations, non-Hispanic whites lost ground to Cubans and especially non-Cuban Hispanics. The non-Hispanic white share of executive, managerial, and professional occupations declined

from 49 to 28 percent between 1990 and 2010 while the Cuban share increased from 25 to 30 percent (surpassing non-Hispanic whites) and the non-Cuban Hispanic share increased from 13 to 27 percent. Meanwhile, the non-Hispanic Black share of the "top" occupational categories held steady at 11.5 percent.

12. In particular, about 222,770 Hispanics (not only immigrants) from Honduras, Nicaragua, Colombia, the Dominican Republic, Venezuela, Mexico, Peru, Argentina, Guatemala, Puerto Rico, El Salvador, Ecuador, and Uruguay added 95,700 people with incomes less than $20,000.

13. Adam Bee, "Household Income Inequality within U.S. Counties: 2006–2010," *American Community Survey Briefs*, U.S. Census Bureau, February 2012, http://www.census.gov/prod/2012pubs/acsbr10-18.pdf; see also Stepick et al., *This Land Is Our Land*.

14. Alejandro Portes, "Dilemmas of a Golden Exile: Integration of Cuban Refugee Families in Milwaukee," *American Sociological Review* 34, no. 4 (1969): 505–18.

15. Seth Bramson, *Speedway to Sunshine: The Story of the Florida East Coast Railway* (Erin, ON: Boston Mills Press, 2003).

16. Paul S. George, "Brokers, Binders, and Builders: Greater Miami's Boom of the mid-1920s," *Florida Historical Quarterly* 65, no. 1 (1986): 27–51; Gary R. Mormino, *Land of Sunshine, State of Dreams: A Social History of Modern Florida* (Gainesville: University Press of Florida, 2005); Melanie Shell-Weiss, *Coming to Miami: A Social History*, Sunbelt Studies series (Gainesville: University Press of Florida, 2009).

17. Even in the case of what was once Miami's largest manufacturing sector—sportswear—Deirdre Clemente argues that place-marketing was essential to its success. Clemente, "Made in Miami: The Development of the Sportswear Industry in South Florida, 1900–1960," *Journal of Social History* 41, no. 1 (2007): 128–48. See also Portes and Stepick, *City on the Edge*; Nijman, *Miami*; Paul S. George, "Passage to the New Eden: Tourism in Miami from Flagler through Everest G. Sewell," *Florida Historical Quarterly* 59, no. 4 (1981): 440–64; John A. Hannigan, "The Postmodern City: A New Urbanization?" *Current Sociology* 43, no. 1 (1995): 151–217; Gregory W. Bush, "'Playground of the USA': Miami and the Promotion of Spectacle," *Pacific Historical Review* 68, no. 2 (1999): 153–72.

18. Marifeli Pérez-Stable and Miren Uriarte, "Cubans and the Changing Economy of Miami," in *Latinos in a Changing U.S. Economy: Comparative Perspectives on Growing Inequality*, ed. Rebecca Morales and Frank Bonilla (Newbury Park, CA: Sage, 1993), 133–59. Saskia Sassen and Alejandro Portes, "Miami: A New Global City?" *Contemporary Sociology* 22, no. 4 (1993): 471–77.

19. Brookings Institution, "Growing the Middle Class," 23.

20. AutoNation is headquartered in Fort Lauderdale (Broward County) while Office Depot is in Boca Raton (Palm Beach County).

21. These neighborhoods are in the centrally located cities of Miami and Miami Beach, which we view as the "urban core" of Miami-Dade County.

22. According to our analysis of change at the census tract level, in the 1980s, when the county overall added nearly 108,000 housing units and about 82,500 occupied housing units, the cities of Miami and Miami Beach together experienced a net loss of 2,650 housing units and more than 10,000 occupied housing units. During this period, only a handful of relatively wealthy central city neighborhoods added more than 300 housing units

each, and only Brickell experienced a substantial increase in occupied housing. Source: Geolytics Inc., Neighborhood Change Database (NCBD), 1970–2000, U.S. Census Bureau, housing tables.

23. Hortense Leon, "Workforce Housing Drives Little Havana Revival," *Florida Real Estate Journal*, April 3, 2007.

24. Marcos Feldman and Violaine Jolivet, "Eyes on Little Havana: Gentrification and the Securitization of Space in the Heart of Miami" *International Journal of Urban and Regional Research* (forthcoming); see also chapter 5 in Jan Lin, *The Power of Urban Ethnic Places: Cultural Heritage and Community Life* (New York: Routledge, 2011).

25. For example, since 1999 the Miami Fellows program, funded by the Kellogg and Knight Foundations, has supported more than one hundred young leaders in civic and arts initiatives. The Knight Arts Challenge and the Miami Foundation's Our Miami initiative support the development of cultural activities and the growth of Miami's "creative class." See Miami Foundation, "Our Miami: Soul of the City,: special supplement to the *Miami Herald*, September 9, 2012, http://ourmiami.org/#!/publications; AEA Consulting, *Building the Arts in Miami: Knight Arts Challenge Interim Review 2008–2011* (Miami, FL: Knight Foundation, October 2012), http://www.knightfoundation.org/publications/building-arts-miami.

26. Douglas Hanks, "In Midtown, Condo Boom's Leftovers Dwindle," *Miami Herald*, September 18, 2012; "Foreigners Responsible for a Fifth of Florida Home Sales," *Miami Herald*, August 27, 2012, Real Estate section; Nick Timiraos, "Foreigners Snap Up Properties in the U.S.," *Wall Street Journal*, June 12, 2012, Real Estate section.

27. Andres Viglucci, "New Towers to Change Miami's Look and Life," *Miami Herald*, March 16, 2003; "Power Developers of Real Estate," *Sun Post*, December 3, 2004.

28. Hannah Sampson, "Art Basel Draws a Crowd, and Hotels Are Selling Out," *Miami Herald*, December 1, 2010.

29. See Marcos Feldman, "The Role of Neighborhood Organizations in the Production of Gentrifiable Urban Space: The Case of Wynwood, Miami's Puerto Rican Barrio (PhD diss., Department of Global and Sociocultural Studies, Florida International University, Miami, 2011), http://digitalcommons.fiu.edu/etd/540/.

30. Brett Sokol, "Heads Up: Rehousing a Miami Collection," *New York Times*, November 29, 2009; Tom Austin, "Private Spaces: Local Collections Add Another Dimension to Miami's Art Scene," *Miami Herald*, December 1, 2010, AB14.

31. Major private collectors—such as the Rubell family, Dennis Scholl, Martin Marguiles, Rosa de la Cruz, and a few others—exemplify the Miami Model because their collections are museum sized and high quality but housed in privately owned warehouses routinely accessible to the art-going public; see Austin, "Private Spaces."

32. Sokol, "Heads Up."

33. The Miami Model was described in 2011 by Dennis Scholl, former director of the Knight Foundation and a major local collector.

34. Among these critics are Rosa de la Cruz and Martin Marguiles. See Anne Tschida, "MAM to PAMM: The Uproar over Renaming Miami's Art Museum Is Just the Latest in a History of Turmoil," *Biscayne Times* monthly magazine, May 2012.

35. Ibid.

36. Joel Engelhardt, "Program Looks to Redirect Development Eastward," *Palm Beach Post*, November 16, 1998, 1; "Hold the Line On Rural, Open Lands," editorial, *Miami Herald*, March 27, 2005, 4L; Neal Peirce and Curtis Johnson, "Will Growth Doom South Florida?," *Sun-Sentinel*, December 3, 2000, 1G.

37. In a 2004 report, Standard and Poor's "cited record growth in Miami's real estate market and an increase in residential migration to the city," in addition to improved financial management, as factors supporting the most recent bond rating upgrade (see Carolyn Salazar, "In Classic Turnaround, City's Finances Earn A+," *Miami Herald*, February 14, 2004, 1B). The City of Miami was however investigated in 2011 and 2012 by the Federal Securities and Exchange Commission for questionable accounting practices used to close a budget hole and mislead investors when selling bonds, leading to warnings from the Moody's ratings agency of a possible credit downgrade (Doug Hanks and Kathleen McGrory, "Moody's to Consider Downgrading City of Miami's Credit Rating," *Miami Herald*, July 25, 2012, 1A).

38. FIU Center for Leadership, Miami Leadership Summit I, Report, January 17, 2012, http://business2.fiu.edu/lead/Events/summit2/MLS1.pdf.

39. Asian Americans made up about 8 percent of summit participants, far more than their proportion in the general population. They were not the most prominent or outspoken participants, but their presence may indicate a trend for the future. We should also caution that because of the convener and location of this event, it may not necessarily be representative of Miami's overall elite. Missing from the summit were representatives of some of Miami's most important employers, such as American Airlines, Carnival Cruises, and the University of Miami.

40. Raymond Mohl, "Elizabeth Virrick and the 'Concrete Monsters': Housing Reform in Postwar Miami," *Tequesta* 61 (2001): 5–37; Mohl, "South of the South?: Jews, Blacks, and the Civil Rights Movement in Miami, 1945–1960," *Journal of American Ethnic History* 18, no. 2 (1999): 3–36.

41. Martin Merzer, *The Billion-Dollar Bet on a Community's Future*, The Children's Trust, 2009, 10, http://www.thechildrenstrust.org/about/campaign-case-study.

42. See Bruce Nissen, "'Social Justice Infrastructure' Organizations as New Actors from the Community: The Case of South Florida," *Journal of Community Practice* 17 (2009): 157–69; Bruce Nissen and Monica Russo, "Building a Movement: Revitalizing Labor in Miami," *WorkingUSA* 9, no. 1 (2006): 123–39.

43. Nissen and Russo, "Building a Movement," 131.

44. See Bruce Nissen, "Living Wage Campaigns from a 'Social Movement' Perspective: The Miami Case," *Labor Studies Journal* 25, no. 3 (2000): 29–50.

45. For a more detailed discussion of the various organizations see Nissen, "'Social Justice Infrastructure,'" and Nissen and Russo, "Building a Movement."

46. Jason Albright, "Contending Rationality, Leadership, and Collective Struggle: The 2006 Justice for Janitors Campaign at the University of Miami," *Labor Studies Journal* 33, no. 1 (2008): 63–80.

47. Charles Rabin, "Displaced Residents: 'Here We Are Now,'" *Miami Herald*, December 22, 2006; Carol J. Williams, "Homeless Take the Football and Run with It," *Los Angeles Times*, February 2, 2007; Marcos Feldman, *How Are the Displaced Scott-Carver Residents*

Faring? The Aftermath of HOPE VI Public Housing Redevelopment in Miami (Miami: Research Institute on Social and Economic Policy, Florida International University, 2007); Michael Vasquez, "Groups Protest UM Biotech Center in Overtown," *Miami Herald*, December 10, 2010; Helen Berggren, "Quality-of-Life Issues Addressed," *Miami Herald*, April 2, 2006; Alfonso Chardy, "Immigrants Are Seeking In-State College Tuition," *Miami Herald*, November 24, 2005, 1B; "Commissioners Vow Improved Bus Service," editorial, *Miami Herald*, November 18, 2001, 3B.

48. See Cynthia Hernández and Carol Stepick, *Wage Theft: An Economic Drain on Florida* (Miami: Research Institute on Social and Economic Policy, Florida International University, 2012). Available from www.risep-fiu.org.

49. Ángel Castillo Jr., "Occupy Havana," letter to the editor, *Miami Herald*, December 22, 2011.

12

How Cubans Transformed Florida Politics and Gained National Influence

SUSAN ECKSTEIN

This chapter documents how Cuban Americans have become politically influential in Miami, and leveraged their local power for national political influence. Their influence has peaked in presidential election years, when candidates for the highest office of the land promoted embargo-tightening measures to curry Cuban American votes in Florida, the largest "swing state," and when national legislators as well as presidential candidates received Cuban American campaign contributions. Most Cuban American voters and the leadership of the Cuban American community pressed for a politically constructed "wall" across the Florida Straits, which they believed would destabilize the Castro-led regime to the point of collapse. Their influence subsided, however, as they became more politically divided in their views toward their homeland, as their leadership became more divided in their party affiliation and policy preferences, and as the emergent Cuban American political class failed to move beyond promoting their narrow ethnic interests and embrace the interests of the growing non-Cuban Hispanic community in their midst.

Cuban Migration: The Magnetism of Miami

Cubans are among the most demographically concentrated of new U.S. immigrant groups. They have mainly settled in Florida, above all in Greater Miami. The influx of Cubans began when hundreds of thousands of opponents of Cuba's 1959 revolution flocked to Miami after Fidel Castro took power. Many thought their stay would be temporary, until Castro was deposed. Instead, not only did they stay, but hundreds of thousands of other Cubans followed in their footsteps.

By the turn of this century more than 60 percent of Cuban immigrants, and more than half of the approximately 1.2 million people in the United States who claim Cuban ancestry, lived in Miami, the once small winter getaway for northern "snowbirds" and retirees.[1] Over the years ever more Cubans gravitated to Miami because they had friends and family there, along with former neighbors, schoolmates, and work colleagues who could help them adjust and re-create their life anew in what Cubans came to consider the "Second Havana."

Washington initially tried to disperse the massive influx of Cubans by making refugee benefits conditional on settling outside South Florida, in order to reduce local labor market pressures. Once the refugee program ended in 1973, however, both new immigrants from Cuba and earlier immigrants who initially had settled elsewhere increasingly gravitated to the Second Havana. For example, 84 percent of Cubans arriving in 2005 noted their intention to settle somewhere in Florida, with Miami their main destination.

Cubans, in turn, attracted other Latin Americans to the city, to the extent that Miami also became dubbed "the northernmost Latin American city." By 2000 Miami was majority Hispanic, and soon thereafter non-Cuban Hispanics came to outnumber Cubans.[2] Miami also came to have the highest percentage of foreign-born residents of any U.S. city, and the third largest number of immigrants in total. Only Los Angeles and New York had more.[3] More significantly, nearly all foreign-born Miami residents came from south of the Rio Grande.[4]

As Cuban and then other Latin American immigrants made Miami their home, non-Hispanic whites moved away. As a result, their percentage of the city's population plunged from 79 to 21 percent between 1970 and 2000.[5] Non-Hispanic whites generally disliked the city's new feeling of "otherness." The Cuban immigrants, in particular, imposed their own cultural world on the city. A bumper sticker reflected white sentiments: "Will the last American out of South Florida please bring the flag."[6]

Cubans made their presence known by clustering in select neighborhoods and municipalities in Greater Miami, where they resisted full assimilation.[7] By the turn of the twenty-first century Hialeah and Westchester were more than 60 percent Cuban, while Hialeah Gardens, Sweetwater, Coral Gables, Miami City, and South Miami had smaller but still substantial Cuban populations.[8] Indicative of how Cuban Americans "stick to their own," even amidst the growing presence of non-Cuban Hispanics, Florida International University's Institute for Public Opinion Research (FIU-IPOR) found that only 14 percent of the more than eighteen hundred Cuban Americans it surveyed in Miami in 2004 lived in neighborhoods where few Cubans lived.[9] After forty or more years in the United States, 40 percent of the first wave of émigrés still lived mainly amongst fellow Cuban Americans, and nearly 80 percent of those surveyed had Cuban American spouses. Even among U.S.-born Cuban Americans, 60 percent married someone of their same heritage.

Where Cuban Americans settled hinged on their social class, not merely their country of origin. Working-class Cuban Americans gravitated to Hialeah, and the poorest to the City of Miami, while moneyed Cuban Americans made their home in Coral Gables and other wealthy communities.[10] The class-based Cuban American communities also were associated with different immigrant waves. The well-to-do communities became home mainly to the first wave of émigrés.[11]

Cubans thereby kept their immigrant and socioeconomic identities alive and distinct from those of the other Hispanics and non-Hispanic whites into whose midst they had moved. Their in-group social ties influenced their political involvements in their adopted land, as detailed next.

Voting and the Making of the Cuban American Political Class

Cubans are unique among immigrants in enjoying a guaranteed path to U.S. citizenship, even when they enter or settle in the country without legal permission. The Cuban Adjustment Act of 1966 entitles all Cubans who arrive in the United States—with or without immigration visas—to qualify for residency status and five years later for citizenship.

Cuban immigrants take their citizenship rights seriously, although to date this is more true of the first wave than of recent émigrés. In 2010, 92 percent of 1960s immigrants had become U.S. citizens—compared to 41 percent of 1990s immigrants and 10 percent of immigrants who arrived during the first decade of this century—and thus eligible to vote and elect people to represent their interests. In 2010 all Cubans who arrived in the United States before 2004 were eligible for citizenship, owing to the 1966 Cuban Adjustment Act.

FIU-IPOR Miami survey data show that Cuban American citizens exercise their voting rights. For example, in 2007, 91 percent of age-eligible Cuban American citizens had registered to vote.[12] While registration rates were high among all voting-age citizens, they were highest among those who emigrated during the first fifteen years of Castro's rule and among those identifying themselves as exiles, and lowest among post–Soviet-era arrivals, whom I refer to as the "New Cubans." The voter registration rate among exiles was even higher than that among age-eligible U.S.-born Cuban Americans.

Beginning in the 1980s, Cuban Americans in Florida (and in Hudson County, New Jersey, which became home to the second largest Cuban immigrant community after the revolution), used their vote to elect "their own" to political office. When given the option, Cuban Americans have typically voted for politicians who share their heritage. Cuban immigrants first won office in municipalities where many of them lived, but with time did so elsewhere as well. They have been elected as mayors, city managers and city council members, state assembly persons (including Speaker of the House), and federal representatives and senators. With only occasional exceptions, they are the only Hispanics to have been elected to public office in Florida.

The Cuban Americans elected to office come from families who fled the revolution early on. Either they themselves immigrated, or their parents did. Cubans who emigrated since 1980, including the hundreds of thousands of Cubans who emigrated in the post-Soviet era, and who by the turn of the century accounted for about half of all Cuban immigrants, remain at the sidelines of the emergent Cuban American political class.[13]

Cuban American politicians and the Cuban American electorate have been committed to Cuban affairs, even if they also concern themselves with local matters. Given that most of the Cuban-born politicians emigrated at a young age, during Castro's first years of rule, and the second-generation Cuban American politicians have yet to step foot on the island, the emergent political class mainly imagines Cuba under Castro. Their politics therefore are shaped by an imagined Cuba that builds on views their parents' generation inculcated in them: views of a paradise lost, with the loss blamed on Fidel, and by implication his brother, Raúl, his right-hand man for decades and since 2008 his successor as head of state. Regardless of which side of the Straits they were born on, Cuban American politicians have very publicly opposed the Castro brothers and advocated policies they believed would bring down the regime. Cuban American politicians' anti-Castro stance won them votes at the polls and helped them secure campaign contributions.

As of 2000, Cuban Americans also held one-third of the top appointed positions in Miami-Dade County, more than any other ethnic group. Given such Cuban American inroads into electoral and appointed office, three-fourths of Miami-Dade residents perceived them as the most politically powerful of the county's ethnic groups.[14]

Leveraging Local Power for National Political Influence

Wealthy Cuban Americans who emigrated soon after the revolution have been instrumental in the electoral success of Cuban Americans. Through adept lobbying, plus political contributions, they have not only managed to get "their own" elected, but also to gain support from non-Cuban lawmakers for national legislation they coveted. They have supported candidates who promote a hard line on Cuba, symbolized by an impermeable embargo that they believed would cause Castro's government to collapse.

Between the early 1980s and the early 2000s Cuban Americans wielded influence through the Cuban American National Foundation, commonly called "the Foundation." The charismatic Jorge Mas Canosa led the Foundation during most of those years, when no other Cuban American group matched it in power brokering. Prior to the founding of the Foundation, the first émigrés had been involved in scores of small organizations, some of which used violent tactics and operated covertly, and none of which influenced mainstream American politics.

President Ronald Reagan channeled the funds that helped launch the Foundation through the National Endowment for Democracy (NED). Florida Democrat Dante Fascell introduced the enabling legislation to establish the NED and became its first director. Using NED funds to help finance political campaigns, the Foundation demanded support for its anti-Castro crusade in return for contributions.[15] Reagan had understood that the new Hispanic group in Florida could help him win reelection and further what was at the time the Republican Party's new strategy to expand its political base in the South. He also recognized that Cuban Americans would support his efforts to defeat left-leaning political movements in the hemisphere, especially in Central America.[16]

Quickly establishing a revenue base of its own, the Foundation formed an associated political action committee (PAC) that channeled campaign contributions to politicians nationwide who supported their anti-Castro cause. A core of members made large annual contributions to both the Foundation and the PAC. At the turn of this century the Foundation claimed fifty thousand members, including the "who's who" of the Miami Cuban American community. Mainly these were Cubans who had emigrated shortly after the revolution and a small number of their U.S.-born children. The Foundation's 170 directors, trustees, and associates reputedly contributed between $1,000 and $10,000 annually to the organization[17] and its PAC, which took in nearly $1.7 million and made $1.3 million in political donations,[18] accounting for all but 1 percent of Cuban American PAC contributions between 1982 and 2000.

The Foundation began in Miami where most of its membership, leadership, and financial contributors lived. And it was in Miami, and in Florida more broadly, where it built up its initial influence-peddling political base. It did so not only by publicly endorsing and privately funding campaigns of candidates sympathetic to its anti-Castro mission, but also by sponsoring a radio station, La Voz de la Fundación (The Voice of the Foundation), that Mas Canosa oversaw. Exiles brought a tradition of radio-listening with them from Cuba, which Mas Canosa put to use.

After consolidating power within the South Florida Cuban American community, the Foundation, under Mas Canosa's tutelage, went on to extend its influence beyond its ethnic and territorial base in Florida, and across the partisan divide, even though most of its members were dedicated Republicans in their private lives. Indicative of its commitment to help elect anti-Castro Cuban Americans to political office, irrespective of their party affiliation or where in the United States they lived, the Foundation's PAC financed campaigns of New Jersey Democrat Robert Menéndez, who began his political career as mayor of Union City, then went on to serve in the U.S. House and, subsequently, the Senate. Menéndez, in exchange, promoted the Foundation's anti-Castro mission, even to the point of defying his party's leadership. In addition to supporting any embargo-tightening legislation up for vote, he publicly opposed President Clinton's efforts in 1999 to improve U.S.-Cuban relations through "baseball diplomacy."[19] And the following year he joined the chorus of South Florida Cuban American politicians who publicly criticized the Clinton administration's decision to return six-year-old Elián Gonzalez to his father in Cuba. Elián, brought ashore after his mother died at sea in their effort to enter the United States without legal permission, became the poster boy of hard-line Cuban Americans' anti-Castro crusade. Menéndez never supported a Cuba-related policy that his mainly Republican Florida campaign financiers opposed.

Modeled after the influential pro-Israel lobby, the Foundation became one of the most effective and the second best financed ethnic lobby in the United States. Its first success at the national level occurred in 1983 when it convinced Congress to allot $10 million to fund Radio Martí, to beam anti-Castro messages to Cubans on the Island. The main sponsor of the bill to finance the radio project was Senator Paula Hawkins, a Florida Republican. Although not Cuban American, she was one of the top ten recipients of Cuban American campaign funds between 1979 and 2000.

Even following the cold war, when Cuba posed no national security threat to the United States, the Foundation's savvy lobbying and campaign donations contributed to passage of several laws that it believed would further its anti-Castro cause. In 1990 Congress passed a bill for which the Foundation had lobbied, establishing the federally funded TV Martí to beam anti-Castro programs to Cuba with visual images. Florida Congressman Dante Fascell, the Democrat who had overseen the NED funding that gave the Foundation its initial financial boost, along with two other key supporters of the legislation, were non–Cuban American beneficiaries of substantial Cuban American campaign contributions. Although the Cuban government blocked reception of the television broadcasts, U.S. taxpayers funded the project for decades.

Then, in 1992 Congress passed the Cuban Democracy Act, for which the Foundation also lobbied. The bill was designed to isolate, and thereby economically strangulate and destabilize the Castro regime by closing embargo loopholes. In particular it prohibited U.S. businesses from trading with Cuba through countries where they had subsidiaries. The bill was sponsored by New Jersey Democratic Congressman Robert Torricelli, the second largest recipient of Cuban American funding between 1979 and 2000. Until the political contributions flowed to his campaign coffers, Torricelli had been an advocate for U.S.-Cuba dialogue.[20] His Senate partner in promoting the bill was Democrat Bob Graham of Florida, the sixth largest recipient of Cuban American political donations during the twenty-one-year period.

The Foundation secured additional support for the embargo-tightening legislation by courting both 1992 presidential candidates with campaign contributions. George H. W. Bush was the fifth largest recipient of Cuban American political donations. Clinton received far fewer dollars, but he announced his support for the pending bill upon attending a Foundation-sponsored event in Miami where he received campaign funds.

Another anti-Castro bill that the Foundation backed, in 1996, further tightened the embargo: the Cuban Liberty and Democratic Solidarity Act, informally known as the Helms-Burton bill after its two key sponsors. Jesse Helms and Dan Burton received substantial Cuban American campaign contributions either shortly before introducing the legislation or while Congress deliberated the bill. Among its provisions, the legislation provided legal basis for U.S. citizens to sue international investors operating on property the Cuban government had expropriated to which they laid prerevolutionary claims. The legislation also called for the U.S. government to deny entry visas to such investors.

Understanding that passage of embargo-tightening measures required wider support than merely legislative sponsors, the directors of the Cuban American PAC strategically channeled funds to candidates nationwide whose support the lobbyists sought. Lawmakers who backed the 1992 and 1996 bills typically received substantially more contributions than those who opposed the legislation, and few recipients of Cuban American dollars voted against the bills.

The 1996 legislation was the last embargo-tightening legislation for which the Foundation lobbied before Mas Canosa died, in 1997. In 2000, after his son, Jorge Mas Santos, assumed the Foundation's helm, Foundation lobbyists failed to block passage of legislation allowing for the sale of food and medicines to Cuba. The Foundation's influence proved to have rested not merely on PAC contributions but also on the astute power brokering of Mas Canosa.

Mas Canosa leveraged influence partly by silencing Cuban Americans who challenged his authority and the policies he advocated. For example, he orchestrated the dismissal of the first Radio Martí director. Although an opponent of Castro, the director opposed TV Martí on grounds that it violated international agreements and he opposed Mas Canosa's domination of the government-funded media projects. With the director's removal from office, Mas Canosa could use the federally funded media projects, along with the Foundation's local radio station, to consolidate his role as the premier gatekeeper communicating on Cuban matters.

Thus, under Mas Canosa's leadership, the Foundation leveraged Cuban American financial success to influence U.S. policy toward Cuba. It advocated for measures to destabilize the Castro-led regime at a time when the United States built bridges with Communist China and Vietnam. The Foundation made use of interest-group politics. But Mas Canosa simultaneously blunted opposition from fellow Cuban Americans who challenged his authority and gatekeeper role on matters pertaining to Cuba.

The Presidential Election Cycle and Exile Policy Influence: 1992–2004

Exiles' national policy influence rested on their leveraging of Cuban American votes and political contributions. In the post–cold war era, when Cuba no longer posed a national security threat to the United States, presidential election years provided exiles with windows of opportunity to persuade not merely legislators but incumbent presidents to champion policies they wanted. Even as exiles' influence over Congress weakened in the latter 1990s, their influence over presidents, who have discretionary power, remained.

Table 12.1. Summary of U.S. embargo tightening and loosening measures and whether incumbent president won Florida (election years, 1992–2004)

Year	Personal Embargo Loosening	Personal Embargo Tightening	Macro Embargo Loosening	Macro Embargo Tightening	Incumbent Wins FL	Incumbent Loses FL
1992		X		X	X	
1994		X				
1995	X					
1996		X		X	X	
1998	X					
1999	X					
2000	[Elián]ᵃ	Xᵇ	X			Xᶜ
2003	Xᵈ					
2004		X			X	

Notes: a. In 2000 Elián González is returned to Cuba amidst Cuban American opposition.
b. The travel cap is codified, amid pressure to lift travel restrictions (but without change in frequency of permitted visits).
c. Al Gore, the incumbent vice president, runs for the presidency, associated with incumbent president's policy regarding Elián.
d. Travel restrictions are loosened for Cuban Americans but tightened for other Americans.

Between 1992 and 2004 Washington policy was intricately linked with the presidential electoral cycle such that government initiatives (1) varied in election versus non-election years; (2) were responsive in election years to concerns and wants of the Cuban American electorate; and (3) were reversed or left unenforced in non-election years, when voter-driven reforms conflicted with non-electoral-based concerns of governance.

Even though Cuban Americans account for less than 1 percent of the U.S. population, they have benefited from concentrating in large numbers in the largest electoral "battleground state," Florida. The state-based winner-take-all electoral college system contributes to the importance of their vote in presidential elections and their ability to leverage their vote for political concessions. In 2000 Cuban Americans accounted for 8 percent of the electorate in Florida, a state that commanded one-tenth of the electoral college votes.[21] Table 12.1 summarizes embargo loosening and tightening policies that were implemented in presidential election and non-election years between 1992 and 2004. It documents whether the policies were implemented by an incumbent and whether the incumbent who implemented the embargo policies won the Florida vote. Embargo policies, in the main, became more restrictive in presidential election years, and less restrictive in off-election years in response to other government concerns.

The post–cold war Cuban American electoral-linked policy cycle began with passage of the Cuban Democracy Act in 1992. George H. W. Bush supported the bill when running for reelection, despite having reservations about it, to curry Cuban American votes in Florida.[22] He strategically signed the legislation in Miami on the eve of the election, and at the ceremony acknowledged Mas Canosa as one of the key forces behind the new law.[23] Indicative that his stance on the bill was electoral-driven is the fact that he had previously vetoed the Mack Amendment, the precursor to the 1992 legislation, because of its extraterritorial claims. Bush had blocked the Mack Amendment, sponsored by then Senator Connie Mack (Senior), in the face of lobbying both by big business, which resented interference with its overseas profiteering, and by foreign governments (such as Canada) that resented U.S. interference with their trade dealings.[24] At the time, appeasing business and foreign allies mattered more to Bush than placating Cuban American hard-liners.

It was in the context of his reelection bid that Bush withdrew his opposition to embargo tightening through extraterritorial means. Like the Mack Amendment, the Cuban Democracy Act prohibited U.S. businesses from third-country trade with Cuba. When pressed to choose between backing interests of business and foreign allies, or courting Cuban American votes in Florida in an election year, the latter mattered more.

In a further indication that his changed stance was electoral-driven, Bush continued to permit U.S. companies to trade with other Communist countries, both from the United States and via other countries. His stance on the pending legislation was not rooted in overarching opposition to economic relations with Communist countries. Bush's opportunism paid off. Three-fourths of Cuban Americans in Florida voted for him, enough to win the state. However, because U.S. policy toward Cuba mattered little to most of the national electorate after the cold war ended, Bush's support for the Cuban Democracy Act did not suffice to win him reelection.

The 1996 election galvanized yet another Foundation-backed policy cycle. Like Bush in 1992, Clinton took advantage of his incumbent status to support new embargo-tightening legislation against the backdrop of his reelection bid. He oversaw passage of the Cuban Liberty and Democratic Solidarity Act. Like Bush before him, in the reelection context Clinton supported legislation he previously had opposed. Clinton had been especially concerned about the internationally unpopular extraterritorial claims of the new bill.[25] Business leaders and foreign governments found the new legislation even more offensive than the Cuban Democracy Act. They considered it an infringement of their sovereignty and trading rights and a violation of the General Agreement on Tariffs and Trade and World Trade Organization principles.

Clinton backed the bill, despite business and foreign government opposition, after the Cuban military shot down planes flown by the exile group Brothers to the Rescue over the Florida Straits in February 1996. Cuba's action stirred émigré fury in Florida. With most Miami Cuban Americans supportive of the so-called Helms-Burton bill,[26] Clinton reversed his stance on the legislation in the context of the heightened anti-Castro fervor in the election year.

Like Bush, Clinton also signed the legislation in Florida. He timed the signing to coincide with the opening of the political primary contest in the state,[27] and he had influential Cuban Americans invited to the signing ceremony.[28] Clinton's approval of the legislation helped him garner about a third of the Cuban American vote in Florida that November, insufficient to break the Republicans' lock on the state's Cuban American electoral bloc but sufficient for him to win the state's electoral college votes and his presidential reelection bid. He was the first Democrat to win Florida in twenty years.

In his memoir, Clinton acknowledged that his support for the bill involved good election-year politics in Florida but that it undermined whatever chance he might have had in a second term to negotiate with Havana authorities a lifting of the embargo in exchange for political and economic change in Cuba.[29] Having considered Florida critical to his reelection, Clinton had worked for four years to cultivate support in the state, including among Cuban Americans. Although he had an interest in making improved U.S.-Cuba bilateral relations and changes in Cuba a hallmark of his presidency, when pressed to choose he prioritized his reelection.

In a further indication that his support for the 1996 legislation was voter-driven, after winning a second term Clinton never enforced a provision of the law that foreign governments and investors found especially egregious: a clause that gave U.S. citizens the right to sue international investors who "trafficked" in property they had owned before the revolution.

Meanwhile, the very enactment of the legislation, with its extraterritorial reach, so angered the international community that member votes in the United Nations General Assembly to condemn the embargo subsequently increased substantially. The United States paid an international price for passing legislation that was never enforced.[30] What was good for winning an election in Florida proved bad for U.S. foreign relations.

In addition, after winning reelection, Clinton never honored provisions of the Helms-Burton legislation that required political and economic change in Cuba before the U.S. government would allow Cuban Americans the rights to visit and send remittances to family on the Island. He relaxed restrictions on what Cuban Americans call the personal embargo, even though the requisite changes had not transpired in Cuba. Clinton, once reelected, argued that cross-border personal ties could lay the groundwork for improved bilateral relations. In essence, Clinton, like Bush before him, reversed policies he had promoted to win votes when they conflicted with concerns of governance—in this case, respect both for the right to travel and for family values.

The 2000 election marked the first time in the presidential electoral policy cycle that no new embargo-tightening measures were introduced. To the contrary, before the election Clinton signed into law legislation that allowed U.S. food sales to Cuba. Agribusiness, with economic interests in numerous farm states, had been lobbying to lift export barriers since the early 1990s to expand their overseas market opportunities.[31] Clinton supported loosening the embargo when not running for reelection and in an election year, when Democrats faced lobbyists more moneyed and influential than Cuban Americans. In 2000 the Florida vote was not his personal concern. While Cuban American lobbyists in the process suffered their first major post–cold war foreign policy legislative defeat, they managed to get a stipulation inserted into the trade bill that Cuba must pay in cash for purchases, to limit the amount of food the Castro government could import. Also in 2000, the Cuban American lobbyists succeeded in getting Congress to legislate a once-a-year cap on Cuban American homeland visits, at a time when congressional momentum was mounting for lifting travel restrictions for all Americans, not merely for Cuban Americans with Island relatives.

The controversy over six-year-old Elián González became the focal point of the 2000 Cuban American policy cycle. After Elián's mother died at sea, the exile community and its supporters argued that he should remain in the United States rather than be returned to his father in Cuba. This episode revealed the political price a presidential candidate incurred by defying Cuban American yearnings. That year Cuban Americans helped George W. Bush win the electoral college vote, with Florida being decisive to the election outcome. Officially, Bush won the state by slightly more than five hundred votes, with more than 80 percent of Cuban Americans backing him. Elián innocently contributed to Bush's exceptionally strong support among Cuban Americans that year. Despite the community's tendency to vote as a bloc, never before had it used the ballot box in such large numbers and in such unity—and in a Florida election officially won by so few votes.

Cuban Americans opposed President Clinton's intervention to honor parental custody rights and return Elián to his father in Cuba. Seventy-nine percent of Miami Cuban Americans felt that Elián should remain in the United States with Miami relatives.³² The Cuban American National Foundation financed Elián's Florida relatives' fight for claims to the boy.

Al Gore, the Democratic presidential nominee in 2000, had been Clinton's vice president. He was damned by association with the Clinton White House even though he very publicly broke with the president and sided with Elián's Miami relatives.³³ In his memoir, Clinton acknowledged Gore's stance to be understandable given the importance of Florida in the election.³⁴ Outrage over the Clinton administration's handling of the Elián case was so strong that Gore did not dare campaign in Cuban American neighborhoods for fear of facing protests, despite his having sided with Cuban Americans in the controversy.³⁵

Gore's experience reveals that when incumbent presidents implement policies unpopular among key constituencies, even a vice president running for the highest office may pay a price at the polls. Cuban Americans were so enraged that the Clinton administration sequestered Elián to return him to Cuba that they went on to defend Bush when his victory was disputed. They intimidated local officials in charge of the recount to the point of helping to shut down the effort to validate the vote.³⁶

When George W. Bush ran for reelection in 2004, after the Elián affair had been put to rest, his support among Cuban Americans in Florida dropped from 82 to 77 percent. Yet, to be assured the support of even three-fourths of Floridian Cuban Americans, Bush acceded to pressure from influential exiles by once again restricting travel and remittances.³⁷ Bush took advantage of his discretionary powers as president to reduce dramatically the rights of Cuban Americans to travel and send remittances to the Island. These were rights that he had expanded during the preceding year. His clampdown placated demands from Cuban Americans at all levels of Florida politics: Republican state representatives, Miami municipal and county officers, the congressional delegation from Miami, and hard-line Cuban American groups, such as Mothers and Women Against Repression, the Cuban Liberty Council, and Unidad Cubana.³⁸ Whereas Clinton had argued that a loosening of travel restrictions would lay bedrock for improved U.S.-Cuban bilateral relations, Bush argued that tightening the personal embargo would hasten regime change on the Island.³⁹ He invited influential, high-ranking Cuban Americans to be present when he gave speeches about strengthening the personal embargo.

George W. Bush's tightening of the embargo in an election year, and loosening of it in a non-election year, further suggests that the Cuba policy was electoral-driven. Bush, like Clinton before him, had expanded Cuban

American travel and remittance-sending rights in an off-election year. When not running for office, both presidents were less accommodating to Cuban American hard-liners and more responsive to bipartisan congressional voices and business and humanitarian interests that favored relaxation of travel restrictions.[40]

Between 1992 and 2004 there was one instance of personal embargo tightening in a non-election year. In 1994, in the context of an immigration crisis, Clinton restricted travel and remittance sending to instances of "extreme hardship" and "extreme humanitarian need," determined on a case-by-case basis.[41] That year, Castro had allowed tens of thousands of Cubans to leave the Island by sea without U.S. entry permission. When Clinton initially refused the boat people admission, outraged exiles turned on the president. They believed that Cubans fleeing Castro were entitled to special immigration privileges. Against this backdrop, Clinton agreed to a request from Mas Canosa to tighten the personal embargo in exchange for him not opposing a revision of the Cuban Adjustment Act requiring Cubans found at sea to be returned to their home country rather than be granted automatic rights to U.S. entry. Cubans who managed to make their way to U.S. shores continued to be entitled to special status. In his memoir, Clinton also admitted that even in this off-election year, he had his 1996 reelection bid in mind when making the deal with Mas Canosa.[42]

Breakdown of the Cuban American Policy Cycle

As of 2008 the political context had changed. The Cuban American community in Florida had continued to increase in size with the annual emigration of at least twenty thousand Cubans in accordance with a bilateral accord that had gone into effect in the mid-1990s, and most new arrivals continued to settle in Florida. By then, however, momentum had built up among non–Cuban American legislators to lift travel restrictions for all Americans and to end economic sanctions against Cuba.[43] Against this backdrop, presidential candidates focused more on whether to maintain or loosen Bush's restrictions than on embargo tightening. And neither candidate could use the highest office to implement vote-getting policies since neither ran as an incumbent. Meanwhile, by 2008 ordinary Cuban Americans had become increasingly divided in the policies they coveted, and influential Cuban Americans ceased to speak in a single voice for policy initiatives.

Miami survey data show that by the time of the 2008 presidential election, Cuban Americans were increasingly divided in their stance toward the personal and trade embargos, toward selling medicine and especially food to Cuba, and toward reestablishing diplomatic ties and engaging in dialogue with the Cuban government. They differed, above all, depending on when they emigrated. The post–Soviet-era arrivals contrast markedly with earlier émigrés in their views toward cross-border relations.[44] Their views differ especially from those of the core of exiles who emigrated in the first years of Castro's rule, the émigré wave from which the Cuban American political class and most campaign contributors emanate.[45]

The varying views of the émigré waves are rooted in their different lived experiences in Cuba. The revolution was a defining and negative experience for the first wave who fled after 1959.[46] Castro's revolution continued to shape their views on Cuban matters even after they had lived most of their lives in the United States. Their hard line on Cuba, even on the people-to-people level, symbolized their continued opposition to Fidel, which they refused to put to rest after the transition of rule to his brother, Raúl.

In contrast, the defining experience for the post–Soviet-era arrivals was the traumatic economic crisis caused by the abrupt ending of Soviet aid and trade. Often emigrating for economic reasons, to improve not only their own lot but, through remittances, that of family they left behind, they favored cross-border ties at both state and personal levels.[47] By the start of this century recent arrivals outnumbered the core of early exiles who emigrated between 1959 and 1964.[48]

Regarding the personal embargo, the émigré waves are especially divided. Indeed, they hold opposing views. In Miami in 2007, on the eve of the 2008 presidential election, approximately three-fourths of the New Cubans (including 80 percent of 1995–2007 émigrés) favored unrestricted travel rights. Approximately the same percentage of the first émigrés favored restrictions on travel.[49]

Reflecting their contrasting views toward the personal embargo, the émigré cohorts differed in their views on Bush's 2004 tightening of travel and remittance-sending restrictions. Distinguishing only between pre- and post-1980 émigrés, Bendixen and Associates found, in their 2006 survey of Miami-Dade and Broward Counties, that 63 percent of pre-1980 émigrés approved, while almost the same percentage (55 percent) of 1980s and later arrivals disapproved, of Bush's 2004 clampdown on cross-border people-to-people rights.[50] Differentiating by year of arrival in more detail, FIU-IPOR found in its 2007 Miami survey that more than twice as many New Cubans as exiles favored a return to the pre-2004, less-restrictive travel and remittance policies.

Although the émigré cohort divide was already in the making at the time of the 2004 election, Bush, running for reelection as an incumbent, had used his discretionary power to tighten the personal embargo to accommodate political pressure from hard-line groups, political contributors, and South Florida Cuban American politicians. The New Cubans were not organized as a political force, and the Foundation, which by then opposed the personal embargo, had become too weak to lobby effectively, for reasons explained later.

When he tightened the personal embargo in 2004, Bush undoubtedly understood where his votes would come from. In Miami, only 31 percent of registered voters, but 57 percent of unregistered voters, felt their lives were restricted by the clampdown.[51] Most Soviet-era émigrés were U.S. citizens and therefore likely to vote, whereas only one-fourth of New Cubans were U.S. citizens.[52] The politically active Soviet-era émigrés who advocated for the tightening of the personal embargo were indifferent to the wishes of recent arrivals.

In 2008, an incipient genealogically based generational divide also was becoming apparent between those born in Cuba and those born in the United States. By then, about half of all Cuban Americans were U.S.-born, and on U.S. Cuba policy, many of them concurred with the views of the New Cubans.[53] For example, two-thirds of U.S.-born Cuban Americans—all U.S. citizens eligible to vote if old enough—disapproved of Bush's 2004 tightening of the personal embargo. Yet, the U.S.-born Cuban Americans and the New Cubans differed in their reasons for opposing the personal embargo. The New Cubans' views were shaped by their continued commitment to friends and family on the Island. In contrast, the views of the U.S.-born were shaped by their U.S. upbringing. They were schooled in U.S. values of compromise and tolerance, even if at home their exile parents socialized them to a hard-line stance toward Castro's Cuba.

Generation-based disputes over policy led the hard-line Island-born to leave the Foundation to form both a new organization, the Cuban Liberty Council (CLC), and a new PAC, the U.S.-Cuba Democracy PAC. Under these circumstances, the Foundation became a shadow of its former self. The new PAC raised more money than the Foundation ever had, while the Foundation lost its financial base to the point that it needed to downsize its staff, close its Washington lobbying office, shut down its radio station, and terminate its PAC-based lobbying efforts. Second-generation Cuban Americans, who dominate the faction loyal to the Foundation, remain committed to their parents' battle with Castro, but they favor a more conciliatory approach to dealing with Cuba consistent with their U.S. upbringing.[54]

Nonetheless, the CLC never attained the influence the Foundation formerly had, its financial base and PAC contributions notwithstanding. It never developed an effective leadership that matched Mas Canosa's. Meanwhile, the organizational split revealed that the Cuban American community no longer spoke in a single voice.

A partisan divide also took hold that eroded exiles' hard-line hegemony. It surfaced among the Cuban American leadership ranks in Miami in 2004, for the first time since Republicans had consolidated their hold over the Cuban American electorate in the 1980s. By 2008, the partisan divide deepened. In the run-up to the 2004 presidential election, U.S.-born Joe García left his post as executive director of the Foundation to join the New Democratic Network, an organization formed to recruit, promote, and fund a new generation of Democratic candidates. Four years later he ran for Congress on the Democratic ticket. Also in 2008, Raúl Martínez, the longtime mayor of Hialeah, who had been a Democrat since the days before Cuban Americans became entrenched in the Republican Party, also ran for Congress. The two of them contested the Miami congressional seats of the staunch Cuban American hard-liner brothers, Mario and Lincoln Díaz-Balart, who had never before faced serious congressional electoral challenges. Although the Democratic candidates lost, they appealed to the Cuban American "generation gap" by focusing less on Raúl and Fidel Castro and more on ending Bush's 2004 restrictions.[55]

Against the growing divide in views among the electorate and the breakdown of hard-liner hegemony at the leadership level, a presidential candidate spoke out for the first time in 2008 for loosening the embargo, although only at the people-to-people level. While John McCain, the Republican candidate, publicly supported continuation of Bush's policies, Barack Obama, the Democratic nominee, announced when campaigning in Florida that if elected he would lift Bush's restrictions on Cuban American travel and remittance-sending rights. Obama argued that Bush's policies left Cubans too dependent on the Castro-led regime and too removed from the transformative message that Cuban Americans carry. While the CLC and the PAC associated with it backed McCain, Obama, without Cuban American PAC money, was not beholden to moneyed Cuban Americans committed to the personal embargo. Under the circumstances, he took the political risk of alienating hard-liners, while appealing to the two-thirds of Miami Cuban Americans, mainly U.S.-born and New Cubans, who favored a return to the travel and remittance policies in place before Bush's 2004 crackdown.[56] Capturing 38 percent of the Cuban American vote, including slightly more than half of young and U.S.-born Cuban American voters, Obama won Florida.

The 2012 election further confirmed that the exile-led hard-line Cuban foreign policy cycle, tied to the presidential electoral cycle, had become history. For one, both Obama, running for reelection, and Mitt Romney, his Republican challenger, promoted no new hard-line Cuba policy. Also Joe García won the congressional seat he previously had lost to a Cuban American Republican. He became the first Cuban American Democrat to win congressional office representing Florida, and he won advocating embargo-loosening on the people-to-people level. In winning, García eroded Cuban American hard-line congressional hegemony. Also, by 2012 Cuban Americans' importance to the Florida electoral outcome had declined. They by then accounted for somewhat less than 6 percent of the state's electorate, down from 8 percent four years earlier.[57] They even represented a minority among the state's Hispanic voters. Given that they differed in their stance on other issues (such as immigration) from other Hispanic ethnics,[58] they were not well positioned to speak for the Hispanic community at large. And the Cuban American community itself had become deeply divided in their partisan loyalty. According to exit polls, 49 percent of Cuban Americans in Florida voted for Obama, while 47 percent voted for Romney.[59]

In Sum

Cuban Americans became the largest immigrant and largest Hispanic group in Miami after the Cuban Revolution. They leveraged their force of numbers to become the most significant ethnic group in South Florida politics, and used their local base to influence national policy toward Cuba. They benefited from residing in the largest "swing" state coupled with savvy targeting of their political contributions.

However, the influential Cuban Americans who promoted a hard line on Cuba and a "wall" across the Florida Straits became increasingly unrepresentative of the Cuban American community, following the arrival of ever more Cubans in the post–cold war years and the development of polar opposite views toward U.S.-Cuba relations among younger U.S.-born Cuban Americans. Concomitant with the Cuban American demographic shift and the diversity of views the shift involved, an emergent organizational and partisan divide eroded the influence of the hard-liners.

The growing non-Cuban Hispanic population of Florida further eroded the influence of the hard-liners, and of Cuban Americans in general. Other Hispanics are not concerned with Cuba and U.S. policy toward it, and Cuban American politicians have failed to speak for the interests of the other Hispanics with whom they differ on key issues.

Unless the Cuban American political class becomes more representative of other Hispanics, their political influence is likely to continue diminishing in the years to come. If they become politically involved, younger, U.S.-born Cuban Americans and post–Soviet-era émigrés are the Cuban Americans best positioned to ally with other Hispanics and represent pan-Hispanic interests. Like other Hispanics, they are less allied with the Republican Party.

Notes

1. This is a remarkable degree of concentration. There are more than four thousand U.S. counties, and less than 1 percent of all Americans are of Cuban origin. Thomas Boswell, *A Demographic Profile of Cuban Americans* (Miami: Cuban American National Council, 2002), ii, 3, 25, 27, 28.

2. Susan Eckstein, *The Immigrant Divide: How Cuban Americans Changed the U.S. and Their Homeland* (New York: Routledge, 2009), 46.

3. See www.skyscrapercity.com/showthread.php?t=448099.

4. Cubans were joined by Puerto Ricans, Nicaraguans, and Colombians, and in smaller numbers by Mexicans, non-Nicaraguan Central Americans, and others from the Caribbean; see U.S. Census Bureau, State and County QuickFacts, Miami-Dade County, Florida, http://quickfacts.census.gov/qfd/states/12025.htm. Latin Americans were lured by the city Cubans remade, at the same time that deteriorating conditions in their home countries induced them to uproot. Not only revolutions but also civil wars, natural disasters, deteriorating economic conditions, and heightened crime and insecurity led rich and poor alike to follow the Cuban example and make Miami their home.

5. Eckstein, *Immigrant Divide*, 46.

6. María Cristina García, *Havana USA: Cuban Exiles and Cuban Americans in South Florida, 1959–1964* (Berkeley: University of California Press, 1996), 74–75.

7. The metropolitan area encompasses almost all of Miami-Dade County. It includes more than two dozen municipalities that range substantially in size.

8. E-Podunk City & County information, www.epodunk.com; Boswell, *Demographic Profile of Cuban Americans*, 3.

9. Eckstein, *Immigrant Divide*, 48.

10. *Miami Herald*, April 24, 2002.

11. Alejandro Portes and Steven Shafer, "Revisiting the Enclave Hypothesis: Miami Twenty-Five Years Later," *Sociology of Entrepreneurship, Research in the Sociology of Organization* 25 (2007), 167.

12. FIU-IPOR, *FIU/Cuba Poll* (2007), cited in Eckstein, *Immigrant Divide*, 93.

13. Eckstein, *Immigrant Divide*, 33.

14. *Miami Herald*, September 4, 2000, 1.

15. Gaston Fonzi, "Who Is Jorge Mas Canosa?," *Esquire*, January 1993, 11; Patrick Haney and Walt Vanderbush, *The Cuban Embargo: The Domestic Politics of an American Foreign Policy* (Pittsburgh, PA: University of Pittsburgh Press, 2005), 43–44.

16. Earl Black and Merle Black, *The Rise of Southern Republicans* (Cambridge, MA: Belknap Press of Harvard University Press, 2002).

17. Eckstein, *Immigrant Divide*, 107, fn. 55.

18. Eckstein, *Immigrant Divide*, 108, fn. 56.

19. "Baseball diplomacy" involved an exchange of games between Cuban All-Stars and the Baltimore Orioles, in Cuba and the United States, to promote cross-border goodwill. After failing to prevent the games, Menéndez helped organize opposition at the U.S. stadium site, in Baltimore. He helped arrange for a large bus caravan to transport protesters from the New York–New Jersey area to the Baltimore game, where they were joined by a smaller contingent from more distant Miami. Exiles associated with the Foundation, an important contributor to his political campaigns, orchestrated the effort to obstruct the playoffs.

20. Morris Morley and Chris McGillion, *Unfinished Business: America and Cuba after the Cold War, 1989–2001* (Cambridge: Cambridge University Press, 2002), 15–16.

21. John Pain, "Cuban-Americans Hit Bush Policies," www.cubanet.org/CNews/y03/ag003/15e4.htm.

22. Morley and McGillion, *Unfinished Business*, 45–46.

23. Lars Schoultz, *That Infernal Little Cuban Republic: The United States and the Cuban Revolution* (Chapel Hill: University of North Carolina Press, 2009), chap. 12.

24. Eckstein, *Back from the Future: Cuba under Castro* (Princeton, NJ: Princeton University Press 1994), 282–83; Morley and McGillion, *Unfinished Business*, 43, 49.

25. Morley and McGillion, *Unfinished Business*, 52–113.

26. FIU-IPOR, *FIU/Cuba Poll*.

27. Morley and McGillion, *Unfinished Business*, 105.

28. Schoultz, *Infernal Little Cuban Republic*, chap. 13.

29. Bill Clinton, *My Life* (New York: Knopf, 2004), 701, 727.

30. The percentage of countries that condemned U.S. economic sanctions against Cuba rose from 33 in 1992 to 73 after the Helms-Burton bill went into effect, and then to 88 percent in 2001. Jorge Domínguez, "Cuba and the Pax Americana," in *A Contemporary Cuba Reader: Reinventing the Revolution*, ed. Philip Brenner, John M. Kirk, William M. LeoGrande, and Marguerite Rose Jiménez (Lanham, MD: Rowman and Littlefield, 2008), 206.

31. Soraya Castro Marino, "Like Sisyphus' Stone: U.S.-Cuban Relations in the Aftermath of September 11, 2001," in *A Contemporary Cuba Reader*, 22; Schoultz, *Infernal Little Cuban Republic*, chap. 13; William LeoGrande, "The United States and Cuba: Strained Engagement," in *Cuba, the United States, and the Post–Cold War World*, ed. Morris Morley and Chris McGillion (Gainesville: University Press of Florida, 2005), 9.

32. FIU-IPOR, *FIU/Cuba Poll 2000*.

33. Though Gore could distance himself from the 2000 legislation that exempted farm exports from the embargo, Elián became such a heated Cuban American controversy that the vice president believed that neutrality on, and indifference to, the issue would cost him the Florida vote.

34. Clinton, *My Life*, 905.

35. Juan Flores, Maria Ilcheva, and Dario Moreno, "Hispanic Vote in Florida: 2004 Election," in *Latinos in the 2004 Election*, ed. Rudy de la Garza, David Leal, and Louis DeSipio (Boulder, CO: Westview Press, 2008).

36. William Finnegan, "The Political Scene: Castro's Shadow," *New Yorker*, May 19, 2004, 70.

37. Flores, Ilcheva, and Moreno, "Hispanic Vote in Florida; Eckstein, *Immigrant Divide*, chaps. 3, 4, 6.

38. Nancy San Martin, "Wary Exiles: A Challenge for Dissident's Cuba Project," *Miami Herald*, January 10, 2003, http://www.cubanet.org/CNews/y03/jan03/10e3.htm.

39. U.S. Department of State, Commission for Assistance to a Free Cuba (CAFC), *Report to the President* (Washington, DC: Government Printing Office, 2004).

40. Schoultz, *Infernal Little Cuban Republic,* chap. 13; LeoGrande "United States and Cuba," 36–44.

41. Felix Masud-Piloto, *From Welcome Exiles to Illegal Immigrants: Cuban Migration to the United States, 1959–1995* (Baltimore, MD: Rowman and Littlefield, 1996).

42. Clinton, *My Life*, 615.

43. Julia Sweig, "A New Stance toward Havana" *The Nation,* May 14, 2007, 11–17.

44. Eckstein, *Immigrant Divide*, 98.

45. Eckstein, *Immigrant Divide*, chap. 3.

46. Silvia Pedraza, *Political Disaffection in Cuba's Revolution and Exodus* (New York: Cambridge University Press, 2007); Eckstein, *Immigrant Divide*, chap. 1.

47. Eckstein, *Immigrant Divide*, appendix.

48. Eckstein, *Immigrant Divide*, table 1.3.

49. Eckstein, *Immigrant Divide*, 97. Although FIU-IPOR included 1985–89 émigrés in the same wave as post–Soviet-era arrivals in its 2000 and 2004 surveys, few Cubans moved to the United States in the latter 1980s.

50. Bendixen and Associates (now Bendixen & Amandi International), "Survey of Cuban and Cuban American Resident Adults in Miami-Dade and Broward" (September 2006), http://bendixenandamandi.com/knowledge-center-archives.

51. FIU-IPOR, *FIU/Cuba Poll.*

52. Eckstein, *Immigrant Divide*, 93.

53. Eckstein, *Immigrant Divide*, 98, 134.

54. Some first-generation immigrants, however, remained loyal to the Foundation. Francisco Hernández, president of the organization, is a case in point.

55. Vaseema P. Nooruddin, "GOP: Cuban Stronghold?" *Politico,* April 21, 2008, www.politico.com/news/stories/0408/9754.html.

56. Eckstein, *Immigrant Divide*, 98.

57. Mark Hugo López and Paul Taylor, *Latino Voters in the 2012 Election* (Washington, DC; Pew Research Center, 2012), http://www.pewhispanic.org/files/2012/11/2012_Latino_vote_exit_poll_analysis_final_11-07-12.pdf.

58. FIU, School of International and Public Affairs, Miami Herald, and Newlink Group, "The Pulse of the Latino Voter: Florida" (2012), http://news.fiu.edu/wp-content/uploads/The-Pulse-of-the-Latino-Voter-Florida-sample.pdf.

59. López and Taylor, "Latino Voters."

Contributors

Amy Turner Bushnell is researcher-in-residence at the John Carter Brown Library and adjunct associate professor of history at Brown University in Providence, Rhode Island.

Raquel Chang-Rodríguez is distinguished professor of Hispanic literature and culture at the City College and the Graduate Center of the City University of New York.

Darién J. Davis is professor of history at Middlebury College in Middlebury, Vermont.

Carmen de la Guardia Herrero is professor at the Universidad Autónoma de Madrid in Spain.

Viviana Díaz Balsera is professor of Spanish at the University of Miami and the author of *The Pyramid under the Cross: Franciscan Discourses of Evangelization and the Nahua Christian Subject in Sixteenth-Century Mexico.*

Jorge Duany is professor of anthropology at the University of Puerto Rico, Río Piedras.

Susan Eckstein is professor of international relations and sociology at Boston University in Massachusetts.

Marcos Feldman is assistant professor of sociology at Northeastern Illinois University in Chicago.

Paul E. Hoffman is Paul W. and Nancy W. Murrill Distinguished Professor and professor of history at Louisiana State University in Baton Rouge.

Richard L. Kagan is Arthur O. Lovejoy Professor Emeritus of History and academy professor at Johns Hopkins University in Baltimore, Maryland.

Jane Landers is Gertrude Conaway Vanderbilt Professor of History and director of the Ecclesiastical and Secular Sources for Slave Societies Project at Vanderbilt University in Nashville, Tennessee.

Rachel A. May is professor of Latin American and Caribbean studies and director of the Institute for the Study of Latin America and the Caribbean at the University of South Florida. She is the author of *Terror in the Countryside: Campesino Responses to Political Violence in Guatemala, 1954–1985.*

Jerald T. Milanich is emeritus professor of the University of Florida in Gainesville.

Gary R. Mormino is Emeritus Frank E. Duckwall Professor of Florida Studies at the University of South Florida in St. Petersburg.

Karen Racine is associate professor of Latin American history at Guelph University in Guelph, Ontario, Canada.

Alex Stepick is professor of global and sociocultural studies at Florida International University in Miami and professor of sociology at Portland State University in Portland, Oregon.

Index

Page numbers in *italics* refer to illustrations.

1Miami, 256
1493 (Mann), 36n42

Abaioa/Abacoa (Indian village), 54, 56
Acapulco, Mex., 123
Achecambei Island, 57
Adams, John, 148, 152
Adams, John Quincy, 22, 148, 157, 178, 185
Adams-Onís Treaty, 22, 157–58
"Additional Material on the Origin of the Name 'Santa Elena'" (Lyon), 66n11
Adorno, Rolena, 80n22
African Americans. *See* Blacks
Africans: Angolans, 137n37; and diet, 15; and first arrival in Florida, 2, 12; free, 2; and Guale Indians, 122; Mandinga, 10, 128; and miscegenation, 118; in Spain, 117. *See also* Blacks
Africans, as slaves: during 2nd Spanish period, 21; activities of, 12, 14, 122; Angolans, 122; and British, 10; costs of, 121; and disease, 109, 122; escaped, 8, 10; global impact on, 9; and Indians, 10, 120, 121; and militias, 123; and miscegenation, 121; mortality of, 12; numbers of, 119; population of, 12; and Spanish, 11, 12; and Spanish exploration, 118–19, 120, 135n25; terms for, 8; trade in, 173; transport of, 119; uprising of, 120
Afro-Cubans, 210, 212, 213, 214, 216, 220
"Afro-Mood and Rumba," 214
Agramón. *See* De Grammont, Michel
Agriculture: conditions for, 15, 70, 75; corn/maize cultivation, 70, 74, 75–76, 110; cotton cultivation, 12; fruit cultivation, 15, 16, 76; grain cultivation, 70, 81n36; grape cultivation, 81n36; Indians and, 73, 79n7, 110; manioc cultivation, 70, 79n7; rice cultivation, 130; seed for, 61; and starving times, 16; sugarcane cultivation, 12, 16; tobacco cultivation, 12; tools for, 15; vegetable cultivation, 16, 76; wheat cultivation, 15, 77, 108, 122. *See also* Foods and beverages
Aguada, P.R., 52
Aguilar, Amalia, 214
Alabama, 8, 62, 63, 73, 103
Alabama River, 75
Alachua County, Fla., 14
Alachua Savanna, 6
Alahambra, The (Irving), 28
Alaminos, Antón de, 3, 60
Alaña, Joseph Xavier, 63
Alcazar Hotel, 27, 28, 199, *200*
Alegría, Ricardo E., 133n10
Alemán, José Manuel, 213
Alexander County, Fla., 80n20
Alfonso XVII, king of Spain, 29
Alger, Russell, 27
Alhambra, 193, 194
Álvarez, Gerónimo, 156
Alvarez de Pineda, Alonso, 58, 71, 79n10, 79n16
Amaguayo, Bahamas, 53
Ambrosio (ranch hand), 137n37
Amelia Island, Fla.: 1812–13 occupation of, 154, 174, 175, 177, 187n11; 1817 MacGregor occupation of, 177–81, 190n52; after Gregor MacGregor's departure, 181–86, 190n68, 190n73; Cuba and, 189n41; description of, 172, 186; English/British and, 172, 173; Indians and, 178; location of, 172; pirates and smugglers and, 172, 173,

Amelia Island, Fla—*continued*
178–79, 181, 183; population of, 171, 173, 174, 178, 180, 182, 184; and race, 182, 183; significance of, 171, 186; and slave trade, 178–79, 181, 183; Spanish and, 172, 173, 185; United States and, 173, 174–75, 184, 185
América Libre (ship), 181, 182
American Airlines, 248, 261n39
American Community Survey, 233
American Medical Association, 25
American Revolution, 20–21, 104, 142, 151, 172
Amichel, 79n11
Amoretta (slave), 132
Amsterdam, Neth., 9, 105
Ana G. Méndez Educational Foundation, 231
Anan/Ania, China, 84
Añasco, Juan de, 135n25
Anastasia Island, 18, 72, 110–11
Andalucía/Andalusia, Sp., 29, 70, 89, 193
Anderson, Sherwood, 27
Andes, 8
Anduaga, Joaquín, 159
Anghiera, Pietro Martire d'/Peter Martyr, 5, 43, 71
Angola, 140n86
Anhaica (Indian town), 74
Animals: alligators, 6; anacondas, 6; areas supporting, 80n18; bears, 15, 81n36; birds, 9, 70; burros, 9; cattle, 9, 14, 15, 61, 77, 108, 112, 122, 140n81; chickens, 9, 15; deer, 14, 81n36; diets of, 15; ducks, 9; earthworms, 9; eels, 57; fish, 24, 57, 70; flying squirrels, 6; game, 81n36; geese, 9; goats, 9, 16, 61; hens, 81n36; in highlands, 73; horses, 9, 18, 60, 140n81; hummingbirds, 6; iguanas, 6; insects, 77; lions, 81n36; pigs and hogs, 9, 15, 18; rabbits, 81n36; rats, 9; sea turtles, 58; sheep, 9, 15, 61; shellfish, 9, 70; small mammals, 70; swans, 9; toucans, 6; turtles, 24; wolves, 15
Annapolis Convention, 147
Antilles, 81n33, 150
Antonio (black), 133n10
Apalache (Indian town), 74
Apalache/Apalachee Indians, 9, 14, 19, 112, 122, 123, 125
Apalache/Apalachee province: agriculture in, 77; British and, 112, 131; Indians from, 123; population of, 110; Ruiz de Salaza Vallecilla's farm on border of, 108; Spanish and, 73, 103, 108; and trade, 108; uprising in, 109
Apalachee Bay, 58
Apalachicola Indians, 9
Apalo, Fla., 100n5
Apuntes ligeros sobre los Estados Unidos de la América Septentrional (Foronda), 156
Arabs, 192
Aranda, Count of, 143, 148
Aranjuez, Sp., 152
Arawak Indians, 2, 65n10
Archiniega, Sancho de, 76, 81n35
Architecture, 13, 27–28, 29, 195, 198, 199, 201, 208n27
Archives of the Indies, 17, 29
Arends, Tulio, 186
Argentina and Argentines, 171, 259n12
Argote, Antonio, 177
Arismendi, Juan Bautista, 176
Aristotle, 79n13
Arkansas River, 111
Arnaz, Desi, 211, 215, 216–17, 222n25
Arredondo, Fernando, 156
Art Basel Miami festival, 251
Articles of Confederation, 147, 152
Ashley River, 131
Asia, 83
Asian Americans, 261n39
Asile (Indian town), 77
Aspiazú, 211
Association for Community Organizations for Reform Now (ACORN), 255
Asturias, Sp., 29, 33
Atahualpa (Inca), 98
Atlantic Ocean, 83–84
Atlantis Hotel, 217
AT&T Cable Company, 213
Aucilla River, 55
Aury, Luis, 181, 182, 183–84, 185, 186, 191n75
AutoNation, 259n120
Aux Cayes, Haiti, 176, 182
Ávila, Father (missionary), 97
Axacán, 105, 106
Ayllón. *See* Vásquez de Ayllón, Lucas
Ays Indians, 7, 66n11, 121, 136n29
Aztecs and Aztec Empire, 3–4, 9, 10, 16, 83

"Babalu"/"Babalu Ayé," 215–17, 222n25
Bahama Channel, 77, 78, 95
Bahamas: Francisco Menéndez in, 10, 132; maps of, 50, *51*; Ponce de León and, 2, 49, 53, 57, 58; Spanish knowledge of, 52; and trade, 111
Bahamians, 212, 217, 243
Bailyn, Bernard, 8
Baltimore, Md., 282n19
Baltimore Orioles, 282n19
Baltimore Patriot and Mercantile Advertiser, 183
Banco Popular de Puerto Rico, 231
Baptist Health System, 248
Barbados, 124
Barcelona, Sp., 28
Barcelona, Venezuela, 176
Barrie, John Francis, 189n41
Barroso, Ary, 214
Batista, Fulgencio, 31, 209, 211, 220n1
Batista, Marta Fernández de, 220n1
Baton Rouge, La., 154, 173
Battle of New Orleans, 22
Battle of Pedernales, 112
Battle of Trafalgar, 150
Bauzá, Graciela, 211
Bauzá, Mario, 211
Bay of Carlos, 59
Bayonne, Fr., 152
Belmar hotel, 217
Benavides, Antonio de, 127, 128, 139n67
Bendixen and Associates, 277, 283n50
Bense, Judith, 9
Berbers, 192
Berlin, Ira, 122
Bermuda, 94, 95, 107, 109
Bernaldo (free black), 120, 135n25
Big Carlos Pass, 59
Biloxi, MS, 112
Biscayan, Johan, 135n24
Biscayne Bay, 55, *55*, 56–57, 72
Bishop, Elizabeth, 5
Bismarck, Otto von, 11
Black Legend, 193, 195
Blacks: activities of, 23, 24; and Calusa Indians, 135n28; and class, 244, 257, 258n11; as convicts, 123; in Cuba, 211; and discrimination, 211, 212, 217–18, 243, 253; free, 24, 117, 118–19, 120, 123–24, 129, 132–33; and Jews, 253; legislation affecting, 24; in Miami, 217–18, 220, 237, 243, 249–51, 253, 257; in Miami/Miami-Dade County, 245, 246; and militias, 137n43; occupations of, 125, 137n43; origins of, 125; as proportion of population, 32, 209; and Puerto Ricans, 233, 237; and race, 243; rights of, 24; socioeconomic characteristics of, 245, 246, 247, 251, 253; and Spanish navy, 132; and tourism, 213. *See* African Americans; Africans; Africans, as slaves; Gracia Real de Santa Teresa de Mose
Boca Raton, Fla., 28, 201, 202, 259n120
Boca Ratone Indians, 63
Bolado, Carlos Vidal, 214
Bolívar, Simón, 176, 182, 183
Bolivia, 171
Bonaparte, Joseph, 153
Bono, Juan/Giovanni, 2
Boston, Mass., 229
Bowman, Charles A., Jr., 190n55
Bradford, William, 11
Brazil and Brazilians, 105, 180, 182, 249
Brickell, Miami, Fla., 249, *250*, 252, 257, 259n22
British. *See* English/ British
British Admiralty, 132
Bronx, N.Y., 228
Brooke, George Mercer, 24
Brothers to the Rescue, 273
Broward, Napoleon Bonaparte, 27
Broward County, Fla., 227, 228, 230, 259n120
Bryant, William Cullen, 195
Buenaventura Lakes, Fla., 229
Buenos Aires, Arg., 16, 154, 181, 191n75
Buffalo, N.Y., 194
Bull, William, 130–31
Burke County, Fla., 80n20
Burton, Dan, 269
Bush, George H. W., 269, 272, 274, 279
Bush, George W., 11, 234, 275–76, 277–78
Bush, Jeb, 234
Bushnell, Amy T., 15–16
Butte, Lord, 20

Cabeza de Vaca, Álvar Núñez, 12, 18, 91, 101n12, 195
Cabezas Altamirano, Juan de las, 107
Cabo de Corrientes, 54, 56

Cabot, John, 52, 65n7
Cachão, 211, 217, 219
Cádiz, Sp., 88, 153, 155
Caicos Island, 53
Calderón, Pedro, 120
Caledonian Mercury, 181, 183
California: Addison Mizner in, 201, 202; architecture in, 28; Cortés in, 134n16; integration in, 212; Juan Garrido in, 134n16; as part of Spanish Empire, 21; Puerto Ricans in, 226, 231; Spanish Craze in, 193, 201
Callava, José, 22
Calle Ocho, Miami, Fla., 249
Caloosahatchee River, 3, 8, 59
Calos (Calusa town), 59, 62
Calusa Indians: archaeology of, 59, 60; avoidance of, by Spanish explorers, 61; and blacks, 135n28; and disease, 62, 63; as fishermen, 63; and food, 14; and Hernando d'Escalante Fontaneda, 18, 59, 121; independence of, from Spanish, 61–62; lands of, 50, 56, 60, 61; languages spoken by, 58, 63; and Menéndez de Avilés, 61, 121; and migration, 62, 63, 67n26; and missionaries, 60, 61, 62, 67n26; and northern Indians, 62–63; and peace with Spanish, 108; and Ponce de León, 3, 4, 50, 52, 57–58, 61, 71; population of, 62; scholarship on, 67n26; towns of, 58–60, 61; and trade, 62
Camargo, Diego de, 71, 72, 79n16
Cambridge, Mass., 229
Camden, N.J., 203, 229
Camden, S.C., 74, 120
Camillus House, 254
Campeche, Mex., 125
Canada and Canadians, 52, 104, 272
Canalejas y Méndez, José, 26
Canary Islands, 16
Canaveral National Seashore, 53, 56
Canbeia Island, 57
Cáncer de Barbastro, Luis, 102n12
Cape Canaveral, Fla., 3, 53, 54, 55, 56, 65n9
Cape de Setos, 56
Cape Fear, 65n9, 78n5
Cape Hatteras, 65n9
Cape Lookout, 65n9, 78n5
Cape of the Cross, 72
Cape Romain, 65n9
Caracas, Ven., 154

Caribbean: climate of, 70; English/British and, 65n7, 124, 171, 172, 173, 175; and Florida, 104; French and, 171; Indians of, 119; migration to, 8; piracy in, 94; religion in, 109; slavery in, 11, 119, 124; Spanish and, 123, 171; United States and, 171, 172
Caribbean Hotel, 217
Carib Indians, 2, 119, 134n14
Carlos (Calusa chief), 58, 59, 60, 121
Carlos III, king of Spain, 21
Carlos Ramírez Orchestra, 215
Carmichael, William, 149
Carmona, Alonso de, 90–91
Carnival Cruises, 261n39
Carolinas: and attacks on Florida, 131; Benavides and, 139n67; climate of, 70; economy of, 126; Francisco Menéndez in, 132; Indians in, 62, 112; piedmont region of, 73; population of, 127; raids on, 128; runaway slaves from, 12, 125, 126–32; slavery in, 11, 12, 124, 126; slave uprisings in, 127; Spanish claims on, 124; and trade, 111; and Yamasee War, 127. *See also* North Carolina; South Carolina
Carrère, John Merven, 27
Cartagena des Indies (now Colombia), 9, 16, 106, 123, 137n43
Casablanca Hotel, 217
Casa Monica, 199
Cassatt, Mary, 194
Castile, Sp., 9
Castillo de San Marcos, 17, 23, 110, 111, 123, 126, 195
Castro, Fidel: and 1994 emigration, 276; Cuban American opposition to, 263, 266, 267, 268, 269, 270, 273, 277, 278, 279; as Cuban head of state, 265, 266, 270, 273, 279; and Cuban Revolution, 31, 167, 168, 263; in Tampa, 31
Castro, Raúl, 266, 277, 279
Catalonia, Sp., 109
Catalyst Miami, 254
Catawba County, Fla., 80n20
Catawba River, 80n20
Catholic Church and Catholics: Africans and, 10; Haitians and, 254; iconography of, 9–10; opposition to, 237; and race, 8; and slavery, 12; Spanish and, 11, 13, 26
Cautio (possible Indian village), 56

Caxambas Ridge, 66n14
Celts, 192
Cendoya, Manuel de, 110
Center for Pan-African Development, 256
Central America and Central Americans, 21, 251, 267
Central Labor Council, 255
Cervantes Saavedra, Miguel de, 25
Chantio (possible Indian village), 56
Charlesfort, 102n19
Charles II, king of Eng., 109
Charles II, king of Spain, 110, 112, 126
Charles III, king of Spain, 142, 147, 148, 150
Charles IV, king of Spain, 148, 150, 152
Charleston/Charles Town, S.C.: and Amelia Island, 181; backers of Gregor MacGregor in, 179, 180; English/British and, 112; establishment of, 109, 124; and globalization, 9; and pirates, 111; slaves and, 124, 127, 131–32; Spanish and, 111, 177; and St. Augustine, 124
Charleston Courier, 182
Charleston Gazette, 179
Charles V, Holy Roman Emperor, 4, 18, 21, 60, 67n22
Charlotte, N.C., 73
Charlotte Harbor, 4, 9, 24, 59, 60, 73
Chase, William Merritt, 194
Chattanooga, Tenn., 74
Chaves, Alonso de, 60, 66n14
Chávez, Hugo, 247
Chequescha (Indian village), 3, 57
Chequiche (Indian village), 57
Chesapeake Bay, 76, 94, 95, 107
Chicago, Ill., 193, 194, 225, 229, 236
Chicora, 72, 75
Children's Trust, 254
Chile, 104, 154, 187n16
China and Chinese, 8, 20, 84, 270
Chirino, Willy, 219
Churchill, Winston, 11
City of Miami, Fla., 244, 249, 261n37, 265
City on the Edge (Portes and Stepick), 242, 253
Clarinda (slave), 132
Clarke, Elijah, 176
Clearwater, Fla., 228
Clemente, Lino de, 176
Clinton, William, 268, 269, 272, 273–74, 275

Clover Club, 214
Coast and Geodetic Survey, U.S., 65n9
Cobbett, William, 152
Coconut Grove, Fla., 201
Codazzi, Agustín, 181
Cofa mission, 100n5
Cofitachequi (now S.C.), 74, 76, 80n27
Coker, Bill, 32
Cole, Nat "King," 217
Coleman, Samuel, 194
Coles, Juan de, 90, 91
Colleton, James, 126
Collier County, Fla., 60
Colombia, 171, 180, 247
Colombians, 225, 235, 244, 259n12, 281n4
Coltrane, John, 217
Columbian Exchange, 7–9
Columbian International Exposition, 194
Columbia restaurant, 33
Columbus, Christopher: depictions of, 1, 194; impact of, 7; modern perceptions of, 11; monument to, 208n27; voyages of, 2, 3, 13, 53; Washington Irving on, 193
Community Benefits Coalition, 256
Community Coalition for a Living Wage (CCLW), 255
Concepción, Chile, 88
Congreso (ship), 183
Congress, U.S., 159, 173, 174, 269, 270, 274, 276
Congress of Vienna, 191n75
Connecticut, 226, 227, 232
Connolly, Nathan, 243, 258n6
Connor, Jeanette Thurber, 29
Connor, Washington, 29
Consejo de Regencia, 153
Constitutional Convention, U.S., 147
Constitutional Triennium, 158
Continental Airlines, 221n14
Continental Army, 173
Continental Congress, 144, 145–46
Cook County, Ill., 228
Cooperativa de Seguros Múltiples, 231
Coosa, Fla., 74–75, 76, 81n28, 135n24
Coppinger, José, 178, 179, 180
Coral Gables, Fla., 28, 201, 264, 265
Córdoba, Sp.: as destination, 28; Garcilaso in, 87, 88, 90, 98; impact of, on colonies, 9; Muslims and, 193, 194; Oré in, 88

Córdoba Salinas, Diego de, 100n3
Cordova Hotel, 27, 199, 200
Coronado, Hernando, 134n21
Cortes (Spanish legislature), 153, 155, 159
Cortés, Hernán/Hernando, 3, 60, 134n16, 137n37
Costa de Caracoles, 60
Coulter, E. Merton, 21
Council of the Indies, 100n5, 109, 136n31, 136n35, 139n67
Covington, Roger, 213, 214
Creek Indians, 22, 63, 77, 103, 112
Cromwell, Oliver, 109
Crónica franciscana de las provincias del Perú (Córdoba), 100n3
Crosby, Alfred, 7, 9, 34n22
Cruz, Celia, 219
Cruz, Juan de la, 137n37
Cruz, Rosa de la, 260n31
Cuba: and Amelia Island Affair, 171, 179, 180, 186, 189n41; blacks in, 10, 120, 123, 132, 133, 136n35, 210; Castro regime in, 31, 263, 265, 266, 267, 268, 269, 270, 276, 277, 278, 279; Chinese in, 20; and communications facilities, 213; Constitution of, 212; de Soto in, 18, 120; diseases in, 63; embargo against, 269–70, 271, 272–74, 275–78, 279, 280, 282n30; Francisco Menéndez in, 10, 132; Hernández de Córdoba and, 60; Indians in, 62, 63, 67n26, 120; Jews in, 212; Joseph Marion Hernández in, 23; and Key West, 25; lotteries in, 20; maps of, 50; Matanzas frontier of, 133; and migration, 133, 209, 212–13, 236, 253; militias in, 123; missionaries in, 62; Oré in, 89–90, 100n5; as part of Santa Elena colony, 101n8; and pirates, 94–95; Ponce de León and, 58, 61; race in, 211, 212; radio and TV in, 268, 269; religion in, 8; and shooting down of exile group planes, 273; Spanish conquest of, 119; Spanish government and, 2, 63, 104, 107, 136n35, 156, 159, 172, 187n16; and trade, 15, 16, 24, 111, 270, 274, 276–77; and United States, 154, 209, 273; uprisings in, 25, 26–27, 209, 212–13, 215, 263. *See also* Havana, Cuba
Cuba (publication), 25
Cuban Adjustment Act of 1966, 265, 276
Cuban All-Stars, 282n19

Cuban American National Foundation, 267–70, 272, 275, 278, 279, 282n19, 283n54
Cuban Bureau of Investigation, 213
Cuban Democracy Act, 269, 272
Cuban Liberty and Democratic Solidarity Act, 269, 272–73
Cuban Liberty Council (CLC), 275, 278–79
"Cuban Parish Records Reveal Immigrant Calusa Indians" (Worth), 67n26
Cuban Pete, 215
Cuban Revolution, 31, 167, 168, 209, 215, 219, 263
Cubans and Cuban Americans: activities of, 20, 24, 25, 212; and arts development, 249–51, 252; birthplaces of, 209; candidates supported and opposed by, 268, 269, 270, 272, 273, 274, 275, 282n19; and class, 242, 252, 254, 257, 258n11, 265; and Congress, 270, 274; and Cuban War of Independence, 26; and culture, 25; and discrimination, 210, 211, 212, 216, 217–18; divisions among, 278–79; dominance of, 225, 235, 236, 253, 263; and economy, 248, 252; as elected officials, 266, 275; and Elián González, 274–75, 282n33; and Florida electorate, 271, 280; languages spoken by, 253; and marriage, 237, 265; and Miami Leadership Summit, 252; and migration, 25, 31–32, 209, 210, 211, 244, 248, 253, 263, 266, 276, 277, 283n49; and music, 210, 211, 213, 214–15, 217, 218–19, 220; in New York City, 210, 212, 213–14; and non-Cuban Hispanics, 232, 265, 280–81; political divisions among, 279, 280; political issues supported by, 253, 266–70, 274, 275, 276–77, 278, 279, 282n19; and population, 224, 228, 244, 271, 281n1; and race and ethnicity, 210, 218, 234, 243, 258n4; and remittances to Cuba, 274, 275–76, 279; and Republican Party, 234, 235, 268, 279, 281; settlement patterns of, 227, 263, 264–65, 266, 281n1; and social reform, 254, 257; and Spanish, 199; and travel restrictions, 271, 274, 275–76, 279; in U.S. censuses, 258n9; and U.S. citizenship, 235, 265, 278; and U.S. government, 264; and voting, 265–66; and wealth, 245–47
Cuban War of Independence, 26–27
Cuesta, Angel L., 29

"Curse of Capistrano, The" (McCulley), 13
Cuzco, Peru, 83, 87, 88
Czechoslovakia, 30

Dade Community Foundation, 249
Dade County, Fla., 228, 244
Daily National Intelligence, 179, 183
Davis, Caleb, 130
Davis, Sammy, Jr., 217
Daytona Beach, Fla., 4, 31, 220n1
Deagan, Kathleen, 129
De Bry, Theodor, 10
Decades (Martyr), 71–72
Declaration of Independence, 152
Deering, Charles, 28
De Gorgues, Dominique, 90
De Grammont, Michel, 110–11, 125
DeLand, Fla., 29
Delaware Bay, 72
Delia (slave), 132
Democrats and Democratic Party, 156, 234, 235, 268
Department of State, U.S., 21
D'Escalante Fontaneda, Hernando, 18, 59, 121
Desi Arnaz and His Orchestra, 215
Desi Arnaz Band, 215
Design District, Miami, Fla., 250
De Soto, Hernando: 19th-century scholarship on, 195, 196; and Atahualpa, 98; and blacks on 1539–43 expedition, 135n24; expeditions of, 7, 9, 18–19, 61, 74, 80n21, 120; fountains and statues dedicated to, 201; Garcilaso de la Vega on, 87, 90–92; illustration of, *87*; and Indians, 96, 134n21; Oré on, 102n12; works by, 195
Dewey, Thomas, 30
Dialogues of Love (Inca Garcilaso de la Vega), 90
Díaz-Balart, Lincoln, 279
Díaz-Balart, Mario, 279
Díaz Biart, Sigfredo, 213
Díaz del Castillo, Bernal, 5
Dickinson, John, 111
Diego (pirate), 125
Diggs, Charles C., Jr., 221n14
Diseases: African slaves and, 12, 109, 122; at Amelia Island, 180; English and, 109; Indians and, 62, 95, 103, 109, 122, 123, 137n41; influenza, 7; measles, 7, 8, 122, 123; plague, 109; at San Miguel de Gualdape, 120; smallpox, 7, 8, 109, 112, 122, 123; tuberculosis, 23; typhus, 8, 109, 122, 123; yellow fever, 7, 8, 23, 109, 122, 123
Disney films, 214
Dobyns, Henry F., 34n20
Dodsworth, Anthony, 112
Dominica, 119
Dominican Republic, 212, 225
Dominicans (people), 218, 225, 235, 237, 244, 251, 259n12
Dominicans (religious order), 13, 95, 244. *See also* Franciscans; Jesuits
Dorantes, Andrés, 120
Drake, Francis, 8, 106
Dry Tortugas, 55, 58
Dunlop, William, 125
Durand, José, 90
Dürer, Albrecht, 10
Dutch, 8, 83, 104, 108, 172
Dutch West India Company, 108
Duval County, Fla., 227

Eakins, Thomas, 194
East Florida Revolution, 175
East Hartford, Conn., 229
Eco de Florida, 25
Ecuadorans, 259n12
Edisto Island, 125
Edisto River, 128
Editorial Cubano de la Música, 213
Eighty Year's War, 108
El Avisador Cubano, 25
El Camino Real, 13
Elcano, Juan Sebastián, 84
El Centro Asturiano, 25–26
El Centro Español, 25–26
El Chicorano, Francisco, 69
El Cubano, 25
El Greco [Doménikos Theotokópoulos], 202
El Internacional, 25
Elizabeth I, queen of Eng., 105, 106
Elliott, Thomas, 127
Elliott Key, Fla., 54
El Morro, 108
El Nirda Island, 57
El Nuevo Día, 231
El Porvenir, 25
El Salvadorans, 259n12

El Telégrafo de las Floridas, 184
El Toreador Cabaret, 214
El Yara, 25
Emerson, Ralph Waldo, 23
Empresas Fonalledas, 231
Emusica, 219
England/Great Britain: and Amelia Island Affair, 171, 179, 180, 186; colonies/territories of, 107, 155; and France, 111, 151, 153; and Louisiana, 20; and migration, 30; and Netherlands, 111; and Spain, 104, 109–10, 111, 148, 149, 150–51, 153, 174, 185; territorial ambitions of, 90, 181; and United States, 142, 146, 149, 158, 172, 174, 175; and War of 1812, 155
English/British: on Amelia Island, 171, 182; attacks by, 77; and disease, 109; and Florida, 107, 171, 172; kidnapping by, 111; and migration, 8; Oré on, 94–95; as pirates, 83, 94–95, 105; and religion, 105; and slavery, 11, 12, 124; and Spanish, 108, 119; and St. Augustine, 106; and trade, 10; Yamasee Indians and, 138n59
Entralgo, Juan, 23
Escampaba/Estantapaca (Calusa town), 58–59
Escobedo, Alonso, 19, 84
Espejo (Chaves), 60, 66n14
Esteban/Estevan (slave), 12, 120, 134n21
Estefan, Emilio, 219
Estefan, Gloria, 215
Estero Bay, 55, 59
"Evacuation of South Florida, 1704–1760, The" (Worth), 67n26
Everglades, 252
Everglades Club, 202
Examiner, 179

Fairbanks, George R., 23, 195–96, 198
Family Compact, 112, 148
Fania Records, 219
Farrow, Jeffrey, 234
Fascell, Dante, 267, 269
Fatio, Susan, 177, 178
Federal Bureau of Investigation, U.S., 213
Federalists, 152, 156
Ferdinand II, king of Aragon, 1, 2, 5, 13, 52, 60, 118

Ferdinand VII, king of Spain, 22, 152–53, 157, 158
Fernández de Ecija, Juan, 107
Fernández de Navarrete, Martín, 78n5
Fernández de Oviedo, Gonzalo, 4, 5, 69–70
Fernandico (slave), 2
Fernandina, Fla., 27, 154, 173, 175, 179, 180. *See also* Amelia Island, Fla.
Ferré, Maurice, 235
First Seminole War, 157
Fitzgerald, F. Scott, 6
FIU-IPOR, 264, 265, 277, 283n49
Flagler, Henry Morrison, 27, 198, 199, 201
Flagler College, 198
Flagler County, Fla., 23
Flemish, 107
Florida (term), 64n3
Florida, 1513–1763: 16th-century perceptions of, 71–72, 74–75; administration of, 172; agriculture in, 77; and Atlantic world, 104; attraction of, 6; boundaries in, 80n24, 94; and Caribbean world, 104; Carib Indians and, 2; climate of, 15, 17; and Columbian Exchange, 7–9; creole nature of, 172; Dutch in, 108; economy of, 108–9, 110, 122–23; English/British and, 105, 107, 112, 132, 172; extent of, 5, 103; first Spanish landfall at, 53; and Fountain of Youth, 5–6; French and, 105–6, 107, 172; geography of, 72–73, 74; and Gulf region, 104; manpower in, 121, 122; maps of, 44, 50–52, 54, 56–57, 58, 64n5, 66n14, 84; naming of, 43, 50, 53; news of, in Spain, 90; Oré in, 88, 89–90, 100n5; as part of Santa Elena colony, 101n8; and Peru, 90; population of, 7–8, 12, 103, 104, 110, 121, 123, 126; purpose of, 104; and religion, 13, 83, 107; as route to New Spain, 83; settlement patterns in, 72, 74, 77–78; Silvestre in, 90; slaves and slavery in, 12, 125–32; Spanish conquest of, 119; Spanish exploration of, 64n3; Spanish institutions in, 13, 14; starving times in, 16; success of, 103; and trade, 14, 15, 16, 106, 110, 123, 172
Florida, 1763–83, 10, 20, 104, 172
Florida, 1783–1821: Andrew Jackson and, 22; and Atlantic world, 104; boundaries of, 21, 142, 145, 150; British and, 171, 172, 173,

181; and Caribbean world, 104; escaped slaves in, 21, 22; Floridablanca and, 141–43; French and, 171, 181; as frontier, 148; Gregor MacGregor and, 176–81; and Gulf region, 104; James Monroe and, 186; and Louisiana Purchase, 151; Mexico and, 181, 191n75; population of, 21, 104, 173; purposes of, 104; and Republic of East Florida, 154; Spain and, 141–43, 155, 156, 171; United States and, 143, 154–55, 157–58, 159, 171, 173; and War of 1812, 155

Florida, 1821-present: 1821 transfer of, to United States, 22; and 1948 presidential election, 30–31; architecture in, 28–29; baseball in, 212; Cubans in, 209, 219, 224, 225, 227, 234, 235, 237, 276; Democratic and Republican Parties in, 234; early 20th-century perceptions of, 28; economy of, 247, 248, 249; electoral college system in, 271, 273; foodways in, 32; histories of, 196; income in, 233; land boom in, 201, 202; and migration, 23; music in, 212; non-Cuban and non-Puerto Rican Latinos in, 235–37, 247; politics in, 234, 235; population of, 24, 30, 31–32, 209, 243; Puerto Ricans in, 224, 225, 226, 227–38; and race, 234; as southernmost U.S. state, 2; and Spanish-American War, 27; Spanish Craze in, 193; and tourism, 6, 28–29; William Clinton in, 273

Florida Bay, 55
Floridablanca, Count of, 141, 142–43, 144, 146, 147–48, 151
Florida Current, 54, 56
Florida Historical Society, 29
Florida International University, 252, 264
Florida Keys: architecture in, 28; as boundary, 5, 119; Cubans and, 63; Indians in, 59–60, 61, 63; maps of, 50, 51, 57; missionaries in, 62; as pirate haven, 25; Ponce de León and, 49, 50, 54, 55, 56, 58, 71; and shipwrecks, 108. *See also* Key West, Fla.
Florida Legal Services, 255, 256
Florida Museum of Natural History, 129
Florida New Majority, 255
Florida State Historical Society, 29
Florida State University, 19
Florida University, 19

Folch, Vicente, 174
Fontainebleau hotel, 215
Fontaneda. *See* d'Escalante Fontaneda, Hernando
Foods and beverages: African, 16, 32; beans, 15, 33; breads, 14, 15, 70, 79n7, 81n36; and class, 15, 16; coffee, 16, 32; corn/maize, 14, 15, 16, 70, 74, 76, 106, 109, 110; costs of, 94; Cuban-Chinese, 32; dairy, 15, 32; eggs, 9; fish and shellfish, 9, 14, 15, 16, 23, 24, 70; fruits, 9, 15, 16, 70, 76; and globalization, 36n42; greens, 33; gruel, 15; guava *pasteles*, 32; herbs, 16; Honduran, 32; *Ilex vomitoria*, 14; Indians and, 14; Jamaican, 32; Korean, 32; mamey *batidos*, 32; mango *helados*, 32; meats, 9, 14, 15, 24, 32, 33, 110; military rations, 106; nuts, 9, 16, 70; okra, 16; peppers, 16; Polish, 32; potatoes, 14, 16, 33; poultry, 33; rice, 32; roots, 70; rum, 14; sassafras, 15; sausages, 33; soldiers and, 76; soups and stews, 33; Spanish, 33; Spanish and, 14–16; squash, 15; sugar, 16; tea, 9; turtles, 58; wheat flour, 70; wines, 15, 81n36, 95. *See also* Agriculture

Foronda, Valentin de, 152, 156–57
Fort Baton Rouge, 20
Fort Brooke, 26
Fort Caroline, 17, 61, 90
Fort Marion, 23, 195
Fort Mose. *See* Gracia Real de Santa Teresa de Mose
Fort Mose Historical Society, 129
Fort Mose Historic Park Museum, 129
Fort Myers, 55
Fort Myers Beach, Fla., 57, 59
Fortuny, Mariano, 194
Foster, Augustus, 175
Fountain of Youth, 5–6
Four Arts Society, 201
France: and Amelia Island Affair, 171; and Brazil, 105; and England/Great Britain, 151, 153; and Florida, 90, 105–96, 171, 181; and Louisiana, 150, 151; revolution in, 148; and Spain, 104, 111, 148, 150, 151, 152–53, 155; territories of, 155
Franciscan Commissary-General of the Indies, 100n5

Franciscans: in Apalache province, 108; and Calusa Indians, 62, 67n26; as chroniclers, 84; historical accounts of, 62, 93, 94, 96, 97; La Rábida, Sp., monestary of, 194; missions of, 13, 62, 67n26, 88, 89, 100n5, 101n8; and *reducciones*, 98; and Ruiz's ranch, 77; in St. Augustine, 19, 106; and Timucua Indians, 94, 106; works by, 19, 45, 84. *See also* Jesuits; Oré, Luis Jerónimo de; *Relación de los mártires de la Florida* (Oré)
Franco, Francisco, 30
Frederic, Philip, 110
Freducci, Ottomanno, 44, 50
Freducci map, 50–52, 54, 56–57, 58–59, 64n5
Free Trade of the Americas, 256
French: and Amelia Island, 171; in Canada, 111; exploration and settlement by, 8, 75, 77, 94, 102n19, 112; and Florida, 61, 105–6, 107, 172; and Gulf coast, 16; and Iberian Peninsula, 141; and Indians, 77; as pirates, 83, 106; and religion, 83; and Spanish, 76, 107, 119; and trade, 17, 106, 111
French and Indian War, 20
French Revolution, 148, 151
Friedman, Robert, 231
Fry, Joseph, 26
Ft. Lauderdale, Fla., 228, 229, 230, 259n120
Fuentes, Carlos, 7

Gainesville, Fla., 77, 123
Galicia, Sp., 30, 33
Galindo, Francisco, 122
Gallegos, Baltasar de, 135n25
Galveston, TX, 21, 181
Gálvez, Bernardo de, 20–21
Gannon, Michael, 13
Garay, Francisco, 71
García, Joe, 279, 280
García, Oria, 209
García de León y Pizarro, José, 185, 189n41
García Menocal, Mario Gabriel, 212–13
Garcilaso de la Vega, El Inca, 87, 88–89, 90, 93, 98, 101n11, 102n20. *See also La Florida del Inca* (Inca Garcilaso de la Vega)
Gardoqui, Diego, 143–45, 146–47, 149
Gardoqui and Sons, 144
Garrido, Juan, 2, 118, 119, 134n16, 135n25
Gaspar (free black), 133n10
General Agreement on Tariffs and Trade, 273

General History of Peru (Inca Garcilaso de la Vega), 88, 89
Genovar, Francis B., 196–98
Gentleman from Elvas, 74
Geographía y descripción universal de las indias (López de Velasco), 57
George II, king of England, 172
George III, king of England, 20
Georgetown, S.C., 78n5
Georgia: Amelia Island defectors in, 180; attacks on, 138n59, 157; climate of, 69; and Florida, 21, 103, 131, 132; Gregor MacGregor in, 176; Indians in, 8, 62, 63, 72, 123, 136n33; missions in, 100n5, 138n59; Patriots Group volunteers from, 174; physical geography of, 72; piedmont region of, 73; runaway slaves from, 132; and slavery, 130, 182, 183; Spanish and, 69, 77; sugar mills in, 113n1
Georgia Sea Islands, 5
Germany and Germans, 30, 107
Gillespie, Dizzy, 214
Godoy, Manuel, 148, 149, 150, 151, 152
Gómez (slave), 120
González, Elián, 268, 271, 274–75, 282n33
González de Barcia, Andrés, 101n13
González (Ponce) de León, Juan, 118, 119
Goodbye Land, The (Iglesias), 30
Goodwill Industries, 248
Gore, Al, 234, 271, 275, 282n33
Goya Foods, 231
Gracia Real de Santa Teresa de Mose: archaeology at, 129; British and, 10, 132; Carolina and Georgia slaves and, 129, 130, 131; as first free black settlement, 12, 47, 129, 138n62; Francisco Menéndez as leader of, 10, 129, 132, 138n62; origin of name of, 139n73
Graham, Bob, 269
Granada, Sp., 193
Grau San Martín, Ramón, 213
Great Abaco Island, Bahamas, 53
Great Britain. *See* England/Great Britain
Great Depression, 30, 248
Greater Miami, Fla., 264, 281n7
Great Gatsby, The (Fitzgerald), 6
Greeks, 15
Grenville, William, 105
Guadalupe, 119

Gual, Pedro, 176, 181, 182, 184, 185, 189n26, 191n75
Guale Indians: and Africans, 120, 121, 122; and Ayllón, 121; and escaped slaves, 125; extinction of, 9; and migration, 111; and Spanish, 122, 123, 136n33; uprisings by, 93, 106, 120, 122, 136n33
Guale province, 94, 103, 105, 106, 110, 136n33
Guanahani Island, 49, 53
Guantánamo, Cuba, 26
Guatemala and Guatemalans, 201, 259n12
Guchi (Calusa town), 58–59
Guillén, Nicolás, 212
Gulf Coast: 19th-century settlement along, 24; and Florida, 104; French and, 16; Indians along, 72, 74, 108; Italian exploration of, 2; La Chua Ranch along, 14; maps of, 51, 55, 58; Spanish expeditions along, 56, 58, 71, 74; and trade, 108
Gulf of Mexico, 143
Gulf Stream, 3, 6, 104
Gustavia, St. Barthélemy, 183

Haiti, 2, 171, 176, 180, 186
Haitian Revolution, 182
Haitians, 182, 237, 243, 245, 254, 257
Hampden, Mass., 228
Hann, John H., 65n10, 66n12, 67n26
Hansel and Raul, 219
Hartford, Conn., 228, 229
Hastings, Thomas, 27, 198
Havana, Cuba: 1555 defense of, 137n43; and 1812 Spanish constitution, 155–56; and calls for Occupy Havana, 219; and Cuban Revolution, 31, 168; departure of Spanish expeditions from, 102n19; diseases in, 109; English/British and, 20, 106; forts at, 108, 123; Francisco Menéndez in, 132; impact of, 9; and Miami, 210, 213; and migration, 210, 218, 219; missionaries in, 63, 89; musicians in, 215, 219; mutual aid societies in, 25; Oré in, 89–90, 100n5; Pedro de Ybarra in, 107; Ponce de León in, 4, 94; and slaves, 122, 123, 127, 128, 136n35, 180; Spanish administration in, 16, 122, 123, 155–56, 174, 179, 180; and Spanish fleet system, 83, 99n1; Spanish forces at, 112; and tourism, 213; and trade, 14, 16, 77, 108, 123, 127; and U.S. FBI, 213; USS *Maine* in, 27; and U.S. trade embargo, 219, 273
Hawkins, Paula, 268
Helms, Jesse, 269
Helms-Burton bill, 269, 273, 282n30
Hernández, Antonio Máximo, 24
Hernández, Joseph Marion, 23
Hernández, Pedro, 101n12
Hernández de Biedma, Luis, 135n25
Hernández de Córdoba, Francisco, 2, 60
Hernandez v. State of Texas, 212
Hernando County, Fla., 227
Herrera, Gonzalo, 156
Herrera y Tordesillas, Antonio: *Historia* by, 56, 64n2; on Ponce de León's 1513 expedition, 3, 50, 52, 53, 54, 55, 56, 57, 58, 59
Hetzel Shoal, 65n9
Heyn, Piet, 108
Hialeah, Fla., 264, 265, 279
Hialeah Gardens, Fla., 264
Hillsborough Bay, 24
Hillsborough County, Fla., 227, 228, 230
Hillsborough River, 24
Hispanic Chamber of Commerce of Metro Orlando, 231
Hispanics. *See* Cubans and Cuban Americans; Puerto Ricans
Hispaniola: agriculture on, 79n7; blacks and, 118, 120, 123; and Florida, 9; Indians and, 58, 119, 134n14; militias and, 123; slaves and, 119, 134n14; Spanish and, 69, 119
Hispano-Americano, 25
Historia general de los hechos de los Castillanos en las islas i tierra firme del Mar Oceano (Herrera), 50, 64n4
History of the Indies (López de Gómara), 72
Hita de Salazar, Pablo, 110
Hoffman, Paul E., 78n5
Holiday, Billie, 217
Holiday in Havana, 215
Hondurans, 244, 259n12
Horne, Lena, 217
Hotel Belmar, 215
Hotel Delmonico, 215
Hotel St. Augustine, 195
House of Representatives, Florida, 235
House of Representatives, U.S., 23, 184, 268
House of Trade, 1, 71

Hubbard, Ruggles, 181, 182
Hudson, Charles, 80n21, 80n27, 81n34
Hudson County, N.J., 266
Hudson River school, 194
Hugo, Victor, 25
Huguenots, 11, 17, 83, 172
Human Services Coalition, 254, 255
Hurricanes, 6, 9, 17, 106, 120, 244, 248

Iberian Peninsula, 141, 152, 153, 192
Illinois country, 111
Illinois State, 226, 232
I Love Lucy, 215
Incas, 102n22, 120
Indian River, 56
Indian River County, Fla., 66n11
Indians: activities of, 14–15, 19, 24, 63, 95; and African slaves, 121; and agriculture, 73, 79n7, 110; and alcohol, 97; attacks by, on Joara and Olamico forts, 76; and Ayllón, 72; contemporary accounts of, 18, 19; decimation of, 2, 11; depictions of, 1; and de Soto, 96, 120; diet of, 14; and disease, 7, 8, 61–62, 63, 95, 103, 109, 122, 123, 137n41; and English/British, 22, 138n59, 172; and Fernandina, 178; and food, 74, 123; Francis Parkman on, 11; and French, 77, 90, 106; Garcilaso de la Vega on, 92–93, 99; and gender roles, 14–15; and geographical names, 2, 79n17; and globalization, 9; and Juan Pardo, 76; kidnapping of, 95; as laborers, 18, 77, 110, 120, 122, 123, 137n41; languages spoken by, 17, 21, 63, 65n10; leasing of fields by, 110; and Menéndez de Avilés, 76–77; and migration, 63, 103, 112–13; and missionaries, 13, 62; and Narváez, 74; and northern Indians, 62–63; Oré on, 95–98, 99, 102n21, 102n22; political organization of, 73, 79n13; and Ponce de León, 53–54; population of, 7, 34n20, 76, 109, 110, 121; and *reducciones*, 97–98, 136n33; and religion, 13, 96, 99, 106; and runaway slaves, 10, 22, 119, 120, 125, 127, 128, 133n11, 140n81, 157; and San Miguel de Gualdape settlers, 71; settlement patterns of, 72, 73, 74, 77; settlements of, 71; as slaves, 11, 62, 76–77, 95, 111, 112, 134n14, 138n55; in Spain, 69, 95; and Spain's enemies, 105; as Spanish allies, 22, 107, 108–9, 125, 154; Spanish perceptions of, 79n13; and Spanish soldiers, 81n35; subsistence practices of, 72, 73, 79n7; terms for, 8; and trade, 73, 77, 106, 108; and tribute, 77. *See also* Calusa Indians
Indians of Central and South Florida, 1513–1763 (Hann), 65n10, 67n26
Institute for Public Opinion Research (FIU-IPOR), 264, 265, 277, 283n49
Interfaith Committee for Worker Justice, 255
Iredell County, Fla., 80n20
Irish, 8, 130, 172, 182
Irving, Washington, 4, 28, 193, 198
Irwin, Jared, 181, 182, 183, 184
Isabella I, queen of Castile and Leon, 5, 13, 118, 119, 194
Italy and Italians, 15, 21, 25, 30, 171

Jacán. *See* Chesapeake Bay
Jackson, Andrew, 22–23, 24, 157
Jackson, Helen Hunt, 194
Jackson, Rachel, 23–24
Jacksonville, Fla., 27
Jamaica and Jamaicans, 16, 71, 94–95, 109, 112, 120, 175, 212
James, Russell D., 10
Jamestown, Va., 12, 78n5
Jaúdenes y Nebot, José de, 148
Jay, John, 144–46, 147, 149
Jay, Sarah, 144
Jay Treaty, 149, 150
Jefferson, Thomas, 149, 152, 154, 156, 182
Jesuits: as missionaries, 13, 60, 61, 63, 76, 90, 93, 95, 96, 98, 105, 106, 122, 135n28; and *reducciones*, 98; in Spain, 95
Jesuits in North America, The (Parkman), 10–11
Jews, 8, 11, 13, 212, 237, 243, 253
Jiménez, Generoso, 215, 219
Joara, 76, 80n21, 81n35, 81n36
Joliet, Wis., 229
Jospo (Yamasee chief), 128–29, 139n70
Juan (slave), 133n10
Juanillo (African), 121, 135n27
Juchi (Calusa town), 59
July Club, Tampa, Fla., 31
Juncal, Port., 176
Junta Central, 153–54, 157
Juntas, 153–54

Jupiter Inlet, 3, 56, 66n11, 73
Justice for Janitors, 255
Juventud Democrática Antifascista de West Tampa, 30

Kansas City, Mo., 193
Kellogg Foundation, 260n25
Kennedy, Paul, 21
Kerry, John, 234
Key Biscayne, Fla., 28
Keys Indians, 63
Key West, Fla.: antipiracy force in, 25; cigar making in, 25; Cubans in, 25, 26, 210; and Cuban War of Independence, 26; early names for, 25; importance of, 25; Indians and, 63; José Martí in, 26; languages in, 25; maps of, 55; Ponce de León and, 50, 55, 56; population of, 25; proximity of, to Cuba, 25; publishing in, 25; and railroad, 248; size of, 25; and Spanish-American War, 27
Kinderlán, Sebastián, 154
King, Martin Luther, 219
Kings County, N.Y., 228
Kissimmee, Fla., 224, 228, 229, 230
Klein, Herbert, 134n12
Knight Arts Challenge, 251, 260n25
Knight Foundation, 249, 260n25, 260n33
Kohl, Johann G., 78n5
Kongo (kingdom), 131, 140n86
Kopp, Belton, 178
Kościuszko, Tadeusz, 182
Krauthammer, Charles, 11
Kruse, Paul, 187n11
Ku Klux Klan, 243

La Casa de Contratación, 1, 71
La Chua Ranch, 14, 82n42, 110, 122–23
La Contienda, 25
La Costa Island, 60
La Cruz (stream), 54
Lady of Cofachiqui/Cofitachequi (Indian), 92, 120
La Florida (Escobedo), 19, 84
La Florida (location). *See* Florida, 1513–1763
La Florida (term), 4, 64n3
La Florida del Inca (Inca Garcilaso de la Vega), 19, 84, 85, 89, 90–93, 98–99
La Fuente, Pilara, 30
La Gaceta, 25

Lake George, 14
Lakeland, Fla., 27
Lake Okeechobee, 55
Lake Worth lagoon, 56
Lam, Wilfredo, 212
La Marseillaise, 182
Languages: African, 132; Algonquin, 95; Arabic, 132; Arawakan, 65n10; Aymara, 88; Ays, 121; Castilian, 135n28; Creole, 254; English, 10, 127, 132, 232, 253, 254; French, 10, 24, 104; Indian, 10; Latin, 88; Miccosukee, 21; Portuguese, 10, 131; Quechua, 87, 88; Taíno, 118; Timucua, 13, 94; Yamasee, 132. *See also* Spanish (language)
Lara, Alonso de, 95
Larson, Lewis H., 79n7
La Salle, René-Robert, Sieur de, 111
Las décadas (Herrera), 64n4
Las Posadas, Andalusia, Sp., 90
Las Tortugas, 58
Latin American Orchestra, 215
Latinos. *See* Cubans and Cuban Americans; Puerto Ricans
La Traducción, 25
Laudonnière, René de, 75, 90
Lavandera, Henry Wallace, 31
La Virgen de los Navegantes (Fernández), 1
La Voz de la Fundación, 268
Lawrence, David, Jr., 254
La Yaguna Island, Bahamas, 49, 53
League of United Latin American Citizens (LULAC), 212
Lears, T. Jackson, 199
Lecuona, Margarita, 222n25
Lee County, Fla., 56, 58, 60, 227
LeFeber, Walter, 147
L'Engle, Susan Fatio, 177, 178
Le Prince (ship), 105
Levique, Juan, 24
Lido Hotel, 215
Lima, Peru, 1, 88, 125
Lincoln County, Fla., 80n20
Lisbon, Port., 118
Little Bahama Bank, 53
Liverpool Mercury, 179
Lobillo, Johan, 135n24
London, Eng., 9, 149, 175
Long Island, N.Y., 202, 229
López, Israel "Cachão," 211, 217, 219

López de Gómara, Francisco, 72
López de Velasco, Juan, 57, 59–60, 66n12
Los Angeles, Calif., 225, 264
Los Mártires, 55
Lotería Nacional Cubana, 20
Louisiana: and Amelia Island Affair, 171; borders of, 151, 155; and Louisiana Purchase, 22, 151, 152, 154, 158; population of, 173; return of, to France, 150; Spanish and, 20, 71, 180, 185, 191n75
Louis XIV, king of France, 111, 112
Louis XVI, king of France, 148
Lower Keys, Fla., 56
Lowery, Woodbury, 78n5
Low-Income Families Fighting Together (LIFFT), 255
Lucayos, Bahamas, 53
Luis (mulatto), 121
Luisa (Indian *cacica*), 134n14
Lummis, Charles F., 194, 204
Luna y Arellano, Tristán de, 17, 61, 74–75, 95, 135n24
Lyon, Eugene, 66n11
Lyric Theater, 223n30

MacGregor, Gregor, 176–81, 188n22, 190n55
MacGregor medal, 178, 189n36
Machado, Gerardo, 213, 215
Machito, 211, 214
Mack, Connie, Sr., 272
Mack Amendment, 272
Macpherson, Captain, 140n81
Mad Dog (Yamasee Indian), 139n70
Madison, James, 154, 157, 187n11
Madison highlands, Fla., 73
Madrid, Sp.: Apalache province officials in, 110; Diego Gardoqui in, 144, 149; and globalization, 9; Oré in, 88; and Peace of Basel, 150; publication of Herrera's *Historia* in, 50; and ratification of Adams-Onís Treaty, 22; U.S. representatives in, 144, 149, 150
Magellan, Ferdinand, 84
Magnolia House, 195
Mahon, John J., 23
Maidique, Modesto, 252
Major, Howard, 203
Málaga Cathedral, 20
Mambo Devils, 217

Mandinga, 10
Manegua Island, Bahamas, 53
Mann, Charles, 36n42
Manuale Peruanum, 100n3
Marathon Key, Fla., 55
Marco Island, Fla., 55, 58, 60, 66n14
Margarita Island, 182
Marguiles, Martin, 260n31
Mariana highlands, 73
Mariguana Island, Bahamas, 49, 53
Márquez Cabrera, Juan, 124
Marseilles, Gil de, 105
Martí, José, 26, 27, 31, 220
Martín, Juan, 135n25
Martínez, Bob, 32
Martínez, Jaime Bartolomé, 102n20
Martínez, Juan, 133n10
Martínez, Raúl, 279
Martínez de Irujo y Tacón, Carlos, 151–52, 156
Martínez Ybor, Vicente, 25
Martín's BBQ, 231
Martyr, Peter/Pietro Martire d'Anghiera, 5, 43, 71
Mas Canosa, Jorge, 267, 268, 270, 272, 276, 279
Massachusetts, 226, 227, 232, 237
Massachusetts Bay, 108
Mas Santos, Jorge, 270
Matança (term), 66n14
Matança Island, 58, 60
Matanzas, Cuba, 108, 133
Matanzas Inlet, 17
Matecumbe Key, 62, 108
Material culture, 9, 10, 15
Mathews, George, 173, 174, 175, 176, 187n11
Máximo Point, 24
Mayaca Indians, 63
Mayaimie Indians, 63
McCain, John, 279
McCarthy, Kevin, 29
McGrath, Campbell, 6
McKay, James, 15
McKean, Sally, 152
McKean, Thomas, 152
McKee, John, 174
McMichael, Andrew, 173
McNeill, William H., 7
Medici, Catherine De, 105

Meinig, Donald, 13, 17
Mejías (African), 134n14
Melbourne Beach, Fla., 4
Melgarejo, Francisco, 133n10
Memoria de las cosas y yndios de la Florida (Fontaneda), 18
Memorial presentado al rey Carlos III y repetido a Carlos IV . . . (Floridablanca), 143
Memorias (Godoy), 151
Méndez de Canzo, Gonzalo, 106, 114n13, 114n14
Mendoza, Jerónimo de, 133n10
Menéndez, Francisco, 10, 128–29, 132, 138n62, 139n70
Menéndez, Pedro, 105
Menéndez, Robert, 268, 282n19
Menéndez de Avilés, Pedro: expeditions by, 18, 121, 135n28; and French, 61, 105; and Hernando d'Escalante Fontaneda, 59; and Indians, 61, 76–77, 135n28; and Jesuits, 105; letters of, 84; outposts established by, 66n11; positions held by, 84; and San Mateo, 105; and Santa Elena, 61, 75, 105; and Spanish Crown, 76, 81n33, 105; and St. Augustine, 15, 29, 59, 61, 75, 105, 121
Menéndez Marqués, Juan, 94, 106
Menéndez Márquez, Francisco, 138n62
Menéndez Márquez, Juan, II, 109
Menéndez Márquez, Pedro, 105, 106
Menéndez Márquez, Thomás, 14
Menéndez Márquez family, 122–23
Mexía, Álvar, 65n10
Mexican Americans, 212
Mexicans: blacks as, 125; in Chicago, 236; in Florida, 235; in Los Angeles, 225; in Miami, 218, 259n12; and migration, 32, 236; in New York City, 225; as ranch hands, 14; in the United States, 234
Mexico: and Amelia Island Affair, 171, 180, 186; blacks in, 120, 123, 135n25; Columbian Exchange in, 8; Cortés and, 60; English/British and, 150; and Florida, 181, 191n75; foods from, 16; as heart of Spanish Empire, 143; and independence from Spain, 153; insurgent groups in, 191n75; and migration, 24; militias in, 123; mining in, 1, 83, 134n16; Narváez and, 12; native empire in, 72; as part of Spanish empire, 119; as part of Spanish Empire, 17, 22; religious iconography in, 10; return of de Soto expedition to, 92; revolutionary forces in, 182; Spanish conquest of, 83; Spanish officials in, 175, 191n75; Texas as part of, 158; and trade, 17; U.S. expeditions in, 157
Mexico City, Mex., 9, 16, 108, 120, 134n16
Miami, Fla.: arts in, 249–52, 260n25, 260n31, 260n33; Bahamians in, 212, 217, 243; baseball in, 213; Bill Clinton in, 269; blacks in, 220, 237, 243, 249, 251, 253, 257, 258n6; Café District in, 251; discrimination in, 211, 212, 218, 243, 253; Dominicans in, 218, 251; economy of, 247–51, 259n17, 259n22, 259n120, 261n37; education in, 254; FBI office in, 213; in fiction, 242; founding of, 243; gentrification in, 248, 249, 252, 257; George H. W. Bush in, 272; Haitians in, 237, 243, 245, 254, 257; and Havana, 210, 213; in Hernando d'Escalante Fontaneda's memoirs, 18; hotels in, 213, 215, 217, 218; immigrant groups in, 255; Indians in, 63; institutionalization in, 242; Jamaicans in, 212; Jews in, 212, 237, 243, 253; labor unions in, 211; Latino intermarriage in, 236–37; music in, 210, 211, 213, 214–15, 217, 218–19; neighborhoods in, 217–18, 225, 249, 250, 251, 252, 253, 255, 257, 259n21, 259n22, 264; and New York City, 210, 214, 219, 251; non-Cuban and non-Puerto Rican Hispanics in, 218, 225, 237, 251, 259n12, 264, 281n4; Overtown neighborhood of, 217–18, 255; persons from, on Amelia Island, 181; population of, 257, 258n9, 259n12, 264; Puerto Ricans in, 212, 214, 217, 218, 224, 225, 228, 230, 236, 237, 251, 259n12, 281n4; and race and ethnicity, 210, 211, 242, 243–47, 249–51, 252–53, 254, 257; recording companies in, 219; renovations in, 223n30; rioting in, 253; scholarship on, 39n88; Second Havana neighborhood in, 264; settlement patterns in, 264–65; social reform in, 254–57; socioeconomic characteristics of, 244–47, 252–53, 257, 258n11; and Spanish-American War, 27; Spanish Craze in, 193, 201; and tourism, 209, 211, 213, 214, 247; and trade, 213; unions in, 215, 254–55; West Indians in, 257. *See also* Cubans and Cuban Americans

Miami Art Museum (MAM), 252
Miami Beach, Fla., 212; arts in, 251; blacks in, 218; Cubans in, 215, 217; discrimination in, 217; economy of, 251; filming of *I Love Lucy* in, 215; gentrification in, 248; Latinos in, 218; maps of, *250*; neighborhoods in, 259n21; and race, 218; real estate in, 249; as symbol of Florida, 28; and tourism, 210
Miami Beach Blue Sail, 215
Miami Black Archives, 223n30
Miami-Dade County, Fla.: education in, 254; and Greater Miami, 281n7; immigrant groups in, 32, 227, 228, 230, 255–56, 266; languages spoken in, 253; neighborhoods in, 259n21; race and ethnicity in, 243–45; socioeconomic characteristics of, 244–47
Miami en Acción, 255
Miami Fellows, 260n25
Miami Foundation, 249, 260n25
Miami-Ft. Lauderdale, Fla., 228
Miami-Ft. Lauderdale-Pompano Beach, Fla., 229, 231
Miami Herald, 252, 254
Miami Latin Boys, 219
Miami Leadership Summit, 252, 261n39
Miami River, 54, *55*, 57, 58, 63
Miami Sound Machine, 219
Miami Workers Center (MWC), 255
Middleton, Arthur, 127–28
Midtown, Miami, Fla., *250*, 251
Milford, Conn., 229
Mina, Francisco Javier, 182
Mining, 1, 16, 83, 119, 134n14, 134n16
Minorcans, 21
Miranda, Carmen, 214
Mirasol, 202
Mirow, M. C., 155
Missionaries: activities of, 13; and Calusa Indians, 60, 61, 62, 67n26; challenges to, 19; Charles F. Lummis on, 194; and Indian sports, 19; and Ponce de León's 1521 expedition, 4; protection of, 107; regions settled by, 73–74; at St. Augustine, 172. *See also* Dominicans (religious order); Franciscans; Jesuits; *La Florida del Inca* (Inca Garcilaso de la Vega); Oré, Luis Jerónimo de
Missions: architecture of, 13; attacks on, 138n59; Axacán, 105; as buffers, 62; construction of, 28; disappearance of, 13, 112–13; locations of, 13, 28, 62, 100n5, 101n8, 111, 136n33, 138n59; mistaking of GA sugar mills for ruins of, 113n1; Nombre de Dios, 106; populations of, 77; protection of, 107; Provincia de Santa Elena, 101n8; Yamasee Indians and, 138n59. *See also* Dominicans (religious order); Franciscans; Jesuits; *La Florida del Inca* (Inca Garcilaso de la Vega); Oré, Luis Jerónimo de
Missions to the Calusa (Hann), 66n12, 67n26
Mississippi, 73, 79n16
Mississippi River: as boundary, 142; French and, 111; Indians and, 92; Spanish and, 92, 120, 144; U.S. navigation of, 144, 145, 146, 149, 150
Mississippi Territory, 155
Mizner, Addison, 29, 201–3
Mizner Industries, 202
Mobile, Ala., 9, 17, 20, 112, 134n21
Mobile Bay, 21
Monaco, Joseph María, 63
Monroe, James: as president, 159, 184, 186; as secretary of state, 171, 173–74, 175, 186, 187n11
Monroe Doctrine, 171, 174, 175, 186
Montaner, Rita, 212
Montiano, Manuel de, 12, 128, 129, 130, 139n71
Montilla, Sp., 98
Moody's, 261n37
Moore, Alexander, 29
Moore, James, 14, 112, 172
Moors, 8, 192
Morales, Francisco, 177
Moré, Beny, 215
Moreno, Luis, 135n25
Morganton, NC, 76
Morgiana (ship), 180
Morison, Samuel Eliot, 5
Morning Post, 190n52
Morton, Joseph, 125
Mosquito Lagoon, *55*, 56, 65n10
Mosquito River, 53
Mothers and Women Against Repression, 275
Mound Key, 59–60, 61, 71
Moyano de Morales, Hernando, 76
Mulberry site, 80n27
Muñoz, Raymond "Monchito," 217

Murden, J., 184
Muslims, 11, 117, 193

Nanipacana, 75
Naperville, Ind., 229
Napoleon I, 150, 151, 152–53, 154, 155, 157
Napoleonic Wars, 171, 172, 173
Narváez, Pánfilo de: 1528 expedition of, 12, 18, 61, 74, 80n22, 120; Cabeza de Vaca on, 91; and first contact, 7; Oré on, 102n12; west Texas Indians on, 134n21; wife of, 18
National Association for the Advancement of Colored People (NAACP), 255
National Endowment for Democracy (NED), 267, 269
National Geographic, 11
National Park Service, U.S., 129
Nat Turner's Rebellion, 24
Naval Academy, U.S., 26
Negrett, Tony, 217
Negro, Jorge, 2
Negro Leagues, 212
Netherlands, 21, 111
New Democratic Network, 279
New England, 17, 109
Newfoundland, 5, 119
New France, 17, 104
New Haven-Milford, Conn., 229
New Jersey, 224, 226, 229, 269, 282n19
New Mexico, 104, 193
New Netherland, 17
New Orleans, La., 20, 22, 150
New Smyrna, Fla., 29
New Spain: administration of, 17; blacks in, 122, 125; borders of, 17, 21; Cortés and, 60; extent of, 64n3; as heart of Spanish Empire, 143; Indians in, 72; and migration, 75; mining in, 83; rivals of, 17; slaves in, 122; and Spanish exploration, 75, 91; Spanish officials in, 95; and trade, 16, 121; troops in, 125; United States and, 157; viceroys of, 95
New York, N.Y.: Addison Mizner in, 202–3; architecture in, 208n27; arts in, 251; and baseball diplomacy protestors, 282n19; Cubans in, 132, 209, 210, 212, 213–14, 217, 219; Diego Gardoqui in, 144, 147; Dominicans in, 225; Dutch merchants in, 110; exhibit of Samuel Coleman's works in, 194; gambling in, 20; harbor of, 18; Luis Onís in, 157; Mexicans in, 225; and Miami, 210, 214, 219, 251; music in, 210, 213–14, 216; neighborhoods in, 225; population of, 264; Puerto Ricans in, 225, 228, 237; Spanish Craze in, 193, 194, 201; Spanish dialects in, 236
New York County, N.Y., 228, 246
New York State, 226, 232, 237
New York Times, 27
Nicaragua and Nicaraguans, 74, 108, 225, 235, 244, 259n12, 281n4
Nombre de Dios mission, 106
North, Lord, 11
North Africa, 21
North Bay, 56
North Carolina, 80n21, 127
Northwest Passage, 105
Nuestra Señora de la Concepción (ship), 102n19
Núñez de Balboa, Vasco, 83

Obama, Barack, 234, 279, 280
Occupy Havana, 257
Occupy Miami, 257
Occupy Wall Street, 257
Ochlockonee River, 55
Ocklawaha River, 14
Ocracoke Island, 132
Ocumare, Venezuela, 176
Office Depot, 259n120
Oglethorpe, James, 10, 132
Ohio, 226
Ohio Shoal, 65n9
Olamico, 76
Olympia, 214
One Man Alone, 219
Onís y González-Vara, Luis de: and French, 174; and United States, 156, 157, 158, 174, 175, 177, 181, 185–86, 187n16
Opa-locka, Fla., 28
Orange County, Calif., 212
Orange County, Fla., 227–28, 229, 230, 236
Orchestra Sacasa, 215
Ordoñez, Alférez Alonso, 136n31
Oré, Luis Jerónimo de, 84, 87–90, 93, 97, 99, 102n21, 107
Oregon Country, 158
Orlando, Fla., 225, 228–29, 230, 231, 234, 236, 237

Orlando-Kissimmee, Fla., 224, 228, 229, 231
Ortiz, Fernando, 210–11
Ortiz, Juan, 18, 19
Ortiz Zárate, Cornelio, 189n26
Osceola (Indian), 23
Osceola County, Fla., 227, 228, 229, 230, 236
Ottoman Empire, 10
Our Miami, 260n25
Outer Banks, 65n7
Ovando, Nicolás de, 119, 133n11
Overtown Music Project, 223n30
Oviedo. *See* Fernández de Oviedo, Gonzalo

Pablo, Don Diego, 131
Pacific Ocean, 83–84
Padrinas, Manuel, 26
Paéz, José Antonio, 183
Paine, Thomas, 11
Paiva, Juan de, 19
Palm Beach, Fla., 29, 201, 202
Palm Beach County, Fla., 227, 259n120
Palm Beach Inn, 201
Palmer, James, 128
Palos, Sp., 3
Panama, 74
Panama-California Exposition, 194
Pan-American Expedition, 194
Panton, Leslie & Co., 10
Pánuco River, 79n11
Papy, William, 24
Pardo, Juan, 76, 77, 81n34
Pareja, Francisco de, 13, 94
Paris, Fr., 9, 149, 251
Parkman, Francis, 11
Parris Island, S.C., 75
Pasco County, Fla., 227
Patagonia, 21
Patriota (ship), 183
Pautz, Patrick Charles, 80n22
Paynes Prairie, 14
Pazos Kanki, Vicente, 180, 181, 184
Peace of Basel, 150
Pearl River, 21, 155
Peck, Douglas T., 78n5
Pee Dee River, 78n5
Pennsylvania, 152, 226, 227, 232, 237
Penobscot River, 71
Pensacola, Fla.: and 1812 Spanish constitution, 156; and 1821 transfer of Florida to United States, 23; and American Revolution, 20; Andrew Jackson and, 22; Apalache refugees in, 112; archaeology in, 16; and Biloxi, Miss., 112; as buffer, 16; diet in, 16; as frontier, 16; importance of, 23; languages spoken in, 24; merchants in, 10; and migration, 23, 24; Narváez and, 134n21; as naval base, 23; population of, 9, 23, 24; race in, 24; Rachel Jackson on, 23–24; Spanish forces at, 112; as Spanish possession, 75, 155; status of, as government post, 16; terms for inhabitants of, 8; and trade, 16, 17; and wealth, 16; and weather, 17
Pensacola Bay, 17, 61, 75, 111–12
People Acting for Community Together (PACT), 254
Perdido River, 154, 155, 174
Pereda, Alonso de, 135n25
Peregrinaciones (Carmona), 90
Perez, Jorge, 251, 252
Pérez, Louis, Jr., 213
Pérez Art Museum Miami (PAMM), 252
Pérez-Galdós, Benito, 25
Pérez Garzón, Juan Sisinio, 153
Pernambuco, Brazil, 182
Persat, Maurice, 181, 185
Peru: blacks in, 120, 135n25; boundaries in, 80n24; Indians in, 72, 96, 97–98; and La Florida, 90; Oré on, 96, 97–98, 99; silver mining in, 1, 16; Spanish and, 17, 74, 83, 90, 97, 99
Pétion, Alexandre, 176, 182
Pew Hispanic Research Center, 209
Philadelphia, Pa.: celebrations in, 195; Constitutional Convention in, 147; deputies of free America in, 176; Philosophical Society in, 156; Puerto Ricans in, 225, 228, 229; Spanish representatives in, 151, 152; Valetín de Foronda in, 156
Philadelphia Aurora, 152
Philadelphia Press, xiiin1
Philip II, king of Spain: and Elizabeth I of England, 106; and French, 75, 77, 83, 105; and Herrera, 50; and Luna, 17, 75; and Menéndez de Avilés, 76, 77; priorities of, in Florida, 104; works dedicated to, 90
Philippines, 21, 104
Phillips Field, Tampa, Fla., 31

Philosophical Society, 156
Piar, Manuel, 176
Pickering, Timothy, 152
Pilgrims and Plymouth Colony, 15
Pinckney, Thomas, 149, 150
Pinckney's Treaty, 150
Pine Island Sound, 55, 59
Pinellas County, Fla., 227
Pinellas Peninsula, 24
Pine Tree Creek, 80n27
Piñon's wife, 133n10
Pirates and piracy: 17th-century, 110; blacks and, 125; Dutch, 83; English, 105; and Fernandina and Amelia Island, 174, 181, 183; French and, 106; Oré on, 94
Pizzo, Tony, 24
Plana Cays, Bahamas, 53
Plant, Henry Bradley, 27, 199
Plants, 9, 72, 73, 74, 80n18. *See also* Agriculture
Plaza Gigante, 231
Pocahontas, 18
Poinciana, Fla., 229
Point of Santa Elena, 75
Pola Island, 57
Politics (Aristotle), 79n13
Polk, Willis, 202
Polk County, Fla., 227, 229
Polo, Marco, 84
Pompano Beach, Fla., 228, 229, 231
Ponce de León, Juan: and 1493 Columbus voyage, 2; 1506 expedition of, 2; 1521 expedition of, 4, 9, 60–61, 67n22, 119; death of, 4, 59, 61; and Ferdinand II, 60; and first contact, 7, 9; and Fountain of Youth, 43; Oré on, 94; and Puerto Rico, 52
Ponce de León, Juan, 1513 expedition of: and first Spanish landfall in Florida, 3, 49, 53; historical accounts of, 3, 49, 50, 52, 53, 64n4; and Indians, 3, 50, 52, 53–54, 57–58, 59, 71, 72; itinerary of, 2–3, 49–50, 52–56, 57, 58, 60, 64n1, 64n2; maps of, 50–52; persons on, 2–3, 119; physical geography discovered on, 71; pilot for, 60; Ponce's report to Charles V on, 4; royal contract for, 2, 52
Ponce de León festivals, 196–98, 199
Ponce de León Hotel, 27, 28, 198, 199, 200
Porter, Cole, 214

Porter, David, 25
Portes, Alejandro, 242, 243, 253
Portobelo, Colón, Panama, 123
Port Royal (now S.C.), 94, 125, 130, 139n66
Port Royal Sound, 75
Portugal and Portuguese, 8, 107, 109, 117, 172
Potano, Fla., 112
Potomac River, 94
Potosí, Bolivia, 1, 16, 102n20
Power University for Social Change (Power U), 255
Poyais, 187n22
Pozo, Chano, 217
Prado, Pérez, 214, 217
Prescott, William Hickling, 10
Presidio de Santa María, 9
Prieto, Martín, 96
Protestants and Protestantism, 10, 11, 23, 83. *See also* Huguenots
Providence Island, 108
Ptolemy, Claudius, 70, 78n4
Publix, 248
Puente, Tito, 211, 214, 217
Puerto Plata, Hispaniola, 135n27
Puerto Rican American Insurance Company (PRAICO), 231
Puerto Rican Professional Association of South Florida (PROFESA), 231–32, 235
Puerto Ricans: and blacks, 237; in Chicago, 236; and Cubans, 232; and discrimination, 212; and education, 236; in Florida, 209, 224, 225, 226, 227–38; and intermarriage, 236–37; in Miami, 214, 217, 218, 251, 259n12, 281n4; and migration, 32, 224, 225; in New York City, 225, 237; and politics, 234, 235, 238; as proportion of population, 209; and race, 233–34; settlement patterns of, 226–30, 231, 237; socioeconomic characteristics of, 230–33, 237–38, 251
Puerto Rico: 1557 defense of, 137n43; and Amelia Island Affair, 171; blacks in, 120, 123, 133n10; and class, 232; and crime, 231; and education, 236; George III on, 20; gold mining in, 119, 134n16; and migration, 236; militias in, 123; and pirates, 94–95; and politics, 235; Ponce de León and, 2, 3, 4, 49, 52, 57, 60; and race, 234; Spanish conquest of, 119; as Spanish possession, 159; and statehood, 235

Puerto Rico Planning Board, 231
Punta de Arracifes, 54, 56
Punta Rassa, Fla., 15
Puritans, 108

Quattlebaum, Paul, 78n5
Québec, Canada, 104
Queen Anne's War, 103, 104, 112
Queens, N.Y., 225
Quincy, NH, 229
Quiñones, John, 235
Quiroga y Losada, Diego de, 125

Radio Martí, 268, 270
Rafael y Sus Rumberos, 215
Rafter, Michael, 176, 178
Ramírez, Alejandro, 179
Ramona (Jackson), 194
Rangel, Rodrigo, 74
Reagan, Ronald, 267
Rebolledo, Diego de, 108, 109
Relación (Cabeza de Vaca), 18, 91, 101n13
Relación de la descendencia de Garcí Pérez de Vargas (Inca Garcilaso de la Vega), 101n11
Relación de los mártires de la Florida (Oré), 84, 86, 88, 89, 90, 93–98, 99, 100n3
Repartimiento system, 122
Report of the Committee Appointed to Frame the Plan of a Provisional Government for the Republic of Floridas, 184, 190n73
Republicans and Republican Party, 152, 234, 235, 267, 268, 279, 281
Republic of East Florida, 154, 175
Republic of the Floridas, 177, 185, 186
Research Institute on Social and Economic Policy (RISEP), 256
Reséndez, Andrés, 80n22
Resino, Dionisio, 8
Retratos de los españoles ilustres con un epítome de sus vidas, 87
R & G Crown, 231
Ribault, Jean de, 17, 75, 90, 94, 105
Riego, Rafael del, 158
Ringling, John, 199
Río de la Plata, 18, 171, 180
Rise and Fall of Great Empires, The (Kennedy), 21
Ritz Carlton Hotel, 201
Ritz Plaza, 217

Rivera Beach, 54
River of Canoes, 56
Riviera Beach, Fla., 55, 56
Roanoke colony, 105
Roberts, John, 214
Roberts Bay, 66n14
Robeson, Paul, 31
Robles (slave), 135n24
Rodríguez, Tito, 214, 217
Rodríguez y Cartaya, Juan, 107
Rogel, Juan, 60, 61, 135n28
Rojas, Rafael, 154
Rolyat Hotel, 199–201
Romans, 192
Rome, Ga., 135n24
Rome, It., 9
Romney, Mitt, 280
Romo de Uriza, Francisco, 112
Roney Plaza, 215
Roosevelt, Franklin D., 31
Root Cause Coalition, 256
Royal Commentaries (Inca Garcilaso de la Vega), 88, 89
Royal Cornwall Gazette, 179
Royal Council of the Indies, 100n5, 109, 136n31, 136n35, 139n67
Royal Ponciana Hotel, 201
Rubell family, 260n31
Rubio, Marco (son), 209
Rubio, Marco, Sr. (father), 209
Ruddock, Alwyn, 65n7
Ruiz, Juana, 2
Ruiz de Salazar Ballecilla/Vallecilla, Benito, 77, 108
Ryder, 248

Salinas, Juan de, 108
Salt River, 56
Salvadorans, 225
Sanabria, Juanito, 217
San Antonio de Enacape, Fla., 61, 100n5
San Buenaventura de Guadalquini mission, 94, 100n5
San Carlos (fort), 172
San Carlos Bay, 3, 57, 59
San Cristóbal (ship), 2
San Diego, Calif., 194
Sands Key, Fla., 55
San Francisco de Potano mission, 100n5

San Germán, P.R., 2, 43, 52
Sanibel Island, Fla., 3, 56, 57
San José de Zápala mission, 100n5
San Juan (colony), 58. *See also* Puerto Rico
San Juan, Fla., 154
San Juan, P.R., 123, 231
San Juan de Boriquén, 119
San Juan de Guacara mission, 100n5
San Juan del Puerto, 108
San Juan de Ulúa, 109
San Juan River, 154
San Lorenzo de El Escorial, Sp., 150
San Luís de Apalache, 74
San Luis de Talimali, 19
San Marco (hotel), 195
San Marcos (fort), 17, 23, 110, 111, 123, 126, 195
San Marcos, Apalache province, 108, 110
San Martín de Timucua mission, 100n5
San Mateo (fort), 90, 98
San Mateo (municipality), 105
San Miguel de Gualdape: agriculture at, 70; destruction of, 120; disease at, 71, 120; foods at, 70–71; founding of, 79n6, 119; hunger at, 70, 71, 120; and Indians, 71; location of, 69, 70, 78n5; Oviedo on, 69–70; population of, 119; scholarship on, 70; survivors on, 69; uprising at, 121–22
San Pedro River, 94
San Salvador, 49, 53
Santa Cruz, 3, 119
Santa Cruz, Alonso de, 71, 77
Santa Cruz de Tarihica mission, 100n5
Santa Elena (colony): Africans at, 121; agriculture at, 75–76; closing of, 106; fortifications at, 121; founding of, 61, 75, 105, 121; French and, 105; as northernmost Spanish settlement, 121; Oré in, 89; rebuilding of, 122; weather at, 75
Santa Elena de La Florida, 94
Santa Fe, N. Mex., 203
Santa Fé River, 14
Santa Isabel de Utinahica mission, 100n5
Santaluce Indians, 63
Santa María, 154
Santa María de Consolación (ship), 2
Santa María del Jacán (Chesapeake Bay), 94, 95
Santa María de Loreto (church), 63
Santa María Island, 54, 57
Santamaría Rodríguez, Ramón "Mongo," 211, 217, 219
Santa Pola Island, 57
Santee River, 72
Santería, 216
Santiago (ship), 2
Santiago, Cuba, 215
Santiago de Chile, 175
Santo Domingo, 94–95, 109, 123, 137n43
Sapelo Sound, Ga., 72, 78n5, 119
Sarah (slave), 132
Sarasota, Fla., 29, 199
Sarasota Bay, 24
Sargent, John Singer, 194
Saturiba (Timucua chief), 90, 135n27
Savannah, Ga., 127, 176
Savannah River, 78n5, 107
Saxony Hotel, 217
Scholl, Dennis, 260n31, 260n33
Scisco, Louis D., 53, 64n1, 64n2, 64n5
Scotland and Scots, 8, 10, 75, 171, 172, 182
Searles, Robert, 109
Second Seminole War, 23
Second Treaty of San Ildefonso, 150, 152
Section D, Cape Henry to Key West (U.S. Coast Pilot), 65n9
Securities and Exchange Commission, U.S., 261n37
Segura, Jean Baptista de, 76
Seminole County, Fla., 227, 228
Seminole Indians, 15, 21, 22, 24, 103, 154, 157
Senate, U.S., 23, 152, 268
"Se Quema Mi Casa" (Covington), 214
Service Employees International Union (SEIU), 254, 255, 256
Seven Years' War, 20, 21, 104
Seville, Sp., 1, 88, 117–18, 133n3, 153, 193, 194, 201
Sewall, Rufus King, 195
Shea, John G., 78n5
Short, William, 149, 150
Siboney Sextet, 215
Sigüenza y Góngora, Carlos de, 111
Silva, Joe, 24
Silvestre, Gonzalo, 90, 93, 98–99
Símbolo católico indiano (Oré), 102n21
Singer, Paris, 202
Slavery, 11–12, 117, 124, 134n12

Slaves: activities of, 123, 137n37; and education, 24; Florida colonists and soldiers and, 136n31; Indians as, 11, 62, 76–77, 95, 111, 112, 119, 133n3; and Indian uprisings, 123; languages spoken by, 8; legal rights of, 12, 117, 134n12; and militias, 123, 128; purchases of, 110; and religion, 8, 12; in Spain, 133n3; Spanish and, 11, 76–77, 117; terms for, 8. *See also* Africans, as slaves; Menéndez, Francisco

Slaves, runaway: and American Revolution, 104; attacks by, 128; as debt payment, 139n71; English and, 130–32; executions of, 127; and gender, 132; and Indians, 21, 119, 121, 127, 128–29, 133n11, 136n29, 140n81; and militias, 132; and miscegenation, 136n29; occupations of, 126; pursuit of, 140n81; and religion, 125–26, 132; return of, 138n55; Spanish and, 127, 139n67; terms for, 8

Smith, Frank W., 198

Smith, John, 11, 18

Smith, Thomas Buckingham, 18, 195, 196, 207n16

Smugglers, 172, 174, 178–79, 181. *See also* Pirates and piracy

Socarrás, Alberto, 211, 214

Solano, Francisco, 89

Soto, Darren, 235

South America: Francis Parkman on, 11; and links to North America, 90, 93, 99, 186; and migration, 244; as part of Spanish Empire, 22, 142; revolutionaries in, 157, 175, 176, 178, 181, 191n75; Spanish dialects in, 236

South Beach, Miami, Fla., 249, *250*

South Carolina: and Amelia Island, 172; economy of, 130; French exploration in, 94; Guale settlements in, 136n33; Patriots Group volunteers from, 174; population of, 130; runaway slaves from, 132; slavery in, 130, 138n60; Spanish settlement in, 61, 121; Stono Rebellion in, 131–32; Yamasee War in, 63. *See also* Carolinas

South Carolina Commons, 131

South Florida Jobs with Justice (SFJwJ), 255

South Miami, Fla., 264

Soviet Union, 30, 31

Spain: and 1783 Treaty of Paris, 142; 1812 constitution of, 155–56, 158; 1820–23 Constitutional Triennium in, 158; Addison Mizner in, 201, 202; and Amelia Island affair, 171–72, 179, 180, 186; and American Revolution, 20–21, 151; and Americas policy, 148; and Asia, 83; blacks in, 117–18, 124, 135n25; calendars in, 79n6; and censorship, 159; civil war in, 30, 153–54; class and race in, 155; economy of, 193; and Eighty Years' War, 108; empire of, 21, 153, 157, 158–59, 160, 172; and England/Great Britain, 104, 109–10, 111, 148, 149, 150–51, 153, 174, 185; fleet system of, 83; and Florida's boundaries, 142; foods in, 33; and France, 104, 111, 148, 150, 151, 152–53, 155; Garcilaso in, 87; Indians in, 69, 95; and *la reconquista*, 13; and Louisiana, 20, 150, 151, 152, 180, 185; and migration, 26; and Netherlands, 104, 111; and news from Florida, 90; Oré in, 88; perceptions of, 193–94, 198, 199; political values and changes in, 143, 146, 148, 152, 158, 159–60; and Portugal, 107; press in, 151; religion in, 13, 26; and repression, 151; and right by conquest, 142, 151; royal family of, 112; Sherwood Anderson on, 27; and slavery, 117, 126, 128, 129, 133n3, 134n14, 138n55, 139n67, 139n71, 179; and trade, 16, 144, 150; and United States, 144, 146–47, 149, 150, 159, 171, 174, 184, 185; wars waged by, 10

Spanish: activities of, 23, 24; and agriculture, 15–16; and Calusa Indians, 108; diet of, 14–16, 23; and Dutch, 83, 108; and English/British, 83, 108, 119; and French and Huguenots, 17, 83, 94, 119; and gender roles, 14–15; and Indians, 14–15, 79n13, 79n17, 108–9, 138n59; literary and artistic depictions of, 10–11; and migration, 8; and miscegenation, 118; persecutions by, 11; and race, 8, 192–93; and religion, 10, 11, 83, 107; and slavery, 11–12; terms for, 8; and trade, 77, 79n13; in Ybor City, 25. *See also* Missionaries

Spanish (language): Africans and, 132; captured Spanish and, 121; dialects of, 236; grammar book for, 13; Indians and, 63; in Key West, 25; Panton, Leslie & Co. employees and, 10; in Pensacola, 24; and Portuguese, 131; predominance of, 254;

public use of, 237; Puerto Ricans and, 232; slaves and, 8, 131; and Spanish-American War, 27; terms from, 14, 29; in Ybor City, 25

Spanish-American War, 27, 193, 199, 201, 204

Spanish Armada, 106

Spanish Craze, 193, 194, 199, 201

"Spanish Element in Our Nationality, The" (Whitman), 203, xiiin1

Spanish fleet system, 83, 99n1

Spanish Harlem, N.Y., 225

Spanish Pioneers, The (Lummis), 194

Spanish Red Cross, 30

Spanish Royal Lottery, 20

Spanish Town, Jamaica, 109

Spanishtown Creek, 24

Spanish War of Independence, 153

Springfield, Mass., 229

SS *Florida* (ship), 213

Stababa (Calusa town), 58–59

Stagg, J. C. A., 187n11

Standard and Poor's, 261n37

Staten Island, N.Y., 18

St. Augustine, Fla.: 1565 thanksgiving in, 15; and 1812 Spanish constitution, 156; 1860s reshaping of, 27; Africans in, 121, 122; and agriculture, 16, 75–76, 104, 106; Amelia Island defectors in, 180; and Apalache province, 110; architecture and buildings in, 27, 28, 106, 111, 195, 198; attacks on, 10, 90, 106, 109, 110–11, 112, 125, 128, 154; Buckingham Smith in, 18; as buffer, 16; celebrations in, 23, 195, 196–98; and Charles Town/Charleston, S.C., 124; consolidation of smaller settlements into, 77; diet in, 16; diseases in, 109, 112, 122, 137n41; English/British and, 130, 139n66; and Florida's transfer to United States, 23; food costs in, 94; forts at, 17–18, 109, 110, 111, 112, 123, 126; founding of, 59, 61, 105, 121; Fountain of Youth in, 6; Francisco Menéndez in, 10; as frontier, 16; harbor at, 104, 105; Henry Morrison Flagler and, 27; histories of, 195; hotels in, 27, 195, 198, 199, 200; importance of, 23; Indians in, 112, 122, 123; John Dickinson in, 111; Joseph Marion Hernández in, 23; labor in, 122; layout of, 13–14; maps of, 55; memorials in, 156; Menéndez de Avilés's grave in, 29; military forces and militias at, 107, 109, 124–25, 128; military forces and militias in, 16; missionaries and, 19, 62, 90, 100n5, 172; as naval base, 104, 105; New Englanders and, 23; Old City Gates of, 17; Oré in, 89, 90, 100n5; and pirates, 110, 111; Ponce de León's and, 4; population of, 106, 109, 111, 122, 124; provisioning of, 106, 108, 109, 110, 123; radio stations in, 31; reconstruction and restoration of, 31, 109; religion in, 23; runaway slaves in, 125–26, 127, 129, 130, 139n66; seawall in, 111; slaves at, 121, 122, 123, 128, 136n29; as Spanish center in East Florida, 174; Spanish Craze in, 194–95; Spanish officials in, 178; status of, as government post, 16; street names in, 199; terms for inhabitants of, 8; and tourism, 31, 195, 199; and trade, 9, 14, 16, 123, 130; and wealth, 16; weather at, 75; William Cullen Bryant on, 195

St. Augustine Historical Society, 196

St. Barthélemy, 183

St. Domingo, 182

Stepick, Alex, 242, 243, 253

Stetson, John, 29

St. Johns River: English/British and, 112; French and, 61, 94, 105–6; Indians and, 108; La Chua ranch near, 14; maps of, 55; physical geography along, 73; and shore line, 65n9; U.S. Army patrols near, 23

St. Lucie (term), 66n11

St. Lucie Fort, 66n11

St. Lucie Inlet, 55, 66n11, 72

St. Lucie River, 56

St. Marys, Ga., 174

St. Marys River, 21

Stono, S.C., 127–28, 131

Stono Rebellion, 131–32, 140n86

St. Petersburg, Fla., 199, 228

Strait of Anián, 84

Straits of Florida, 3, 31, 52

St. Sebastian River, 66n11

Stuart, Mary, 106

Suárez, Tony, 229, 235

Su instrucción reservada (Floridablanca), 143

Sunshine, Silvia, 25

Surruque Indians, 65n10

Suwannee River, 14, 110

Swedes, 8

Sweetwater, Fla., 264
Switzerland and Swiss, 21, 251

Taino Indians, 2, 17
Take Back the Land, 256
Tallahassee, Fla., 19, 73, 74, 122
Tampa, Fla.: and 1948 presidential election, 31; architecture in, 28; cigar making in, 29, 30; Cubans in, 199, 209; and Cuban War of Independence, 26; Fidel Castro in, 31; foods in, 33; and Great Depression, 30; health care in, 25; in Hernando d'Escalante Fontaneda's memoirs, 18; hotels in, 27–28, 199; José Martí and, 26, 31; Manuel Padrinas in, 26; and migration, 29, 33; mutual aid societies in, 25–26; origins of, 26; Puerto Ricans in, 225, 228, 230, 236, 237; and Spanish-American War, 27; and Spanish Civil War, 30; and Spanish Craze, 199; Spanish in, 24, 25–26; and trade, 15
Tampa Bay, 18, 55, 61, 73, 74, 120
Tampa Bay Hotel, 27, 199
Tampa–St. Petersburg-Clearwater, Fla., 228
Tapia, Crispin de, 124
Teleco mission, 100n5
Tennessee, 174
Tenochtitlán, Mex., 3, 134n16
Ten Thousand Islands, 18, 24, 71
Ten Years' War, 26
Tequesta (Indian village), 18, 54, 57, 58, 63
Tequesta (Spanish mission settlement), 63
Tequesta Indians, 3, 7, 63
Texas: and Adams-Onís Treaty, 22; French settlement in, 111; Indians in, 134n21; and Mexico, 158; Narváez in, 74; as part of Spanish Empire, 21; Puerto Ricans in, 226, 227, 231; Spanish Craze in, 193; Spanish missions in, 111
Thirty Years' War, 108–9
Thompson, Martin, 176
Thornton, John, 131, 140n86
Thurmond, Strom, 30
Tiffany, Louis, 27
Timucua Indians: activities of, 109, 122; language of, 13, 14; and migration, 109; population of, 8; raids by, 90, 125; and religion, 106, 122; uprising of, 109, 123

Timucua province, 94, 103, 108, 110, 123
Tocobaga Indians, 9, 18, 108
Toledo, Francisco, 97, 98
Toledo, Sp., 201, 202
Tolomato Cemetery, St. Augustine, Fla., 31
Tonantzin (Aztec goddess), 10
Tony Negrett and His Authentic Cubans, 217
Torre, Pedro de la, 135n25
Torres, Manuel, 176, 189n26
Torres y Ayala, Laureano de, 138n55
Torricelli, Robert, 269
Tortugas Islands, 3
Tourism: in 1920s, 28–29; blacks and, 213; and class, 28; and Fountain of Youth, 6; and Havana, Cuba, 213; and Miami, Fla., 209, 211, 213, 214, 247; and Miami Beach, Fla., 210; and St. Augustine, Fla., 31, 195, 199
Townshend, Charles, 20
"Tracking the Calusa Overseas" (Worth), 67n26
"Track of Ponce de Leon, The" (Scisco), 53, 64n1, 64n2, 64n5
Trade goods: agricultural products, 108; ambergris, 108; barrel staves, 173; cattle, 15, 110; chert, 73; clothing, 108; coffee, 16; copper, 73; corn, 14; cotton, 173; deerskins, 14, 106, 111; flint, 73; foods, 77; freshwater pearls, 73; gold, 1, 16; guns, 108, 111; hides, 14, 95; meat, 14; pelts, 77; quartz, 73, 80n20; rice, 173; sarsaparilla, 77; sassafras, 106; silver, 1, 16, 106; slaves as, 111, 173; sugar, 16; tar, 173; turpentine, 173; wines, 95; wood, 173
Treaty of Amity, Settlement, and Limits between the United States of America and His Catholic Majesty, 22, 157–58
Treaty of Friendship, Limits, and Navigation between Spain and the United States, 150
Treaty of Paris (1763), 132
Treaty of Paris (1783), 142
Treaty of San Lorenzo, 150, 151
Treaty of Tordesillas, 5
Treviño Guillamas, Juan, 107
Trewman's Exeter Flying Post, 179
Truman, Harry S., 30
Turner, Nat, 24
Turtle Mound, 53, 55, 65n10

TV Martí, 269
Twelve Years' Truce, 108
Two Friends (ship), 182

Udall, Stewart, 11
Ulibahali (now GA), 135n24
Unidad Cubana, 275
Union City, N.J., 268
United for Dignity for Immigrant Workers Rights, 255
United Nations General Assembly, 273
United Provinces, 108
United States: and Amelia Island Affair, 178, 180, 184; and China, 270; cities in, 249; class in, 257; consumption in, 28; and Cuba, 154, 209, 273, 282n30; discrimination in, 212; Dutch mania in, 193; Egyptian mania in, 193; and England/Great Britain, 142, 146, 149, 158, 172, 174, 175; and expansion, 145, 149, 152; and Florida, 142, 154–55, 157–58; Foronda on, 156; and Gregor MacGregor, 176, 177; Japanese mania in, 193; leisure in, 28; Mexican mania in, 193; and neutrality, 148–49; non-Puerto Rican Hispanics in, 211–12, 221n10, 234, 264; political organization of, 143, 144, 145–46, 147, 148; political values of, 143, 158; position of, in North America, 141; and production, 28; and Protestant work ethic, 28; Puerto Ricans in, 226–27, 230, 231, 232, 233; and recognition of former Spanish territories, 159; and religion, 204; and right by conquest, 142; and Spain, 144–47, 149, 159, 171, 174, 184, 185; and Spanish Civil War, 157; Spanish Craze in, 193; and trade, 144, 145, 147, 150, 272; and Vietnam, 270; and War of 1812, 155
United States Coast Pilot for the Atlantic Coast, 54
University of Miami, 213, 214, 248, 255, 261n39
University of Puerto Rico, 232
University of Salamanca, 201
Univisión, 32
Upper East Side, Miami, Fla., 249, 250
Upper Keys, Fla., 55, 56, 57
Upper Peru, 171
Uruguayans, 259n12

U.S.-Cuba Democracy PAC, 278
USS *Maine*, 27

Valdés, Fernando, 107
Valdés, Miguel, 215
Valdés, Pedro de, 107
Valencia, Sp., 194
Valladolid, Juan de, 118
Vandera, Juan de la, 76
Vásquez de Ayllón, Lucas: claims by, 69, 70; colony of, 70, 78n5; death of, 71; expeditions of, 72; and founding of San Miguel de Gualdape, 119; and Guale Indians, 121; and Gulf coast exploration, 2; and Indians, 72; location of colony of, 69; Oré on, 102n12; Oviedo on, 69; at Spanish Court, 69; on "terrestrial gems," 73
Vásquez de Coronado, Francisco, 12, 102n12
Velasco, Luis de (Indian), 95
Velasco y Ruiz de Alarcón, Luis de (Spaniard), 95
Venezuela, 65n7, 89, 171, 180, 182, 183, 247
Venezuelans, 235, 244, 249, 259n12
Venice, It., 9
Veracruz, Mex., 1, 16, 125
Vermillion Bay, La., 71
Vespucci, Amerigo, 1
Vespucci, Juan, 84
Viar, Juan Ignacio de, 148
Villafañe, Angel de, 75
Villaret, Auguste Gustave de, 181
Villa Vizcaya, 201
Villa Zorayda, 198, 207n16
Virginia, 107, 109, 127
Virginius (ship), 26
Virgin of Guadalupe, 10
Visigoths, 192
Vivanco, Juan de, 100n5
Vizcaya, Sp., 120
Volusia County, Fla., 227, 236

Wage Theft Ordinance, 256
Wallace, Henry, 30–31
Walt Disney World, 224, 232
Walting Island, 49
Warm Mineral Springs, Fla., 6
War of 1812, 22, 155, 172, 181
War of the Convention, 150

War of the League of Augsburg, 111
Warren, Harris Gaylord, 190n55
Wars of Religion, 77, 105
Washington, D.C., 22, 179–80, 183, 186, 208n27
Wateree River, 76, 80n27
Weber, David, 5
WeCount!, 255
Weddle, Robert, 79n11, 79n16
Welsh, 8
West Africa, 8
Westchester, Fla., 264
West Hartford, Conn., 229
West Indians, 257
West Tampa, Fla., 30
White, Stanford, 202, 208n27
Whitman, Walt, 194
Wiencek, Henry, 19
Wild Coast, 105, 111, 112
William Morris Agency, 217
Wilmington, Del., 229
Winn-Dixie, 248
Winyah Bay, 65n9
Withlacoochee River, 55
Wolfe, Tom, 242

Wood, Peter, 127, 131
World Fuel Services, 248
World Trade Organization, 273
Worth, John, 67n26
Worth Avenue, 202
Wynwood, Miami, Fla., 249, 250, 251
Wynwood Art District, Miami, Fla., 251
Wynwood Art District Association, 251
Wynwood Cafe District, Miami, Fla., 249

Xavier Cugat Orchestra, 215

Yamasee War, 63, 127, 132
Yamasee/Yamassee Indians, 10, 63, 112, 125, 127, 128–29, 138n59
Ybarra, Pedro de, 107
Ybor City, Fla., 20, 25, 26, 33
Yglesias, Jose, 30
Yribarren, Joseph de, 189n34

Zacatecas, Mex., 83
Zéspedes, Vicente Manuel de, 21
Zorro, 10
Zúñiga y Cerda, José, 112

www.ingramcontent.com/pod-product-compliance
Lightning Source LLC
Chambersburg PA
CBHW021337230426
43666CB00006B/318